Implementing
the Conservation Title
of the Food Security Act
of 1985

Implementing the Conservation Title of the Food Security Act of 1985

Ted L. Napier, Editor

SOIL
AND WATER
CONSERVATION
SOCIETY

Published for
North Central Region Research Committee 149,
Changing Institutional Environment for the On-farm Adoption
of Soil and Water Conservation Practices,
and North Central Region Research Committee 111,
Natural Resource Use and Environmental Policy,
by the
Soil and Water Conservation Society
7515 Northeast Ankeny Road
Ankeny, Iowa 50021-9764

Library of Congress Catalog Card No. 90-9687

ISBN 0-935734-22-8

Library of Congress Cataloging in Publication Data

Main entry under title:

Implementing the Conservation Title of the Food Security Act of 1985 /
   Ted L. Napier, editor
   ISBN 0-935734-22-8
   1. Land use, Rural—Government policy—United States—Congresses.
   2. Soil conservation—Government policy—United States—Congresses.
   3. Water conservation—Government policy—United States—Congresses.
   4. Environmental policy—United States—Congresses.
   5. Agriculture and state—United States—Congresses.
   6. Farms—Government policy—United States—Congresses.
 I. Napier, Ted L.
II. Soil and Water Conservation Society (U.S.)
HD256.I46 1990
333.76'16'0973—dc20

90-9867
CIP

Contents

III. Micro-level Economic Impacts of the Conservation Title

IV. Barriers and Facilitators to Implementation of the Conservation Title at the Farm Level

V. Wildlife Impacts of the Conservation Title

VI. Future Policy Needs After the Conservation Title of the Food Security Act of 1985

VII. Summary and Conclusions

Contributors

Alfred Berner, Group Leader
Farmland Wildlife Population and Research Group, Minnesota Department of Natural Resources, Madelia

Jon Brandt, Co-Director
Food and Agricultural Policy Research Institute, University of Missouri, Columbia

Gordon Bultena, Professor
Department of Sociology, Iowa State University, Ames

Silvana M. Camboni, Associate Director
Ohio State University Research Foundation, Columbus

Richard T. Clark, Associate Professor
Department of Agricultural Economics, University of Nebraska, North Platte

Randal C. Coon, Research Specialist
Department of Agricultural Economics, North Dakota State University, Fargo

Michael R. Dicks, Assistant Professor
Department of Agricultural Economics, Oklahoma State University, Stillwater

Barbara B. Dunkelberg, Research Associate
Department of Agricultural Economics, Purdue University, West Lafayette, Indiana

Brenda L. Ekstrom, Research Associate
Department of Agricultural Economics, North Dakota State University, Fargo

David E. Ervin, Branch Chief
Resource Policy Branch, Resources and Technology Division, Economic Research Service, U.S. Department of Agriculture, Washington, D.C.

J. Dixon Esseks, Associate Professor
Center for Government Studies, Northern Illinois University, DeKalb

Jerald J. Fletcher, Associate Professor
Division of Resource Management, West Virginia University, Morgantown

Klaus Frohberg, Research Scholar
International Institute of Applied Systems Analysis, Center for Agricultural and Rural Development, Iowa State University, Ames

R. Mack Gray, Assistant to the Chief
Strategic Planning and Budget Analysis, Soil Conservation Service, U.S. Department of Agriculture, Washington, D.C.

Doug Haney, Research Associate
Department of Agricultural Economics, Iowa State University, Ames

Paul Harte, Program Specialist
Agricultural Stabilization and Conservation Service, U.S. Department of Agriculture, Washington, D.C.

Thomas Hebert, Legislative Assistant
Senate Committee on Agriculture, Washington, D.C.

Douglas Helms, Historian
Soil Conservation Service, U.S. Department of Agriculture, Washington, D.C.

John S. Hickman, Assistant Professor
Extension Agronomy, Kansas State University, Manhattan

Thomas J. Hoban, Assistant Professor
Department of Rural Sociology, North Carolina State University, Raleigh

John P. Hoehn, Assistant Professor
Department of Agricultural Economics, Michigan State University, East Lansing

Eric Hoiberg, Professor
Department of Sociology, Iowa State University, Ames

Matthew Holt, Research Associate
Department of Economics, Iowa State University, Ames

Derald Holtkamp, Graduate Assistant
Department of Agricultural Economics, Iowa State University, Ames

Bengt Hyberg, Agriculture Economist
Resource Technology Division, Economics Research Service, U.S. Department of Agriculture, Washington, D.C.

James B. Johnson, Professor
Department of Agricultural Economics, Montana State University, Bozeman

Stanley R. Johnson, Professor
Department of Economics, Iowa State University, Ames

James J. Jones, Policy Analyst
Office of Policy Analysis, U.S. Environmental Protection Agency, Washington, D.C.

Keith Kozloff, Research Associate
Department of Agricultural and Applied Economics, University of Minnesota, St. Paul

Steven Kraft, Associate Professor
Department of Agribusiness Economics, Southern Illinois University, Carbondale

Peter J. Kuch, Senior Policy Analyst
Office of Policy Analysis, U.S. Environmental Protection Agency, Washington, D.C.

Paul Lasley, Associate Professor
Department of Sociology, Iowa State University, Ames

F. Larry Leistritz, Professor
Department of Agricultural Economics, North Dakota State University, Fargo

Jay A. Leitch, Associate Professor
Department of Agricultural Economics, North Dakota State University, Fargo

Michael Linsenbigler, Agricultural Program Specialist
Agricultural Stabilization and Conservation Service, U.S. Department of Agriculture, Falls Church, Virginia

Stephen B. Lovejoy, Associate Professor
Department of Agricultural Economics, Purdue University, West Lafayette, Indiana

James A. Maetzold, Program Analyst
Strategic Planning and Policy Analysis Staff, Soil Conservation Service, U.S. Department of Agriculture, Washington, D.C.

William H. Meyers, Professor
Department of Agricultural Economics, Iowa State University, Ames

Timothy Mortensen, Research Assistant
Department of Agricultural Economics, North Dakota State University, Fargo

Ted L. Napier, Professor
Department of Agricultural Economics and Rural Sociology, Ohio State University, Columbus

Amy Purvis, Graduate Research Assistant
Department of Agricultural Economics, Michigan State University, East Lansing

Mark Reeff, Resource Specialist
International Association of Fish and Wildlife Agencies, Washington, D.C.

Ann Robinson, Soil Conservation Coordinator
Izaac Walton League of America, Minneapolis, Minnesota

Colin P. Rowell, Extension Assistant
Department of Agricultural Economics, Kansas State University, Manhattan

Jerry R. Skees, Assistant Professor
Department of Sociology, University of Kentucky, Lexington

Vernon Sorenson, Professor
Department of Agricultural Economics, Michigan State University, East Lansing

Kurt Stephenson, Graduate Research Associate
Department of Sociology, University of Kentucky, Lexington

Louis E. Swanson, Associate Professor
Department of Sociology, University of Kentucky, Lexington

Steven J. Taff, Assistant Professor
Department of Agricultural and Applied Economics, University of Minnesota, St. Paul

C. Robert Taylor, Alfa Professor
Department of Agricultural Economics and Rural Sociology, Auburn University, Auburn, Alabama

Leland C. Thompson, Assistant Professor
Department of Agricultural Economics, Iowa State University, Ames

Greg Traxler, Research Assistant
Department of Economics, Iowa State University, Ames

Patrick Westhoff, Research Associate
Center for Agriculture and Rural Development, Iowa State University, Ames

Jeffrey R. Williams, Associate Professor
Department of Agricultural Economics, Kansas State University, Manhattan

Robert Wolcott, Director
Economics and Environmental Resource Division, Office of Policy Analysis, U.S. Environmental Protection Agency, Washington, D.C.

Abner Womack, Co-Director
Food and Agricultural Policy Research Institute, Department of Agricultural Economics, University of Missouri, Columbia

Preface

This text is the product of a national symposium convened in Columbus, Ohio, on March 1-2, 1989. The symposium was sponsored by the North Central Region Research Committee-149; the North Central Region Research Committee-111; the Farm Foundation; the Soil Conservation Service, U.S. Department of Agriculture; and the U.S. Environmental Protection Agency. The contributions of these sponsors are greatly appreciated.

The primary objective of the symposium was to provide a forum for the presentation and discussion of research findings on problems associated with implementing the Conservation Title of the Food Security Act of 1985. Papers were commissioned from a variety of regions in the United States and by researchers from various disciplines.

The text begins with an outline of the various components of the Conservation Title. Present implementation procedures and policies are discussed. The history of conservation programs in the United States is followed by a summary of some of the problems associated with implementing the Conservation Title. Basically, contributors conclude that implementation of the Conservation Title is an evolutionary process that is not yet complete.

The second section is devoted to the assessment of the macro-level economic impacts of Conservation Title programs, with particular emphasis on the Conservation Reserve Program. Evidence provided by the contributors suggests that the Conservation Title programs have positive and negative impacts and that the impacts are not evenly distributed geographically.

The third section focuses on the micro-level economic impacts of Conservation Title programs. The studies reported in this section graphically demonstrate the potentially adverse impacts of Conservation Title programs on local, regional, and state populations. The papers in this section suggest that conservation programs should be integrated with nonmetropolitan, community, and regional development programs.

The fourth section focuses on factors that facilitate and impede participation in Conservation Title programs. A variety of variables are discussed from the perspective of economics and sociology. The findings reported strongly suggest that effective implementation of complex conservation legislation, such as the Conservation Title, is extremely difficult and expensive.

The fifth section examines the contributions made by Conservation Title programs to wildlife habitat and production. Presenters conclude that Conservation Title programs have enhanced wildlife habitat and production. They also argue that the potential exists for considerable improvement in wildlife habitat as additional land is enrolled in set-aside programs and as other components of the Conservation Title are implemented.

The sixth section looks at future directions for soil and water conservation in the United States. The contributors anticipate the maintenance of conservation programs designed to remove highly erodible land from crop production by the use of economic incentives. Regulatory approaches are recognized as legitimate but not preferred.

The last chapter synthesizes the contributions made by various authors. Broad policy issues are identified and a research agenda to address them is offered for consideration. Contributions by physical and social scientists will be required to address adequately the research issues discussed.

Ted L. Napier
Ohio State University

I

An Historical Perspective of the Conservation Title

1

The Conservation Title of the Food Security Act of 1985: An Overview

Ted L. Napier

Passage of the Conservation Title as an element of the Food Security Act of 1985 prompted many natural resources specialists to label it the most significant environmental legislation enacted in U.S. history. Academicians, conservationists, and politicians predicted that the title would revolutionize soil and water conservation efforts in the United States.

While there is justification for this enthusiasm, it must be recognized that well-intended legislation may not achieve intended objectives; in fact, such legislation may produce unintended consequences that are not desirable for specific segments of society. Therefore, national environmental policies, such as the Conservation Title, should be examined carefully to determine what the probabilities are that the expected outcomes will be achieved.

Basic Components of the Conservation Title

The Conservation Title consists of four basic programs: the Conservation Reserve, conservation compliance, sodbuster, and swampbuster.[1] Each of these programs is designed to achieve a specific objective, but the purpose of the entire title is to provide a comprehensive set of environmental policies to guide national soil and water conservation efforts.

The Conservation Reserve Program. The Conservation Reserve Program (CRP) was created to achieve multiple objectives: conservation of soil re-

[1]Daniel Conrad, Soil Conservation Service, Columbus, Ohio, provided information about recent changes in implementation procedures for specific Conservation Title programs.

sources, reduction of surplus stocks of agricultural products, enhancement of wildlife habitat, and maintenance of farm income. While it may be impossible to achieve all of these goals with a single program (*1*), the legislative intent was to accomplish several objectives simultaneously.

The goal of CRP is to retire 45 million acres of highly erodible cropland from agricultural production for a period of 10 years. Cropland is defined as any land that was in crop production two of the five years between 1981 and 1985.

Landowners who enroll land in the CRP receive an annual rent from the U.S. Department of Agriculture (USDA). The amount of rent per acre is agreed upon at the inception of the contract period. Highly erodible land must constitute at least one-third of a field or a minimum of 50 acres to qualify for inclusion in the program. All highly erodible land is eligible for inclusion in the CRP, but no more than 25 percent of the cropland in a single county may be enrolled.

Land is enrolled in the CRP using the designation of highly erodible fields. To be defined as highly erodible, a field must satisfy one or more of the following conditions: (1) land with an erosion index of 8 or greater and an annual soil loss of T (tolerance) or more; (2) land in capability class VI, VII, or VIII; (3) land in capability class II through V with an annual soil loss of 3T or more; (4) land in capability class II through V with an annual soil loss of 2T or more and gully erosion; and (5) land in capability class II through V with an annual soil loss of 2T or more and a landowner who is willing to plant trees on the enrolled land. The definition has changed considerably from the 3T criterion used early in the program.

Some land not classified as highly erodible may also be enrolled in the CRP. Land areas 66 feet to 99 feet wide along streams or wetlands may be enrolled as filter strips even though the land is not subject to erosion. The purpose of filter strips is to trap sediment and farm chemicals transported from highly erodible land.

Farmed wetlands may also be enrolled in the CRP as of January 1989, even though the land may not be subject to erosion. Farmed wetlands are former wetlands that are cropped periodically as weather conditions permit.

Land subject to scour erosion may also be enrolled in the CRP even though such land may not be defined as highly erodible. Land adjacent to streams may be severely eroded by streamflow during floods. Whole fields or "redefined fields" may be enrolled in the CRP to prevent this type of erosion. Site determination of the land eligible for inclusion must be made before the scour-prone land can be bid into the CRP program.

Land enrolled in the CRP must be protected by groundcover. Tree and shrub planting are encouraged, but grass cover is acceptable. The federal government will pay 50 percent of the initial costs of establishing groundcover, but will not pay for maintenance.[2] Mowing is permitted to control weeds, and spraying for insect pests is acceptable.

Agricultural products cannot be produced on CRP land for the duration of the contract period. Hay may be harvested under crisis situations, such as the drought of 1988, but only with the authorization of the secretary of agriculture. In certain situations the secretary of agriculture may authorize crop production on CRP land, but the land released from the CRP must be cultivated in a manner that satisfies the conditions of conservation compliance and sodbuster provisions. CRP rental payments are reduced on a formula basis when revenues are generated from crop production on enrolled land. The issue of who assumes the costs of re-establishing groundcover on CRP land used for authorized crop production has not been clarified because row-crop production on set-aside land has not been authorized to date. Trees grown on CRP land may be harvested for commercial use. This action was taken to encourage tree planting.

A number of requirements were established to determine eligibility for participation in the CRP. The first requirement is that a person desiring to enroll land in the program must demonstrate his or her right to retire land from crop production for an extended time period. Landowners qualify to do so unless they are encumbered by leasing arrangements with tenants. Tenants may enter into contracts to retire cropland, assuming they have controlled the land to be enrolled for 10 years prior to the date of the bid submission.

Persons qualified to enroll highly erodible land in the program are required to submit bids. The bids submitted are evaluated and a decision is made to accept or reject each. If a bid is accepted, a contract is written that specifies the conditions of the agreement.

CRP agreements are binding for the duration of the contracts, even when enrolled land is transferred to a new owner. A new landowner may renegotiate certain aspects of the contract but must comply with the agreement. A new owner may request revision of practices used on the land, changes in groundcover, and modifications in scheduling of groundcover applica-

[2]Lack of cost-sharing for maintenance of groundcover on CRP acres will significantly affect landowners' willingness to enroll land in filter strips. Filter strips require extensive maintenance to remain effective in reducing erosion. When landowners learn of the maintenance costs associated with filter strips, they will likely be reluctant to enroll land in the program unless the rental fees reflect maintenance costs.

tion or mowing of enrolled land, but he or she cannot renegotiate annual rental fees. Distribution of CRP rents among owners and tenants may also be renegotiated by new owners because they have never had the land in owner-tenant agreements. Any changes in the original contracts must be approved by the county Agricultural Stabilization and Conservation Service (ASCS) committee. The person who originally entered into the contract is responsible for any penalties for violation of CRP agreements; however, the new owner receives CRP rents.

CRP agreements are considered void if the original landowner(s) who entered into the contract dies. All owners who signed the original contract must be deceased for the contract to be declared void. The estate of deceased persons is not encumbered with the original CRP leasing arrangement.

The federal government establishes upper bounds on rents for each bidding period. Bids above the cap are not accepted. Special bid pools may be created for specific areas or producer groups that may exceed established caps, but this action requires approval by the secretary of agriculture.

After the sixth round of bidding, the caps became strongly influenced by local rent values. CRP rental fees cannot exceed local land rents. This is to minimize disruption of local rental markets.

Tenant rights to land enrolled in the CRP are protected by program implementation procedures. Landowners must share CRP rents with tenants when there have been written or oral owner-tenant agreements. There are no standardized rules for division of rental fees among owners and renters; however, the tenant must release the land for enrollment in the program. The owner and tenant engage in bargaining to determine the distribution of the CRP rent.

Penalties established for violation of CRP contracts are substantial. Violation of CRP contracts can result in the loss of access to a variety of farm programs such as price support programs, government crop insurance, Farmers Home Administration loans, Commodity Credit Corporation storage loans, farm storage loans, and CRP payments.[3] Violators may also be required to return CRP rental fees plus interest and monies contributed for cost-sharing of groundcover expenses.

About 15 percent of all CRP contracts will be randomly validated for compliance via field checks by Soil Conservation Service (SCS) person-

---

[3]The probability that Conservation Title programs will achieve their stated objectives is strongly influenced by the continuance of USDA farm programs and the future viability of U.S. agriculture. If the agricultural sector should increase its economic viability substantially and USDA farm programs should be abolished or substantially reduced, few incentives will remain for landowners to comply with Conservation Title program requirements.

nel each year. SCS field staff members will visit the land selected for evaluation and determine whether or not the land is in compliance with the contract. SCS staff members will report their findings to ASCS. If there are violations, ASCS will inform landowners that they will not be eligible for participation in USDA programs for that year. The CRP participant may become eligible for USDA programs the following year if he or she complies with contractual agreements.

Conservation Compliance. The conservation compliance provision of the Conservation Title basically states that owners of highly erodible land must have an approved farm conservation plan developed by January 1, 1990, and have that plan fully implemented by January 1, 1995. Failure to meet these requirements will result in the loss of access to federal farm program benefits similar to those forfeited by violation of CRP agreements. The five-year time period for implementation is to provide landowners adequate time to spread costs of implementing the farm plan over several years. Landowners who take no action until January 1, 1995 must fully implement the farm plan before they become eligible for farm program benefits.

Partial financing of conservation practices to implement conservation plans is available through ASCS cost-sharing, but the opportunity to do so is constrained by the availability of cost-share funding. There is no established percentage for cost-sharing of conservation compliance practices.

The original intent of the conservation compliance program was to institutionalize incentives to encourage landowners to reduce soil erosion to T on highly erodible land by 1995. However, the legislation provided that the chief of SCS could modify criteria to prevent hardship for individual landowners. This right was exercised in 1988 with the adoption of the "alternative conservation systems" approach (2). The intent of alternative conservation systems is to prevent landowners from being forced out of farming by conservation compliance.

ASCS is required to do status reviews of conservation compliance farm plans. About 15 percent of the farm plans will be randomly selected each year for assessment by SCS field staff relative to compliance. SCS will report its findings to ASCS and a determination will be made whether or not farm program benefits are received for the year in which the assessment is made. Landowners who are denied farm program benefits in a particular year may qualify for benefits the following year, if they act to comply with conservation compliance expectations.

Land enrolled in the CRP is subject to conservation compliance regulations when the contracts expire, assuming landowners wish to return the idled land to crop production. An approved conservation plan must be fully implemented before highly erodible land enrolled in the CRP can be returned to crop production.

Sodbuster. The sodbuster provision of the Conservation Title was designed to prevent landowners from bringing highly erodible land into agricultural production without an approved farm conservation plan. Land cultivated at least once between 1981 and 1985 was declared exempt from the legislation. The penalties for violation of sodbuster are the same as those for violating CRP agreements.

Unlike other components of the Conservation Title, the sodbuster provision requires complete implementation of an approved conservation plan before highly erodible land can be cultivated for the first time. If highly erodible land is cultivated for the first time without complete implementation of an approved plan, the landowner may be required to forfeit all farm program benefits for the entire farm until the plan is fully implemented.

There are minor exceptions to the sodbuster provisions at the farm level, such as well heads, areas where brush piles have been located for several years, old farmsteads that have not been operated for several years, fence rows, and "odd acres." Very small areas of highly erodible land may be converted to crop production without implementation of a conservation plan, but conversion of land other than that noted above is subject to the sodbuster provision.

Swampbuster. The swampbuster component of the Conservation Title basically states that landowners cannot convert wetlands to crop production without loss of access to government farm programs. Claims for exemption from the regulation must have been filed prior to September 17, 1988.

Wetlands are presently defined as land composed primarily of hydric soils and covered primarily with plants usually found on wet soils. The area defined as a wetland must be permanently flooded or seasonally covered with water for 15 consecutive days during the growing season. The area can have no previous history of drainage.

Under present implementation procedures, landowners who wish to drain a wetland for crop production must prepare a petition to do so. The proposal to drain a wetland must be filed with the SCS state conservationist and with the U.S. Department of the Interior's Fish and Wildlife Service (FWS). Extensive justification must be provided for the conversion of established wetlands, and both agencies must approve the proposed action.

At present, the only legitimate reasons for conversion of wetlands to crop production are "third-party" and "minimum-effect" actions. Third-party action refers to public and private actions that result in the inadvertent draining of a wetland on another landowner's property. For example, if local, state, or federal governments should engage in any development action— construction of airports, highways, government housing, public facilities— that results in the drainage of a wetland on private property, the owner of the affected land is permitted to convert the drained wetland to crop production without loss of government support programs. Actions taken by private landowners that result in inadvertent draining of a wetland on an adjacent farm are also considered third-party actions.

Minimum effects are defined as actions taken by landowners that will disturb but not destroy an existing wetland. Landowners who wish to modify existing wetlands must prepare an environmental impact statement and submit a petition to SCS and FWS. The petition must be approved by both agencies before drainage can proceed. Landowners who farm cropland created by approved wetland conversions are eligible for government farm programs.

Landowners may petition to substitute newly created wetlands for established wetlands removed by drainage. Landowners may have good farm management justifications for removing established wetlands but are prevented from doing so for environmental reasons. The minimum-effects provision permits the creation of wetland areas to replace wetlands removed by drainage. Such proposals must be evaluated and approved by SCS and FWS.

Assessment of Conservation Title Programs

The foregoing overview of the components of the Conservation Title outlines the intent of the legislation and highlights the complexity of the rules and regulations governing its implementation. Many of the problems associated with implementation of the Conservation Title cannot be understood without knowledge of the interdependency of the various components of the legislation.

Also, the procedures used to implement certain aspects of the Conservation Title are being elaborated constantly and are becoming more specific over time. Some of the problems associated with implementing the Conservation Title programs discussed in other chapters of this text are a partial function of the uncertainties about the future directions of the programs.

REFERENCES

1. Napier, Ted L. 1988. *Anticipated changes in rural communities due to financial stress in agriculture: Implications for conservation programs.* In John E. Mitchell [editor] *Impacts of the Conservation Reserve Program in the Great Plains.* U.S. Forest Service and Range Management Society of America, Fort Collins, Colorado. pp. 84-90.
2. Napier, Ted L. 1990. *The evolution of U.S. soil conservation policy: From voluntary adoption to coercion.* In John Boardman, Ian Foster, and John Dearing [editors] *Soil Erosion on Agricultural Land.* John Wiley Publishers, London, England.

2

New Authorities and New Roles: SCS and the 1985 Farm Bill

Douglas Helms

Since passage of the Soil Conservation Act in 1935, the U.S. government has tried in various ways to promote soil conservation. Federal policymakers have promoted research; created an agency of technically trained people to carry soil conservation information to the farming community; encouraged the growth of conservation districts; shared in the cost of establishing soil conservation practices on farms and ranches; and tried innovative approaches, including long-term contracts, such as those in the Great Plains Conservation Program.

Title XII, Conservation, of the Food Security Act of 1985 (Public Law 99198), added a new array of soil conservation provisions designed to link soil conservation to eligibility for other U.S. Department of Agriculture (USDA) programs. The framers of the various clauses especially wanted to eliminate the possibility that commodity price support programs encouraged poor soil conservation practices or the loss of wetlands.

The Environmental Movement Extended

Inclusion of provisions in the 1985 farm bill to reduce soil erosion can be seen as an extension of the environmental movement. Traditional soil conservation groups, the National Association of Conservation Districts (NACD) and the Soil and Water Conservation Society (SWCS); USDA officials who were favorable to the concept; members of Congress and their staffs; and academics all contributed. But major changes in legislation require active lobbying from some groups. The environmental groups' new emphasis on soil erosion was not a turning of attention away from earlier issues, such as preserving woodland, wild rivers, wetlands, and reducing pollutants in air and water. Rather, it represented a wider view encompassing agricultural land. Many individuals and organizations in the environmental movement who lobbied for the act are now monitoring the progress. They and the older soil conservation groups—NACD and SWCS—came to be known as the "conservation coalition."

While soil erosion would undoubtedly have attracted the attention of environmental groups eventually, events in the U.S. farm community accelerated the process. In the early 1970s, only a couple of years after passage of the National Environmental Policy Act, events brought soil erosion to the attention of the public. After several decades of U.S. agricultural surpluses, grain prices began rising in the early 1970s as the Soviet Union purchased large quantities. Grain exports in 1973 were double those in 1972. Prices of wheat, soybeans, and corn in 1974 were 208 percent, 133 percent, and 128 percent, respectively, of what they were in 1970 (2). In response, USDA eased production controls, including the requirement that "set-aside" be held out of production as a condition of participation in price-support programs. Secretary of Agriculture Earl L. Butz proclaimed, "For the first time in many years the American farmer is free to produce as much as he can" (5).

USDA encouraged production in the belief that increased foreign demand was a long-term trend that might well make price supports and production controls unnecessary. Early on, the rush to produce also threatened some long-established conservation measures. By late 1973, according to Butz, USDA was receiving reports of the "heedlessness of some producers." He wrote in the *Journal of Soil and Water Conservation* that reports from the northern Great Plains told of "plowing up grassed waterways, shallow hilltops, and steep slopes...and tearing out windbreaks that took many years to establish." From the southern Great Plains, there were "reports of speculators breaking ground and preparing to plant cotton on thousands of acres of native rangeland that have never been used for crops before" (5). Farmers converting to irrigation did remove wide windbreaks, but, later, an SCS survey found that new plantings of narrower windbreaks had more than offset windbreak losses in most Great Plains states during the period 1970 to 1975 (28). Whatever the actual magnitude of the loss, aerial views of the shifts from some older, wide windbreaks to irrigation systems vividly illustrated what took place.

An SCS survey of cropland expansion in July 1974 found that farmers had converted 3.6 million acres of grassland, 400,000 acres of woodland,

and 4.9 million acres of idle land to cropland. About 4 million of the 8.9 million converted acres had inadequate erosion control. At the time, public attention centered on the Great Plains, but land conversions took place in all regions. The eroding land was scattered throughout the United States, with the heaviest concentrations in the Corn Belt, western Great Plains, southern Coastal Plain, eastern Piedmont and Coastal Plain, and the southern High Plains (15). During the early 1980s, the prospects that domestic and export demands might absorb all U.S. production would prove illusory as good crop years worldwide and loss of markets, in part because of crop embargoes, took a toll. But the trend that began in 1973 continued. Food and feed grains were planted on 294 million acres in 1972, 318 million acres in 1973, 326 million acres in 1974, and 363 million acres in 1981 (41). Thereafter, cropland devoted to food and feed grains went into a slight decline.

Total land in crops had declined in the 1950s and 1960s. The land brought into production during the 1970s and early 1980s actually restored the U.S. cropland base to its level immediately following World War II. It was not the same cropland in all cases because some cropland was converted to other uses. The expansion involved some land not used for production over the past 40 or so years (16).

The expansion of acreage in grain crops also turned people's attention to soil erosion. Questions arose about the wisdom of expanding grain production for export, hoping to reduce the balance of payments, but at the same time causing more soil erosion as a consequence. Was this a case of mortgaging the future? While some of the attention focused on trade and agricultural production policies, the effectiveness of soil conservation programs also came under scrutiny—both the technical assistance activities of SCS and the financial assistance programs administered by the Agricultural Stabilization and Conservation Service (ASCS). In the late 1970s the General Accounting Office (GAO) issued several reports on conservation activities, including *To Protect Tomorrow's Food Supply, Soil Conservation Needs Priority Attention,* which reviewed the Agricultural Conservation Program (ACP). ACP provided costsharing money for soil conservation practices with farmers. Critics of the program believed much of the cost-share money was spent not on soil conserving practices but on practices that enhanced production of crops that were already in surplus and costing the government through price support payments. A related criticism was that the more prosperous farmers, often owners of the best land, were in a better position to take advantage of cost-sharing; thus, much of the money was spent on less erodible land rather than on the land most at risk. Finally, program reviewers believed that both the ACP funds and SCS technical assistance should be targeted to the most critical erosion areas, rather than being distributed evenly across the country (11, 25). Some of the criticism was ahistorical, taking the view that little had been done in the way of conservation in the past. That view gave little recognition to shifting gains and losses over time in the soil conservation movement.

Congress' most significant act in response to the concern over soil erosion, however, was passage of the Soil and Water Resources Conservation Act of 1977 (RCA). The RCA process, as it came to be called, required the USDA to report to Congress on four interrelated topics: the status and condition of America's natural resource base, the present and likely future demands on these resources, the programs needed to protect and enhance these resources for sustained use, and any new approaches that may be needed (12). Government observers in the United States often scoffed at the prospect of another study as a way of evading a difficult issue. In retrospect, the RCA seems to have become one of the instrumental factors in passage of the conservation provisions of the 1985 farm bill. Previous studies of conservation needs by SCS had concentrated on identifying conservation problem areas and needed conservation work. The studies started under RCA concentrated on quantifying soil erosion. Earlier, in the Rural Development Act of 1972, Congress provided for a continuing land inventory and monitoring program that collected information for the RCA studies. The National Resources Inventories (NRI), which became linked to the RCA process, had compiled information on land cover, small water areas, flood-prone areas, irrigated land, conservation needs for various land uses, water erosion, wind erosion, prime farmland, potential for new cropland, land capability classification, and wetlands. The availability of this information, as well as the public comment process established under RCA, provided a forum for numerous individuals, organizations, other government agencies, and academics to express their opinions. The inventories supplied the raw material of analysis and debate. Conferences and special volumes flourished as soil erosion became one of the main environmental issues in the late 1970s and early 1980s (37, 38).

Austerity Begets Targeting

Under RCA, USDA analyzed the data and submitted a program of recommendations to Congress. It fell to the incoming USDA administration in 1981 to complete the proposed program and forward it to Congress. The formulation of the program and the discussions of legislative initiatives took place in a climate in which there would be little additional money for soil conservation; rather, there might be less. As Congress, USDA agencies, and public interest groups debated the final RCA report and recommendations, Congress completed the 1981 farm bill (*12*). The Agriculture and Food Act of 1981 (Public Law 97-88) included several major conservation provisions.

The Farmland Protection Policy Act sought to minimize "the extent to which federal programs contribute to the unnecessary and irreversible conversion of farmland to nonagricultural uses." Throughout much of the 1960s and 1970s, the continuing loss of fertile and generally fairly level land, especially "prime farmland," to development meant that the major soil conservation topic was prime farmland and planning development in agricultural areas, rather than soil erosion. The National Agricultural Lands Study, an interagency-sponsored study of the problems and issues, was completed in early 1981 (*9, 29*). Another provision of the act, the Conservation Loan Program, made it possible for farmers to borrow from the Commodity Credit Corporation to install conservation practices. The Matching Grants for Conservation Activities would go to local units of government through state soil conservation agencies. The RCA report submitted to Congress had included matching grants. The Special Areas Conservation Program would accelerate technical and financial assistance to farmers and ranchers in areas with severe soil erosion or other resource problems. USDA would contract with farmers or ranchers to carry out conservation. SCS, in the Great Plains Conservation Program, had developed long-term contracts with farmers covering the whole farm or ranch that served as a model for the special areas program. The information gathered in the RCA process to identify soil erosion problem areas would be used to identify special areas. USDA did not include special areas in the report submitted to Congress, but Congress added a section on it (*19, 30*).

The administration did not request additional funds for the matching grants and special areas. The RCA recommendations, however, included a proposal on "targeting" as another way to direct funds and people to problem areas. USDA did not have additional funds for special areas, but did start a targeting program. The action came under existing law and did not require legislative authority. The RCA report to Congress recommended that soil conservation programs be moved away from the traditional first-come, first-served allocation and shifted to designated resource problem areas where excessive soil erosion, water shortages, flooding, or other problems threatened long-term agricultural productivity. SCS and ASCS were to devote an additional five percent of their technical and financial assistance to the targeted areas until 25 percent of their funds were going to targeted areas

(*39, 40*). From its national office, SCS designated 10 targeted areas in 1982. In 1983 the states submitted proposals for additional targeted areas.

In 1983 SCS undertook another program to shift resources to problem areas. The areas of the country that created soil conservation districts early on had laid claim to SCS people and funds because the agency worked through districts. But years later, in the 1980s, the areas with the greatest concentration of SCS personnel did not tally with the greatest erosion problem areas being identified in studies. SCS began adjusting the formulas for allocating funds and personnel to states by giving greater weight to resource problems. In cases where the one or two people stationed by SCS at the district office constituted the major part of the operation, the changes seemed ominous. Also, districts tended to see themselves as having a broader natural resource role than just soil conservation. At any rate, when Congress heard from the districts, the issues of targeting and adjusting the formula for allocating monies to states had become inseparable. Congress in 1984 froze the adjustments (*23, 24, 34*). Under the conservation provisions of the Food Security Act of 1985, the obligation to make highly erodible land and wetland determinations and to help farmers with conservation plans caused SCS to put people and resources where they were most needed.

A Changing Climate

Meanwhile, other events shaped the legislative climate in which the conservation sections of the 1985 farm bill would be considered. The Great Plains, scene of the renowned Dust Bowl of the 1930s, provided some of the impetus. Between 1977 and 1982 wheat farmers planted large tracts of grassland in Montana (1.8 million acres), South Dakota (750,000 acres), and Colorado (572,000 acres). In some places the resulting wind erosion proved a nuisance to neighboring farmers as windblown dust covered irrigated pasture and piled up against fences. Some vocal and effective local landowners wanted action, especially Edith Steiger Phillips of Keota, Colorado. She persuaded county commissioners in Weld County to take action against out-of-state interests who plowed up adjacent grassland for wheat production (*33*). She and others created sufficient sentiment for action that Colorado Senator William Armstrong introduced a bill (S. 1825) in 1981 that would deny USDA program benefits, including price support payments, to farmers who converted fragile land to cropland. The bill applied only to land west of the 100 meridian that had not been in crops during the preceding 10 years. Owners would not be eligible for price supports on that land unless they entered into a long-term agreement with the secretary of agriculture to protect it with soil conservation practices. The bugabear of outside investors looking for tax breaks and a quick return on investment usually showed up in discussions of the Great Plains and soil conservation. Certainly, there were some large operations, but surveys conducted after the outcry indicated that Coloradans had owned most of the converted land for some time before planting it to small grains. They responded, it seems, to the prospects of more profit in grain production than from rangeland (*18, 20*).

The Armstrong bill, dubbed the "Sodbuster Bill," did not become law in its first version, but it did occasion congressional hearings and furthered discussion. The Colorado Cattlemen's Association, the American Farm Bureau Federation, and traditional soil conservation and environmental groups testified in favor of the bill. The grassroots actions to support legislation gave greater credence to Washington-based pressure for linking soil conservation and commodity programs. In addition to Weld County, other counties in Colorado and Petroleum County in Montana passed ordinances to try to prevent plowing of native grassland (*20, 26*).

The bill provided a forum for the conservation groups to promote a broader conservation section. NACD, for example, testified that denial of participation in USDA programs because of sodbusting should not be limited to price-support programs. Other suggestions further defined the marginal land in terms of land capability classification and set in process an attempt to define fragile land and, eventually, highly erodible land (*17*).

In 1981 Senator Armstrong incorporated many of these suggestions in an amendment, "Agricultural Commodity Production on Highly Erodible Land," to an agricultural appropriations act. It passed the Senate but was eliminated in the conference committee (*35*). In the next congressional session he introduced S.663, "Prohibition of Incentive Payments for Crops Produced on Highly Erodible Land." The bill still pertained to sodbusting, or land that had not been cultivated during the past 10 years. The sodbuster bill drew wide support from such organizations as the American Farm Bureau Federation and the National Farmers Union. Peter C. Myers, chief of SCS, spoke for the department in support of the bill (*36*).

During 1983 there were additional hearings on the sodbuster and other soil conservation initiatives that eventually came to be included in the farm bill. While USDA supported the sodbuster provisions, the department consistently held that soil conservation initiatives in other bills introduced in 1983 and 1984, such as a conservation reserve program or a certified voluntary set-aside, should await consideration of the 1985 farm bill (*32*).

During the interim period between the 1981 and 1985 farm bills, the PIK

(Payment-in-Kind) program provided an example of how farm programs could deflect conservation aims. USDA needed to reduce crop surpluses to boost prices and hopefully reduce the cost of price support programs. Out of several options, USDA officials in the early 1980s selected PIK, just one of several tools at their disposal that could be used in price support programs. It offered the possibility of reducing crop surpluses, which were depressing prices, by paying farmers in-kind, with farm commodities, to reduce their planted acreage. Proponents of tying conservation to the farm programs often held that commodity programs encouraged farmers to push their cropland base to the limit in order to be able to participate in annual set-aside programs. Conversely, farmers who voluntarily put erodible land into pasture, forests, or cover crops found that such land was not eligible for programs like PIK. The voluntary set-aside, a key element in some bills introduced in Congress, sought to address this problem. Reports that the "conservation-use acres" under PIK achieved less for conservation than projected also highlighted the problems of programs in which conservation was a secondary benefit (*3, 9, 22*).

Another Opportunity

The 1985 farm bill provided the next opportunity to incorporate conservation into agricultural programs. Developments in the farm economy also made for some significant changes. U.S. farmers had lost significantly in export markets. During the embargoes on grain to the Soviet Union, other countries increased production and exports. The rising value of the dollar further weakened the American farmer's position as an exporter. Farmers were caught in the price-cost squeeze, especially those who had bought land and equipment in the 1970s and who were faced with long-term, high interest loans on land and equipment whose value had declined. The percentage drop in farmland values in the five years after 1981 was the greatest for any five-year period since the Civil War (*21*). Many farmers had little borrowing equity for operating loans. In such a climate the security of price support programs became crucial. With the dramatic increase in the cost of commodity programs ($17.7 billion in fiscal year 1985), the administration began looking for ways to reduce costs in the future. Not only were individual farmers in trouble, but the whole farm credit system administered by USDA and the Farm Credit Administration was tottering. All these matters required attention from Congress (*4*).

Urban interests had for some time bargained with farm state representatives in giving their support to agricultural programs. In some cases, the legislation benefited both sides, as in the school lunch and food stamp programs. In what turned out to be a very prophetic analysis, Don Paarlberg, an agricultural economist who served in the Eisenhower, Nixon, and Ford administrations, reasoned at the beginning of the Reagan years that the food programs were popular enough to stand on their own. The newer scenario was more likely to be urban congressmen voting for farm legislation if that legislation included performance in soil conservation provisions (*31*). The Paarlberg prophecy came to pass in the 1985 farm bill. The conservation coalition, representing the traditional environmental groups with urban support and the primary soil conservation organizations, mobilized their forces for a strong conservation section.

The conservation provisions were tied to USDA programs. Any sort of government intervention has never been popular with the farming community. But the proponents had several ready arguments. Farmers did not have to participate in programs; so conservation seemed an equitable trade for public taxpayer support of farm programs. Also, experience and years of analysis of USDA programs pointed out how conservation programs and price support programs worked at cross-purposes. The conservation programs had encouraged voluntary dedication of land to its best uses, frequently to less intensive uses, such as pasture, hay, and rangeland. Another element of public support brought about adjustments through rental or contracting arrangements. But the price support programs sent the message to farmers that they should maintain their cropland base in order to participate to the maximum in price support programs. There was less incentive to adjust production to price or to make the land use changes that matched land to its best uses. In a sense, farmers who voluntarily retired land to less intensive uses were penalized because they reduced the size of their potential payments under commodity programs.

The farmers of the conservation sections in the 1985 farm bill act had years of experience and observation and studies to rely on in writing the provisions. There had been congressional hearings on various bills after 1981. Many of the provisions that eventually appeared in the bill were laid out earlier in a report, "Soil Conservation in America: What Do We Have to Lose?", issued by the American Farmland Trust (*1*). Coalition members presented extensive testimony early in 1985 before the Senate Agriculture Committee. Some of the more active participants included Ken Cook, now of The Conservation Foundation, Bob Gray of the American Farmland Trust, Norm Berg, Washington representative for SWCS, Maureen Hinkle of the National Audubon Society, Neil Sampson of the American Forestry Association, Charlie Boothby of NACD, and Justin Ward of the Natural Resources

Defense Council. In mid-March Sierra Club lobbyists Dan Weiss and Rose McCullough and club members visited hundreds of members of Congress to press their conservation agenda. The group had also worked with USDA officials. The movement to link conservation with commodity programs benefitted from the presence of two strong conservation advocates in the department in John Block, secretary of agriculture, and Peter Myers, chief of SCS and, later, assistant secretary for natural resources and the environment. Block had earlier announced that he believed use of soil-conserving practices was a reasonable request to make of farmers receiving USDA assistance. Myers served as the liaison to Congress and reported weekly to John Block. Wayne Chapman of SCS, who was serving as a legislative fellow with the House Committee on Agriculture, provided communication between the Congress and the department. Numerous individuals in SCS and other USDA agencies provided analysis on various provisions included in the bill (6, 10).

Under the support and chairmanship of Congressman Ed Jones of Tennessee, the Subcommittee on Conservation, Credit, and Rural Development of the House Committee on Agriculture had long been the incubator for new soil conservation legislation, including many forerunners of the conservation provisions in the 1985 farm bill. During April 1985, Senator Richard Lugar of Indiana chaired sessions of the Senate Committee on Agriculture, Nutrition, and Forestry on the reauthorization of the 1981 farm bill. At these meetings the conservation coalition laid out its agenda.

The Matter of Implementation

As with many laws, it was not the framing of the law but the writing of rules and guidelines for implementation that has created the most debate and disagreement. SWCS sponsored a special conference, "American Agriculture at the Crossroads," in the fall of 1987 to discuss implementation issues (27). There have been some disagreements over how rigorously the Conservation Reserve Program (CRP) should be restricted to the most highly erodible land; the uses of the CRP land, especially for grazing and hay; the treatment of cover crops, such as alfalfa in a crop rotation, under conservation compliance; the definitions of wetlands for swampbuster; and, finally, the implementation of conservation compliance.

Probably the most difficult jobs in implementing the conservation provisions have been those of the SCS soil conservationists in field offices who work directly with farmers. Excluding the national office, four technical centers, and the state offices, there are about 7,000 SCS employees in the field. SCS estimated that work on the conservation provisions would require about 70 percent of that staff's time until 1995. To date, much of the time has gone to making highly erodible soil determinations; updating field office technical guides with conservation systems for that particular region, its soils and traditional cropping patterns, and writing conservation plans. A field is considered highly erodible if one-third of its soil map units, or as much as 50 acres in it, are highly erodible. About 120 million acres on 1.7 million out of the 2.3 million farms in the United States are affected. SCS concentrated first on conservation compliance and is now turning its attention to making wetland determinations. Of the estimated 70 million acres of wetlands, about 5 million acres have potential for conversion to cropland and thus are affected.

Not only has there been a high work load, but there has also been the stress associated with rendering unpopular options. Conservation compliance has resulted in a role change for soil conservationists. They can still be, as they have been in the past, friends with farmers. But at times they may need to make determinations on highly erodible land or wetlands that are unwelcomed. The ability to work with the farmer toward a mutually acceptable solution is a challenge for soil conservationists. Because of this need, states have begun to focus more of their training for field office employees on stress management, conflict resolution, and public relations skills to prepare them to deal more effectively with the publics that they serve.

The Food Security Act also has some implications for the work of SCS. Operating soil conservation programs under the conservation provisions will lead to greater integration of economic analysis into farm conservation planning and the design of conservation practices. The process has already started. Researchers in experiment stations have, from the early days of the soil conservation movement, undertaken economic analysis of soil conservation programs to assist farmers and to promote the programs. At other times, researchers have tried to analyze motivation to reveal why farmers adopt conservation practices. Will farmers adopt conservation practices only if it can be demonstrated conclusively that they are profitable? Are farmers significantly motivated to adopt conservation practices by the conservation ethic? What needs, other than economic viability, do farmers have that may provide the incentive for conservation? Future analyses of the response to conservation compliance legislation may provide some answers to these questions. Conservation compliance focuses more attention, both on the part of the farmer and SCS, on the benefits, costs, and motivations involved in soil conservation.

Also, the economic aspect should influence the range of options available to farmers. That is to say, it should influence the design of conservation systems. One criticism of soil conservation practices has been that too often practices have not been designed for small farmers with limited resources. This, of course, is not a new concern. When speaking of working with minority groups, Kenneth E. Grant, then administrator of SCS, said in 1972, "We may have to invent ways to install practices that do not require expensive specialized equipment or costly materials" (14). The number of minority farmers has continued to decrease drastically, but there have been significant increases in the number of small and part-time farmers. With conservation compliance, the need exists to design systems and practices for limited-resource farmers and part-time farmers that are economically feasible. Economists should be involved, along with the engineers, agronomists, and earth scientists, in working out a whole range of options with varying degrees of effectiveness and cost efficiency.

Conservation compliance also provides an opportunity to reduce the gap between conservation measures planned and conservation measures applied. Of all the people SCS assisted with conservation plans in 1968, only 65 percent actually applied at least one conservation practice. A few years later, the figure had dropped to under 60 percent, and, indeed, 65 percent was viewed as a reasonable goal (14).

A little historical perspective on this matter is in order. When Hugh Hammond Bennett was successful in securing emergency relief administration funds to conduct demonstration projects in 1933, there were other competitors for conservation funds. Bennett successfully argued against an emergency terracing program and made the case that there was more to soil conservation than terracing. When the Soil Erosion Service started contacting the farmers in demonstration project areas, they worked out conservation plans for the whole farm. The concept was and is good. But the agency has still had to struggle with a couple of problems. First, in judging progress in soil conservation on the land or the employee's effectiveness, completion of plans could too readily be confused with accomplishments. Conservation compliance has changed the focus. The farmer is more likely to look at his or her operation as a whole when making decisions about the crop rotations, cover crops, and other aspects of a conservation system. Planning and application of conservation practices should correlate more closely than ever before.

The Food Security Act should also lead to greater coordination of SCS recommendations to farmers with advice to the farmers from other federal agencies and the state extension services. Again, the historical reasons are illustrative. The early proponents of SCS argued successfully that attention to soil conservation from USDA was lagging and that a separate agency was appropriate. Opponents of a service devoted solely to soil conservation held that soil conservation was only one aspect of farm management. Any assistance to farmers in soil conservation should be delivered along with other assistance in animal or crop production and the other facets of farm management. But SCS has maintained its independence. In delineating responsibilities within USDA to avoid conflicts soil conservation has been treated as a separate component of farm management. Admittedly, the boundaries were blurred. With the requirements of conservation compliance, farmers are likely to insist that USDA speak with one voice and that farmers receive information on soil conservation that is coordinated with advice on other farm matters that they received from other agencies.

The Food Security Act emphasis on linking soil conservation to other assistance available from USDA and trying to add some consistency to program objectives is only the latest of numerous devices tried. We—society— have relied on research, science, technology, and education in delivering information on soil conservation directly to farmers. As a society we have helped pay for conservation through cost-sharing. Through purchase or rental, we have tried to retire or change the uses of erodible land. Appeals to farmers have varied from stewardship to profitability as a reason for soil conservation. None of these ways to promote soil conservation proved a panacea, but all had and have merit. The results of the conservation provisions have not run their course. In our complex society we dare not hope for perfection. But we can recognize the legislation as a significant addition to the quest and our work toward an enduring agriculture.

REFERENCES

1. American Farmland Trust. 1984. *Soil conservation in America: What do we have to lose?* Washington, D.C. 131 pp.
2. Batie, Sandra A. 1983. *Crisis in America's croplands?* The Conservation Foundation, Washington, D.C. 131 pp.
3. Berg, Norman A., and Robert J. Gray. 1984. *Soil conservation: The search for solutions.* Journal of Soil and Water Conservation 39(1): 18-22.
4. Browne, William P. 1988. *Private interests, public policy, and American agriculture.* University Press of Kansas, Lawrence. 294 pp.
5. Butz, Earl L. 1973. *Produce and protect.* Journal of Soil and Water Conservation 28(6): 250-251.
6. Chapman, E. Wayne. 1987. *Rationale and legislation for the creation of the Conservation Reserve Program.* In *Symposium Proceedings, Impacts of the Conservation Reserve Program in the Great Plains.* General Technical Report RM-158. U.S. Forest Service, Fort Collins, Colorado. pp. 9-13.
7. Cook, Kenneth A. 1981. *Problems and prospect for the Agricultural Conservation*

Program. Journal of Soil and Water Conservation 36(1): 24-27.

8. Cook, Kenneth A. 1981. *RCA and the art of the possible.* Journal of Soil and Water Conservation 36(6): 330-333.

9. Cook, Kenneth A. 1981. *The National Agricultural Lands Study goes out with a bang.* Journal of Soil and Water Conservation 36(2): 91-93.

10. Cook, Ken. 1983. *Soil Conservation: PIK in a poke.* Journal of Soil and Water Conservation 38(6): 475-476.

11. Cook, Ken. 1986. *Pinch me, I must be dreamin!* Journal of Soil and Water Conservation 41(2): 93-94.

12. Davis, R. M. 1978. *RCA: Your role in conservation's future.* Journal of Soil and Water Conservation 33(6): 267-269.

13. Glasser, Lawrence. 1986. *Provisions of the Food Security Act of 1985.* Agricultural Information Bulletin No. 498. U.S. Department of Agriculture, Washington, D.C. pp. 46-50.

14. Grant, Kenneth. 1972. *Annual message, Conference of State Conservationists, September 25, 1972.* Soil Conservation Service, U.S. Department of Agriculture, Washington, D.C. 25 pp.

15. Grant, Kenneth E. 1975. *Erosion in 1973-1974: The record and the challenge.* Journal of Soil and Water Conservation 30(1): 29-32.

16. Heimlich, Ralph E. 1985. *Soil erosion on new cropland: A sodbusting perspective.* Journal of Soil and Water Conservation 40(4): 322-326.

17. Heimlich, Ralph E., and Nelson L. Bills. 1984. *An improved soil erosion classification for conservation policy.* Journal of Soil and Water Conservation 39(4): 261-266.

18. Huszar, Paul C. 1985. *Dusting off the sodbuster issue.* Journal of Soil and Water Conservation 40(6): 482-484.

19. Jeffords, James M. 1982. *Soil conservation policy for the future.* Journal of Soil and Water Conservation 37(1): 10-13.

20. Laycock, W. A. 1981. *History of grassland plowing and grass planting on the Great Plains.* In *Impact of the Conservation Reserve Program in the Great Plains.* General Technical Report RM-158. Rocky Mountain Forest and Range Experiment Station, Forest Service, U.S. Department of Agriculture, Fort Collins, Colorado. pp. 3-8.

21. Lindert, Peter H. 1988. *Long-run trends in American farmland values.* Agricultural History 62(summer): 45-85.

22. Mekelburg, Milton E. 1983. *New approaches to commodity programs and conservation goals.* Journal of Soil and Water Conservation 38(4): 324-325.

23. Myers, Peter C. 1984. *A new look at funding technical assistance.* Journal of Soil and Water Conservation 38(1): 38-39.

24. Myers, Peter C. 1985. *Targeting: How good is the aim?* Journal of Soil and Water Conservation 49(3): 282-283.

25. Sampson, R. Neil. 1981. *Farmland or wasteland: A time to choose.* Rodale Press, Emmaus, Pennsylvania. 422 pp.

26. Society of Range Management. 1983. *Symposium on the plowing of fragile grasslands in Colorado.* Rangelands 5(2): 61-65.

27. Soil and Water Conservation Society. 1988. *American agriculture at the crossroads: A conservation assessment of the Food Security Act.* Journal of Soil and Water Conservation 43(1): 1-112.

28. Soil Conservation Service, U.S. Department of Agriculture. 1980. *Field windbreak removals in five Great Plains States, 1970 to 1975.* Washington, D.C. 15 pp.

29. Soil Conservation Society of America. 1981. *An interview with Robert Gray.* Journal of Soil and Water Conservation 36(3): 62-68.

30. Soil Conservation Society of America. 1982. *Twenty questions, John Block.* Journal

of Soil and Water Conservation 37(1): 7-9.
31. Soth, Lauren. 1981. *Farm and conservation policy decisions Reagan will face.* Journal of Soil and Water Conservation 36(1): 22-24.
32. U.S. Congress. 1982. Congressional Record. S. 12376, September 28, 1982.
33. U.S. Congress. 1982. *Prohibition of price supports for crop produced on certain lands.* House of Representatives, Committee on Agriculture. 97th Congress, 2nd session, Washington, D.C.
34. U.S. Congress. 1983. *Senate, Committee on Agriculture, Hearing, prohibition of incentive payments for crops produced on highly erodible land.* 98th Congress, 1st session, Washington, D.C. 106 pp.
35. U.S. Congress, House of Representatives. 1984. *Agriculture, rural development, and related agencies appropriation bill, 1985.* House Report 98-809, 98th Congress, 2nd session. Washington, D.C.
36. U.S. Congress, House of Representatives, Committee on Agriculture. 1984. *Hearings, miscellaneous conservation.* 98th Congress, 1st session, Serial No. 98-13. Washington, D.C. 503 pp.
37. U.S. Department of Agriculture. 1981. *1980 appraisal. Part I. Soil, water, and related resources in the United States: Status, condition and trends.* Washington, D.C. 327 pp.
38. U.S. Department of Agriculture. 1981. *1980 appraisal. Part II. Soil, water, and related resources in the United States: Analysis of resource trends.* Washington, D.C. 296 pp.
39. U.S. Department of Agriculture. 1981. *1981 program report and environmental impact statement, revised draft, Soil and Water Resources Conservation Act, 1981.* Washington, D.C.
40. U.S. Department of Agriculture. 1982. *A national program for soil and water conservation: 1982 final program report and environmental impact statement.* Washington, D.C. 163 pp.
41. U.S. Department of Agriculture. 1987. *Agricultural statistics, 1987.* Washington, D.C.
42. U.S. Department of Agriculture. 1988. *Conservation systems workshop.* Produced for the U.S. Department of Agriculture by the Cooperative Extension Service. University of Illinois, Urbana.

3

Implementing the Conservation Title of the 1985 Food Security Act: Conservation or Politics?

Richard T. Clark and James B. Johnson

The Conservation Title (Title XII) of the 1985 Food Security Act has three major subtitles. Subtitle B, Highly Erodible Land Conservation, contains the provisions that have become popularly known as "conservation compliance" and "sodbuster." This subtitle requires farmers of highly erodible land (HEL) to implement a locally approved soil conservation plan by certain dates in order to remain eligible for most USDA programs.

Subtitle C, Wetland Conservation, is also known as "swampbuster." This subtitle requires that farmers not physically alter and plant crops on natural wetlands if they want to remain eligible for other U.S. Department of Agriculture (USDA) benefits.

Subtitle D, Conservation Reserve, is a voluntary land retirement program for HEL and other lands deemed unsuitable for cultivation.

The Soil Conservation Service (SCS) and the Agricultural Stabilization and Conservation Service (ASCS) have the major roles in implementing these conservation subtitles. ASCS is the overall administrator of these subtitles, but SCS has significant responsibilities as well. For the first time SCS is working with farmers in a nonvoluntary role.

The Extension Service has responsibility for coordination of education and information related to Title XII. Other USDA agencies, such as the Federal Crop Insurance Corporation (FCIC), Forest Service (FS), and

26

Farmers Home Administration (FmHA) also have roles in implementing the conservation subtitles.

Implementation—From Whose Perspective?

Dicks and Grano (7) suggest that implementation is the final step in the three-step evolution of government programs. The first two steps are development and legislation.

Development is the time during which research into ways of achieving objectives is conducted. In this phase the probable economic impacts of alternative actions may be examined.

During the legislative step, choices of alternative actions are made on the basis of social and political feasibility. Based on the Dicks and Grano assertion then, the Conservation Title of the 1985 Food Security Act is conservation, but it is also politics. This statement certainly comes as no surprise.

Once legislation becomes law, the implementation strategy is developed by the agency charged with the responsibility. Legislation upon which implementation strategy is based can be quite specific or general. Leitch (18) argues that bills are often deliberately written to allow discretion so that lawmakers and administrators are not locked into unforeseen situations. General legislation provides only limits on actions and general guidance. As Dicks and Grano (7) suggest, the Conservation Title legislation is general; therefore, the implementing agencies in USDA had broad discretionary powers in determining specific implementation strategies.

The USDA agencies responsible for implementing the conservation provisions fully exercised their discretionary authority as reflected in the implementation paperwork. The legislation itself covers four, three-column pages. Final rules and discussions cover 26 pages. In addition, ASCS has large implementation manuals for the Conservation Reserve Program (CRP) and for highly erodible land and wetland conservation. Beyond these manuals are reams of national and state notices issued to clarify Title XII procedures. SCS has processed several trees (forests) upon which implementing directions are written! SCS even issued in 1988 a "Food Security Act Manual" that not only described its responsibilities but also those of other USDA agencies.

Dicks and Grano (7) conclude: "Thus, the performance of the legislated program(s) depends almost entirely upon the implementation process." The attitude of the implementing agency is crucial to the eventual outcome. What if the U.S. Fish and Wildlife Service had been the implementing agency for Title XII?

Dicks and Grano quote T. K. Jayuraman (*14*) who was addressing watershed projects:

"Good ideas do not fully materialize unless proper care is taken at the implementation stage. The saddest thing...is that, whilst so much time and attention was paid to technological component(s) in the earlier stages of preplanning, planning, and the feasibility study preparation, there was not much attention paid to the problems of the actual implementation."

There is little doubt that this is also true of the Conservation Title, particularly the CRP. Only about two months lapsed between passage of the law and the first CRP sign-up. This was not the fault of the implementing agency. Legislated goals made it imperative that action happen fast. In retrospect, the first set of rules and regulations for CRP were quite complete, and the dedicated civil servants are to be complimented.

Leitch (*18*) notes three federal perspectives to the implementation process: administration, congress, and the agencies. The Reagan Administration was primarily concerned with the budget; therefore, major actions were to limit spending and get government out of agriculture. The administration was content to let others worry about implementation. Congress is concerned with getting reelected. Congressional members will listen to their constituents and special interests. Agencies are expected to implement laws that congress wants within policy guidelines set forth by the administration. These perspectives may be helpful to keep in mind as implementation of Title XII is discussed.

Even with acceptance of the Dicks and Grano view of the evolutionary steps of governmental programs, one additional step merits emphasis. That step comes after implementation by the designated agency. It is acceptance and implementation by the directly affected public, in this case those farmers of highly erodible land and wetlands. So when one asks, "How is implementation going?", one must also ask, "From whose perspective?"

Wetland conservation will have impacts on fewer farmers. It is also less advanced in its implementation. For these reasons, Subtitle C is not addressed here.

Conservation Reserve Program

Is CRP Meeting the Goals? The primary purpose of CRP, as expressed in the final rules and regulations (*39*), is "...reducing the amount of erosion occurring on our nation's cropland.... The other objectives listed in Section 704.1 are secondary benefits." Other objectives are to (1) protect our longterm capability to produce food and fiber, (2) reduce sedimenta-

Table 1. Acres eligible for and accepted into the Conservation Reserve Program through 1988.

Region*	Eligible	Accepted	Accepted/Eligible (percent)
	acres		
West and Intermountain	7,746,800	2,507,126	32.4
Northern Great Plains	13,813,700	5,885,359	42.6
Central Great Plains	17,535,600	5,293,258	30.2
Southern Great Plains	17,753,300	4,942,617	27.8
Lake States	6,150,300	2,261,660	36.8
Corn Belt	21,753,800	3,921.830	18.0
Northeast	4,192,200	161,598	3.9
Southeast	12,347,600	3,156,462	25.6
Total United States	101,535,800	28,130,290	27.7

Source: Unpublished information from the U.S. Department of Agriculture.
*Regions including the following states: West and Intermountain—AK, AZ, CA, HI, ID, NV, OR, UT, WA; Northern Great Plains—MT, ND, SD, WY; Central Great Plains—CO, KS, NE; Southern—NM, OK, TX; Lake States—MI, MN, WI; Corn Belt—IL, IN, IA, MO, OH; Northeast—CT, DE, MD, ME, MA, NH, NJ, NY, PA, RI, VT; Southeast—AL, AR, FL, GA, KY, LA, MS, NC, SC, TN, VA, WV.

tion, (3) improve water quality, (4) create fish and wildlife habitat, (5) curb production of surplus commodities, and (6) provide needed income support for farmers.

A sense of how well CRP is meeting the primary goal can be attained by examining the enrollment of eligible land. The Corn Belt, East, and Northeast have the poorest track record of enrolling land, when percentages of eligible land enrolled is considered (Table 1). However, with about 28 percent of the land eligible for CRP enrolled through 1988, progress is being made. In addition, SCS estimates of erosion reduction are phenomenal.

The impacts on sedimentation and water quality have not been estimated directly. If erosion has been reduced, some sedimentation and water quality benefits may have been realized. The addition of filter strips as a CRP practice was an attempt to increase the direct water quality benefits of CRP and a recognition that CRP was not providing enough of such benefits.

Reduction of crop acreage bases for commodity program crops could have some impact on the total supply of program crops. Table 2 outlines progress relative to the reduction of base acreages.

Major Implementation Issues. When attention is directed only to the numbers, such as enrollment and base reduction, one becomes quite euphoric about progress with CRP. And there may be good reason to be euphoric.

Yet, implementation of the conservation reserve has not been without problems.

Definitional Changes. Eligibility criteria are important in determining who can play the game. There was a change in the definition of eligible land before the first sign-up began but after publicity had been sent out. This change—from two times the soil tolerance (T) to 3T—was brought about through political lobbying by environmental groups. The main effect of this definitional change was a reduction in eligible land from about 104 million acres to about 70 million acres (*9*). The criterion was changed again prior to the third sign-up to include those acres in land capability classes II through V that were eroding at 2T or greater if they had significant gully erosion. Finally, for the fourth and subsequent bids the criterion became land with an erosion index of 8 or more if this land were eroding at a rate of T or more. The latter change increased the pool of eligible land to an estimated 122 million acres (*6*). It also made land eligible that, under current farming practices, does not have a major erosion problem—a defeat for the major program goal. This latter change did appease those who had argued that the definition for CRP land and conservation compliance should be compatible (*2, 8*). The periodic changing of the eligibility criterion made information and education programs difficult. It also confused bidders, who

Table 2. Acres of program crop bases and base acres placed in the CRP through 1988.

Region*	Corn and Sorghum Base	Corn and Sorghum CRP	Oats and Barley Base	Oats and Barley CRP	Wheat Base	Wheat CRP	UP Cotton Base	UP Cotton CRP
				million acres				
West and Intermountain	0.89	.008	3.61	.663	8.07	.931	2.08	†
Northern Great Plains	5.72	.300	10.09	1.529	24.92	1.959	—	—
Central Great Plains	18.31	1.209	1.43	.301	21.19	1.994	†	†
Southern Great Plains	9.10	.906	.95	.079	16.51	1.934	8.73	1.074
Lake States	14.15	.609	3.43	.437	4.91	.373	—	—
Corn Belt	40.11	1.558	1.15	.116	7.56	.522	.26	†
Northeast	2.94	.034	.52	.017	.55	.007	—	—
Southeast	9.89	.588	.70	.071	8.44	.681	4.50	.085
Total United States	101.11	5.211	21.88	3.213	92.15	8.400	15.58	1.160

Source: Base acres are for 1986 from "The Conservation Reserve Program: Progress Report and Preliminary Evaluation of the First Two Years." USDA report, November 1988, and CRP acres from unpublished USDA data provided by James R. McMullen, ASCS.
*See table 1 for states contained in each region.
†Less than 1,000 acres.

found themselves ineligible under certain specifications of the criterion and eligible under other specifications of the criterion. The eligibility criterion of land for CRP has been the primary source of SCS state-level appeals in Nebraska.[1]

Early in CRP, the definition of an "agricultural commodity" seemed to exclude alfalfa and perennial grasses. It was not until an amendment[2] was passed that this definition was clarified. Now, alfalfa and perennial grasses in rotation are acceptable "agricultural commodities" for CRP eligibility. This is another change brought about by the political process. The erosion control impact of this definitional change is difficult to assess. If highly erodible land that was in alfalfa for at least four of the five years from 1981-1985 can now be placed in permanent CRP cover, the expected average annual erosion should be less under CRP than under the cropping rotation.

Bidding and Bid Acceptance Procedure. The bidding concept appeared to be sound. Farmers would bid their eligible land according to their returns foregone. Cropland with lower net returns would be bid at lower levels than more productive, erodible cropland, thus minimizing the government's costs for retiring land. An early analysis by the Economic Research Service (ERS) showed that costs per ton of erosion reduction could be minimized by targeting highly erodible land for bidding and accepting bids in ascending order up to some predetermined acreage level (*12*). That procedure was not as efficient as others in reducing surplus crop production. Although this early analysis did not include land that was highly erodible because of wind erosion, the analysis demonstrated how a bidding procedure and conservation reserve could work.

The bidding procedure did work fairly well through the first three sign-ups. Then it became apparent that USDA was not likely to lower the pool bid maximums. Bidders grouped their bids at the previous pool bid maximums. The bid system became an offer system.

Politics seems to have entered the setting of pool bid maximums, and certain bidders apparently received inside information. In one Nebraska pool the maximum was raised $5 per acre for the fourth sign-up. Bids from certain counties within that pool grouped at a bid level that was $5 per acre higher than the previous pool bid maximum. Bidders in other counties in the pool apparently did not receive the insider's information because their bids were all grouped at the prior pool bid maximum. The word that the pool maximum was to be raised apparently was leaked from congres-

[1]Personal conversation with Russell Shultz, assistant state conservationist, SCS, Nebraska, 1988.
[2]ASCS, USDA. 1987. Notice CRP-54. January 23.

sional sources prior to the bidding period.

It has been stated that within-state pool boundaries were set to spread the payment out over congressional districts (31). One of the authors of this paper helped to set the pool boundaries in Nebraska. These boundaries were set to coincide with the type of agriculture and to help target erosion. After the first sign-up the maximum pool bids became known. It became apparent what would have happened in Nebraska without pool boundaries. Highly erodible (from water erosion) land in eastern Nebraska would not have been bid at the lower bid levels set for the western Nebraska wind erosion areas. If bid caps that would attract the eastern Nebraska land would have been used for a statewide pool, bidders in western Nebraska would have bid to receive the windfall gains from CRP participation. Budget exposure under CRP would have exceeded per acre benefits from program crop payments and net returns from production. A change in the bid acceptance criteria from maximums per acre to least cost per ton of erosion reduced would have eliminated the need for intrastate pools.

Some cleverness on the part of those setting pool maximums might also have resulted in a wider range of bids. If the maximum bids to be accepted had occasionally been lowered, bidders would have kept bidding rather than offering. But the politics of such an action were such that this behavior did not occur.

The secretary of agriculture has the flexibility to accept bids according to criteria other than those being used. As Dicks (6) argues, a complete evaluation of CRP requires a look at its performance against all goals. He shows that through the first four sign-ups the program had a net cost of $14 per acre when compared to erosion and supply control benefits. Is that too large a cost for the remaining, unmeasured benefits? If the secretary decides it is, the discretionary authority to alter the bid acceptance criteria could permit an improvement in the cost/benefit ratio.

Reichelderfer and Boggess (31) state: "The evidence suggests that implementation of the CRP in 1986 was suboptimal in the sense that the net government cost of the program could have been reduced while simultaneously increasing the level of erosion reduction and supply control achieved."

Dicks and associates (9) show that a bid selection criterion of minimizing the net cost per ton of erosion reduction would have increased supply and erosion control benefits above those being realized under the current bidding procedures for the same total federal outlay. In their analysis, net costs were equal to rental costs minus supply control cost savings. The net cost of each bid was then divided by the total pretreatment erosion and bids with the lowest cost per ton were chosen first until the budget limit was achieved. This alternate bid selection criterion could produce more of certain benefits than the bidding procedure in use. Why hasn't this alternate procedure been used? Maybe the answer is politics.

The Bid Limit. The maximum bid level set for each pool has had a profound effect on overall performance of CRP. The only significant change in the concept came about with the sixth sign-up period. This change, because of an amendment to a funding bill, indicated that county maximums were to be set no higher than local land rental rates, regardless of the pool maximum.[3] Beyond that, each bid was to be accepted only if it did not exceed the local rental rate for comparable land. The cash rental rate was to be a major determinant of that maximum. Just prior to the bidding period, other local rental rates, including crop-shares, were included in the calculations of comparable rental rates.[4] Permitting the use of crop-share was needed in states, such as Nebraska, where it is the predominant lease arrangement (*15*). In more than half of the states some county maximums were set below pool maximums.[5] The number of individual bids rejected because of county maximums is unknown. This revised procedure created considerable paperwork and delayed acceptance of bids and notification of bidders.

The procedure was then changed again. Counties were notified that their maximums for the seventh sign-up would be the same as the pool.[6]

Limiting maximums to land rental rates may make sense for a budget-conscious administration, but it makes little economic sense from the bidder's perspective. The CRP retires resources other than land. Many of the costs of other resources can be stopped when land is retired (e.g., fertilizer, diesel fuel, hired labor, seed, irrigation fuel, and repairs on equipment). However, costs of some resources cannot be so easily turned off. What happens to operator management and labor? If there is alternative employment that provides a labor return equal to or greater than CRP, then the charge against the CRP land could logically be zero. Otherwise, idled labor needs to be compensated through payment.

The ownership costs of a machinery complement continue when land is idled unless some of the machinery is sold. It is difficult to sell off excess machine capacity. How do you sell 40 percent of a 24-foot combine? These costs need to be charged to CRP unless adequate alternative uses of the machinery are available. Consequently, the CRP bid was expected to cover machinery ownership costs in instances where the machinery

---

[3]ASCS, USDA, 1988. Notice CRP-92, January 29.
[4]ASCS, USDA. 1988. Notice CRP 94. February 11.
[5]ASCS, USDA. 1988. Notices CRP 95 and 96. March 3 and March 14, respectively.
[6]ASCS, USDA. 1988. Notice CRP 104. July 13.

capacity is idled. USDA apparently has not fully recognized that CRP payments in many cases properly include compensation for factors of production other than land.

What will be the effect of strengthening commodity prices on break-even bid levels? It is estimated that a break-even CRP bid in eastern Nebraska would be $81 per acre with a current corn price of $2.50 per bushel and an ASCS yield of 60 bushels per acre. That exceeds the present eastern Nebraska maximum by $11 per acre. The fact that pool bid maximums are too low to attract corn acres was dramatically demonstrated when the corn bonus was offered in the fourth bid period. About 1.9 million acres of the total 3.1 million acres of corn base reduction in the first seven sign-ups occurred in the fourth sign-up.[7]

Farm-level Implementation Problems. Once a bidder has land accepted into the CRP, some problems have occurred. One major problem, particularly in wheat-producing areas of the Great Plains, is pest control. Establishment of permanent grass, especially native species, in the Great Plains often requires several years. During the interim period, CRP acres are infested with annual and noxious weeds. While CRP rules are clear that noxious weeds are to be controlled, they are less clear about annual weeds. Weeds are to be controlled if they threaten establishment and maintenance of the stand; seldom is that the case for annual weeds. Weeds do not necessarily create a problem on CRP land itself; however, weeds on CRP land present problems for adjacent land and landowners.

Chemical sprays will control broadleaf weeds, but grassy weeds present another problem. High incidences of these grassy weeds have been documented on CRP land in western Nebraska.[8] These weeds are susceptible to wheat streak mosaic virus; they are also known overwintering areas for wheat leaf curl mites that spread the disease. Anecdotal evidence indicates that wheat fields next to CRP land have a higher incidence of wheat streak mosaic than others. While the cause and effect is unproven, the concern continues, as expressed by the Great Plains Agricultural Council.[9]

Landlord-tenant relations on CRP lands are a problem in the Great Plains and elsewhere, even though some disagree (*17*). While this does not appear to be a problem that keeps some people from bidding (*10*), it is the problem that has generated the most inquiries to state and county exten-

[7]Unpublished data from E. Wayne Chapman, Extension Service, March 16, 1987, and James R. McMullen, ASCS, January 3, 1989.
[8]Letter from Dr. John E. Watkins, extension plant pathologist, to Dr. Jim Bushnell, associate director, Nebraska Cooperative Extension Service. November 4, 1988.
[9]Report of the Implementation Subcommittee, Conservation Title Task Force, Great Plains Agricultural Council. May 1988.

sion faculty. Tenants complain that landlords try to remove them so landlords can receive the entire CRP payment. ASCS rules are quite clear that tenant history will be maintained on cropland entered into CRP. Yet, ASCS cannot legally force a landlord to maintain the "same" tenant prior to signing a CRP contract. The signed contract (and in cases of tenant relationships, it must be signed by all parties, including the tenant) is viewed by ASCS as a 10-year written lease between landlord and tenant. The only way the tenant will be changed after the CRP contract is signed is if the tenant leaves voluntarily. A landlord can, prior to lease signing, change tenants, and usually legally because leases tend to be verbal and year-to-year, at least in Nebraska and South Dakota (15). ASCS' only legal concern is the maintenance of tenant history, not the legal arrangements between tenants and landlords. Some landlords have illegally removed tenants, but this practice does not appear widespread.

Determining who receives what share of the CRP payment is the most common problem between landlords and tenants. Unless the CRP contract specifies otherwise, the CRP payment will be split the same as it is for commodity program payments. Most CRP contracts designate the shares to be received. Nebraska county ASCS committees review the share arrangements. Reversal of the shares of CRP payments from shares received in other farming operations appears common. A recently introduced bill in the Montana legislature follows this convention; it would require the state to provide 20 percent of CRP payments on state land to tenants.[10] CRP contract shares based on the cost contributions of involved parties suggest that share reversal is appropriate. This is particularly true of share leases when the landlord typically received 25 percent to 40 percent of the crop and when the CRP tenant will be responsible for stand establishment and maintenance. With CRP, the landlord would receive 60 percent to 75 percent of the payment.

The Future of CRP Lands. Several individuals have addressed the issue of what will happen to CRP acres once the contracts expire (1, 3, 16, 25), but few concrete suggestions have been put forth. A recent survey of CRP contract holders in Montana inquired of their intended use of CRP land when contracts expire.[11] This random survey of tenants and owner-operators revealed that 44 percent intended to crop CRP land, 39 percent intended to leave it in grass, and one percent intended to gift it to others. Surpris-

[10]Senate Bill 32. Montana State Senate. 1989. Sponsored by Senator Jenkins.
[11]Unpublished survey results, James B. Johnson and James E. Standaert. Department of Agricultural Economics and Economics, Montana State University, Bozeman. 1989.

ingly, none had intentions of selling his or her CRP land, but landlords who were nonoperators were not surveyed. The remaining 16 percent was comprised of nonrespondents and those who may have had other uses in mind that were not listed on the questionnaire. Whether or not the contract holders will carry out their intentions, of course, is speculation at this point. Cacek (3) argues that CRP land will have more permanence after the program than the Soil Bank land because of conservation compliance. CRP is targeted to marginal cropland, while the Soil Bank was not. If it is a desirable goal to maintain CRP in permanent cover, attention should be initiated on how to bribe contract holders.

Highly Erodible Lands

Agency Responsibilities. Many agencies are involved in the implementation of the highly erodible land (HEL) subtitle. Any USDA agency that provides covered benefits has responsibilities. Farmers who apply for loans through the Farmers Home Administration (FmHA) or for insurance through the Federal Crop Insurance Corporation (FCIC) or its affiliates activate actions by these two agencies related to the Conservation Title. If a farmer is not eligible for USDA benefits, it is up to the USDA agency to which the farmer applies for benefits to deny those benefits. Local conservation districts are responsible for final approval of conservation plans in most areas.

ASCS and SCS have substantial responsibilities for conservation eligibility determination, conservation planning, and enforcement. Among the specific responsibilities (41) of ASCS are determining (1) whether a person produced an agricultural commodity on a given field, (2) whether land was planted to an agricultural commodity or was in an approved set-aside program in any of the years 1981 through 1985, (3) whether to permit exchange of crop acreage bases of one crop for an acreage base of another crop that leaves higher crop residue, and (4) the history of landlord and tenant arrangements on specific land parcels. ASCS also establishes the official field boundaries and approves field boundary changes. Because ASCS administers price and income support programs, the agency must also rule on eligibility of those who request such benefits. Enforcement is another major ASCS responsibility.

SCS responsibilities are much broader for highly erodible land than for CRP. The implications of SCS actions are more encompassing. SCS is responsible for determining whether (1) land is highly erodible, (2) HEL is predominant in a field, (3) the conservation plan that a person is actively applying is based on a local SCS field office technical guide and is approved by the appropriate authorities, and (4) the conservation plan is adequate for the production of an agricultural commodity on highly erodible land. A potentially broad set of responsibilities was given to SCS when the final rule stated "...SCS will provide such other technical assistance for implementation of the provisions of this part as is determined to be necessary" (41).

The direct responsibilities given to SCS read as though SCS is not part of the enforcement process. But exemption (b) under section 12.5 of the final rule states (41):

"As further specified in this part, no person shall be ineligible for the program benefits described in section 12.4(a) as the result of production of an agricultural commodity on highly erodible land if such production is in compliance with an approved conservation plan or conservation system."

When this statement is examined in conjunction with specific SCS responsibilities, one might conclude that SCS is as responsible for enforcement of compliance as ASCS. In fact, section 510.44 of the SCS Food Security Act manual (43) suggests that SCS is to assist ASCS with compliance checks. Furthermore, section 510.70 states that SCS employees who observe violations of conservation rules must report those violations to ASCS.

Leaving the role of providing technical assistance to farm managers on a demand basis and moving to a quasi-regulatory role has placed many SCS employees in an uncomfortable position, and rightly so. Many people in the land grant university complex have experienced similar feelings when others have attempted to define an agenda for the complex and place land grant personnel in uncomfortable situations.

Conservation Compliance Versus Sodbuster Rules. The major difference between conservation compliance and sodbuster is the timing of the requirements for developing and implementing conservation plans. Conservation compliance is an exemption from the rules for highly erodible land that produced a commodity crop at least one year of five from 1981 through 1985. This exempted land must have an approved conservation plan by January 1, 1990. That plan must be fully implemented by January 1, 1995. Highly erodible land without that cropping history is known as "sodbusted" land if, after the law was passed, this land is used to produce an agricultural commodity crop. Sodbusted land must have an approved conservation plan fully implemented prior to producing an agricultural commodity to remain eligible for USDA benefits.

After January 1, 1990, all HEL will be under the same set of rules with one major exception. HEL that is converted from native vegetation (i.e., rangeland or woodland) to crop production after December 23, 1985, must have a basic conservation system as the conservation plan (42). Other highly erodible land will be allowed to use alternative conservation systems in the conservation plan.

One easily missed implication of the merging of rules for conservation compliance and sodbuster after January 1, 1990, is the importance of developing a plan for highly erodible cropland prior to the deadline. Those with a plan in hand by January 1, 1990, will have until January 1, 1995, to fully implement the plan. Those with highly erodible land who wait until after January 1, 1990, to develop a conservation plan will have to implement fully the approved plan immediately before a commodity crop can be produced if the producers are to maintain eligibility for USDA benefits.

Agency Progress with HEL Implementation. Completing conservation plans is the first step in local implementation of the HEL sections. Table 3 shows progress on this count through December 31, 1988. SCS had set a goal of completing 65 percent of the necessary plans by the end of 1988. At that point, the agency appeared to be on target. The remaining acres needing plans could well be the toughest, however. SCS goals may have been met by doing the easy ones first. A cursory study of completion rates in Nebraska revealed that northeastern Nebraska has the highest level of

Table 3. Progress in conservation planning for highly erodible land as of December 31, 1988.

	Highly Erodible Land		
Region*	Base	Fields Planned	Planned/Base (%)
	——— acres ———		
West and Intermountain	12,594,000	7,333,000	58.2
Northern Great Plains	25,159,000	15,460,000	61.4
Central Great Plains	31,821,000	21,985,000	69.1
Southern Great Plains	21,699,000	13,529,000	62.3
Lake States	6,018,000	3,260,000	54.2
Corn Belt	27,360,000	16,588,000	60.6
East	3,240,000	2,252,000	69.5
Northeast			
Southeast	14,786,000	8,770,000	59.3
Total United States†	142,677,000	89,177,000	62.5

Source: Unpublished data provided by Dwight M. Treadway, Extension Service, USDA, November 1988, and January 1989.
*See table 1 for states contained in each region.
†Numbers may not add due to rounding of individual state estimates.

uncompleted plans. That area is also known to be one with high levels of soil erosion and low historical participation in conservation programs. Less than 250 farm managers attended six workshops sponsored jointly by SCS, the Cooperative Extension Service, and the Montana Grain Growers Association held throughout Montana in November and December of 1988. SCS estimates that more than 60 percent of Montana's cropland is HEL. It is expected, therefore, that at least 60 percent of the state's 23,000 farms would require conservation plans. An attendance of 250 of a possible 14,000 farmers is not overwhelming interest.

Legislative History and Alternative Conservation Systems. Early action related to Title XII centered on CRP. The HEL and wetland subtitles of the law waited in the wings for rules and regulations until June 27, 1986 (*38*). Even then action was slow. A reading of the legislation and interim rules indicated that these sections had potential ramifications far beyond the CRP.[12]

Once the interim rules and regulations were issued, the action began. The interim rules specified that erosion would be controlled to T unless "impracticable" and then to 2T. The matter of impracticality was a judgment made by the local professional soil conservationist after considering the economic consequences. Apparently, SCS tried to determine how to deal with the concept of what was practicable. At least one SCS national technical center offered guidelines to state offices for dealing with this definitional nightmare.[13] In fact, SCS was in the process of developing a limited set of soils for which alternative conservation systems could be applied. Then, on June 29, 1987, a new interim rule was issued (*40*). This rule, which was subsequently made final (*41*), clarified that T will be a goal but not a requirement. The final rule (*41*) states:

"A conservation plan or a conservation system developed...must be based on and in conformity with the SCS field office technical guide. For highly erodible croplands which were in production prior to December 23, 1985, the applicable conservation systems...are designed to achieve *substantial*[14] reductions in soil erosion, taking into consideration economic and technical feasibility and other resource factors."

If the interim rule was not clear, later actions by SCS were. It is well known that some SCS state conservationist's jobs were on the line because

---

[12]Richard T. Clark. 1986. "The Sleeping Giant in the 1985 Farm Bill." University of Nebraska news release, August 1, 1986.
[13]Economics Technical Note No. 4. West NTC, Bulletin No. W200-7-2.
[14]Emphasis added.

they were too rigid in their use of T as a requirement. Wilson Scaling, chief of SCS, made it quite clear to SCS employees that use of alternative conservation systems was the SCS policy.[15] It is also clear that it was easier for Scaling to take such a stand than to follow a rigid T standard and place SCS in an even larger enforcer role. In 1985, not long after being appointed to the position of chief, Scaling stated (33):

"Above all, SCS recognizes that most agricultural land in this nation belongs to individuals. These people have the right to manage their land in the way they know best. Everywhere a government has tried to make these decisions for people that effort has failed. Centralized authority does not work.... Our nation must rely on the common sense of our farmers and ranchers to do what is right."

A rather interesting item concerning the apparent movement away from T as a requirement by SCS is found in the conference committee report of the original legislation. In the discussion of ineligibility of exempted highly erodible land (Section 1212 of the Food Security Act), the conferees state:[16]

"If a rigid standard of 'T' value is mandated for an acceptable conservation plan, even if erosion had been reduced from say 30 tons per acre to 7-8 tons per acre through the application of cost-effective conservation measures, the producer could be required to either install a very expensive additional practice such as terraces or convert the land to grass or trees from cropland in order to continue to be eligible for program benefits. It is not the intent of the Conferees to cause undue hardship on producers to comply with the provisions. Therefore, the Secretary should apply standards of reasonable judgement of local professional soil conservationists and consider economic consequences in establishing requirements...."

To most readers, it is clear that conferees did not want T used as a standard, yet those who drafted the interim rules stated T as a requirement. Once the standard became known, the political pressure began building. Some of that pressure arose from Nebraska, where public meetings with congressional representation were held. Farm-state congressional members applied pressure[17], and the rules were changed. They were changed to conform with the original congressional intent. USDA still came away with "egg on its face." It appeared to the general public and many soil conser-

[15]"A Visit with the Chief on the 1985 Farm Bill." Videotaped remarks by Wilson Scaling, chief, Soil Conservation Service, to SCS employees, May 4, 1988.
[16]U.S. House of Representatives. 1985. Food Security Act of 1985, the Committee of Conference-Conference Report. 99th Congress, 1st Session, Report 99-447.
[17]Beeder, David C. 1987. "Erosion Controls Called 'Heavy-handed'." Omaha World Herald, April 14.

vation professionals that USDA was caving in to political pressure (13, 32, 37). Haas (13) sums it up best:

"The ACS [alternative conservation systems] has turned out to be a highly flexible system that is adequate to satisfy the requirements of law. But it connotes a system that is substandard to the professional conservationist—one that does not conform to his or her standards for technical excellence."

If the policy that SCS intended to pursue was not already clear, it became perfectly clear to all within SCS on May 3, 1988.[18] Apparently, the trickle-down theory was not working well. Scaling's bulletin clearly states:

"ACS are to be included in all field office technical guides where there is highly erodible land subject to the compliance provision of the 1985 Food Security Act.[19] ACS will be developed for all HEL soils,..."

Prior to this bulletin, some SCS state offices were developing alternative conservation systems but only for certain targeted HEL soils.

Will alternative conservation systems be the downfall of conservation compliance? A good question, but one without a good answer, at least now. On the positive side, it has been known for years that reducing soil erosion to T can be costly (30) and that private economic incentives for soil conservation are weak (35). The added costs of achieving the last increments of soil erosion reduction are high. Use of alternative conservation systems may encourage a cost-effective approach to soil conservation.

But not having any standard other than the "substantial reduction" can lead to inconsistent plans between farms and neighbors. Problems from inconsistency will become apparent after enforcement begins in 1990. Such inconsistency and the apparent USDA waffling could strengthen attitudes reported by Nowak and Schnepf (27). More than 50 percent of USDA county-level administrators responding to their survey thought farmers believe that enforcement of conservation compliance will be relaxed. Nearly half also thought farmers believe the timetable for implementation of conservation compliance would be changed. Scaling (34) is not worried about consistency. He states, "Adaptation and flexibility to meet local needs is perhaps more desirable than complete consistency." Hopefully, he is right. The answer is not in.

Economic Analysis—Where Is It? The rules and regulations repeatedly suggest that an acceptable conservation system should be determined, in part, by economic evaluation.

[18]USDA, Soil Conservation Service. 1988. National Bulletin No. 180-8-31. Subject: CPA-Inclusion of Alternative Conservation Systems in Field Office Technical Guides. May 3.
[19]Emphasis not added.

Glenn Stoddard, executive director of Wisconsin's Land Conservation Association, states (37), "Alternative conservation systems may be needed to prevent economic hardship, but there has been no attempt to use explicit economic criteria in their development." That statement, though not documented, squares with our experience. In both Montana and Nebraska the development of alternative conservation systems by SCS was largely done by agency conservation agronomists with minimal input by agency economists and little, if any, review by university personnel or commodity organization leaders. The senior author of this paper asked the question, "Have you been involved in developing alternative conservation systems in your state?", to a group of state SCS economists from the Midwest who were attending an in-service training session.[20] From this group representing 12 states, only three felt they had been involved. One of the three admitted that he had been asked to do an economic analysis, but it had not been used in making the decision on alternative conservation systems. It is difficult to provide economic analysis if not asked—and, seemingly, equally as difficult if the economist offers.

SCS is not alone in neglecting the economics of alternative conservation systems. University research is also sparse, partly because conservation research typically has not attracted a lot of research dollars.

Some need may remain for the economic analysis of alternative conservation systems to allow farm managers some basis for selecting a plan that will have the most favorable (or least unfavorable) farm income impacts. Most of the plans we have observed in Montana and Nebraska have been quite general. These plans place heavy emphasis on crop residue management. We all know there are several cropping system and tillage method combinations that will meet a goal of "30 percent residue cover at planting." During the period 1990-1995, many farmers will be trying to meet such goals with an economically efficient management system. Some within SCS recognize the need for using economics in conservation planning, yet it will take cooperation and the desire by SCS line administrators to utilize and help develop economic evaluations of alternative conservation systems.[21]

Conservation Compliance and State Law. In some cases relaxation from the T standard has put state conservation laws and agencies at odds with

[20]Richard T. Clark, panel participant for the 1985 Food Security Act, Midwest NTC, in-service training for economists, Lincoln, Nebraska. June 29, 1988.
[21]"Integrating Economics into the Conservation Planning Process," a report by the SCS Economic Application Work Group, Paul A. Dodd, chairman. Issued as National Bulletin No. 450-9-7, January 30, 1989.

the federal rules. Nebraska's Erosion and Sediment Control Act is a case in point.

This law has a complaint section. If a neighbor successfully files a complaint about erosion damage, the offending farmer must develop a plan that will lower estimated erosion to T (*4*). The law grants exclusions to farmers who have and are following farm unit conservation plans. Because of the difference in erosion goals and the exclusion clause, Nebraska natural resource districts (NRDs) (conservation districts in most states) were quite concerned about alternative conservation systems. The Nebraska Natural Resources Commission, acting on behalf of the NRDs, negotiated a compromise with SCS. All Nebraska conservation compliance plans that do not reduce erosion to T will now contain the following statement.[22]

"All parties acknowledge that this plan does not reduce average annual soil losses in field no.(s)_____to the levels required under the Nebraska Erosion and Sediment Control Act, that this plan does not constitute a 'farm unit conservation plan' as defined in the act, and that implementation of this plan may not protect the landowner and/or operator from complaints filed pursuant to the act."

On-Farm Implementation—A Potential Problem. Acceptance and implementation of conservation plans by farmers represent the most important phase of the entire process. It appears that ASCS and SCS are depending primarily on "self-certification" for ensuring compliance. Beginning in 1990, farmers will need to certify that they are in compliance whenever they apply for benefits for any of the affected USDA programs. But will this faith be adequate?

Research suggests that farmers' recognition of the soil erosion problem is a key to their voluntary adoption of soil-conserving practices (*23, 26, 28*). Is there any reason to believe things will be different under the present rules? Research also has shown that farmers perceive lower levels of erosion on their own farms than do conservation professionals (*26, 28*). If nothing else, the compliance process should improve problem recognition. Of course, being told and accepting are not necessarily synonymous.

One of the reasons that acceptance is difficult for some is that the direct costs of sheet and rill erosion and wind erosion are not obvious. Even the long-run costs of these appear to be small (*29*). Lovejoy and Napier (*19*) suggest that farmers will not adopt conservation practices to solve erosion problems when the long-run impacts are small. If conservation practices

[22]USDA, Soil Conservation Service, Nebraska Bulletin No. 300-8-32, June 29, 1988.

simultaneously solve other problems, the probability of adoption increases.

Conservation cannot be "sold" to farmers on the basis of farm benefits from erosion control. Better information about intergenerational problems and offsite costs are needed. Some have suggested that programs aimed at altering attitudes may be helpful (19, 28). But changes in attitudes must also be accompanied by changes in behavior—an additional step that is not easy to bring about.

Napier and Forster (22) suggested in 1982 that mandatory methods are essential for erosion control. They cited many references to studies that showed farmers strongly oppose laws or regulations that impose environmental standards and land use controls. A recent survey concludes that farmers believe soil conservation is not an appropriate area for governmental intervention (20). Furthermore, Napier (21) reports that Ohio farmers believed they should not be responsible for assuming the economic costs of adopting soil erosion control practices. Indeed, farmers have been permitted to take this view for years. Fletcher (11) suggests that since the beginning of soil conservation programs landowners have had the implicit right to allow erosion if they so chose.

Does Title XII signal a change in this traditional view of property rights? If it does, there is a lot of convincing to do. Napier and Forster (22) stated, "Evidence suggests that educational approaches to soil erosion control typically have little effect when employed alone." Maybe Title XII, combined with educational efforts, will do the job. But Title XII must be enforced if it is to be that tool. Self-certification is inadequate. ASCS and SCS should seriously consider how they will jointly check compliance and bring credibility to the laws. Will politically appointed agency heads be able to handle the heat? A positive answer is in doubt. Concerns with the political nature of implementation continue.

Even if farmers accept the fact that they must comply with the Conservation Title requirement, those same farmers must implement the plans. Farmers who have not used conservation tillage methods will not learn overnight. High-residue systems require different management than those that rely on more tillage. Some plans call for more than 50 percent residue cover after planting. That will be difficult to achieve under the best of management.

It has also been demonstrated that farmers do not properly perceive their use of conservation tillage (5). Studies show that the costs of conservation methods compared to conventional methods are important in bringing about change (11, 24, 36). While emphasis on the farm benefits of erosion control may not sell the program, information on comparative costs and risks appear to offer promise. The time is right for a major effort to bring together what is known about the costs of alternative conservation systems and to provide evaluation methods for farm managers to determine probable farm income impacts of the use of alternative systems. Farmers will be requiring that kind of information while they are learning to implement plans. They will also need technical assistance on how to accomplish correctly the elements of their plans.

Where Is Conservation Without Commodity Programs? If 1990 results in a major change in commodity programs, HEL conservation could become much less effective. The "mandatory" or economically essential nature of conservation compliance would be lost for many farmers if the administration does away with price and income support programs. There will still be strong incentives for farmer compliance in the Great Plains, however, because of FCIC insurance. The bottom line is that conservationists need to keep a close watch on the 1990 farm bill. Major changes in the commodity program may necessitate major changes in the Conservation Title.

Conclusions

The major on-farm implementation problems for CRP, particularly in the Great Plains, will be the weed and insect host nature of CRP. Landlord-tenant relationships will also continue to create headaches. On a macro scale, it will be difficult to meet CRP goals in the face of constrained federal budgets. A change in bidding and bid acceptance criteria may be helpful for achieving erosion and other goals within tight budgets. Negative impacts on local economics in areas of high CRP participation is a problem that merits watching. Of course, the future of CRP after the contracts expire must not be forgotten.

The major conservation problem for the HEL section of the Conservation Title is successful implementation of conservation plans. Good, sound economic analyses of alternative means for implementing the plans could help. But no major desire is evident among those with line decision-making authority in SCS to see that economics becomes a functional part of technical assistance and plan development. Furthermore, concern exists about the nature of conservation plans. A majority of conservation plans will likely require few if any changes from current farming practices, even in areas plagued with high levels of erosion. Enforcement of plans is another concern. Procedures have not been worked out for effective enforcement. Without adequate enforcement, the best plans may be meaningless. More than education will be needed in some areas.

Is Title XII conservation or politics? No doubt both, but with too much emphasis on the latter.

REFERENCES

1. Bartlett, E. T. 1987. *Social and economic impacts of the Conservation Reserve Program.* Impacts of the Conservation Reserve Program in the Great Plains: Symposium Proceedings. General Technical Report RM 158. Rocky Mountain Forest and Range Experiment Station, Forest Service, U.S. Department of Agriculture, Fort Collins, Colorado. pp. 52-54.
2. Benbrook, Charles M. 1988. *First principles: The definition of highly erodible land and tolerable soil loss.* Journal of Soil and Water Conservation 43(1): 35-38.
3. Cacek, Terry. 1988. *After the CRP contract expires.* Journal of Soil and Water Conservation 43(4): 291-293.
4. Clark, Richard T. 1987. *Nebraska's Erosion and Sediment Control Act—LB 474. Crop focus—87.* Cooperative Extension Service, University of Nebraska, Lincoln. pp. 111-114.
5. Dickey, Elbert C., Paul J. Jasa, Byn J. Dolesh, Lisa A. Brown, and S. Kay Rockwell. 1987. *Conservation tillage: Perceived and actual use.* Journal of Soil and Water Conservation 42(6): 431-434.
6. Dicks, Michael. 1987. *More benefits with fewer acres please!* Journal of Soil and Water Conservation 42(3): 170-173.
7. Dicks, Michael R., and Anthony Grano. 1988. *Conservation policy insights for the future.* Journal of Soil and Water Conservation 43(2): 148-151.
8. Dicks, Michael R., and John W. Putnam. 1986. *Conservation reserve and compliance: A paradox.* Journal of Soil and Water Conservation 41(6): 403-406.
9. Dicks, Michael R., Katherine Reichelderfer, and William Boggess. 1987. *Implementing the Conservation Reserve Program.* Economic Research Service, USDA Staff Report. AGES 861213.
10. Esseks, J. Dixon, and Steven K. Kraft. 1988. *Why eligible landowners did not participate in the first four sign-ups of the Conservation Reserve Program.* Journal of Soil and Water Conservation 43(3): 251-256.
11. Fletcher, Jerald J. 1986. *Conserving soil: Economic insights.* Journal of Soil and Water Conservation 41(5): 304 and 309-310.
12. Grano, Anthony, Neil Schaller, Richard Clark, Wen-Yuan Huang, Clayton Ogg, and Shu-Eng Webb. 1985. *Analysis of policies to conserve soil and reduce surplus crop production.* Economic Research Service, USDA, AER 534.
13. Haas, Joseph W. 1988. *Professional integrity and practical politics.* Journal of Soil and Water Conservation 43(5): 394-396.
14. Jayuraman, T. K. 1982. *Evaluation of implementation phase of rural development projects: A case study from Gujarat, India.* Agricultural Administration 10: 55-100.
15. Johnson, Bruce, Larry Jansen, and Michael Lundeen. 1986. *Farmland rental markets: Current issues, practices and conditions.* Staff paper 1986-11. Department of Agricultural Economics, University of Nebraska, Lincoln.
16. Kleckner, Dean. 1988. *Implementing CRP: A private perspective.* Journal of Soil and Water Conservation 43(1): 18-20.
17. Larson, Greg. 1988. *Implementing CRP: A state/local perspective.* Journal of Soil and Water Conservation 43(1): 16-18.
18. Leitch, Jay A. 1987. *Policy questions from CRP in the midwest.* Impacts of the Conservation Reserve Program in the Great Plains: Symposium Proceedings. General Technical Report RM-158. Rocky Mountain Forest and Range Experiment Station,

Forest Service, U.S. Department of Agriculture, Fort Collins, Colorado. pp. 91-94.
19. Lovejoy, Stephen B., and Ted L. Napier. 1986. *Conserving soil: Sociological insights.* Journal of Soil and Water Conservation 41(5): 304-308.
20. Molnar, Joseph J., and Patricia A. Duffy. 1988. *Public perceptions of how farmers treat the soil.* Journal of Soil and Water Conservation 43(2): 182-185.
21. Napier, Ted L. 1987. *Anticipated changes in rural communities due to financial stress in agriculture: Implications for conservation programs.* Impacts of the Conservation Reserve Program in the Great Plains: Symposium Proceedings. General Technical Report RM-158. Rocky Mountain Forest and Range Experiment Station, Forest Service, U.S. Department of Agriculture, Fort Collins, Colorado. pp. 84-90.
22. Napier, Ted L., and D. Lynn Forster. 1982. *Farmer attitudes and behavior associated with soil erosion control.* In Harold G. Halcrow, Earl O. Heady, and Melvin L. Cotner [editors] *Soil Conservation Policies, Institutions, and Incentives.* Soil Conservation Society of America, Ankeny, Iowa.
23. Napier, Ted L., and Silvana M. Camboni. 1988. *Attitudes toward a proposed soil conservation program.* Journal of Soil and Water Conservation 43(2): 186-191.
24. Napier, Ted L., Cameron S. Thraen, Akia Gore, and W. Richard Goe. 1984. *Factors affecting adoption of conventional and conservation tillage practices in Ohio.* Journal of Soil and Water Conservation 39(3): 205-209.
25. Newman, James B. 1987. *Overview of the present land use situation and the anticipated ecological impacts of program implementation.* Impacts of the Conservation Reserve Program in the Great Plains: Symposium Proceedings. General Technical Report RM-158. Rocky Mountain Forest and Range Experiment Station, Forest Service, U.S. Department of Agriculture, Fort Collins, Colorado. pp. 55-59.
26. Nowak, Peter J. 1983. *Obstacles to adoption of conservation tillage.* Journal of Soil and Water Conservation 38(3): 162-165.
27. Nowak, Peter J., and Max Schnepf. 1988. *A national survey of county-level USDA program administrators: The conservation title of the Food Security Act of 1985.* Soil and Water Conservation Society, Ankeny, Iowa.
28. Osterman, Douglas A., and Theresa L. Hicks. 1988. *Highly erodible land: Farmer perceptions versus actual measurements.* Journal of Soil and Water Conservation 43(2): 177-182.
29. Putnam, John, Jimmy Williams, and David Sawyer. 1988. *Using the erosion-productivity input calculator (EPIC) model to estimate the impact of soil erosion for the 1985 RCA appraisal.* Journal of Soil and Water Conservation 43(4): 321-326.
30. Raitt, Daryll D. 1983. *Soil erosion—a threat to land quality.* Lower Grand Subbasin, Northern Missouri River Tributaries Basin. River Basin Report. Economic Research Service, Soil Conservation Service, and Forest Service, U.S. Department of Agriculture, Washington, D.C.
31. Reichelderfer, Katherine, and William G. Boggess. 1988. *Government decision-making and program performance: The case of the Conservation Reserve Program.* American Journal of Agricultural Economics 70(1): 1-11.
32. Sand, Duane. 1988. *Viewpoint: Where are the conservationists?* Journal of Soil and Water Conservation 43(4): 278.
33. Scaling, Wilson. 1985. *A continuing commitment to conservation service.* Journal of Soil and Water Conservation 40(5): 399.
34. Scaling, Wilson. 1988. *Implementing conservation compliance and sodbuster: A federal view.* Journal of Soil and Water Conservation 43(1): 22-24.
35. Seitz, Wesley D., and Earl R. Swanson. 1980. *Economics of soil conservation from the farmer's perspective.* American Journal of Agricultural Economics 62: 1,084-1,088.
36. Seita, Parveen P. 1987. *Consideration of risk in soil conservation analysis.* Journal

of Soil and Water Conservation 42(6): 435-437.

37. Stoddard, Glenn M. 1988. *Alternative conservation systems: Controlling the damage.* Journal of Soil and Water Conservation 43(3): 214.

38. U.S. Department of Agriculture. 1986. *Highly erodible land and wetland conservation: Interim rule.* Federal Register 51(124): 23,496-23,514.

39. U.S. Department of Agriculture. 1987. *Conservation Reserve Program: Final rule.* Federal Register 52(28): 4,265-4,276.

40. U.S. Department of Agriculture. 1987. *Highly erodible land and wetland conservation: Interim rule with request for comments.* Federal Register 52(124): 24,132-24,133.

41. U.S. Department of Agriculture. 1987. *Highly erodible land and wetland conservation: Final rule and notice of finding no significant impact.* Federal Register 52(180): 35,194-35,208.

42. U.S. Department of Agriculture. 1988. *Highly erodible land and wetland conservation: Final rule correction.* Federal Register 53(26): 3,997-3,999.

43. U.S. Department of Agriculture, Soil Conservation Service. 1988. *National Food Security Act Manual.* Title 180, 2nd edition. Washington, D.C.

II
Macro-level Economic Impacts of the Conservation Title

4

Implications of Current and Proposed Environmental Policies for America's Rural Economies

Michael R. Dicks, Bengt Hyberg,
and Thomas Hebert

Two issues returned to the top of the agricultural policy agenda in the 1980s, conservation and rural development. The conservation movement regained the momentum it had in the 1960s, pressing for and receiving legislation to control agricultural sources of environmental pollution. Rural development initiatives are also in vogue again as the nation becomes more aware of the plight of financially troubled farmers and rural communities.

The Food Security Act of 1985 (FSA) contains provisions and programs to reduce agriculture's contribution to environmental degradation and improve the financial well-being of farmers and rural economies. As the stage is being set for debates on a new farm bill, the conservation movement has added several items to its agenda and many areas in rural America continue their increasingly desperate call for assistance.

Unless new, innovative measures are devised to aid and strengthen rural economies, commodity programs and environmental issues could continue to aggravate the financial stress in rural communities. Analyzing the impacts of FSA's conservation provisions on rural communities illustrates the linkage between policies that affect agriculture and the health of farm-dependent communities. Understanding this linkage offers guidance for developing future environmental provisions that positively effect rural economies.

A Crisis in Rural America

Since the early 1980s, newspapers throughout the United States have carried headline stories decrying the farm crisis. Reflecting their concern, the

Senate subcommittee on intergovernmental affairs noted that "the public has learned of serious financial problems facing America's farmers, and the massive drops in real farm income and farm land values that occurred during this decade. Attention has been focused on the direct, often dramatic impacts on individual farmers, their families, and on small businesses in America's agriculturally dependent communities" (*15*). The subcommittee described the magnitude of the financial strain in the following paragraph:

"The large gains in net farm incomes obtained in the 1970s vanished in the 1980s, falling from an average $41 billion ($1982) for the 1970s to an average $25 billion between 1980 and 1984—a 40 percent decline. This decline in net farm incomes was accompanied by a decline in individual wealth of $146 billion (1982 to 1985) as a result of an average 30 percent reduction in land values. This reduction in wealth is equivalent to the combined assets of IBM, General Electric, Eastman Kodak, 3M, Proctor and Gamble, Dow Chemical, McDonalds, RCA, Upjohn, Weyerhaeuser, and CBS. The decreased wealth during the 1980-1984 period led to (1) a 20 percent real decline in the tax base; (2) a 100 percent increase in tax delinquency rates; (3) sharp declines in nonfarm incomes, employment, and property values; (4) tax increases, or cuts in public services of as much as $200 per capita in farm dependent counties; and (5) an increased importance of government payments to farm income."

The enormous drop in net farm income and wealth led to farm foreclosures, business closings, and increased unemployment in rural areas. For the first time in more than a decade, nonmetropolitan areas exceed metropolitan areas in unemployment. The increasing disparity in unemployment between urban and rural centers led to renewed migration to urban centers by rural inhabitants. This migration had been reversed temporarily in the 1970s after having occurred almost constantly through the 1900s.

Declines in net farm income and wealth, a shrinking rural tax base to support local government, increased rates of rural unemployment, and renewed migration from rural communities motivated farm legislation designed to bolster farm income. FSA added a record $16.7 billion in direct government payments to net farm income in 1987. Although this support increased net farm income to the average level for the 1970s, the exodus from rural areas and the financial squeeze on rural, local government continues.

Dependence of Rural Economies on Agriculture

Agriculture provides employment opportunities and a source of demand for goods and services in rural economies. More than 8 million people were employed on U.S. farms in 1985, including 2.5 million hired farm workers and 2.9 million farm operators. The remaining 3.8 million people received no cash wages or salary but a "token" cash allowance, room and board, or payment-in-kind (8). Additional employment is generated through farm-related activities, such as processing, transportation, storage, and marketing of agricultural inputs and outputs. Persons employed in agricultural production or related activities purchase a portion of public and private goods and services in rural economies. These economic and employment links between agriculture and the industries supplying its inputs and marketing its output determine how a change in the agricultural sector will affect the rest of the economy.

The total economic activity generated by agriculture accounts for about 18 percent of the total value of all U.S. output (gross national product) and 21.3 million jobs (full-time equivalents). Actual crop and livestock production activities produced only 2 percent of gross national product (GNP) and 2.7 million jobs in 1984. Input activities (purchase of equipment, supplies, feed, seed, fertilizer, labor, and financing) accounted for an additional 2 percent of GNP and 2 million jobs. The remaining 14 percent of GNP and 16.6 million jobs generated by agriculture is the result of output activities (transport, storage, processing, manufacture, distribution, and sale of agricultural products) (6).

The more highly dependent upon agricultural production as the main source of employment and income, the more sensitive rural economies are to policies that affect agriculture. Agricultural production serves as the backbone for economic activity in more than 514 U.S. counties (Figure 1), providing more than 20 percent of total employment and income (1).

Employment in farm-dependent rural communities is generated largely as a result of agricultural production and associated input and output activities. Farmers and workers in the input and output industries will spend their incomes for food, durable and nondurable goods, recreation, and private and public services generating additional economic activity in the household consumption and service sectors of the economy. Workers in the household consumption and service sectors of the economy will, in turn, spend their incomes for goods and services generating additional employment in the local economy, ad infinitum.

Dependence of Agriculture on Rural Economies

While rural economies depend upon agriculture as a source of employment, agricultural producers also depend upon rural economies for employment. Almost 48 percent of all farm operators received income from non-farm employment, averaging $10,722 of additional income and 211 days employment. In addition, less than one-third of all hired farm workers worked 150 or more days on a farm, but accounted for more than three-quarters of the total worker-days of hired farm work. Hired farm workers earned an average of $3,247 from hired farm work and $2,579 from non-farm work (8).

In addition to providing off-farm employment to farm workers and operators, rural economies create a tax base with which to support schools, churches, police and fire protection, business centers, road maintenance, and other public and private goods and services. The health of the rural economic infrastructure and agriculture are interdependent. A reduction in agricultural employment will result in either a reduced or more expensive (per capita) infrastructure. A reduction in infrastructure as a result of events exogenous (or endogenous) to agriculture will result in a reduction in agricultural production or a higher per unit production cost as transportation and transaction costs rise.

The effect of agricultural policy on a community increases with the community's dependence on agriculture. This dependence may vary from year to year as other major industries experience expansions or contractions. For instance, many communities in the Great Plains are highly dependent on the energy and military sectors as well as agriculture. Thus, a contraction in the agriculture sector would exacerbate the financial squeeze felt

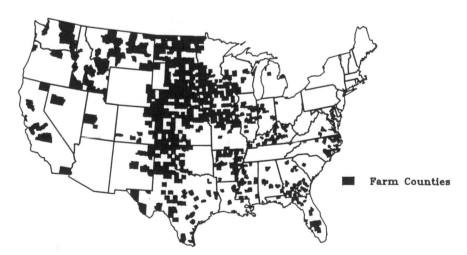

Figure 1. Nonmetro counties dependent on farming (13).

by farm-dependent communities already suffering from the effects of a contraction in the energy or defense sectors.

The New Environmental Legislation

The Conservation Title of the FSA is a major piece of environmental legislation directly affecting agriculture. This title contains four main provisions; the Conservation Reserve Program (CRP), conservation compliance, sodbuster, and swampbuster, each of which may induce permanent changes in land use. These land use changes have the potential to limit the quantity of agricultural output and alter its composition, affect the mix of purchased inputs, and change the level of net farm income.

Since the passage of FSA, several new environmental acts or amendments to older acts have been passed and proposed. These include the 1987 Water Quality Act and amendments to two other environmental acts—the Federal Insecticide, Fungicide, and Rodenticide Act (FIFRA) and the Endangered Species Act. These new acts and amendments will compel farmers to move toward more environmentally conscious farming.

Passage of the Water Quality Act established new programs to control agricultural contribution to surface water and groundwater degradation. This act differs from previous legislation by providing regulatory authority to reduce nonpoint pollution of surface and groundwater.

Amendments to the FIFRA legislation were made in 1988. These amendments represent a major compromise between the National Agricultural Chemicals Association and the environmental coalition. The amendments require the reregistration of all pesticides registered prior to November 1, 1984, under new, more stringent guidelines; the education of all commercial applicators (including farmers); storage, transport, and disposal of restricted pesticides; and indemnification of those who use these pesticides. In addition, there currently is a proposed amendment to FIFRA that would prohibit the application of a pesticide when the level of that pesticide in groundwater exceeds the Environmental Protection Agency (EPA) standard. The level requiring action by EPA is to be based on Safe Drinking Water Act standards. The Endangered Species Act prohibits use of pesticides determined harmful to endangered species in counties inhabited by these species.

Effects of the Environmental Legislation on Rural Economies

Each of these environmental programs and policies has the potential to provide significant benefits to society through increases in water quality, wildlife habitat, and recreation. However, the strategy used to implement these provisions is critical to achieving net social benefits without creating equal or greater social and private costs. The implementation of several of these policies in areas highly dependent upon agriculture may adversely affect specific areas of the United States.

The effects of agricultural and environmental programs will be different when viewed from a local rather than a national perspective. Local economies are not as resilient as the national economy because they are not as diversified, nor are they as able to reallocate resources among sectors. The loss of businesses from the local economy may cause firms in adjoining communities to expand service, resulting in a loss of employment in the local economy, but not for the nation.

The farm-dependent counties correspond closely with areas where soil erosion, surface and/or groundwater contamination from agricultural chemicals, and or groundwater depletion are serious problems (Figures 1, 2, and 3). Each of these environmental problems has increased in the last few decades. Reducing crop production in farm-dependent counties by idling cropland or by reducing agricultural chemical use will erode the economic base of those communities.

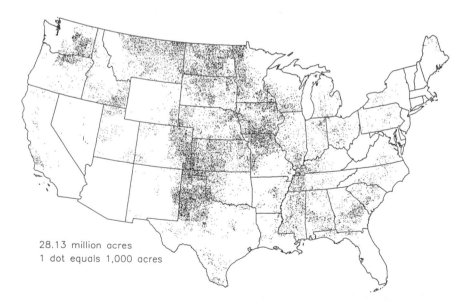

28.13 million acres
1 dot equals 1,000 acres

Figure 2. Conservation Reserve Program enrollment through 1988 (9).

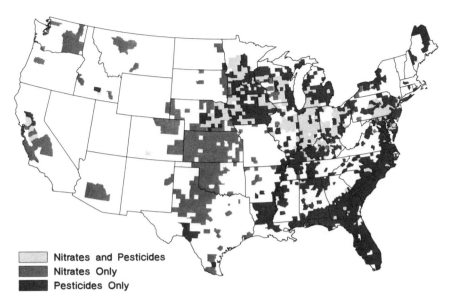

Figure 3. Areas of potential groundwater contamination from agricultural chemicals by type of contamination (7).

The conservation provisions of the FSA could reduce crop acreage 40 million to 90 million acres by 1995 (3). In addition, the FSA conservation provisions, in conjunction with other environmental provisions, will place downward pressure on yields and upward pressure on production costs by limiting chemical input use and imposing various land use restrictions.

Some $3 billion was spent on pesticides in 1984. This represented a five-fold increase in use since the 1950s. An estimated $12 billion in commodities would have been lost to competing weeds, insects, fungi, rodents, bacteria, and other pests without application of these chemicals (12).

Upon application, agricultural chemicals are either absorbed by plants, percolate into the soil (and eventually into groundwater), or carried by runoff into waterbodies (lakes, ponds, streams, etc.). In areas where erosion is a problem, groundwater contamination is less likely to be a major problem because agricultural chemicals are carried away in runoff. Thus, agricultural areas that are relatively free of highly erodible cropland that rely on groundwater for domestic uses will come under the greatest pressure to limit pesticide use.

Areas with concentrations of highly erodible cropland remaining in production will need to implement conservation plans to meet the requirements of the conservation compliance provision. These areas may also come under pressure to reduce the use of pesticides (FIFRA and the Endangered Species Act) and fertilizers (Water Quality Act) because less runoff might initiate greater percolation. The provisions of the Water Quality Act will put additional pressure on farmers with highly erodible cropland to curb erosion through the implementation of best management practices. This act will also enable the targeting of regulations, requiring reduced chemical utilization or other land use restrictions, in potential groundwater contamination areas. Increased production costs per unit associated with the implementation of best management practices and/or land use restrictions may tighten the financial squeeze on farmers.

The environmental programs and provisions will target cropland that is concentrated in agriculturally dependent, rural communities. Each will have differing impacts concurrent with the initial stages of implementation, full implementation, and program termination. In general, most will reduce agricultural output and may increase commodity prices. Some will provide off-setting payments, maintaining or increasing net farm income. However, a reduction in agricultural production, accompanied by a price (income) increase, may maintain net farm income but still reduce net economic activity as the level of employment necessary to facilitate input supply and output processing declines as a result of reduced output (14). Because average net returns (1970s) are less than one-third of the total revenue generated by crop production activities, maintaining net farm income while eliminating the production activity will have a net impact of reducing economic activity (expenditures) by as much as two-thirds. The greater the proportion of production expenditures for goods and services produced outside the local economy, the less the net impact of reducing output. Also, the level of stocks will affect the impact of reduced output on local economies. If stocks are sufficient to meet local demand, marketing and processing services will remain constant.

Reducing erosion or other environmental contaminants may provide economic benefits to rural economies in the form of reduced expenditures associated with rural clean water systems (pumping, purification, and delivery), road maintenance, and flood control. However, where reduced costs for these activities are achieved through displacement of labor, economic activity may be reduced unless alternative employment opportunities exist.

The Economic Impacts of the CRP

Analysis of the CRP provides an illustration of the impacts of environmental programs and policies on rural economies. More than 28 million acres (less than 10 percent of U.S. cropland) were enrolled in the CRP as of the end of 1988. The overall effect of the CRP on the U.S. economy presumably is minor (less than one percent of GNP). Moreover, this minor impact is spread across most of the United States because some 75 percent of all U.S. counties have participated in the CRP and may show some reduction in economic activity.

However, 80 percent of the acreage enrolled in the CRP is concentrated in less than 18 percent of the U.S. counties (Figure 2). A majority of these counties are located in the Mountain States and Southern Plains. The extent to which local land markets, agribusinesses, and economies are likely to be affected depends upon the actual level of CRP participation, the level of output reduction, the expenditures generated by the rental and establishment cost-share payments, and the local economy's ability to adapt to changes in local expenditure patterns.

To estimate the relative magnitude of the impacts of the CRP on national, regional, state, and local economies, Dicks and associates (4) used the Forest Service's national interregional input-output model (IMPLAN) (2). IMPLAN was employed to measure direct (reduction in crop production), indirect (reduction in the associated agricultural input and output industries), and induced impacts (reduced demand for goods and services providing support to these agricultural industries).

Economy-wide impacts of CRP enrollment are determined on the basis of changes in feed and food grains, cotton, and soybean production; increases in hay, forestry, and pasture establishment; and changes in household consumption activities. Because the IMPLAN model is based upon interindustry transactions that occurred in 1982, estimates represent the partial economic impacts that would occur if the level and interaction in the current economy were identical to that found in the 1982 economy.

The CRP reduces total gross output and employment in all sectors of the national, regional, and local economies in all three stages of the program (cover establishment, full implementation, and program termination).[1] The reduction in economic activity due to decreases in agricultural production and the related decrease in the use of agricultural inputs are somewhat offset by the temporary infusion of rental payments.

During the cover-establishment stage, total gross output and employment decline in the agricultural production sector as cropland is retired from production, rental payments are made to participants, and cover crops are established. In the full-implementation stage, economic activity declines

[1]The analysis does not include an examination of nonmarket economic activity, such as recreation and water quality.

in all sectors. The agricultural input sector declines more rapidly during this stage than the other sectors because expenditures for cover establishment were completed in the first stage. The economic activity that results from returning some of the CRP land to production (at program termination) increases total gross output in all sectors.

The general effects of the CRP on smaller economies are similar, but larger than those observed for the national economy. The greatest impacts are observed in the Northern Plains, Southern Plains, and Mountain States. These are regions with a large number of farm-dependent counties and high rates of enrollment in the CRP (44 percent of the eligible land). When smaller, more agriculturally dependent areas are examined, the CRP has an even greater effect on agricultural activity.

The reduction in total gross output in the agricultural production sector is approximately 3 percent nationally under full implementation, compared to decreases of 3.5 percent in the Mountain Region, 10.3 percent in Montana, and 20.9 percent in northeastern Montana. Employment declines range from 3.5 percent in the Mountain Region to 21.4 percent in northeastern Montana. Economic activity can be expected to increase after CRP contracts expire as retired land reverts to alternative uses, but the level of activity will not recover to pre-program levels.

The reduction in cropland use also reduces total gross output in the agricultural input sector (Figure 4). This reduction occurs both during the program and after rental payments end. Nationally, under full implementation, the input sector's total gross output declines about 2 percent. In agriculturally dependent rural areas, such as northeastern Montana, the CRP effects on the input sector are magnified, with total gross output losses in the input sector of 15.7 percent.

The CRP will have little impact on the agricultural processing sector during the period when rental payments are made, provided stock levels remain high. Rental payments, treated as ordinary disposable income, are used by farmers to purchase goods that include many of these high-valued, processed agricultural goods. As a result, economic activity in the agricultural processing sector can increase as rental payments and disposable farm incomes increase, even when planted crop acreage declines, because the rental payments more than offset the loss in employment in the agricultural input and production sectors.

If stock levels were reduced and no longer sufficient to fill processing needs, reduced agricultural output would also lower the regional grain handling and marketing activities. Nationally, if stocks declined and sufficient grain were unavailable, the agricultural processing sector would be affected.

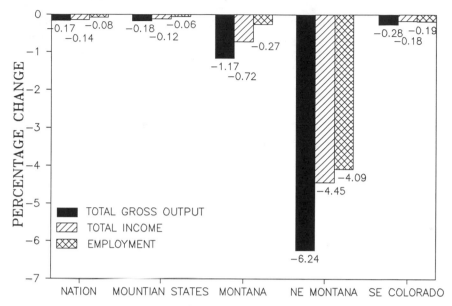

Figure 4. A comparison of economic effects of a fully implemented, 45-million-acre CRP in the United States, Mountain States, Montana, northeastern Montana, and southeastern Colorado.

Grain would be imported to maintain the high-value processing activities, however. Grain handlers and marketers in port areas and regions containing high-value processing activities would be affected.

Generally, slightly reduced levels of income, total gross output, and employment will occur in the household and other nonagricultural sectors at the regional level as a result of CRP. When net farm income increases as a result of CRP, activity in the household sector will increase. For example, in Montana and northeastern Montana the rental payment is 1.6 times greater than cash rent for the land (implying increased net farm income), slightly increasing economic activity in the household-expenditure sector. The increased household expenditures partially offsets the reduced economic activity associated with reduced crop output.

Factors not included in Dicks and associates' analyses (4), but important in determining the impact of these rental payments on economic activity, are farm size, income level, and age and location of the recipient. The greater the level of gross farm sales, income level, age, and the greater (shorter) the distance to the rural (urban) business center, the smaller the stimulation to the local economy. Rental payments presumably are spent according to a typical expenditure pattern (food, housing, recreation, etc.)

for an average income person in the specific local or regional economy.

The existence of alternative economic opportunities in an area affects the impact of the CRP on a region's economy. The total economic impact of the CRP on southeastern Colorado, which includes two metropolitan areas and has a large military influence, is much smaller than on Montana and northeastern Montana (Figure 4). This smaller impact occurs in spite of the fact that southern Colorado has a significant proportion of its cropland acres enrolled in the CRP. The decline in total gross output for the national economy is 0.17 percent under full implementation, while for northeastern Montana, a less diversified economy, the decline is 35 times greater (6.24 percent).

As CRP enrollment approaches 45 million acres nationally, the number of acres enrolled in a local area increase, thus exacerbating the decline in economic activity in such regions as Montana while barely affecting other regions, such as southeastern Colorado. The difference stems from the fact that southeastern Colorado, as of 1987, had already nearly reached the maximum enrollment permitted by FSA. Montana, on the other hand, has a substantial amount of cropland that could still enter the CRP.

After termination of the CRP, the agricultural processing, other manufacturing, and household-expenditure sectors are also affected by the conserving cover established on the CRP land. In the South and Delta States, timber has been established on most CRP land. Once timber thinning and harvest begins, communities within these regions will experience a stronger recovery in the agricultural processing and household-expenditure sectors than communities where grass was the primary conserving cover.

Environmental and Commodity Policies and Rural Economies

Environmental programs and policies currently being implemented and those being proposed for implementation will certainly provide significant environmental benefits. Some will provide monetary incentives for participation, while others may regulate action through denial of available benefits and levying of fines. Each program, regardless of strategy, will tend to reduce output and economic activity in rural communities, particularly farm-dependent communities.

Commodity programs being devised and implemented independent of the environmental programs and policies will provide additional environmental benefits (however small) and reduce output. Most will offer some form of price and income support, providing incentives for producers to maintain current crops and production practices. Like the environmental programs and provisions, commodity programs that reduce output will reduce economic activity in rural communities. Again, these impacts will be greatest in farm-dependent communities. However, retiring cropland under commodity programs will not have the same effect as reducing an equal amount of production under a conservation program. The commodity program will spread impacts over a different, more widely distributed number of counties compared with the more limited, concentrated set targeted by conservation programs.

FSA moved closer than any farm legislation in the past to bring consistency to commodity and environmental programs and policies. However, in general, these programs have been detrimental to specific farm-dependent economies. Continued reduction of economic activity in these communities may precipitate a collapse of the community infrastructure, including the loss of wholesalers and retailers, government and public services, and the deprivation of equipment, buildings, and transportation systems. In areas where farm-dependent communities are needed to be productive in the future, the infrastructure should be maintained until the cost of maintenance exceeds the future costs of rebuilding.

An Alternative Policy Approach

An alternative to maintaining assistance to farm-dependent communities through government intervention would be to promote a change from surplus crops produced with environmentally damaging practices to deficit crops (net import) produced with environmentally sound practices. Alternative opportunities include agriculture-based industrial materials, aquaculture and mariculture (fish and shellfish) products, low-input or sustainable agriculture, and biotechnology.

Developing agricultural products for industrial uses will provide farmers with an increased variety of crops and less dependency on traditional agricultural markets. Seven crops have already shown significant potential as sources of industrial materials and are slated for commercialization over the next three to five years. About 100,000 acres of these crops were in production in 1987. Another five crops are currently being examined with commercialization likely in the next 5 to 15 years.

Shifts in consumer preference towards fishery products as a substitute for other protein sources offers farmers an alternative production enterprise. A larger aquaculture industry will increase the demand for high-protein feed grains and reduce the growing U.S. trade deficit for edible fish ($5 billion).

Sustainable agriculture is an alternative to current production methods. Sustainable implies using available resources in such a way as to guarantee the continuous availability of those resources. Alternative, regenerative, organic, low-input farming systems are included within the scope of sustainable agriculture. While all of these alternatives have different ends and means, they all share a common goal of producing agricultural products economically with minimal adverse effects upon human health, natural resources, environmental quality, and rural economies (*11*).

Alternative opportunities have the potential to (1) provide alternative employment and income-earning opportunities to farmers and rural communities, (2) develop new markets for domestic products, (3) develop new sources of inputs for industry and new products for consumers, (4) reduce the U.S. trade deficit, (5) reduce the adverse effects on human health and the environment associated with agriculture, and (6) reduce the need for government intervention in agriculture.

The potential land acreage devoted to future aquaculture and industrial crops is unlikely to be anywhere near the 70 million to 100 million acres of excess capacity considered to exist in 1987 (*5*). But aquaculture, which now uses almost 500,000 acres, could eventually utilize 2 million to 3 million acres, and industrial crops that currently utilize only about 100,000 acres may utilize as many as 10 million acres in the future. Moving toward sustainable agriculture could lower production costs and yields, further reducing excess capacity.

Summary

Current developments do not indicate a wholesale departure from traditional agriculture, but rather a growing need for diversification. The next major farm legislation will likely increase the emphasis on conservation, environmental quality, human health and food quality, and continue the current trend of reducing government support for traditional commodities.

The increased presence of environmental and consumer demands in the agricultural policy forum may increase the financial squeeze already felt by many U.S. farmers and rural communities. Reducing output of traditional commodities will have serious implications for farm-dependent communities if alternative employment and income-generating activities are not provided.

Diversification through the adoption of alternatives could have significant impacts on commodity prices and the economic viability of rural areas. Market structure and geographic distribution could change. Labor markets in rural areas may change as the demand for management increases in response to the adoption of alternatives.

It is important to understand the synergistic effects of reducing government support for traditional agricultural commodities, increasing requirements for environmental quality, and the adoption of alternative opportunities on various agricultural sectors, markets, and economies. Policymakers and implementing agencies will require information describing the potential actions and interactions of the various policies, programs, and alternatives.

REFERENCES

1. Ahearn, Mary, Susan Bently, and Thomas Carlin. 1988. *Farming dependent counties and the financial well-being of farm operators.* AIB No. 544. Economic Research Service, U.S. Department of Agriculture, Washington, D.C.
2. Alward, G., and C. Palmer. 1985. *Implan user's guide, Version 1.1.* Forest Service, U.S. Department of Agriculture, Washington, D.C.
3. Barbarika, Alexander, and Michael R. Dicks. 1988. *Estimating the costs of compliance.* Journal of Agricultural Economics Research 40(3): 12-20.
4. Dicks, Michael R., et al. 1988. *Community impacts of the Conservation Title of the 1985 Food Security Act.* In Proceedings, Great Plains Agricultural Council, Las Cruces, New Mexico, June 7-9, 1988. Great Plains Agricultural Council, Lincoln, Nebraska. pp. 9-46.
5. Dvoskin, Dan. 1988. *Excess capacity in U.S. agriculture: An economic approach to measurement.* AER-580. Economic Research Service, U.S. Department of Agriculture, Washington, D.C.
6. Harrington, David, G. Schluter, and P. O'Brien. 1986. *Agriculture's links to the national economy.* AIB No. 504. Economic Research Service, U.S. Department of Agriculture, Washington, D.C.
7. Neilson, Elizabeth G., and Linda K. Lee. 1987. *The magnitude and costs of groundwater contamination from agriculture: A national perspective.* AER No. 576. Economic Research Service, U.S. Department of Agriculture, Washington, D.C.
8. Oliveira, Victor J., and E. Jane Cox. 1988. *The agricultural work force of 1985: A statistical profile.* AER-582. Economic Research Service, U.S. Department of Agriculture, Washington, D.C.
9. Osborn, Tim, Felix Llacuna, and Michael Linsenbigler. 1989. *The conservation reserve program: Implementation and accomplishments, 1987-1988.* Statistical bulletin No. 785. Economic Research Service, U.S. Department of Agriculture, Washington, D.C.
10. Petrulis, M., et al. 1987. *How is farm financial stress affecting rural America?* AER-568. Economic Research Service, U.S. Department of Agriculture, Washington, D.C.
11. Schaller, Neill. 1988. *Alternative agriculture gains attention.* Agricultural Outlook (October): 26-28.
12. Smezdra, Phillip. 1986. *Major changes coming in pesticide law.* Agricultural Outlook (October): 24-26.
13. Sommer, Judith E., and Fred K. Hines. 1988. *The U.S. farm sector: How agricultural exports are shaping rural economies in the 1980s.* AIB No. 541. Economic Research Service, U.S. Department of Agriculture, Washington, D.C.
14. Sonka, Steven T., and Earl O. Heady. 1975. *Income and structure of American*

agriculture under future alternatives of farm size, policies and exports. CARD Report No. 53. Center for Agricultural and Rural Development, Iowa State University, Ames, Iowa.

15. United States Senate, Committee on Governmental Affairs. 1986. *Governing the Heartland: Can rural governments survive the farm crisis?* SS-176. U.S. Government Printing Office, Washington, D.C.

5

Economic Efficiency Effects and Government Finance Impacts of the Conservation Title: Policy and Program Implications

David E. Ervin

Virtually everyone commenting on the Conservation Title of the 1985 Food Security Act (FSA) has pronounced it the most important soil and water conservation act since the 1930s. In support of that pronouncement, the Conservation Reserve Program (CRP) and the conservation compliance, sodbuster, and swampbuster provisions may ultimately apply to 380 million acres of actual and potential cropland, more than one-half of the U.S. total. Obviously, the scope of impact is great.

That impact can take very different shape and form depending upon the rules of implementation. Others suggest that the potential for differential impact exists (5). In essence, the character of those implementation rules defines the degree to which the various provisions add new value to or subtract value from the U.S. resource base (i.e., efficiency effects) and/or affect government receipts and expenditures.

Defining Efficiency and Government Finance Relationships

Economists take special care to distinguish between efficiency and government finance impacts because they can and usually do have quite different economic implications. Efficiency effects refer to reallocations of society's resources, including nonmarket environmental products, which lead to increases (benefits) or decreases (costs) in the value (quantity and/or price) of goods and services provided to current and/or future generations. Examples relevant to the CRP include improved water quality due to land use changes and the associated loss in social net returns to crop production. A comparison of the total CRP benefits with its total costs yields the net economic efficiency effects for society.

Government finance impacts are changes in the public treasury's inflows (receipts) or outflows (expenditures), or internal budget reallocations. However, these financial effects can either have efficiency consequences and/or represent a transfer between the private sector and government.[1] That is, efficiency and government finance are overlapping sets, but not coincidental sets. Consider two effects from the potential decline in excess crop production due to CRP enrollment. Reduced excess supply results in lower government storage cost (and budget expenditure), which is also an efficiency benefit because the funds can be spent on another government or private activity with higher economic value. Second, the lower level of excess crop production reduces government expenditure for price support payments. Because those payments are intended to support farm income, they represent a transfer from taxpayers to agricultural producers. Thus, the reduction in commodity program expenses allows a return of part of the transfer or a reallocation to other government activities. An economic efficiency benefit would be created only if it is assumed that the return or reallocation produces greater economic value in its new use. In the absence of information about interpersonal values, economists generally assume that the ultimate economic value of the transfer is the same regardless of who receives it. Therefore, a reallocation of the transfer is generally assumed not to have efficiency consequences.

Clearly, economic efficiency and government cost are related but different concepts. That is, an improvement in government finance due to expenditure reduction (e.g., a price support payment decline) does not necessarily imply an improvement in efficiency. Some efficiency effects have government finance consequences. And some government finance impacts have efficiency consequences. But there is not a general correspondence. It depends upon the specific program in question.

Most importantly, both can be valid social objectives for different reasons. Care should be taken, however, in intertwining them because they may be competitive. An increased emphasis on one may diminish the other. Reichelderfer and Boggess (12) illustrate that actual 1986 CRP enrollment could have been altered to improve both government cost and some efficiency dimensions. However, their finding in that particular case does not

---

[1]This discussion abstracts from the concept that an increasing total level of government taxation may have efficiency cost consequences for the total economy because the focus is on one small set of government programs.

run counter to the basic notion advanced here that the interrelationships between the two goals needs to be recognized explicitly and incorporated into program decision-making.

Efficiency and Government Finance Effects

The CRP idles cropland for a 10-year period through voluntary, compensatory contracts with owners and operators of highly erodible cropland. By constraining the amount of land available for crop production, the CRP supposedly raises production costs, reduces output supplies, and increases market prices.[2] This primary crop production effect is counterbalanced against improved conservation and environmental services from the enrolled land. An important secondary goal is to control excess crop supplies and thereby reduce government commodity program costs through lower output levels and higher market prices (thus requiring lower deficiency payments).

Termed the "program ineligibility" provisions, conservation compliance, sodbuster, and swampbuster seek to remove federal agricultural program incentives to farm highly erodible cropland, unbroken pasture or prairie, and wetlands, respectively, without conservation safeguards. The presumed intent, therefore, is to increase the flow of environmental services from that land. By threatening the removal of agricultural program benefits, the desired effect is to change the practices used to farm such land, which may raise production costs over current cropping methods. At the aggregate level, production cost increases translate into lower crop supplies and higher food prices. The program ineligibility provisions do not have explicit government cost objectives. However, their net effect is probably to limit potential budget exposure for commodity program payments by raising the cost of program crop production on land subject to the conservation requirements, thus reducing supplies and increasing crop prices. Some farmers may even refrain from participating in commodity programs rather than meet the conservation requirements.

The Conservation Title provisions use different methods but have similar final effects. The same sets of efficiency benefits and costs and govern-

[2]This interpretation of the CRP's effects is dependent upon the assumption that the enrolled land would have been in crop production without the CRP in place. If an equivalent supply-reducing amount of land had been withdrawn by another mechanism in the absence of the CRP, then the assumed crop supply reduction and increased prices would have occurred in either case. Consequently, it would be inappropriate to attribute the supply reduction and price increases to the CRP

ment finance effects generally apply to each (with the exception of CRP compensation). A listing of the probable generic impacts provides perspective on the range of those effects and their interrelationships.[3] Recall from above that the efficiency and government finance lists are not additive because they overlap. Each measures a different economic phenomenon.

The following are among the efficiency benefits:

► Increased conservation and environmental services (e.g., erosion reduction, wildlife habitat).

► Reduced losses from excess crop supplies (e.g., storage and transportation payments and export subsidies).

► Noncancellation of secondary benefits (e.g., reduced pollution from agricultural processing firms).

► Increased producer welfare due to higher crop prices.

Among the efficiency costs are the following:

► Reduced consumer welfare due to lower crop outputs and higher prices.

► Conservation cover establishment costs on CRP land.

► Unemployment or underemployment of immobile agricultural production resources (e.g., labor and machinery).

► Noncancellation of secondary costs (e.g., increased environmental externalities from firms supplying conservation cover inputs, such as air pollution from grass seed production).

Government revenue/cost savings include the following:

► Reduced commodity program expenses for deficiency and paid diversion payments due to less base acreage (direct) and higher market prices (indirect).

► Reduced storage and transportation payments and export subsidies.

► Lower administrative costs for traditional agricultural commodity programs on diverted base acres.

► Lower traditional government erosion control expenditures.

Added government expenditures include the following:

► CRP rental payments.

► Conservation cover establishment cost-sharing.

► Administrative costs for CRP land enrollment and maintenance and conservation compliance, sodbuster, and swampbuster implementation.

The following discussion focuses on the CRP because that program contains the most prominent government cost dimension. While all of these efficiency and government finance effects are possible, their relative magnitude can vary according to the manner in which the particular pro-

[3]See Ervin and Dicks (7) for a more complete explanation of these effects.

grams are implemented. The balance of these effects becomes the explicit or implicit result of conservation policy choices. Such a conclusion is not startling. But it deserves careful consideration because the pursuit of different mixes of efficiency and government finance objectives can yield quite different economic effects for society.

Alternative CRP Paths

The CRP was born in 1984-1985 amid three important social and economic conditions in the agricultural economy: (1) public perception of high damages to cropland and off-site resources (e.g., rivers and lakes) caused by soil erosion, (2) propensity of U.S. agriculture to produce more program crops than could be sold at market prices, and (3) public preference that agricultural commodity and conservation programs be consistent. Not surprisingly, the CRP has as its primary goal the reduction of cropland erosion and, second, the control of excess crop production, along with a host of ancillary objectives. The two major goals for the most part can be interpreted as efficiency and government cost concerns, respectively.

Congressional design of the CRP was patterned after the Soil Bank Program of the 1950s and 1960s with two exceptions. First, enrollment was to be targeted to that land with the greatest erosion problem. Second, an owner/operator bid procedure with maximum acceptable bid limits would replace the Soil Bank offer system. Participating CRP owners/operators receive annual payments equal to their successful bids, plus a one-time payment of one-half of the eligible costs necessary to establish a conservation cover. In exchange for payment, participants agree to implement approved conservation cover and not harvest commercial agricultural crops from the enrolled land during the contract (except if the secretary of agriculture declares an emergency, such as the 1988 drought period). Once the contract expires, the owner/operator is free to resume cropping on the land, but risks losing the farm's agricultural program benefits unless the cropping practices satisfy an approved soil conservation plan. Readers should consult Dicks and associates (4) for a full explanation of program details.

It is important to emphasize the different nature of economic effects derived by pursuing the two primary goals. Consider the erosion reduction objective first. Cropland erosion generally causes a variety of costs, beginning with the diminished productive capacity of the soil (on-site impacts) and ending with the deposition of the eroded soil and attached substances (e.g., agricultural chemicals) away from the eroding field (off-site damages). Average annual on-site damages have been estimated at $1.1 billion for all

U.S. cropland (*1*). Idling highly erodible cropland with the CRP reduces the on-site productivity damages, assuming the land would have remained in crop production otherwise. The productivity damages avoided are thus savings to current and future generations in the form of lower production costs and crop prices; these savings are, therefore, an economic efficiency benefit.[4]

Off-site damages are clear examples of negative externalities. Operators of erodible cropland often farm in such a manner that eroded soil and attached substances leave their farms, creating costs for other parties. Ribaudo (*13*) and Clark and associates (*2*) have estimated that the annual costs of off-site effects range from $4 billion to $5 billion per year. Again, the enrollment of CRP land will diminish those costs, presuming, as above, that the cropland would have continued to cause the erosion damages without the CRP. If that presumption is correct, then the off-site costs avoided are also an efficiency benefit.

Of course, these benefits come at some efficiency cost if it is assumed that the CRP land would have been in production without price supports. Under that presumption, diverting land from production raises the cost of producing a given amount of crops, thereby reducing supplies and raising consumers' food costs. Thus, the main cost of adding the CRP land is to reduce the economic welfare of food consumers.[5]

Pursuit of the second CRP goal, control of excess crop production, produces both government finance and additional efficiency effects. By reducing crop production, two beneficial government finance effects are created. First, the crop deficiency payments (target price minus market price or loan rate) or annual paid diversion payments received for the CRP acres normally participating in commodity programs are avoided. This is a direct

[4]There is growing evidence that on-site productivity losses are recognized by private landowners (*6, 9, 11*). The degree of that recognition and ensuing private action is still under investigation. Even with such private erosion control action, society may choose to achieve a different erosion reduction level for other reasons (e.g., intergenerational transfers). Thus, the CRP-induced erosion control changes from private levels may yield a social efficiency benefit. But the social cost of that erosion reduction needs to be weighed against those benefits.

[5]Farmers, unlike consumers, may actually receive higher net income for two reasons. First, participating CRP farmers receive annual rental payments that presumably cover all of their expected loss in net income from enrolling land. Second, because of an inelastic (i.e., price responsive) demand curve for most agricultural crops, the idling of CRP acres may push prices higher so that total remaining crop revenue increases and more than offsets increased production costs. Thus, farmers in the aggregate, CRP participants and nonparticipants, will benefit. Again, such an increase in farm net income presumes that the aggregate supply reduction would not have occurred without the CRP.

cost-saving. Second, the reduced crop production, if significant, pushes up market prices, thereby lowering the deficiency payment rate on remaining program crop production. Weighing against these direct and indirect government cost-savings are additional CRP rental and conservation cover cost-share expenses, plus any net increases in administrative costs. The unknown net government finance impact represents either a net cost saving for return to the taxpayer or expenditure on other programs, or a net new government cost requiring additional tax revenues or reallocation from other programs.

In addition to the government finance effects, the reduction of excess crop production generates at least three efficiency benefits. First, the resources devoted to storing and transporting the surplus commodities are freed for other uses. Second, any direct export subsidies necessary to enable foreign purchases of the prior crop production on CRP land are avoided. Finally, society saves the difference between the social cost to produce the excess supply and the amount U.S. consumers would pay for the excess consumed domestically, often referred to as "deadweight loss."

A particular CRP implementation path yields effects relevant to the primary and secondary goals simultaneously. As a result, there emerges a mixture of efficiency and government finance effects. That is a necessary program outcome. However, the preceding discussion should make it clear that the simple addition of efficiency and government finance effects to derive a total economic impact is inappropriate and can be confusing. That is, saved commodity program expenditures are not equivalent to efficiency benefits, and CRP rental expenses are not equivalent to efficiency costs.

Implementation of CRP

CRP Summary, Rounds 1-7. Slightly more than 28 million acres were enrolled in the CRP through the seventh sign-up round (1986-1988). Table 1 provides the essential information on the enrollment pattern and government costs by region. Note first the heavy concentration of acres in the Northern Plains, Southern Plains, and Mountain regions, accounting for 61 percent of the enrolled acres but only 46 percent of the acres available to the CRP. Dicks' analysis implies that the relationship of the region's maximum acceptable CRP rental bid to the average cropland cash rental is an important reason for that outcome (*3*). Second, note that the three highest enrollment regions also have the lowest average rental rate, which comprises the largest CRP government cost component.

From these partial data we cannot determine the relative economic efficiency or the government finance impacts of the implementation pattern. To shed more light on that comparison, a more comprehensive study of CRP enrollment is necessary.

Projected CRP Efficiency and Government Finance Effects. The major efficiency and government finance impacts of full CRP implementation were recently estimated by an Economic Research Service study team (*14*). The projections pertain to a 45-million-acre CRP based on experience through the first six CRP sign-ups, 1987 crop market conditions, and projected agricultural economic events over the 1988-1999 period.

Table 2 presents the two principal government finance impacts, CRP rental and cost-share payments (column 3) and direct and indirect commodity program cost-savings (column 4), for estimated enrollment levels (column 1). Column 5, environmental benefits, is a compilation of estimated effects, including enhanced soil productivity, improved surface water quality, reduced wind erosion damages, and increased wildlife recreational values. Neither the CRP cost components nor the environmental benefits should be construed as complete government finance or economic effi-

Table 1. Comparisons of Conservation Reserve Program enrollment by region, 1986-1988.

Region	Acres Enrolled* (millions)	Percent of Total Enrolled	Percent of Total Cropland Available for Enrollment†	Average Rental Payment‡	Average Cost-share‡
			%	$/acre/year	
Northeast	.16	.56	4.31	62.77	48.43
Appalachia	.94	3.34	6.75	54.97	39.30
Southeast	1.38	4.91	3.87	44.52	38.66
Delta States	.85	3.02	3.01	45.21	32.07
Corn Belt	3.92	16.67	23.52	81.12	41.96
Lake States	2.26	8.03	8.18	58.78	30.97
Northern Plains	6.94	24.67	19.08	43.75	35.29
Southern Plains	4.47	15.89	12.48	40.52	50.35
Mountain	5.65	20.08	14.35	39.96	32.11
Pacific	1.56	5.54	4.45	51.03	32.24
United States	28.13	100	100	49.71	37.82

*Source: Agricultural Stabilization and Conservation Service, U.S. Department of Agriculture, Washington, D.C.

†Source: Young, C. E., and C. T. Osborn, editors, (*14*). Available cropland incorporates the restriction that normally no more than 25 percent of a county's cropland can be enrolled in the CRP.

‡The average rental payment and cost-share reflects the nominal values over the 1986-1988 period.

Table 2. Projected Conservation Reserve Program enrollment, government finance and environmental effects, and region averages in 1987 dollars.

Region	Enrollment*	Average Available for CRP Enrollment	Average Annual Rental and Cost-Share Payments†	Average Annual Commodity Program Savings†	Average Annual Environmental Benefits†
	— million acres —		$/acre		
Northeast	.73	10.0	52	40	73
Appalachian	1.97	4.7	49	28	43
Southeast	1.90	2.7	39	18	37
Delta States	1.43	2.1	40	94	46
Corn Belt	7.65	16.4	62	60	25
Lake States	3.79	5.7	52	39	56
Northern Plains	9.63	13.3	43	32	8
Southern Plains	6.78	8.7	38	26	12
Mountain	8.47	3.0	37	13	10
Pacific	2.65	3.1	45	45	14
Total average	45.00	69.7	46	40	21

*Source: Young, C. E. and C. T. Osborn, editors, (14). Available acreage incorporates the restriction that normally no more than 25 percent of a county's cropland can be enrolled in the CRP.

†The average annual figures were derived by computing the total present value of the respective variable over 1986-1899, then dividing by the total CRP acre-years generated in the respective region, i.e., the total acres enrolled by year summed over the 14-year period. Thus, the values smooth any variation over time and reflect 1986 values.

ciency measures. Rather, they are the most complete indicators of these respective effects, given available data and research.

Several brief explanatory comments are necessary to interpret the figures properly. Enrollment projections were based on trends through the sixth sign-up in early 1988, but were adjusted to reflect the changing regional distribution of maximum available acreage (column 2) as the 45 million total was approached.[6] This resulted in an increasing proportion for the Corn Belt in the later rounds.

The average annual figures in columns 3-5 were derived by first calculating the total present value (1986 dollars) for each variable over the CRP's assumed life of contracts (1986-1999). Then, the total present value is divided by the sum of estimated CRP acre-years over the 14-year period in the respective region, that is, the total enrolled acres summed over years. As calculated, the annuities do not represent a particular year but are necessary when the enrollment levels are uneven through time and per acre figures are desired. Analyses with these average figures assume implicitly that the acreage distributions of those variables are similar over different regions, or that each acre generates the average. For example, assume that the environmental benefit value in the Lake States is constant over all eligible acres, whereas the corresponding average in the Northeast is heavily influenced by a small percentage of high-benefit acres. Obviously, comparing the economic effects of enrollment paths over the regions can be misleading if all acres are assumed equal to the mean.

Finally, the commodity program cost-savings deserve special comment. As noted, these values incorporate the direct savings of deficiency payments on base acres enrolled in the CRP and the indirect savings from higher market prices as the CRP reduces crop supplies (14). The direct savings can be calculated in a straightforward manner for each region by multiplying the particular crop deficiency payment rate by the respective base acres diverted into the CRP in each year. However, the indirect savings are the result of aggregate supply reductions at the market level and, therefore, must be attributed or decomposed to individual regions.

To derive regional indirect savings, the total indirect savings by crop were weighted by the regional (1986) share of total production (bushels harvested) of the particular crop. This procedure implicitly assumes that the CRP's

[6]The maximum available acreage incorporates the CRP restriction that enrollment is limited to 25 percent or less of a county's cropland. Maximum eligible acreage for a region will, of course, exceed the available acreage if the 25 percent restriction is binding for one or more counties.

national supply effect by crop is composed of regional adjustments reflecting a specified 1986 crop production pattern. In the absence of better information on the regional crop enterprise shifts induced by the CRP, such an arbitrary procedure is necessary. Of course, this approach can be faulty to the extent that enrollment of acres normally growing a particular crop is much more concentrated in one or more regions than predicted by the specified crop production base.

A comprehensive economic efficiency comparison of alternative CRP implementation paths would include consideration of all of the benefits and costs previously listed (7). Similarly, a comprehensive government finance analysis of the alternatives requires inclusion of the expenditure and receipt categories explained earlier. Such analyses were not possible with available data.

Some rudimentary comparisons of table 2 values may nonetheless suggest probable implications of pursuing different paths. One justification for conducting such comparisons is that the three reported average values likely represent the largest economic and fiscal effects of the CRP. The only major missing piece of information is the economic efficiency cost (loss in consumer welfare) of CRP enrollment by region, which could not be estimated for this analysis.

First, consider the approach of enrolling land to minimize average annual rental and cost-share expenses (column 3). Most emphasis would be placed on the Mountain, Southern Plains, Southeast, Delta, Northern Plains, and Pacific regions (assuming that additional enrollments would not significantly increase the average bid rate). To a considerable extent, the present enrollment pattern (Table 1) follows this pattern.

Next, consider a strategy to emphasize environmental benefits.[7] In this case, the Northeast, Lake States, Delta, and Appalachian regions would be targeted for heavier enrollments than other areas.[8] Noteworthy are the relatively low environmental benefit values for the Northern Plains, Mountain, Southern Plains, and Pacific regions, which fared well under the average rental cost criterion. It is worth emphasizing that most estimates of the

[7]Use of the average annual environmental benefits measure for projected enrollment is faulty to the degree that a different sign-up pattern would have yielded significantly different regional benefit values and distributions. For example, the inclusion of new environmental goals apart from erosion control, such as groundwater protection, could alter the figures.
[8]This assumes again that the regional acreage distributions of environmental benefits are largely similar. Obviously, some acres from all regions may have high environmental benefit values and merit enrollment. The argument here concerns only regional averages and emphasis. A full economic analysis would compare the marginal benefit-cost shifts for regional enrollment variations, rather than average values.

environmental value component are not mature methodologies with substantial corroboration. In particular, the wind erosion damages avoided, concentrated in the Southern Plains, Mountain, and Northern Plains regions, have a wide estimation range because of little previous research (*14*).

Finally, what if the focus is shifted to government commodity program cost savings? The Delta region, although small in potential enrollment size, leads the average cost-savings figures due to reduced cotton production. In the next group are the Corn Belt, Pacific, Northeast, and Lake States regions representing about 35 million available acres. Again, the Southern Plains and Mountain Regions do not appear to represent areas of great potential commodity program savings, but the Northern Plains States exhibit fairly sizeable avoided program payments.

The combination of one or both of the cost-savings categories with the efficiency benefit criterion is tempting, given the CRP's multiple objectives. The resulting value is a mixture of different economic dimensions. Some might add commodity program cost-savings to environmental benefits and subtract or divide by rental and cost-share costs. But the resulting ratio requires a careful interpretation. For example, the environmental benefits divided by CRP rental and cost-share expenses measures the real economic benefits provided by a transfer of funds from taxpayers or other government programs. However, it omits consideration of the efficiency costs of such an action. Regardless of this interpretive difficulty, the ratio can be a legitimate program implementation measure.

It is appropriate to subtract the commodity program savings from the CRP rental payments to derive a net government cost figure (ignoring other government cost and revenue effects). Only the Delta region provides a net gain (due to cotton program savings) while the Pacific breaks even, and the Corn Belt shows a slight deficit. The remaining regions run an annual government cost deficit of more than $10 per acre. Recall also that neither the cost nor the revenue measure is complete. For example, avoided storage and transportation costs are not included in the cost savings and increased administrative expenses are omitted from the CRP expenditure side.

Summary and Implications

There is little question that implementation of a major government program is a complex political and administrative process predominated by uncertainty. Competing political and economic theories exist as to the driving forces behind such programs. For example, Gardner (*8*) advanced and tested the notion that agricultural commodity programs are efficient income redistributional measures, that is, a combination of distributional and efficiency objectives. Reichelderfer and Boggess (12) articulated the position that the political preference function for the CRP probably reflects a multiplicity of objectives with unknown and uncertain weights on each objective.

In light of these thoughts, a clear understanding of the concepts of efficiency and distributive effects and their interrelationships in conservation program implementation is very important. Herein, an attempt was made to differentiate the concepts of economic efficiency and government finance, and to demonstrate that the two objectives can be competitive in the CRP case when viewed from a regional implementation perspective. Preliminary empirical analysis suggests that different regions would be emphasized for environmental efficiency and government finance reasons and that the present enrollment pattern does not match either objective well. These ex-post revelations are unfortunately not very helpful to the CRP implementation process begun over two years ago.

Lindblom (10) characterized government policymaking as a process of incremental decision-making or "muddling through" in which goals and procedures become intertwined because of the complexity of the policy choices under incomplete and uncertain information. Only with the provision of more reliable and complete information on the policy choices and tradeoffs can the desired outcomes be approached more efficiently. In that vein, government agencies, universities, and other groups should strive to be proactive in the policy process and provide such information in the program design and implementation stages.

REFERENCES

1. Alt, K., C. T. Osborn, and D. Colacicco. 1989. *Soil erosion: What effect on agricultural productivity?* Agriculture Information Bulletin 556. Economic Research Service, U.S. Department of Agriculture. Washington, D.C.
2. Clark, E. H., J. A. Haverkamp, and W. Chapman. 1985. *Eroding soils: The off-farm impacts.* The Conservation Foundation, Washington, D.C.
3. Dicks, M. R. 1987. *February CRP sign-up brings enrollment to almost 20 million acres.* Agricultural Outlook AO-129. U.S. Department of Agriculture, Washington, D.C. p. 31.
4. Dicks, M. R., K. Reichelderfer, and W. Boggess. 1987. *Implementing the Conservation Reserve Program.* Staff Report AGES861213. Economic Research Service, U.S. Department of Agriculture, Washington, D.C.
5. Dicks, Michael R., Bengt Hyberg, and Thomas Hebert. 1989. *Implications of the current and proposed environmental policies for America's rural economies.* In Ted L. Napier [editor] *Implementing the Conservation Title of the Food Security Act of 1985.* Soil and Water Conservation Society, Ankeny, Iowa. pp. 51-66.

6. Ervin, D. E., and J. W. Mill. 1985. *Agricultural land markets and soil erosion: Policy relevance and conceptual issues.* American Journal of Agricultural Economics 67(5): 938-942.
7. Ervin, D. E., and Michael R. Dicks. 1988. *Cropland diversion for conservation and environmental improvement: An economic welfare analysis.* Land Economics 64(3): 256-268.
8. Gardner, Bruce L. 1987. *Causes of U.S. farm commodity programs.* Journal of Political Economy 95(2): 290-310.
9. King, D. A., and J. A. Sinden. 1988. *Influence of soil conservation on land values.* Land Economics 64(3): 242-255.
10. Lindblom, Charles E. 1959. *The science of muddling through.* Public Administration Review.
11. Miranowski, J. A., and B. D. Hammes. 1984. *Implicit prices for soil characteristics in Iowa.* American Journal of Agricultural Economics 66(5): 745-749.
12. Reichelderfer, Katherine, and William G. Boggess. 1988. *Government decision-making and program performance.* American Journal Agricultural Economics 70(1): 1-11.
13. Ribaudo, M. O. 1986. *Reducing soil erosion's offsite benefits.* AER 561. Economic Research Service, U.S. Department of Agriculture, Washington, D.C.
14. Young, C. E., and C. T. Osborn, editors. *The Conservation Reserve Program: An economic assessment.* Agricultural Economics Report. Economic Research Service, U.S. Department of Agriculture, Washington, D.C.

6

National and Regional Impacts of Targeting the Conservation Reserve Program

Klaus Frohberg, Doug Haney, Matthew Holt,
Derald Holtkamp, S. R. Johnson, W. H. Meyers,
Leland C. Thompson, Greg Traxler,
and Patrick Westhoff

Soil and water conservation continues to be an important focus of environmental policy at national and state levels. Soil productivity and the potential for water contamination by sediment and agricultural chemicals, such as fertilizers and pesticides, in recent years have prompted a series of major conservation policies and environmental protection programs.

The Food Security Act (FSA) of 1985 includes continued support for the Agricultural Conservation Programs (ACP). ACP is a cooperative effort by federal and state agencies and agricultural producers to restore and protect land and water resources and the environment. ACP provides cost-sharing to farmers who implement resource conservation practices on agricultural land. Assistance for conservation planning is provided by the Soil Conservation Service, Forest Service, and Cooperative Extension Service.

The Conservation Reserve Program (CRP) authorized by FSA encourages farmers to idle highly erodible land (HEL), converting it to permanent vegetative cover. The farmer may enter into a 10-year CRP contract with the U.S. Department of Agriculture (USDA) and receive annual rental payments of up to $50,000 per farm per year on the acres. Payment is made through the Agricultural Stabilization and Conservation Service (ASCS). At least two-thirds of a field must be highly erodible and have been cropped between 1981 and 1985, for CRP eligibility (4).

By changing the targeting criteria, significant potential exists within the CRP for enhanced benefits of erosion abatement. Including land adjacent to water bodies, flowing streams and river waterways may reduce erosion and improve water quality. Termed "buffer strips," these lands are removed from production and placed into the CRP with a vegetative cover to limit sedimentation and prevent upland erosion materials from reaching waterway channels. This targeting of buffer strip areas as eligible CRP land has the potential to increase environmental benefits of the CRP.

Noting that data for use in identifying land adjacent to streams, rivers, and other water bodies are generally lacking, our source in estimating eligible buffer strip acres was the 1982 NRI. Once we identified the eligible buffer strip land, we used post sign-up records to identify overlap with regular CRP land. Also, buffer strip land had to be eligible for CRP sign-up in accordance with county limits. We used the CARD modeling systems to evaluate impacts of targeting alternatives for erosion, government cost, agricultural commodity prices, and farm income. Baseline projections were from the *1988 FAPRI Ten-Year International Outlook (2)*, prepared in March 1988 prior to the drought.

Buffer Strip Area and CRP Allocation

Buffer Strips. Unfortunately, reliable data on land area adjacent to streams, lakes, ponds, and other water bodies are generally not available. Several alternative data sets, including the 1982 Natural Resource Inventory (NRI), exist for approximating this area. The 1982 NRI, a comprehensive survey of the natural resource and cropland base in the United States, is specific to the substate (multicounty) level. The NRI reports acres in water bodies between 2 and 40 acres, and less than 2 acres, as well as acres in small perennial streams narrower than 600 feet. NRI data, however, do not provide information on land class or erodibility levels of land adjacent to the water bodies—information necessary for identifying potential buffer strip area. Also, the NRI does not report bank lengths for the water bodies.

The basic data records in the 1982 NRI are primary sampling units (PSU) representing a predetermined land area. For instance, most PSUs represent a quarter section (a one-half mile square area containing 160 acres), although some 40-acre and 640-acre areas are included. Significantly, distance to the nearest water source is recorded for each PSU. Although the type of water source is not listed, this information can be used to allocate the county water body data to land classes. Of course, these data have low statistical validity at the PSU level. Other data for miles of privately owned river length by state were used in conjunction with the NRI in determining potential buffer strip areas and checking consistency of the NRI data and river length to date (4).

First, county-level data were obtained from the 1982 NRI for acres of land in streams and water bodies. All water bodies (lakes, ponds, etc.) were assumed to be circular. County-level estimates of shore length for water bodies were computed as:

$$WL_i = 2\pi[(ASQM_i/\pi)^{\frac{1}{2}}]; \quad i=1, ..., 3,112 \text{ counties} \tag{1}$$

where $ASQM_i = AWB_i \times 0.00156$, WL_i denotes the total county shore length for water bodies in thousands of miles, $ASQM_i$ is the total county water body area in acres reported by the NRI, and 0.00156 is a factor (involving π) used to convert acres to square miles. Equation 1 was derived from the standard relations for the area and circumference of a circle.

Second, total acres of small perennial streams (streams up to 600 feet wide), denoted APS_i, were summarized by county from the NRI. State-level data on stream bank length then were apportioned to a county level. County-level total acres in water were computed as

$$ATOT_i = AWB_i + APS_i; \quad i=1, ..., 3,112 \tag{2}$$

The values from equation 2 were used to construct a set of homogeneous weights for proportionately converting the state-level bank length data to a county level. Specifically, if CBL_i denotes county bank length, then

$$CBL_i = SBL \times (ATOT_i / \sum_{i=1}^{N} ATOT_i) \tag{3}$$

where N is the number of counties in state S.

The estimates from equation 3, combined with the shore length estimates from equation 1, approximate the total area available for buffer strips in a county. Unfortunately, these estimates provide no information about the land group or erodibility of land.

Land Classes. "Distance to water" information contained in the NRI were combined with the above area estimates to approximate classes of land along streams and water bodies. Specifically, the NRI data were used to measure endogenous crop acres within a specified distance to water (such as 100 feet) for each county and each land class within a county. A set of weights for apportioning county-level bank and shore length to different land classes then was developed. Endogenous crop acres in land class 1 simply were divided by endogenous crop acres in all the land classes for a given county. This procedure, however, overestimated the shore and bank length for a land class because a county has more land than that in endogenous crops.

The expression for determining water length (shore length plus bank length) for a land class in a county was:

$$SL_{il} = CBL_i \times (land_{il}/land_i^{end})^p + WL_i \times (land_{il}/land_i^{end}) \qquad [4]$$

where $i = 1, ..., 3112$, $l = 1, ..., 8$, SL_{il} is miles of water length for land class l in county i, $land_{il}$ is total privately owned acres in county i, and $land_i$ represents the total land base in county i (CBL_i and WL_i were previously defined).

In equation 4, the denominator for the weights adjusting county bank length, CBA_i, is total acres owned privately in county i, $land_i^p$. This value was used because the bank length data already are adjusted to reflect privately owned land along river and stream banks. Likewise, the denominator in the weights for adjusting county shore length, WL_i, is the total county land base, $land_i$. Total county area is used because, unlike the bank length data, no distinction is made between private and public water bodies in the NRI data base.

Future CRP Allocations and Buffer Strip Scenarios

When allocating CRP land for the scenarios, a number of issues had to be considered. No more land in a county can be put into a CRP than is eligible. In addition, total future CRP and buffer strip allocations at the county level had to match the targeted levels specified in the scenarios. The scenarios evaluated included a base run where a 45-million-acre CRP enrollment was imposed without targeting any CRP land to buffer strips (*45/0*). There were three alternative scenarios, as follows: 5 million acres of the 45 million acres of CRP land targeted to buffer strips (*45/5*), 20 million acres of the 45 million CRP acres targeted to buffer strips (*45/20*), and the CRP expanded to 65 million acres and 25 million acres targeted to buffer strips (*65/20*).

The legislated limit for county CRP sign-up is 25 percent of the total land base. Some evidence suggests, however, that this 25-percent limit has been relaxed in previous sign-ups, and questions arose about the viability of the 25-percent limit in the buffer strip scenarios. For the 45/5 scenario the 25-percent limit was continued. But a 35-percent county limit was applied for the other scenarios, largely to obtain sufficient eligible land to meet the 20- and 25-million-acre buffer strip targets. Also, buffer strip width had to be expanded. The widths used were 100-foot buffer strips for the 45/5 scenario, 230-foot strips for the 45/20 scenario, and 300-foot strips for the 65/20 scenario.

Buffer Strips and CRP Eligibility. With the data on buffer strip width, county and land class, water body and stream length, past CRP enrollment (through the first four sign-up periods), and the total acres available for future sign-up, future CRP enrollment could be allocated. But several important decisions remained for determining county and land class CRP participation.

For instance, the definitions used for regular and buffer strip CRP did not preclude the possibility that past CRP sign-up had occurred in eligible buffer strip areas and that future CRP sign-up on land meeting the existing eligibility criteria could include targeted buffer strip area. The potential overlap between regular CRP acres and buffer strip CRP acres had to be reflected in allocating future CRP acres. That is, we had to know the potential land area available for CRP meeting the standard eligibility definition, the potential land area meeting the buffer strip criterion, and the overlap area satisfying both CRP criteria.

The 1982 NRI again was used to determine total acres eligible for buffer strips for a prespecified buffer strip width. The NRI data were scanned to obtain all acres of endogenous crops within 100, 230, and 300 feet of water. These values then were aggregated to obtain total area available for buffer strips at a county and land class level; this value was denoted as $bland_{il}^{e}$.

Next, the overlap in the two definitions was determined. That is, it was necessary to estimate the eligible CRP land in buffer strips also satisfying the > 2T and land class 2-8 criteria. This was accomplished using two definitions of regular CRP-eligible land: (1) Denoting land eligible for regular CRP within t feet of water (t=100, 230, 300) as $land_{il}^{e, \leq t}$ and (2) denoting land eligible for regular CRP greater than t feet from water as $land_{il}^{e, >t}$. By definition,

$$land_{il}^{e} = land_{il}^{e, \leq t} + land_{il}^{e, >t}; \quad t=100, 230, 300 \tag{5}$$

The union set of all available CR land satisfying both the regular CR and the buffer strip eligibility was:

$$land_{il}^{eu} = land_{il}^{e \leq t} + bland_{il}^{e} \tag{6}$$

where i=1, ..., 3112, l=1, ..., 8, t=100, 230, 300, and $land_{il}^{eu}$ is the union set of all CRP land that fits both definitions.

County-Level Estimates. The final step was to convert the value from equation 6 into a value that is both allocable and eligible for the CRP with the county-level sign-up limits applied. For the county-level percentage limits, the land that was both allocable and eligible under the 25 percent rule was as follows:

$$\text{land}_{il}^{eu} \qquad \qquad \text{if } \sum_l \text{land}_{il}^{eu} \leq 0.25 \sum_l \text{land}_{il}$$

$$\text{land}_{il}^{aeu} = \text{CRP}_{il}^{p} \qquad \text{if } \text{CRP}_{il}^{p} > \text{land}_{il}^{eu} \qquad \qquad\qquad [7]$$

$$\text{fct}_i^1 \times \text{land}_{il}^{eu} \qquad\quad \text{otherwise}$$

An identical definition for allocable and eligible CRP land under the 35-percent county limit rule can be obtained by replacing .25 with .35 in equation 7. Expressions similar to equation 7 can be used to obtain regular CRP land both allocable and eligible, $\text{land}_{il}^{ae, > 2T}$, and buffer strip land both allocable and eligible, bland_{il}^{ae}.

Given that the union set of land allocable and eligible for future CRP sign-up was used in the allocation model, it was also necessary to reflect previous CRP enrollment of buffer strip areas. Unfortunately, these data simply were not available. Given the lack of available data, an ad hoc adjustment then was made for past CRP sign-up data. Because $\text{land}_{il}^{e, \leq t}$ and $\text{land}_{il}^{e,t}$ were known from the NRI, adjustments in past sign-up data could be made to reflect overlap with buffer strip area. In particular, a proportion ($\text{land}_{il}^{e, \leq t}/\text{land}_{il}$) was applied to all present CRP sign-up land to estimate total land allocatable and eligible for buffer strips not already in previous CR sign-up.

Results

The evaluation of likely economic impacts of targeting eligible CRP land to include buffer strips was conducted in the early spring of 1988 prior to the drought. Thus, results of the analyses are best viewed as an exercise given the conditions in the agricultural commodity markets, abstractions required to quantify eligible buffer strip area and eligible CRP land and to allocate the regular and buffer strip land to future CRP sign-up adhering to both the legislated county limits and the scenario specifications. The economic conditions for agriculture have changed significantly, of course, since the spring of 1988.

Two economic modeling systems were used in the exercise. First, the CARD/FARPI multi-market commodity modeling system was applied to obtain national results. This system provides estimates of land use, agricultural market prices, and government cost over a projected time horizon. Second, the scenarios were evaluated using results from the CARD/FAPRI multi-market commodity market analyses in CARD static mathematical programming models at the producing area (PA) level, maximizing annual returns over short-run variable costs for crop production.

Multi-Market Commodity Model Analysis. The multi-market commodity model analysis of the CRP alternatives proceeds from a baseline. The baseline scenario is from the CARD/FAPRI multi-market commodity models reflecting macroeconomic conditions and the commodity market situation for the spring of 1988. The policy assumptions, summarized in table 1, are for the different CRP scenarios, indicated as 45/0, 45/5, 45/20, and 65/25. For the 65-million-acre CRP scenario adjustments in the commodity program, parameters were made to achieve a more level path in stocks and market prices over the 10-year evaluation period.

The CARD/FAPRI 10-year projections for U.S. agriculture are quite sensitive to the macroeconomic conditions in the United States and in foreign countries. Additional details on the policy assumptions and the macroeconomic conditions are provided in the 10-year report (2). Generally, the macroeconomic conditions projected are consistent with a continuation of the situation as in the spring of 1988.

State and Regional CRP Enrollment. The actual sign-up information used for the evaluation is through the fourth period, in which sign-up was concentrated in the Great Plains and Mountain States. Future sign-up in these states will be limited by the rule that no more than 25 percent of the cropland in a given county can be in the CRP.

For the 45/0 scenario, future CRP enrollment is projected as heaviest in the Corn Belt, where current enrollment is limited but much eligible land is available for the CRP. A shift toward the Corn Belt for CRP acreage implies that the rental rates will increase, because land values are higher in the Midwest than in the Great Plains and the Mountain States. Detailed projections of sign-up are provided in table 2. For the 45/5 scenario, targeting 5 million acres of buffer strips is projected to have limited effects on state CRP enrollment. This is partly because the future sign-up in the targeted areas is already projected for heavy increases in the 45/0 or baseline. The 45/5 scenario results in a modest increase in CRP acreage in the Corn Belt, the Northeast, the Delta, and the Appalachian regions.

For the 45/20 scenario, increasing the number of target acres to 20 million, the result for regional/state sign-up is more significant. In general, the direction of the impacts is the same as for the 45/5 scenario; but the magnitudes are larger. CRP enrollment drops sharply in such states as Texas, Colorado, and Kansas where the baseline sign-up was high and targeted or buffer strip acres are few. Enrollment increases in Kentucky and the Mississippi River Basin where the baseline sign-up was low and targeted acres exist.

When the CRP is increased to 65 million acres with 25 million acres in buffer strips, the regional composition of the CRP again changes greatly. Increased enrollment is most dramatic in states where eligible acres

Table 1. Major program assumptions of alternative scenarios.

Policy Instrument	45-Million-Acre CRP			65-Million-Acre CRP, 25 Targeted (65/25)
	0 Targeted (45/0)	5 Targeted (45/5)	20 Targeted (45/20)	
		million acres		
Total CRP acreage				
1988-1989	28	28	28	32
1989-1990	38	38	38	48
1990-1991	45	45	45	60
1991-1992	45	45	45	65
Targeted CRP acreage				
1988-1989	None	2	5	5
1989-1990	None	4	14	15
1990-1991	None	5	20	22
1991-1992	None	5	20	25
Acreage reduction	10-20% of corn base acres and 10-27.5% of wheat acres must be idled to receive deficiency payments	Same as 45/0	Same as 45/0	Rates are adjusted to offset half the changes in planted area that would result from CRP changes
Paid diversions	0-10% of corn base may be idled for an additional payment; no diversion for wheat	Same as 45/0	Same as 45/0	Rates are adjusted to offset half the changes in planted area that would result from CRP changes
Generic PIK certificates	Heavy usage in making payments, including 50% of CRP payments until 1990-1991 and 25% thereafter	Same as 45/0	Same as 45/0	Same as 45/0

Table 2. State CRP enrollment under the baseline (45/0) and three targeting options: a 45-million-acre CRP with 5 million (45/5) and 20 million target acres (45/20) and a 65-million-acre CRP with 25 million target acres (65/25).

State	Enrollment Through 4th Sign-up	0 Targeted (45/0)	5 Targeted (45/5)	20 Targeted (45/20)	25 Targeted (65/25)
			(thousand acres)		
Alabama	308	822	766	763	1,044
Arkansas	97	415	541	841	1,030
California	138	244	286	730	819
Colorado	1,423	2,143	1,993	1,593	2,128
Delaware	0	13	22	29	45
Florida	51	188	169	125	198
Georgia	280	774	717	638	978
Idaho	547	1,260	1,176	916	1,417
Illinois	277	1,822	2,200	2,371	3,704
Indiana	146	997	1,184	1,399	2,157
Iowa	1,253	4,482	4,331	3,547	5,723
Kansas	1,391	2,675	2,608	2,105	3,300
Kentucky	282	778	861	1,255	1,660
Louisiana	43	175	236	333	501
Maine	12	56	50	113	104
Maryland	3	93	127	186	274
Massachusetts	0	14	13	35	46
Michigan	69	389	477	690	1,058
Minnesota	1,194	2,803	2,724	2,083	3,344
Mississippi	396	800	871	1,078	1,425
Missouri	904	2,359	2,587	2,785	4,010
Montana	1,146	3,053	2,765	2,848	3,638
Nebraska	802	2,073	2,036	1,695	2,668
New Jersey	0	53	57	83	121
New Mexico	440	297	264	411	408
New York	25	260	316	519	777
North Carolina	61	510	600	841	1,122
North Dakota	713	2,105	2,042	1,601	2,507
Ohio	103	584	712	1,195	1,753
Oklahoma	709	1,264	1,230	1,074	1,622
Oregon	437	645	587	632	817
Pennsylvania	34	450	541	760	1,151
South Carolina	139	242	231	279	400
South Dakota	456	1,347	1,232	943	1,448
Tennessee	252	863	846	1,312	1,620
Texas	2,253	4,939	4,586	3,215	5,065
Utah	191	253	328	698	593
Vermont	0	15	20	92	84
Virginia	26	250	245	473	548
Washington	688	1,251	1,133	804	1,265
West Virginia	0	45	49	353	335
Wisconsin	235	998	1,010	953	1,493
Wyoming	159	201	235	546	526
Other states	0	0	0	58	71
Total	17,683	45,000	45,000	45,000	65,000

1990 Enrollment — *45 Million Acre CRP* / *65 Million Acre CRP*

are concentrated and where current sign-up is limited. Enrollment increases over baseline levels in every region. The largest gains in CRP occur in the Corn Belt. Table 2 shows results for each of these scenarios by state and used in the CARD/FAPRI multi-market commodity model analysis.

Baseline (45/0). The baseline results are summarized first, because the scenarios are evaluated as comparisons to these projections. In general, the area planted to major program crops increases slowly from 1988-1989 forward. Total area idled declines gradually beginning in 1989-1990. The area idled by annual programs falls more rapidly as the CRP increases. Given normal weather in the United States and abroad, corn prices are projected to increase gradually from the lowest levels in 1986-1987. Soybean prices increase more rapidly in 1988-1989 but adjust in the following year as production responds to the price increase and demand is similar to that of the previous year.

One important consequence of the large acreage reduction and expanding imports in the projection period is a decline in stocks of corn or feed grains and wheat. By 1991-1992, these stocks were reduced to normal levels. The rules of operating the program, summarized in table 1, were set to utilize these stocks on an even basis, generating a relatively smooth market price path for the grains involved and not inducing significant shocks for the livestock economy.

Net CCC expenditures, which decline slightly from FY 1987, are projected to decrease more significantly in FY 1988 and reach a $10 billion level by FY 1991. A large portion of the decline in FY 1988 is a result of reduced loan outlays. Generally, the baseline shows increasing prices, a slow reduction in stocks, continued use of acreage reduction provisions in the commodity programs, and a growing world demand for agricultural commodities stimulated by moderately optimistic macroeconomic conditions.

Base Acreage Adjustments. Increasing the CRP reduces the number of base acres eligible for government payments. After the fourth sign-up, the total CRP enrollment of 17.7 million acres had reduced the base acreage of the seven program crops modeled by 11.2 million acres (Table 3). Projections of future reductions in base acreage depended on CRP enrollment by state. For each state and commodity, the 1990 base reduction was set equal to the 1987 base reduction multiplied by the ratio of the 1990 state CRP to the 1987 state CRP. National base reductions for each of the commodities were simply the sum of the state reductions.

Table 3. Base reductions under the baseline (45/0) and three targeting scenarios: 5 million targeted acres in a 45 million acre CRP (45/5); 20 million targeted acres in a 45 million acre CRP (45/20); 25 million targeted acres in a 65 million acre CRP (65/45).

	1987-1988	1988-1989	1989-1990	1990-1991	1991-1992	1988-1992 Average	Change from Base	Percent Change
				million acres				
Wheat								
45/0	4.96	6.85	9.29	11.00	11.00	9.54		
45/5	4.96	6.72	9.12	10.80	10.80	9.36	−0.18	−1.8
45/20	4.96	6.45	8.75	10.36	10.36	8.98	−0.55	−5.8
65/25	4.96	7.26	10.88	13.61	14.74	11.62	2.09	21.9
Corn								
45/0	2.32	5.03	6.83	8.08	8.08	7.01		
45/5	2.32	5.21	7.07	8.38	8.38	7.26	0.26	3.6
45/20	2.32	5.35	7.26	8.60	8.60	7.45	0.45	6.4
65/25	2.32	6.41	9.61	12.01	13.01	10.26	3.26	46.5
Barley								
45/0	1.28	1.82	2.47	2.93	2.93	2.54		
45/5	1.28	1.72	2.34	2.77	2.77	2.40	−0.14	−5.4
45/20	1.28	1.69	2.30	2.72	2.72	2.36	−0.18	−7.1
65/25	1.28	1.84	2.76	3.45	3.74	2.95	0.41	16.2
Sorghum								
45/0	1.34	1.77	2.40	2.84	2.84	2.46		
45/5	1.34	1.74	2.36	2.80	2.80	2.43	−0.04	−1.5
45/20	1.34	1.56	2.11	2.50	2.50	2.17	−0.29	−12.0
65/25	1.34	1.81	2.72	3.40	3.68	2.90	0.44	17.9
Oats								
45/0	0.55	0.98	1.33	1.58	1.58	1.37		
45/5	0.55	0.97	1.31	1.56	1.56	1.35	−0.02	−1.3
45/20	0.55	0.88	1.20	1.42	1.42	1.23	−0.14	−10.1
65/25	0.55	1.06	1.59	1.98	2.15	1.70	0.33	23.9
Cotton								
45/0	0.74	1.01	1.38	1.63	1.63	1.41		
45/5	0.74	0.95	1.29	1.53	1.53	1.33	−0.09	− 6.2
45/20	0.74	0.90	1.06	1.17	1.17	1.08	−0.34	−23.9
65/25	0.74	1.06	1.41	1.68	1.79	1.49	0.07	5.1
Rice								
45/0	0.00	0.01	0.01	0.01	0.01	0.01		
45/5	0.00	0.01	0.01	0.01	0.01	0.01	0.00	27.5
45/20	0.00	0.01	0.02	0.02	0.02	0.02	0.01	92.2
65/25	0.00	0.01	0.02	0.02	0.02	0.02	0.01	117.1
Total								
45/0	11.19	17.47	23.71	28.07	28.07	24.33		
45/5	11.19	17.32	23.50	27.85	27.85	24.13	−0.20	−0.8
45/20	11.19	16.84	22.70	26.79	26.79	23.28	−1.05	−4.3
65/25	11.19	19.45	28.99	36.15	39.13	30.93	6.60	27.1

After the fourth sign-up, the wheat base had been reduced by almost 5.0 million acres because of the CRP. Alternatively, the corn base had been reduced by only 2.3 million acres. In the baseline scenario, however, future CRP enrollment is projected to reduce corn base acreage almost as much as wheat.

Results of scenarios for base acreage reduction also are summarized in table 3. For the 45/5 scenario, more corn acres are enrolled in CRP when 5 million acres are targeted to buffer strips. Except for rice, the amount of base acreage enrolled in the CRP falls for each of the other major crops. The changes are relatively small; the largest absolute effect is the 300,000-acre reduction for the corn base in 1990.

Targeting 20 million acres to buffer strips in the 45 million acre CRP magnifies the effects observed in the 45/5 scenario. Total base acreages enrolled in the CRP falls by almost 1.3 million acres in 1990, because much of the targeted land is located where fewer program crops are grown. The greatest absolute effects are for wheat and corn, but the largest proportional effect is for cotton. In 1990, almost half a million fewer base cotton acres are enrolled in the CRP under the 45/20 scenario than in the baseline.

For the 65/25 scenario, buffer strips reduce total base acreage by 11 million acres from the 45/0 levels. Other than rice (where the baseline CRP enrollment is low) the largest percent increases in CRP enrollment occur for corn. This follows because the eligible acreage is concentrated in the Midwest and Upper Mississippi River Basin. Enlarging the CRP necessarily has a significant effect on corn and wheat supply and will be apparent on the price paths that are developed.

Planted Acreage. Planted acreage for the major crops is determined in the CARD/FAPRI model by parameters of government programs and economic conditions. Increasing base acreage enrolled in the CRP for a given commodity tends to reduce the planted acreage of that crop. But this direct effect is countered by changes in other government programs and increases in market prices, which in turn affect participation and planted acreage.

In the baseline, planted acreage for wheat, corn, and cotton expands between 1987 and 1991. Relaxation of idle land requirements for commodity programs and increased market prices more than offset the effect of the expansion in CRP acreage. In contrast, the barley and sorghum area contracts until 1990. For soybeans, cotton, and rice, large acreage increases are projected for 1988, but they change little between 1988 and 1991. Planted acreage for oats falls in part because fewer corn set-aside acres require a cover crop.

Investigating the impacts of the targeting and CRP scenarios for planted acreage shows significant supply effects. The 45/5 scenario shows little effect on planted acreage. In fact, for all eight major crops, the planted acreage differs from the baseline by less than 1 percent (Table 4). Corn and soybean acreage falls slightly, while wheat, barley, sorghum, and cotton acreage increases.

Targeting the 20 million acres to buffer strips under the 45/20 scenario increases sorghum and cotton area planted by about 2 percent above the baseline level. This is because of the sharp drop in CRP enrollment as a result of targeting in Kansas and Texas. Acreages in wheat, barley, and oats increase by smaller amounts. Corn, soybeans, and rice acreages fall compared to the baseline.

Results for the 65/25 scenario suggest more significant impacts. Increasing the size of the CRP to 65 million acres reduces total planted acreage in the eight major crops by more than 5 million acres by 1991. This effect would have been larger had annual acreage diversion parameters for the commodity programs not been relaxed. For example, the 1991 acreage reduction program for corn was reduced from 10 percent to 5 percent to adjust for the supply-reducing effects of the CRP. The 20 million acre increase in 1991 CRP acres can be accounted for as follows: the planted acreage in the eight program crops is reduced by 5.3 million, the land in annual acreage retirement programs falls by 60 million acres, 5.7 million acres of the expanded CRP come from nonprogram crops, and the total land use increases by 3.0 million acres because of higher crop prices.

Market Prices. In the CARD/FAPRI multi-market commodity model, market prices for major commodities are determined by the interaction of supply and demand. Given domestic production and beginning stocks, domestic use, exports, and ending stocks, prices are jointly determined. Thus, for example, lower production will result in higher prices, lower exports, lower domestic use, and reduced carryover stocks.

In the baseline, prices for wheat, corn, barley, and sorghum are projected to increase for the next five years. The 45/5 scenario showed little impact on planted area or acreage base, which in turn will cause little impact on market prices.

Price changes are more pronounced under the 45/20 scenario because production shifts are larger than under the baseline or the 45/5 scenario. The direction of the changes, however, is the same as for the 45/5 scenario. These results are summarized in table 5. The largest price effect is for cotton (-6.5 percent), which also had the largest proportional change in planted

Table 4. Planted acreage under the baseline (45/0) and three targeting scenarios: 5 million targeted acres in a 45 million acre CRP (45/5); 20 million targeted acres in a 45 million acre CRP (45/20); 25 million targeted acres in a 65 million acre CRP (65/45).

	1987-1988	1988-1989	1989-1990	1990-1991	1991-1992	1988-1992 Average	Change from Base	Percent Change
				million acres				
Wheat								
45/0	65.8	65.3	72.0	73.8	73.7	71.2		
45/5	65.8	65.4	72.2	73.9	73.9	71.4	0.2	0.2
45/20	65.8	65.6	72.5	74.3	74.3	71.7	0.5	0.7
65/25	65.8	65.0	71.3	72.7	72.1	70.3	−0.9	−1.3
Corn								
45/0	65.7	66.9	67.8	69.1	73.1	69.2		
45/5	65.7	66.8	67.7	68.9	72.9	69.1	−0.1	−0.2
45/20	65.7	66.7	67.5	68.8	72.7	68.9	−0.3	−0.4
65/25	65.7	66.4	66.7	67.8	71.2	68.0	−1.2	−1.7
Barley								
45/0	11.0	11.0	10.7	10.6	11.3	10.9		
45/5	11.0	11.1	10.7	10.6	11.3	10.9	0.0	0.2
45/20	11.0	11.1	10.7	10.6	11.3	10.9	0.0	0.2
65/25	11.0	11.1	10.7	10.7	11.2	10.9	0.0	0.2
Sorghum								
45/0	11.8	11.6	11.1	11.4	12.7	11.7		
45/5	11.8	11.6	11.2	11.5	12.7	11.8	0.1	0.4
45/20	11.8	11.7	11.4	11.7	13.0	12.0	0.3	2.1
65/25	11.8	11.7	11.1	11.5	12.6	11.7	0.0	0.2
Oats								
45/0	18.0	14.3	13.7	13.3	13.0	13.6		
45/5	18.0	14.3	13.7	13.3	13.0	13.6	0.0	0.0
45/20	18.0	14.4	13.8	13.4	13.1	13.7	0.1	0.7
65/25	18.0	14.3	13.6	13.1	12.7	13.4	−0.2	−1.1
Cotton								
45/0	10.4	12.0	11.6	11.5	11.8	11.7		
45/5	10.4	12.0	11.6	11.6	11.8	11.8	0.0	0.4
45/20	10.4	12.1	11.8	11.8	12.0	11.9	0.2	1.6
65/25	10.4	12.0	11.6	11.5	11.7	11.7	0.0	−0.3
Rice								
45/0	2.4	2.9	2.9	2.9	3.0			
45/5	2.4	2.9	2.9	2.9	3.0	2.9	0.0	0.0
45/20	2.4	2.9	2.9	2.9	2.9	2.9	0.0	−0.3
65/25	2.4	2.9	2.9	2.9	2.9	2.9	0.0	−0.3
Soybeans								
45/0	57.4	62.0	64.6	67.6	61.9	62.8		
45/5	57.4	62.0	64.5	62.6	61.8	62.7	0.0	−0.1
45/20	57.4	62.0	64.5	62.6	61.8	62.7	0.0	−0.1
65/25	57.4	61.4	63.9	61.4	60.6	61.8	0.9	−1.5
Total								
45/0	242.5	245.9	254.4	255.2	260.4	254.0		
45/5	242.5	246.1	254.5	255.3	260.4	254.0	0.1	0.0
45/20	242.5	246.4	255.0	256.1	261.1	254.7	0.7	0.3
65/25	242.5	244.7	251.7	251.6	255.0	250.8	−3.2	−1.3

Table 5. Market prices under the baseline (45/0) and three targeting scenarios: 5 million targeted acres in a 45 million acre CRP (45/5); 20 million targeted acres in a 45 million acre CRP (45/20); 25 million targeted acres in a 65 million acre CRP (65/45).

	1987-1988	1988-1989	1989-1990	1990-1991	1991-1992	1988-1992 Average	Change from Base	Percent Change
				dollars per bushel				
Wheat								
45/0	2.56	2.86	3.00	3.05	3.09	3.00		
45/5	2.56	2.86	3.00	3.05	3.09	3.00	0.00	0.0
45/20	2.56	2.85	2.99	3.04	3.09	2.99	(0.01)	-0.2
65/25	2.56	2.89	3.11	3.23	3.33	3.14	0.14	4.7
Corn								
45/0	1.71	1.91	2.00	2.05	2.11	2.02		
45/5	1.71	1.92	2.01	2.06	2.13	2.03	0.01	0.6
45/20	1.71	1.92	2.02	2.08	2.15	2.04	0.02	1.2
65/25	1.71	1.95	2.10	2.19	2.31	2.14	0.12	5.9
Barley								
45/0	1.80	2.02	2.07	2.15	2.11	2.09		
45/5	1.80	2.01	2.07	2.14	2.10	2.08	(0.01)	-0.4
45/20	1.80	2.01	2.06	2.13	2.09	2.07	(0.02)	-0.7
65/25	1.80	2.02	2.12	2.18	2.19	2.13	0.04	1.9
Sorghum								
45/0	1.60	1.74	1.91	2.04	2.03	1.93		
45/5	1.60	1.74	1.91	2.04	2.03	1.93	0.00	0.0
45/20	1.60	1.73	1.89	2.03	2.02	1.92	0.01	-0.6
65/25	1.60	1.76	1.97	2.13	2.16	2.01	0.07	3.9
Oats								
45/0	1.65	1.46	1.52	1.60	1.65	1.56		
45/5	1.65	1.47	1.52	1.60	1.66	1.56	0.00	0.3
45/20	1.65	1.47	1.52	1.61	1.66	1.57	0.01	0.5
65/25	1.65	1.47	1.52	1.62	1.69	1.58	0.02	1.1
Cotton*								
45/0	0.630	0.602	0.584	0.593	0.606	0.596		
45/5	0.628	0.597	0.575	0.582	0.594	0.587	(0.009)	-1.6
45/20	0.626	0.586	0.551	0.545	0.551	0.558	(0.038)	-6.4
65/25	0.632	0.605	0.589	0.600	0.615	0.602	0.006	1.0
Rice†								
45/0	6.96	5.91	6.18	6.49	6.59	6.29		
45/5	6.96	5.91	6.18	6.49	6.59	6.29	0.00	0.0
45/20	6.96	5.92	6.20	6.52	6.62	6.32	0.02	0.4
65/25	6.96	5.93	6.22	6.57	6.68	6.35	0.06	0.9
Soybeans								
45/0	5.63	6.14	5.23	5.24	5.79	5.60		
45/5	5.63	6.15	5.25	5.26	5.80	5.62	0.01	0.3
45/20	5.63	6.15	5.25	5.28	5.81	5.62	0.02	0.4
65/25	5.64	6.42	5.63	5.86	6.48	6.10	0.50	8.9

*Dollars per pound.
†Dollars per hundredweight.

acreage. In the 65/25 CRP scenario, higher prices for all eight of the major commodities were projected. Prices increased most dramatically for corn (5.9 percent) and soybeans (8.9 percent), because much of the increased CRP acreage is from the Corn Belt. These higher prices have a significant influence on the cost of operating the commodity programs.

Government Cost. Government costs of the CRP and commodity programs are calculated using an accounting framework designed to replicate the actions of the Commodity Credit Corporation (CCC). Government costs are computed on a cash basis, so when a CRP payment is made in Payment-In-Kind (PIK) certificates instead of cash, it is not recorded as a cost to the CRP. If this certificate then is used to repay a corn loan, the cost is ascribed to the corn program. Thus, the certificates are not lost, but they skew the allocation of recorded costs by commodity.

For the baseline or 45/0 scenario, government cost of the agricultural commodity programs is projected to fall dramatically in FY 1988 to about $14 billion from levels in excess of $20 billion in FY 1986 and 1987 (Table 6). More modest declines occur in out-years. It is assumed in the analysis that 50 percent of the rental payments will be made in certificates until 1992. Thus, the true CRP costs are almost double those reported. In FY 1992, the certificate proportion of the CRP payment is assumed to fall to 25 percent. The rental rate of $52.78 per acre, up from $48.70, is projected because the land bid into the CRP is more productive.

In planted acreage, the cost impacts of the 45/5 scenario are minimal. The conclusion from the analysis is that modest targeting of the CRP can occur at the 45 million acre level without significant impacts on government costs, prices, or planted acreage. Even when the number of targeted acres is increased to 20 million, total government cost is not significantly affected (only 1.1 percent higher). Holding state bid rates constant, the national average bid rate for future sign-up is $53.86. Cotton program costs rise by as much as $390 million for 1992 as a result of lower prices and increased program acreage. Were it not for cotton, total government costs actually would fall for this scenario. The high cost of the cotton program could be reduced if the program acreage reduction rate were increased to offset the reductions in CRP acreage.

When the CRP is expanded to 65 million acres, the net impact on government costs depends on the magnitudes of two effects working in opposite directions. Base acreage reductions result in higher commodity prices and reductions in deficiency payments. But larger total rental payments must be made on the expanded CRP acreage. With state bid rates assumed con-

Table 6. Government costs under the baseline (45/0) and three targeting scenarios: 5 million targeted acres in a 45 million acre CRP (45/5); 20 million targeted acres in a 45 million acre CRP (45/20); 25 million targeted acres in a 65 million acre CRP assuming constant (65/25 Lo) and increased (65/25 Hi) state bid rates.

	Fiscal Year 1988	Fiscal Year 1989	Fiscal Year 1990	Fiscal Year 1991	Fiscal Year 1992	1988-1992 Average	Change From Base	Percent Change
			billion dollars, cash accounting					
Wheat								
45/0	1.21	1.70	1.65	1.74	1.53	1.57		
45/5	1.21	1.70	1.66	1.74	1.53	1.57	0.00	0.0
45/20	1.23	1.72	1.68	1.75	1.54	1.58	0.02	1.1
65/25 Lo	1.19	1.56	1.36	1.33	1.05	1.30	(0.27)	− 17.1
65/25 Hi	1.19	1.57	1.39	1.38	1.08	1.32	(0.24)	− 15.6
Feed Grains								
45/0	8.89	6.37	4.41	3.46	3.27	5.28		
45/5	8.86	6.34	4.33	3.32	3.19	5.21	(0.07)	− 1.3
45/20	8.86	6.32	4.31	3.21	3.06	5.15	(0.13)	− 2.4
65/25 Lo	8.67	5.94	3.78	2.28	2.11	4.56	(0.72)	− 13.7
65/25 Hi	8.67	5.97	3.85	2.36	2.16	4.60	(0.68)	− 12.8
Cotton								
45/0	0.77	0.73	0.73	0.66	0.54	0.69		
45/5	0.79	0.77	0.79	0.74	0.61	0.74	0.06	8.2
45/20	0.81	0.86	0.98	1.04	0.93	0.92	0.24	34.7
65/25 Lo	0.76	0.71	0.69	0.62	0.48	0.65	(0.03)	− 5.0
65/25 Hi	0.76	0.71	0.69	0.62	0.48	0.65	(0.03)	− 5.0
Soybeans								
45/0	(1.71)	(0.17)	0.29	(0.00)	(0.10)	(0.34)		
45/5	(1.71)	(0.18)	0.27	(0.01)	(0.07)	(0.34)	(0.00)	− 0.8
45/20	(1.71)	(0.18)	0.28	(0.02)	(0.07)	(0.34)	(0.00)	− 1.1
65/25 Lo	(1.72)	(0.23)	0.11	(0.04)	(0.08)	(0.39)	(0.05)	− 15.5
65/25 Hi	(1.72)	(0.23)	0.11	(0.04)	(0.08)	(0.39)	(0.05)	− 15.5
CRP								
45/0	0.83	1.08	1.23	1.15	1.73	1.21		
45/5	0.83	1.09	1.24	1.17	1.75	1.22	0.01	0.7
45/20	0.83	1.09	1.25	1.17	1.75	1.22	0.01	0.9
65/25 Lo	0.98	1.43	1.71	1.76	2.56	1.69	0.48	39.9
65/25 Hi	0.98	1.59	2.04	2.23	3.34	2.04	0.83	68.7
Other								
45/0	4.01	3.47	2.91	2.80	2.75	3.19		
45/5	4.01	3.46	2.91	2.80	2.75	3.19	(0.00)	− 0.1
45/20	4.01	3.46	2.90	2.79	2.74	3.18	(0.01)	− 0.3
65/25 Lo	4.00	3.43	2.83	2.72	2.68	3.13	(0.06)	− 1.8
65/25 Hi	4.01	3.43	2.84	2.73	2.68	3.14	(0.05	− 1.6
Total								
45/0	14.01	13.18	11.23	9.81	9.71	11.59		
45/5	14.00	13.19	11.20	9.76	9.75	11.58	(0.01)	− 0.1
45/20	14.03	13.27	11.40	9.92	9.95	11.71	0.13	1.1
65/25 Lo	13.88	12.84	10.48	8.68	8.80	10.93	(0.65)	− 5.6
65/25 Hi	13.89	13.05	10.92	9.28	9.66	11.36	(0.23)	− 2.0

stant, the average net cost saving to the government averages approximately $650 million per year over the next five years. If the assumed average bid rates increase by 40 percent (to $75.49 per acre), the cost savings fall to $230 million per year; beyond 1992, government costs are essentially unchanged.

Mathematical Programming Analysis. The mathematical programming models used to evaluate CRP levels and targeting were for five producing areas (PAs). The models incorporate prices and acreages from section 2 and the CARD/FAPRI multi-market commodity analysis. These PAs are in the Upper Midwestern region, covering the Mississippi River Basin. Detailed descriptions of the models are provided in Holtkamp and associates (*3*). Generally, the models use a static linear programming framework. Each PA is modeled as a representative farm. The maximization is for net returns over variable costs of crop production. The livestock sector is not endogenous. But livestock is included in terms of feed demand requirements that are constant for the CRP scenarios. Crops are identified in rotations typical of those in the Upper Mississippi River Basin. Budgets for crop production and for erosion are from ARIMS (*1*).

The PA models include constraints for land (three groups), machinery, operator labor, and commodity acreage bases. The commodity acreage bases are keyed to scenarios and the CARD/FAPRI results. For the analysis, it is important to determine the tradeoffs between commodity program payments, increased cost of the CRP and, perhaps, production cost. Participation in commodity programs is endogenized, using program and market price differentials and the value of the acreage base assuming that current commodity programs are continued. Finally, CRP enrollment is exogenously specified given the allocation developed in section 2 and the state results previously reported.

Base Run and Scenarios. The evaluations were for scenarios compared to a base run. The base run (45/0) assumes that the CRP is fully implemented (Table 7). Again, commodity program and market prices, reduced acreage requirements, and other variables are for 1990 and are from the CARD/FAPRI March 1988 baseline.

45/5 Scenario Compared to the Baseline. Results comparing the 45/5 scenario to the baseline are summarized in table 8. Projected corn and soybean prices under the 45/5 scenario are up slightly. Acreage enrolled in the CRP is down in PAs 39 and 41 and up in PAs 40, 42, and 43. Relatively

Table 7. Estimates of net income, production, land use, pesticide use, and land rental value for the baseline 45/0 scenario by producing area.

	Producing Area				
	No. 39	No. 40	No. 41	No. 42	No. 43
	million dollars				
Net income, crops	1,688	868	3,321	1,825	585
	million units				
Production					
Corn (bushels)	497.66	183.80	1,220.73	665.97	175.48
Soybeans (bushels)	154.03	38.33	364.98	229.37	52.14
Wheat (bushels)	111.00	31.27	29.71	67.76	72.95
Hay (tons)	6.02	10.31	9.78	1.19	0.82
	million acres				
Land use					
Corn	4.25	1.69	10.41	5.61	1.57
Soybeans	4.50	1.25	10.42	6.51	1.57
Wheat	2.25	0.55	0.57	1.19	1.22
Hay	1.62	2.33	2.39	0.42	0.32
Set aside	0.75	0.33	2.06	0.90	0.21
CRP	1.46	0.67	3.72	1.08	0.59
Idle land (percent of total land)	14.9%	14.7%	19.5%	12.6%	14.7%
CRP (percent of total land base)	9.8%	9.9%	12.6%	6.8%	10.8%
	million acres				
Commodity program					
Corn base	3.46	1.93	12.57	4.87	0.92
Wheat base	2.14	0.10	0.16	1.26	0.76
Participation					
Corn	2.88	1.61	10.25	4.04	0.77
Wheat	1.48	0.07	0.05	0.75	0.45
Base reduction					
Corn	0.34	0.21	1.73	0.23	0.07
Wheat	0.24	0.01	0.05	0.20	0.13
Participation rate					
Corn	0.83	0.83	0.82	0.83	0.84
Wheat	0.69	0.64	0.30	0.60	0.59
Tillage method					
Conventional	8.88	4.84	17.63	9.43	3.38
Reduced tillage	3.73	0.73	6.17	4.10	1.28
No-till	0.00	0.25	0.00	0.19	0.00
	million pounds of active ingredient				
Pesticide use					
Alachlor	13.11	3.76	30.85	14.68	4.16
Atrazine	5.75	2.29	13.95	7.37	2.05
Dual	0.00	1.92	0.00	0.32	0.00
Sencor	1.92	0.47	4.47	2.63	0.61
Treflan	3.56	0.82	8.29	4.66	1.06
	dollars per acre				
Land rental values					
Soil class one	65.99	28.50	43.73	57.97	38.26
Soil class two	68.77	60.66	80.33	85.17	91.94
Soil class three	99.55	86.80	82.51	105.45	104.72
CRP shadow price	98.76	91.34	112.20	112.86	107.00

Table 8. Percentage difference estimates as compared to the baseline (45/0) for the 45/5 scenario, by production area.

	Producing Area				
	No. 39	No. 40	No. 41	No. 42	No. 43
	%				
Net income, crops	−0.2	−0.3	−0.5	0.2	−0.1
Production					
Corn (bushels)	1.0	−0.2	0.4	−1.8	−2.0
Soybeans (bushels)	−0.1	−0.3	0.4	−1.0	−2.2
Wheat (bushels)	.0	0.0	3.3	−1.1	0.1
Hay (tons)	−0.2	−0.1	0.0	0.6	0.1
Land use					
Corn	0.9	0.0	0.6	−2.0	−4.2
Soybeans	−0.2	0.1	0.5	−1.4	−4.2
Wheat	0.0	0.0	3.3	−1.7	−1.4
Hay	0.0	0.0	0.0	0.0	0.0
Set aside	0.3	−0.3	0.5	−1.5	−0.9
CRP	−2.5	1.2	−3.4	20.9	10.0
Idle land (percent of total land)	−1.5	0.6	−2.0	10.7	8.9
CRP (percent of total land base)	−2.4	1.1	−3.4	21.0	11.9
Commodity program					
Corn base	0.3	−0.1	0.5	−1.0	−0.1
Wheat base	0.0	0.0	0.0	0.0	0.0
Participation					
Corn	0.3	−0.6	0.5	−1.0	−0.6
Wheat	14.6	20.9	111.9	21.8	25.4
Base reduction					
Corn	−2.9	1.4	−3.4	21.0	1.4
Wheat	−2.9	1.4	−3.5	21.1	9.6
Participation rate					
Corn	0.1	−0.5	0.0	−0.0	−0.5
Wheat	14.6	20.9	111.9	21.8	25.4
Tillage method					
Conventional	0.5	0.0	0.1	−0.3	0.6
Reduced tillage	0.0	−1.0	1.6	0.0	1.6
No-till		0.0		−86.5	
Pesticide use					
Alachlor	1.0	−0.3	0.3	−0.9	−1.9
Atrazine	1.0	−0.1	0.7	−1.9	−1.4
Dual		−70.7		−91.1	
Sencor	−0.1	−0.5	0.3	−3.1	−1.6
Treflan	−0.2	−0.5	0.2	−0.9	−1.7
Land rental values					
Soil class one	−0.3	0.4	−1.8	1.8	0.0
Soil class two	−0.2	0.1	−1.9	6.9	0.0
Soil class three	−0.3	−0.1	−1.9	3.3	0.0
CRP shadow price	−0.5	−0.3	−0.6	4.5	−0.2

large increases in CRP enrollment are implied for PAs 42 and 43.

Planted acreages for corn, wheat, and soybeans were down in PAs 42 and 43, but the other PAs had relatively small changes in land use patterns. Set-aside and base acreage changes follow the changes in CRP enrollment. Acres of corn participating in commodity programs changed little. Commodity programs are still quite profitable compared to growing corn outside the commodity programs.

In assessing overall results, the changes are relatively minor. Production patterns remain similar, and changes in net farm income are negligible. Use of all pesticides is down in PAs 40, 42, and 43 because of changes in crop rotation and tillage practices and in total acreage planted. The shadow or imputed price for CRP enrollment in PA 42 indicates that the CRP rental rate required to actually buy out the level of CRP imposed for PA 42 would be considerably higher than that used in the CARD/FAPRI model evaluation.

45/20 Scenario Compared to Baseline. The major change between this scenario and the baseline and the 45/5 scenario is increased targeting of CRP land. Generally, the quality or productivity of the CRP land available for targeting is higher than under existing regulations. Thus, the larger impacts are on net income and on the imputed rental rates for the CRP land compared to the baseline (Table 9). Changes in planted acres in the PAs are similar to those for the 45/5 scenario. Shadow prices for CRP enrollment are up significantly for all PAs, primarily because higher quality land is being removed as buffer strips.

65/25 Scenario Compared to Baseline. Projected prices for corn, soybeans, and wheat prices are up significantly. And, of course, CRP enrollments are up in all PAs because of the increase in the total CRP and the large share of buffer land available for targeting nationally in these PAs.

Results of the analysis are consistent with those obtained by comparing the 45/5 and 45/20 scenarios. Net farm income is up in all PAs as a result of CRP payments and higher commodity prices (Table 10). Government program participation is down. Government cost for operating the combined commodity and CRP is reduced. Planted acreage and production of all crops is generally down or unchanged in all of the PAs except 43. CRP shadow prices increase in all PAs, primarily because of the larger quantity of land in the CRP and targeting of the CRP to buffer strips. Tillage practices are similar to those in the baseline. Thus, the major impacts follow from higher CRP restrictions, targeting, and higher commodity prices.

Table 9. Percentage difference estimates as compared to the baseline (45/0) for the 45/20 scenario, by production area.*

	Producing Area				
	No. 39	No. 40	No. 41	No. 42	No. 43
			%		
Net income, crops	9	7	10	11	9
Production					
Corn (bushels)	9	6	4	−4	16
Soybeans (bushels)	−1	−6	4	−5	−10
Wheat (bushels)	−1	0	−22	−5	−17
Hay (tons)	−3	0	0	−22	0
Land use					
Corn	9	7	4	3	17
Soybeans	−1	−4	4	−4	−11
Wheat	0	0	−22	−5	−18
Hay	0	0	0	−28	0
Set aside	3	0	3	−2	−2
CRP	−26	−4	−22	30	18
Idle land (percent of total land)	−16	−3	−13	16	13
CRP (percent of total land base)	−26	−5	−22	30	18
Commodity program					
Corn base	5	0	3	−1	−1
Wheat base	−8	−10	−26	−21	−19
Participation					
Corn	3	0	3	−1	−1
Wheat	20	17	118	20	23
Base reduction					
Corn	−26	−4	−22	30	18
Wheat	−26	−4	−22	30	18
Participation rate					
Corn	−2	−0	1	0	0
Wheat	31	30	193	52	53
Tillage method					
Conventional	4	−1	−1	−1	−1
Reduced tillage	0	4	14	−2	−4
No-till		0		−65	
Pesticide use					
Alachlor	8	9	2	3	15
Atrazine	9	7	4	2	17
Dual		−73		−84	
Sencor	−2	−5	8	−6	−10
Treflan	−3	−4	1	−7	−10
Land rental values					
Soil class one	16	55	24	20	16
Soil class two	28	24	13	17	8
Soil class three	20	19	13	13	7
CRP shadow price	34	15	11	15	8

*Assumed variables: price change from base—corn, +1.5%; wheat, 0%; soybeans, +1%; hay, 0%. Deficiency payment— corn, $0.67; wheat, $0.96. Set aside requirement—corn, 20%; wheat, 10%.

Table 10. Percentage difference estimates as compared to the baseline (45/0) for the 65/20 scenario, by production area.*

	Producing Area				
	No. 39	No. 40	No. 41	No. 42	No. 43
			%		
Net income, crops	16	15	17	21	18
Production					
Corn (bushels)	−4	11	−4	2	4
Soybeans (bushels)	1	−38	−4	−5	4
Wheat (bushels)	−4	0	−26	−36	−39
Hay (tons)	−2	0	0	−100	−11
Land use					
Corn	−4	11	−4	2	3
Soybeans	0	−40	−4	−5	3
Wheat	−4	0	−26	−100	−41
Hay	−1	0	0	−100	−3
Set aside	−2	−5	−4	−6	−7
CRP	19	50	28	103	70
Idle land (percent of total land)	12	32	17	61	50
CRP (percent of total land base)	19	50	28	113	70
Commodity program					
Corn base	1.6	−5.3	−3.7	−4.8	−4
Wheat base	−13.5	−18.0	−41.3	−32.9	−28
Participation					
Corn	−1.7	−5.5	−3.9	−4.7	−5
Wheat	−2.9	7.1	71.4	25.3	10
Base reduction					
Corn	18.8	50.1	28.0	102.8	70
Wheat	18.8	50.1	28.0	102.8	70
Participation rate					
Corn	−3.2	−0.2	−0.2	0.1	−0.5
Wheat	12.2	30.7	191.7	86.8	52.6
Tillage method					
Conventional	9.2	1.0	−0.9	−5.0	−2
Reduced tillage	−30.3	−50.6	−12.5	−9.3	−22
No-till		0.0		−100.0	
Pesticide use					
Alachlor	−5.0	13.7	−4.3	4.6	3
Atrazine	−4.3	9.5	−4.1	1.6	3
Dual	0.0	−99.4	0.0	−100.0	0
Sencor	−0.1	−37.8	76.5	−6.6	3
Treflan	−0.2	−35.6	−100.0	−3.2	3
Land rental values					
Soil class one	33.9	122.0	45.0	51.9	51
Soil class two	50.1	61.5	39.9	46.1	27
Soil class three	35.6	49.0	40.2	37.0	23
CRP shadow price	41.7	34.2	18.7	30.3	20

*Assumed variables: price change from base—corn, +7%; wheat, +6%; soybeans, +12%; hay, 0%. Deficiency payment— corn, $0.56; wheat, $0.77. Set aside requirement—corn, 20%; wheat, 10%.

Summary. Results from the PA models, together with the price changes simulated by the CARD/FAPRI multi-market commodity model, suggest that farmers in the Midwest are not collectively worse off as a result of the CRP options analyzed. And the farmers in these Midwestern PAs are better off for the 45/20 and 65/25 options. The fact that net returns for farmers are higher in these options is a result of the CRP payments and the higher commodity prices that result from the reductions in available cropland because of targeting increasing CRP limits. Results not shown but available from the models indicate an increase in total erosion levels because the potential erosion levels on some of the buffer strip lands are not as high as those for the other eligible CRP land.

Summary and Conclusions

This CRP targeting exercise used the 1988 CARD/FAPRI baseline to emphasize the important interrelationships between commodity programs and the CRP. In effect, the analysis entailed substituting CRP for acreage reduction required to participate in commodity programs. Total cropped acres stay more or less the same, and the targeting criteria determine the impact by crop. The result for government costs in the short run is highly dependent on the level of stocks available for Payments-in-Kind, and that moderates market prices. In future years, tightness in available land for planted acres will cause higher commodity prices. The higher commodity prices increase consumers' cost for the CRP in the out-years. An important aspect of targeting the CRP is that it places societal priorities on the idled acres of cropland.

Mathematical programming results are subordinate to the CARD/FAPRI baseline and CRP and targeting scenario results. Important questions for targeting relate to whether it will significantly impact the type of farming by region. The five PAs selected for analysis were from the Corn Belt, where the major impacts of targeting the CRP would be felt. Generally, the programming analysis results show little impact on net farm income. For the 65/25 scenario, with higher market prices and higher assumed CRP rental payments, net farm income is higher. This increase is partly because acreage planted outside the commodity programs produces crops sold at higher market prices. Other impacts of the CRP are on the input utilization pattern detailed in the discussion of results. The overall conclusion, except for the 65/25 scenario, is that these impacts are relatively small.

Generally, the trade-off between commodity program deficiency payments and CRP rental, at least for the 45/5 and 45/20 scenarios, is almost even.

Thus, government costs, market prices, production, exports, and other indicators of performance of the sector are affected only modestly. The increase to 65 million acres for the CRP and the targeting of 25 million acres to buffer strips produces more significant changes. Government costs are reduced slightly, and market prices rise more rapidly because more land is taken out of production. In fact, some savings are estimated. But these estimates of savings are highly sensitive to the parameters of the commodity programs and the CRP rental rates assumed. And the programming analysis results for shadow prices on CRP land constraints are higher than the rental rates assumed.

Finally, a cautionary note is in order for the 65 million CRP scenario. This scenario is tight in the idle versus planted acreage. If the demand for exports were to increase more rapidly than projected, a considerably higher commodity price path would result from the targeting requirement to include 25 million acres in the CRP and to increase CRP limit to 65 million acres.

REFERENCES

1. English, Burton C., Elwin G. Smith, and George E. Oamek. 1987. *An overview and mathematical representation of the National Agricultural Resource Interregional Modeling System.* Staff paper. Center for Agricultural and Rural Development, Iowa State University, Ames.
2. Food and Agricultural Policy Research Institute. 1988. *FAPRI ten-year international outlook.* Center for National Food and Agriculture Policy, Department of Agricultural Economics, University of Missouri, Columbia, and Center for Agricultre and Rural Development, Trade and Agricultural Policy Division, Department of Economics, Iowa State University, Ames.
3. Holtkamp, Derald J., Greg Traxler, and Klaus K. Frohberg. 1988. *Documentation of the CARD state production modeling system.* Center for Agricultural and Rural Development, Iowa State University, Ames.
4. United States Department of Agriculture. 1987. *ASCS background information: Conservation and environmental protection programs.* BI No. 5. Agriculture Stabilization and Conservation Service, Washington, D.C.

7

The Food Security Act of 1985: Conservation Reserve Implications

Abner Womack, William H. Meyers, Jon A. Brandt, Stanley R. Johnson, and Patrick Westhoff

Our focus is the market-level economic impact of the conservation components in the Food Security Act (FSA), particularly the Conservation Reserve Program (CRP). Analysis is derived from a large-scale econometric model of U.S. agriculture maintained by the Food and Agricultural Policy Research Institute (FAPRI), sponsored by the University of Missouri and Iowa State University. This scenario examines U.S. agriculture over the next 10 years, assuming a continuation of current programs.

Estimated results are predicated on two sets of important information. First, general economic information is consistent with November 1988 baseline projections by the Wharton Econometric Forecasting Associates group (3). In general, these projections imply moderately expanding U.S. and world economies with a slowdown in 1989 and 1990 but no recession through 1995. Real interest rates are projected to remain relatively high; however, inflation will remain in check at four to five percent per year.

Second, FSA provisions continue through 1990-1991 and are maintained through the next farm bill with slight modifications (1). Target price supports to farmers are assumed frozen at 1990 levels. A total of 40 million acres would be placed in the CRP. Export-enhancement programs would be phased out gradually after 1990. Use of PIK certificates would continue, but at a lower percentage rate of payments.

Conservation Reserve Land Use

Since the FAPRI model represents major crops and livestock categories only, conclusions are restricted to this general area of the U.S. agricultural economy. Also, the assumption of 40 million total acres in the CRP is consistent with 30 million acres of land in crops examined by the model as indicated in table 1.

Imposing these conservation acreages implies a total of 33 million acres by 1989, moving up 7.5 million from the 1988 level of 25 million. An additional 7 million is projected to enter the program in 1990.

Acreage equations are conditioned to represent land moving into the CRP, and consideration is given to regions where land would be available. Rental rates presumably will have to be raised significantly before this additional land can be induced into the 10-year reserve. One reason is that a larger share of future enrollment must come from areas with higher land rent, such as the Corn Belt (Figures 1-3). Another reason is that higher rental rates will be necessary to reverse the declining trend in new enrollment. Throughout the country, a high proportion of marginal land that is eligible for the CRP has already been enrolled. Higher rental rates will be required to induce additional acres into the reserve.

Acreage Control Programs and Stock Objectives

A key management objective of a farm program at the national level is to ensure that normal carryover levels are achieved. In years with ample production, stocks are accumulated; in years with low production, stocks are released. This implies a predetermined stock objective. With some notion of expected prices, it is possible to estimate total demand that

Table 1. Base reductions due to the CRP.

	1987-1988	1988-1989	1989-1990	1990-1991
	million acres			
Wheat	5.0	7.6	9.6	11.4
Corn	2.3	2.9	4.0	5.0
Sorghum	1.3	1.9	2.5	3.0
Barley	1.3	2.0	2.4	2.9
Oats	0.6	0.9	1.1	1.4
Cotton	0.7	1.0	1.3	1.6
Rice	0.0	0.0	0.0	0.0
Total base reduction	11.2	16.3	21.0	25.3
Reduced soybean acreage	2.1	2.9	3.9	4.7
Other	4.4	6.3	8.2	9.9
Total CRP acreage	17.7	25.5	33.0	40.0

incorporates domestic and foreign markets. Combining these estimates implies a desired total level of production that, in turn, suggests government program levels with required percentages of set-aside and paid land diversion. When supplies are tight, acreage reduction rates are minimized. But

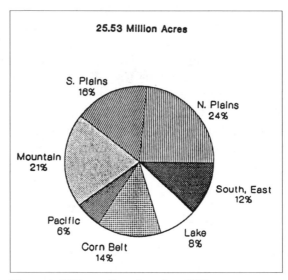

Figure 1. CRP enrollment, spring 1988.

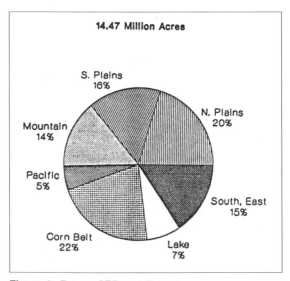

Figure 2. Future CRP enrollment.

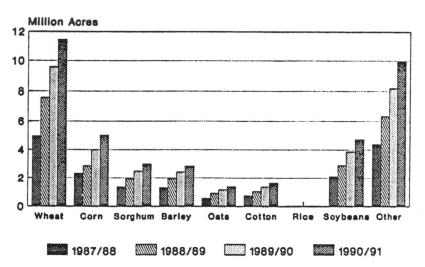

Figure 3. CRP enrollment by crop.

when stocks are excessive, set-aside restrictions are higher. As an example, set-aside requirements for wheat producers were 27.5 percent for the 1988-1989 crop year, but after the drought dropped to 10 percent for the 1989-1990 crop. Similarly, corn set-aside restrictions fell from 20 percent in 1988-1989 to 10 percent in 1989-1990.

An objective of this analysis was to hold total corn stocks between 1.5 billion and 2.0 billion bushels and wheat between 0.7 billion to 1.0 billion. Given the combination of projected demand strength plus land idled in the CRP, Acreage Reduction Program (ARP) rates were held at low levels throughout the projection period. By the mid-1990s, ARP rates were reduced to 10 percent for feed grains and 5 percent for wheat. Exceptions were cotton and rice, where prices remained near loan rates and ARP rates had to be held at the 20 percent level.

Given these program management guidelines, total wheat reserves reached an estimated maximum of about 780 million bushels in 1992-1993. Corn stocks peaked at about 1.7 billion bushels at the same time. Thus, this combination of factors—40 million CRP acres, modest demand growth, and normal stock carryover—reduces the cropland idled in annual programs from an average of 48 million acres in the 1985-1988 period to about 13 million acres in the 1993-1997 period. This is similar to the set-aside levels in 1978, 1979, and 1982, but carryover stocks in these past years were significantly higher (Figures 4 and 5). Projected plantings of program crops remain at or slightly above levels of the mid-1970s.

Projected Prices, Producer Returns, and Program Participation

Farm prices for feed grains and wheat are projected to average at or near the mid-range of the respective target prices and loan rate prices through 1992-1993. Although stocks were reduced drastically by the drought, we expect that low set-aside programs would tend to moderate this situation over the next four years. Projected farm prices of corn average about $2.10 per bushel and wheat about $3.25, significantly below drought prices of 1988. Farm prices are projected to average about 10 percent higher, or about $2.30 per bushel for corn and $3.60 per bushel for wheat, during the 1993-1997 period.

With government target prices for program participants frozen at 1990 levels and input costs increasing at four to five percent per year, it is likely that participant producer returns will decline over time. Farmers not participating in government programs will find exactly the opposite situation. Market price increases narrow the return gap. The average advantage for farmers participating in the wheat program over nonparticipants drops to about $10 per acre for 1993-1997, compared to $20 to $30 per acre in the

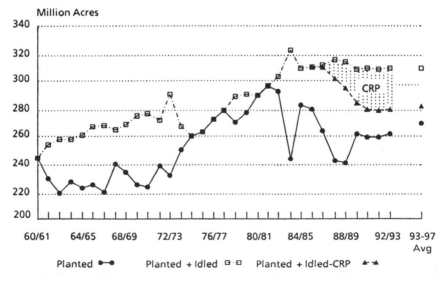

Figure 4. U.S. crop acreage (corn, wheat, soybean, barley, sorghum, oats, rice, cotton).

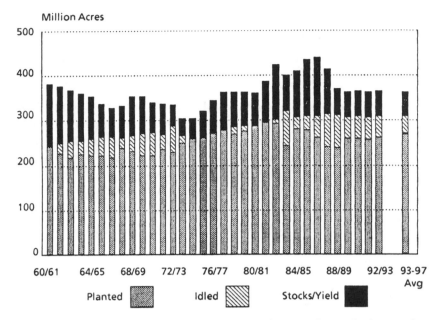

Figure 5. U.S. Crop acreage and inventories (corn, wheat, soybeans, barley, sorghum, oats, rice, cotton.

earlier years. Program participation for wheat is estimated to drop about 15 percent, from 85 percent in 1988 to 70 percent during the 1993-1997 period. Corn participation is expected to drop about 20 percent during the same period.

This has implications for the conservation compliance program. As participation rates decline, nonprogram planted area increases, averaging 156 million acres from 1993-1997 or nearly 35 million acres above current levels. Obviously, these acres are not subject to conservation compliance practices mandated by FSA.

A set of cross-purposes tends to emerge. The desire by Congress to reduce overall budget exposure implies lower government support. Reduced support results in lower participation by farmers and, hence, a substantial amount of planted area shifting out of government programs. Increased area in the CRP contributes to supply management and helps increase prices. This also tends to reduce participation rates and increase planting outside the programs. The increase in CRP acres improves soil conservation, while lower program participation rates have the opposite effect. Insofar as the conservation compliance provisions increase the cost of program participation, the compliance requirement itself will reduce participation and increase plantings outside the program.

Area Constraints

Projecting planted and idled land in the near future is difficult. Should the U.S. and world economies slip into another recession, or if weather patterns turn more favorable, then excess capacity is likely. Stocks would be expected to build, necessitating larger ARP rates. On the other hand, with robust domestic and foreign economies, perhaps combined with another drought, stocks would decline and annual land set-aside could be reduced to zero.

While these scenarios are possible, they do not reflect the most likely set of events conditioning this longer term evaluation. Favorable economic conditions were assumed—no recessions, no boom period. Weather was assumed to be normal, implying yield growth at intermediate trend levels. This combination suggests moderate growth in U.S. and world livestock industries. Both domestic and foreign food grains, feed grains, and high protein demand were, therefore, projected at moderate to strong growth rates.

Impacts on land use are reflected in figure 4. Total area planted and idled for major crops tends to remain about 310 million acres. But the mix of planted, set-aside, and CRP acreages changes significantly. In 1987-1988, 243 million acres of land were planted, with 60 million in set-asides and 13 million in the CRP. By 1992-1993, this mix, conditioned by our assumptions, is about 263 million acres planted, 30 million in the CRP, and 17 million in set-aside programs.

If a drought should occur during this period, acreage in the following year will necessarily increase to replenish depleted stocks. The 1988 drought reduced stocks by about 50 percent, prompting an expected increase in plantings of 21 million acres in the following year. In the years beyond 1990-1991, the area idled in annual programs is less than 20 million acres, and stock levels are much lower than in 1988. This would imply either releasing land from the CRP or allowing prices to remain high enough to bring additional land into cultivation. This kind of land expansion occurred in the 1970s, but it also brought with it increased soil erosion problems.

Some Conclusions

Baseline analysis conducted by the FAPRI suggests that a continuation of FSA conditioned on moderate economic expansion and normal weather, may lead to tightness in land area by the early 1990s, should the 40-million acre CRP be implemented. Tightness refers to the availability of reasonably productive land at current levels of government supports and market prices. National Resources Inventory data indicate that additional land is available (2). However, incentives would probably have to exceed those of the early 1970s to bring it into production.

Several conclusions could be drawn, but the most likely is that land still fallow is less productive and that much higher prices would be required to bring this land into the production stream. But this may jeopardize the conservation objective.

One important objective of FSA was to reduce soil loss through conservation programs. The 40-million to 45-million-acre CRP was designed to remove highly erodible land from crop production. If the objective of achieving at least the 40-million-acre CRP remains a high priority, then other counter measures may need to be considered. One may be to allow CRP participants to "buy back" their contract for a year in the event of a drought. This would conflict with the conservation objective and be opposed by environmental interests. Another option may be to carry sufficient stocks to offset the potential production shortfall in poor weather years. This strategy may be achievable with normal weather over the next few years. However, stock rebuilding may be constrained by land base availability, particularly as we move toward the 40-million-acre CRP objective. Higher stocks imply additional costs to the government. This is inconsistent with the goal of reducing program management costs.

As is often the case for any set of national objectives that may require different strategies, compromise and balance is often the result. This balance cuts across several related issues. Considering the total picture, achieving one objective of placing 40 million acres in the CRP for 10 years may be in conflict with stabilization and other program objectives. It will be worthwhile for policymakers to evaluate these tradeoffs more carefully as decisions are made to open the CRP for new enrollment over the next two years.

REFERENCES

1. Food and Agricultural Policy Research Institute. 1989. *U.S. and world agricultural outlook.* FAPRI –1-89, University of Missouri, Columbia, and Iowa State University, Ames.
2. Reichelderfer, Katherine. 1988. *Policy issues arising from implementation of the 1985 farm bill conservation provisions. In Increasing Understanding of Public Problems and Policies—1988.* Farm Foundation, Oak Brook, Illinois.
3. Wharton Econometric Forecasting Associates. 1988. *U.S. economic outlook 1988-1991.* Bala-Cynwyd, Pennsylvania.

8

Supply Control Aspects
of the Conservation Reserve

C. Robert Taylor

The Conservation Reserve Program (CRP) seeks to take 40 million to 45 million acres of highly erodible cropland out of production by 1990. Land in the CRP must be placed in grass or tree cover. Multiple objectives of the CRP, as stated in the legislation, are to reduce wind and water erosion, protect long-run capabilities to produce food and fiber, create better habitat for fish and wildlife, reduce surplus agricultural commodities, and provide farm income support. The supply control feature may have the greatest immediate economic impact on agriculture. CRP rental payments will have a direct impact on farm income, while increases in relative crop prices resulting from supply control will have a positive indirect impact on income.

CRP Policies Evaluated

Estimates of the aggregate economic impacts on consumers, producers, and taxpayers as a result of expanding the CRP to 45 million acres (CRP-45) and to 65 million acres (a potential modification of current legislation) (CRP-65) are discussed here. Current legislation calls for expanding the reserve to 40 million to 45 million acres by 1991.

Table 1 provides a regional distribution of the current CRP land and projections for the 45-million-acre and 65-million-acre reserves. Projections for CRP-45 and CRP-65 are based on the regional cropland eligible by virtue of its erodibility. Base bite associated with the CRP, which is the reduction in farm program acreage as a result of land being placed in the

CRP, was assumed to be proportional to base bite in CRP sign-ups 1-6.

Economic impacts of the CRP scenarios were estimated using AGSIM, a computer model of crop and livestock production in the United States. AGSIM is based on a large set of statistically estimated supply-and-demand equations for major agricultural commodities. Supply equations in the model show how agricultural producers respond to changes in commodity prices and farm programs; demand functions show how domestic and foreign consumers react in response to changes in commodity prices.

Baseline Assumptions

Assumptions about future target prices, deficiency payments, and set-aside rates have a critical impact on absolute and relative estimates of the impacts of CRP on producers, consumers, and taxpayers. It was assumed that the target price and set-aside features of the Acreage Reduction Program (ARP) in the Food Security Act of 1985 would be extended through the 1996 crop year. Table 2 provides the assumed target prices for 1990 through 1996. Full deficiency payments were assumed, as were normal crop yields. Unless noted, estimated economic effects are for the average of the 1993-1996 period. It is assumed that CRP policies will be fully implemented by the beginning of the 1991 crop year.

Estimated Effects of CRP-45

Because the CRP reduces production of agricultural commodities, crop prices can be expected to increase after market adjustments occur. Full

Table 1. Acreage in the CRP.

Region	Signups 1-6	Projected Through 1990	Expanded CRP Program
		1,000 acres	
Alabama	435	625	759
Southeast*	811	953	1,156
Delta states†	778	1,514	2,063
Appalachian states	863	2,072	3,611
Plains states	10,141	17,433	21,360
Western states	6,709	9,325	11,080
Corn Belt states	5,631	12,496	22,866
Northeast and other states	157	582	2,104
U.S. total	25,525	45,000	65,000

*Georgia, Florida, and South Carolina.
†Arkansas, Louisiana, and Mississippi.

implementation of a 45-million-acre conservation reserve, as called for in current legislation, would increase crop prices 8.3 percent (Table 3) over prices that would prevail with the 25 million acres now in the CRP. Although full implementation of current CRP legislation would take an additional 20 million acres of land out of agricultural use, the net effect on planted acreage would be only 9.4 million acres. The net effect on acreage planted is less than the amount of land put into the CRP primarily because of producers' response (on nonbase acreage) to the higher prices resulting from supply reduction. Acreage idled under the ARP program would decline by 3 million acres, partly because of the base acreage reduction feature of the CRP and partly because of slightly reduced participation in the ARP program as a result of higher crop prices.

Higher crop prices translate into higher feed prices for livestock producers. Livestock producers respond to higher feed prices by reducing production, which increases livestock prices. After all supply-and-demand adjustments have occurred, full implementation of a 45-million-acre CRP is estimated to increase livestock prices 2.5 percent (Table 3). Table 4 presents the estimated effects of a 45-million-acre CRP on regional crop income and national livestock producers' income.

Net income to farmers increases in all regions with CRP-45 because of increased crop prices and CRP rental payments. Nationally, crop income increases slightly more than $3 billion annually (Table 4). The largest income gains are in the Corn Belt and Great Plains, where much of the CRP land is anticipated to come out of production (Table 1).

Livestock feed cost increases with CRP-45 are more than offset by the livestock price increases resulting from supply adjustment. Income to livestock producers and processors of livestock products is estimated to increase $376 million annually (Table 4).

Because crop prices increase with implementation of the CRP, consumers of agricultural products suffer negative impacts. Table 5 provides estimates of the effects on consumers of crop and livestock commodities.

Under CRP-45, domestic consumers of agricultural crop products will

Table 2. Policy assumption for the 1990 through 1996 period.

Crop	Target Price	Set-aside Rate
Corn	$2.84/bu	20%
Sorghum	2.69/bu	20%
Barley	2.43/bu	20%
Cotton	0.73/lb	20%

Table 3. Estimated effects of the CRP on prices.

Commodity	Change in Prices for:	
	45-Million-Acre CRP	65-Million-Acre CRP
All crops	8.3%	19.6%
Corn ($/bu)	$0.17	$ 0.40
Sorghum ($/bu)	0.19	0.37
Barley ($/bu)	0.15	0.27
Oats ($/bu)	0.22	0.54
Wheat ($/bu)	0.22	0.43
Soybeans ($/bu)	0.31	1.02
Cotton lint ($/lb)	0.01	0.02
All hay ($/T)	9.30	21.26
All livestock products	2.5%	5.9%

Table 4. Effects of the CRP on crop and livestock income.

Region	Change in Net Income* Relative to CRP-25	
	CRP-45	CRP-65
	—— million $/year ——	
Crop production in:†		
Alabama	18	50
Southeastern states	31	113
Delta states	120	313
Appalachian states	108	324
Plains states	1,028	2,656
Western states	470	1,156
Corn Belt states	1,147	3,132
Northeastern states	109	196
U.S. total	3,031	7,940
Livestock producers	376	1,003

*Change in net crop income includes CRP rental payments and ARP deficiency payments.
†From production of corn, grain, sorghum, barley, oats, wheat, soybeans, cotton, and all hay.

be subject to negative impacts. The total impact: $4.4 billion annually, which is $18 per person per year. Domestic consumers of livestock products will be subject to negative impacts of $3 billion annually, or $12 per person per year.

Average rental rate for the 25 million acres now in the CRP is $48 per year nationally and about $41 per year in the Southeast. Because the removal of land from agricultural production increases prices, placing additional land in the CRP is not as attractive unless rental rates increase to reflect the increased profitability of production. Inducing an additional 20 million acres into the reserve will require an estimated average rental rate of $52, and that rate must increase to $57 for the last sign-up required to complete the 45-million-acre reserve.

Treasury costs for farm programs under CRP-45 will not be significantly affected (Table 5). Reduced ARP payments about equal the increased CRP rental payments.

Estimated Effects of CRP-65

Tables 3-5 display the effects of expanding the CRP to 65 million acres as a means of providing additional conservation benefits and supply control. Although this policy would place an additional 40 million acres in the CRP, a net of only 20 million acres come into production in the United States in response to higher crop prices. ARP acreage would decrease more than 5 million acres. Thus, an estimated 15 million acres of new cropland—less than 5 percent of our current cropland—would come out of crop production.

Crop prices would increase 19.6 percent over prices prevailing with a 25-million-acre CRP, and 11.6 percent over prices with full implementation of the 45-million-acre CRP. Livestock prices would increase 5.9 percent with CRP-65 (Table 3).

Table 5. Estimated effects of the CRP on consumers and the federal budget.

	Change in Benefits for	
Group	CRP-45	CRP-65
	———million $/year———	
Domestic consumers of major crops*	−4,386	−10,153
	(−18.12)	(−41.95)
Foreign consumers and producers of crops	−3,015	−6,980
	−1,978	−2,403
Consumers of livestock products	(−12.46)	(−28.84)
U.S. Treasury cost†		
ARP payments	−1,094	−1,503
	(−4.52)	(−6.21)
CRP payments	1,015	2,839
	(4.57)	(11.73)

*Numbers in parentheses are estimates of per capita costs for domestic consumers.

†Numbers in parentheses are estimates of per capita costs for domestic taxpayers.

The expanded CRP would increase crop income by $7.9 billion and $4.9 billion annually over CRP-25 and CRP-45, respectively. Livestock producers would gain an estimated $1 billion annually (Table 4).

Domestic consumers of crop and livestock commodities would suffer negative impacts of $42 and $29 per capita per year, respectively (Table 5). Foreign consumers and producers also would be subject to negative impacts, but not as much as domestic consumers and producers. Although exports would fall in response to higher domestic prices, the value of exports would not change significantly.

Inducing 65 million acres into the CRP in normal price and yield years would require an increase in rental payments from $48 per acre at present to an average of about $60 per acre for the 40-million-acre addition to the CRP. The rental rate for the last acres added to CRP-65 would be about $72 per year.

Treasury costs for the CRP program would increase $2.8 billion annually, while ARP payments would decline by $1.5 billion. Net treasury cost would thus increase $1.3 billion a year.

Both positive and negative economic effects of the expanded CRP scenario considered here might be reduced somewhat if the set-aside requirement were reduced along with implementation of the expanded CRP.

Effects on Commodity Stocks

A side effect of increased commodity prices resulting from either CRP scenario is a reduction in stocks of most commodities. A meaningful way of summarizing stock levels is to use the acreage equivalent of stocks, that is, the acreage that would be required to produce the amount of crops in storage, given normal crop yields. For the crops considered here (see note two to Table 4), the acreage equivalent of stocks for crop year 1986-1987 was about 136 million acres. Because about 300 million acres are planted each year, the stock levels for 1986-1987 are equal to almost 45 percent of the production during a normal crop year. Largely because of the 1988 drought, estimated stocks at the end of the 1988-1989 crop year were 62 million acres.

The acreage equivalent of stocks assuming normal weather over the 1993-1996 time period, is estimated to be 59, 54, and 50 million acres, respectively, for CRP-25, CRP-45, and CRP-65. Of course, in drought years stocks would be considerably below these estimated levels. Because of lower stock levels, prices and farm income would be more sensitive to weather with an expanded CRP. Under CRP-65, stock levels might get low enough in drought years to warrant public concern unless land were released from the CRP.

Effects of the 1988 Drought

The severe drought in many parts of the United States in 1988 caused prices of many crops to increase considerably by the end of the crop year. Because stocks of most commodities were at high levels going into 1988, the price effects of the drought should be dissipated in one or two years if yields return to normal in the 1989-1990 crop year. As a result of the near-term price effects of the drought, however, bid prices might have to be raised over the estimated rental rates discussed previously to induce land into the CRP.

If bid prices are not raised to adjust for the 1988 drought, CRP sign-ups may fall short of the legislative goal of 40 million to 45 million acres by 1991. This being the case, the agricultural benefits of CRP-45 shown in tables 3 and 4 will not be realized.

Conclusions

Estimated benefits and costs of the CRP (Tables 3-5) are those manifested in the marketplace for agricultural commodities. Producers benefit from a CRP directly through rental payments and indirectly through higher commodity prices. Consumers lose through higher food prices. Taxpayers break even with CRP-45 and lose slightly with CRP-65. For the scenarios considered here, losses to consumers and taxpayers exceed the benefits to producers. Collectively averaging the gains and losses to domestic producers, consumers, and taxpayers, the net cost of CRP-45 is $5 per capita per year; the net cost of CRP-65 is about $15 per capita per year.

The small net per-capita cost associated with production and consumption of agricultural products must be weighed against nonmarket conservation benefits, such as reduced erosion (about 21 tons per acre per year), which reduces sedimentation and increases future productivity of soil, and by additional wildlife values created by the CRP.

From a budget deficit standpoint, the tradeoff between ARP payments and CRP payments with CRP-45 is almost one-to-one. Placing additional land into the CRP reduced ARP payments by more than 50 cents for each dollar of CRP rental payments. Reduced ARP payments come about largely because of increased crop prices, and thus reduced deficiency payments and reduced participation when land is taken out of production with the

CRP. The base acreage reduction that occurs with the CRP also reduces ARP payments.

In the Southeast, the CRP program is speeding up the conversion of some marginal cropland to short-rotation timber. Because economic considerations currently favor timber production, this land will likely stay in timber indefinitely unless the agricultural crop export situation improves substantially. Thus, terminating the CRP program at the end of the 10-year contract will not likely bring land back into production in the Southeast.

The extent to which land in other parts of the United States will come back into production after the 10-year contract depends largely on prevailing prices. Because of the economics of large machinery, however, many small or irregularly shaped fields will remain in soil-conserving uses. Continued development of markets for private hunting on land in soil-conserving uses and in timber also will tend to keep land in the CRP from returning to crop production.

Because of the economics of timber production and hunting leases, a significant portion of land in the CRP, especially CRP-45, may remain out of crop production even when rental payments cease upon expiration of the 10-year contract. Thus, supply control aspects of the CRP may continue past the contract period.

9

Water Quality and the Conservation Title

Stephen B. Lovejoy, James J. Jones,
Barbara B. Dunkelberg, Jerald J. Fletcher, and
Peter J. Kuch

America's agricultural sector is increasingly being required to recognize and account for the impacts of its production practices on environmental resources. In recent years water quality has received greater attention as one of the determinants of desirable production practices. The general public and its representatives in Washington, D.C., are suggesting that the country needs clean water along with food and fiber production. The government, as well as agricultural and environmental groups alike, should strive to provide these desired commodities and amenities.

In the past, the U.S. Environmental Protection Agency (EPA) concentrated its water quality efforts on assisting municipalities with the construction and operation of sewage treatment plants and on regulating industries to reduce discharge of pollutants into the nation's surface waters. Recent investigation, however, suggests that point-source pollution reductions will be inadequate to achieve society's water quality goals. Agriculture's role in nonpoint-source water pollution has been well documented. Now, environmentalists, as well as the EPA, are increasingly examining how to control agricultural discharges to improve water quality and at the same time maintain food and fiber production.

The U.S. Department of Agriculture (USDA) has responded to the social forces that are suggesting that agricultural practices be less environmentally degrading. USDA's recent work on the National Program for Soil and Water Conservation for 1988 through 1997 illustrates the Department's concern over water quality and, in general, the off-site impacts of agricultural production practices. Although first priority is still to reduce the damage caused by excessive soil erosion, the damages mentioned include off-site as well as on-site damages. In addition, the number two priority in the 10-year USDA program is to "protect the quality of surface and ground-water against harmful contamination from nonpoint-sources."

Interest in the water quality impacts of agricultural production practices suggests that agriculture will be called upon more frequently to examine the water quality impacts of alternative agricultural programs and policies. As compared to estimating changes in gross soil erosion resulting from agricultural policies, however, the tools for estimating the water quality impacts of agricultural policies are not as refined. In the 1970s and early 1980s a group of researchers with Resources for the Future (RFF), in Washington, D.C., began constructing a model to estimate the water quality impacts of various point and nonpoint sources. This model has been used in several situations, such as the Resources Conservation Act (RCA) process, to provide baseline information on the impacts of cropland production practices on nutrient loadings in the nation's surface waters. This type of national model for estimating the water quality impacts associated with alternative policies is essential. At the same time that Americans desire cleaner water, they also want the most efficient, effective policies for achieving their water quality goals.

A Water Quality Model

Concern for water quality impacts of agricultural practices led the Soil Conservation Service (SCS) and EPA, in cooperation with Purdue University, to revive the water quality model that was originally constructed by Leonard Gianessi and Henry Peskin at RFF. This model provides directional estimates of water quality impacts to decision-makers for use in policy deliberations.

Many water quality models (ANSWERS, AGNPS, CREAMS, etc.) are oriented toward small watersheds. Much less work has been done on regional or national models. When assessing degradation of surface water quality by agricultural production at the national level, it is useful to examine the endowment of the United States in terms of surface water. The United States has thousands of rivers, lakes, reservoirs, and creeks into which flow billions of gallons of water every day. Obviously, some method to represent these water bodies is vital for wise use of the resources.

The Water Quality Model, as developed by RFF and later adapted by Purdue University, attempts to represent an aggregate picture of the nation's water resources by concentrating on the major rivers, streams, and lakes in the nation. To do this, the Water Quality Model establishes nodal points at mouths of rivers, entrances to reservoirs, forks of major tributaries, major population centers, and beginnings of estuaries. This method yields 1,300 nodal points around the nation, which are used in 44 distinct subnetworks and then aggregated for national estimates. For instance, the Mississippi River subnetwork has 124 rivers and 78 lakes and reservoirs. Nationwide, the average distance between nodal points is 66 miles.

A first question in the analysis of water quality is: What are the sources of various pollutants? Data developed by Leonard Gianessi at RFF suggest that rural land uses, including cropland, generate large quantities of sediment, phosphorus, and nitrogen. Nearly all suspended sediments come from rural land uses, and more than 80 percent of total phosphorus and nitrogen comes from rural land uses. When these are the pollutants of concern, the loadings emanating from rural land must be considered in any policies or proposals to reduce the degradation of water resources.

The Water Quality Model is unique in its ability to examine the issues surrounding sources of pollutants entering surface waters. The model is data-intensive, in the sense that substantial information on point-source polluters, rural land uses, urban nonpoint-source pollution, and technical coefficients are necessary. Point sources of pollution in the model consist

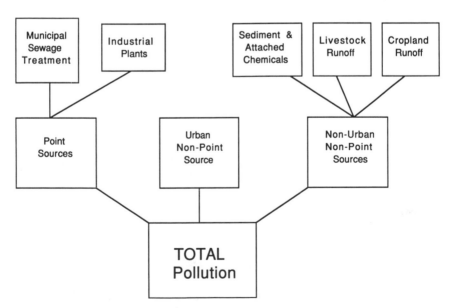

Figure 1. Water quality model description.

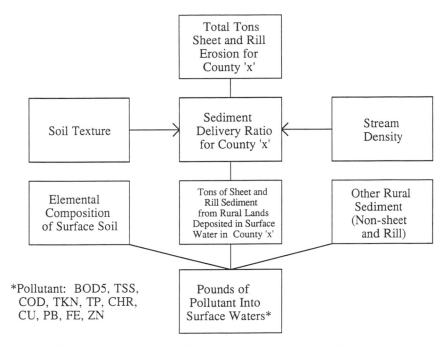

Figure 2. Sediment and related pollutants models for water quality model.

of industrial discharges as well as discharges from municipal treatment plants (Figure 1). Nonpoint-sources can be divided into rural and urban. Rural pollutants can best be described by separating out sediment originating from various rural land uses, nutrients from animal agricultural practices, and nutrient runoff from cropland (Figures 2-4).

Of great interest to many policy analysts are estimates of how various agricultural policies might affect the loadings of various agricultural pollutants. The first challenge encountered in this type of analysis is to interpret a policy or program. As evidenced by many pieces of legislation, including the Food Security Act, the true impact often comes from creative rule-making rather than from the actual statute. Determining the influence of a policy or program on land use is often difficult as well. Only after land use changes are established can one begin to examine the impacts upon water systems.

In examining the water quality implications of alternative policies, we enlisted the cooperation of Stan Johnson and the Center for Agricultural and Rural Development (CARD) at Iowa State University. With CARD's assistance in providing estimates of changes in land use and changes in

erosion, we were able to estimate the impacts of specific policies or programs on water quality parameters, for example, loadings of total suspended
solids (TSS), total phosphorus (TP), and total Kjeldahl nitrogen (TKN).
The 1982 National Resources Inventory (NRI) served as the baseline; CARD
estimated changes in cropping and erosion for each potential policy.

After establishing the analytical capability, the next question in policy
analysis revolves around which policies to examine. The policy arena,
especially in agricultural/environmental areas, has been and continues to
be extremely fluid. During the past several years, the Conservation Reserve
Program (CRP) has changed dramatically in terms of its definition of highly
erodible land and additional eligibility criteria. These broadened criteria
now include filter strips, cropped wetlands, and other acres that are not
highly erodible but deemed worthy of protection for some other environmental amenity. In addition, conservation compliance has shifted from national
standards toward locally based standards, as evidenced by alternative conservation systems. Selecting the appropriate policies becomes even more
important when considering that these analyses are not inexpensive, either
in terms of direct dollars or human resources.

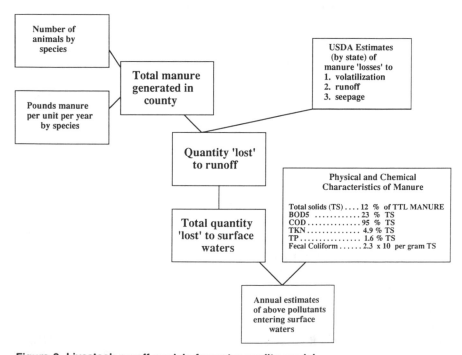

Figure 3. Livestock runoff models for water quality model.

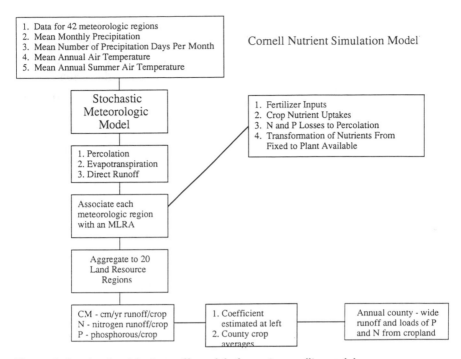

Figure 4. Cropland nutrient runoff models for water quality model.

In response to the question of policy examination, we formulated a series of possible scenarios for the CRP and conservation compliance that, we believe, cover a range of potential policies. We were particularly concerned with conservation compliance because it can be viewed as a longer term program, at least longer than the 10-year CRP, assuming that target prices stay high enough to encourage wide-scale enrollment in commodity programs. In addition to looking at conservation compliance as a national soil erosion standard, we incorporated indices of economic hardship. Most environmentalists, while wanting to protect environmental resources, do not want to force large numbers of agricultural producers out of business, nor do they want to pay $10 for a bowl of corn flakes or $5 for a diet soft drink. Assisted by the CARD staff, we established a mechanism for relaxing conservation compliance constraints, if producer rents in a county fall by more than 25 percent.

Further, the present lack of criteria to target compliance to achieve water quality goals is of considerable concern. Although conservation compliance is already targeted for erosion control (highly erodible land), a means of identifying areas with water quality problems might help in future policy deliberation. EPA's Office of Water, using a number of sources, has compiled a ranking of U.S. counties by their agricultural nonpoint-source contamination problems. Although distinctions between any two counties are probably meaningless, dividing them into quartiles provides a reasonable prioritization scheme. The assumption is that controls on erosion and pollutant loadings in counties in the first and second quartiles (counties with the greatest problems) would provide greater water quality benefits than would controls on erosion and pollutant loadings in the third and fourth quartiles.

Simulation Results

Water quality impacts of policies are determined by examining the estimated land use, for example, cropping patterns, in comparison with the 1982 NRI and thereby estimating changes in erosion and loadings of suspended solids, as well as phosphorus and nitrogen. All results are reported by USDA crop reporting regions (Figure 5).

One of the most significant policies in the 1980s has been the CRP, enacted to retire up to 45 million acres of highly erodible cropland. The first scenario examined simulates 1990 cropping patterns, assuming that 45 million acres have been enrolled in CRP but with no erosion restrictions (no conserva-

Figure 5. USDA crop reporting regions.

Table 1. Baseline, 1990: Changes in cropland erosion and in nonurban nonpoint total suspended solids, total phosphorus, and total nitrogen with a 45-million-acre Conservation Reserve Program.

Region	Cropland Erosion	Total Suspended Solids	Total Phosphorus	Total Nitrogen
		Percent Change From 1982 NRI Base		
		Total NonUrban Nonpoint Pollution		
		%		
Northeast	− 27	− 9	− 14	− 13
Appalachia	− 15	− 5	− 5	− 6
Southeast	− 36	− 11	− 19	− 18
Delta	− 15	− 7	− 10	− 11
Cornbelt	− 56	− 38	− 46	− 45
Lake States	− 62	− 40	− 51	− 47
Northern Plains	− 10	− 4	− 5	− 5
Southern Plains	+ 36	+ 7	+ 11	+ 11
Mountain States	− 6	− 1	− 1	− 1
Pacific	− 12	− 1	− 1	− 2
National total	− 35	− 13	− 14	− 18

tion compliance) in place. The CRP certainly fulfills its goal of reducing gross erosion on cropland. Our estimates indicate an overall reduction of 35 percent in the nation's gross erosion. By region, the variation ranges from a 62 percent reduction in the Lake States to an increase of 36 percent in the Southern Plains (Table 1). The impact of a 45-million-acre CRP on total nonurban nonpoint pollution is, of course, lower than its impact on cropland alone because other rural lands, such as range, pasture, and forest, are not affected.

As table 1 indicates, the analysis projects a 13 percent reduction in TSS, a 14 percent reduction in TP, and an 18 percent reduction in TKN nationally. Regionally, the results vary from high reductions in pollutant loadings in the Lake States and the Corn Belt regions to moderate increases of 7 percent and 11 percent in the Southern Plains. The estimated increases in erosion and pollution in some regions that occur in this scenario are not necessarily inconsistent with the overall goals of the CRP policy if it maintains a national perspective and if the emphasis is on aggregate loadings.

When conservation compliance policy is imposed on top of the 45-million-acre CRP, the impact on pollutant loadings from rural land is even more dramatic. If all counties in the 48 contiguous states were to reduce cropland erosion to a 10-ton national standard (2T), except in any counties where economic hardship would result, gross cropland erosion would be reduced 44 percent nationally (Table 2). Changes in erosion in the 10 crop reporting regions vary from a 65 percent reduction in the Lake States to a 7 percent increase in the Southern Plains. In this scenario, total rural non-point TSS is reduced by 16 percent, TP by 18 percent, and TKN by 23 percent. Again, the Lake States and Corn Belt regions achieve the highest reductions in these pollutants, with several other regions making dramatic decreases in erosion and pollution.

The issue of targeting for water quality is receiving a great deal of attention. Some observers suggest that standards should be more strict in areas with the greatest problems. Using the EPA ranking described previously, we imposed conditions in which the top quartile of counties, in terms of their agricultural nonpoint pollution problems, would not crop acres that had erosion rates greater than 2T, regardless of any resulting economic hardship. The second, third, and fourth quartiles behave as in the previous scenario: They must reduce erosion to 2T unless economic hardship results (producer rents fall by more than 25 percent). Compared to the previous policy alternative, some additional reductions in erosion and pollution result; cropland erosion is reduced 47 percent overall and TSS declines by 17 percent, TP by 19 percent, and TKN by 25 percent (Table 3). The Lake States

Table 2. Conservation compliance, 1990: Changes in cropland erosion and in nonurban nonpoint total suspended solids, total phosphorus, and total nitrogen with Policy No. V28. All quartiles reduce to 2T except in economic hardship.

Region	Cropland Erosion	Percent Change From 1982 NRI Base		
		Total NonUrban Nonpoint Pollution		
		Total Suspended Solids	Total Phosphorus	Total Nitrogen
		%		
Northeast	−49	−16	−26	−24
Appalachia	−25	−9	−8	−10
Southeast	−47	−14	−25	−23
Delta	−23	−11	−15	−16
Cornbelt	−61	−41	−49	−48
Lake States	−65	−42	−53	−50
Northern Plains	−22	−9	−11	−12
Southern Plains	+7	+1	+2	+2
Mountain States	−17	−2	−3	−3
Pacific	−41	−4	−4	−5
National total	−44	−16	−18	−23

Table 3. Conservation compliance: Changes in cropland erosion and in non-urban nonpoint total suspended solids, total phosphorus and total nitrogen with Policy No. V40. First quartile reduces to 2T, others to 2T except in economic hardship.

		Percent Change From 1982 NRI Base		
		Total NonUrban Nonpoint Pollution		
Region	Cropland Erosion	Total Suspended Solids	Total Phosphorus	Total Nitrogen
			%	
Northeast	− 48	− 16	− 25	− 24
Appalachia	− 25	− 9	− 8	− 10
Southeast	− 57	− 11	− 14	− 15
Delta	− 22	− 11	− 14	− 15
Cornbelt	− 63	− 43	− 51	− 50
Lake States	− 65	− 42	− 54	− 50
Northern Plains	− 27	− 11	− 14	− 15
Southern Plains	− 10	− 2	− 3	− 3
Mountain States	− 21	− 2	− 4	− 4
Pacific	− 42	− 4	− 4	− 5
National total	− 47	− 17	− 19	− 25

and Corn Belt regions again show the greatest reductions, and all regions exhibit declines in erosion and pollution loadings.

Summary

Controlling erosion on cropland offers a partial solution to water quality problems. Reducing erosion reduces loadings of sediment, phosphorus, and nitrogen. But the changes resulting from a national standard are far from uniform, and they may not be correlated with the severity of water quality problems or the degree to which agriculture is responsible. The CRP has resulted in substantial reductions in erosion, as will conservation compliance. Reduction of pollutant loadings from rural land also has been significant. Although targeting of conservation compliance suggests further loading reductions, additional information on the costs of such a policy must be assembled. In addition, the information presented here should be considered in terms of the benefits gained by reducing pollution regionally and nationally.

Policy should promote the public's well-being and not a narrow special interest group. In addition, decisions that determine policies are rarely clear-cut and nearly always involve value judgments. The role of the public and its elected representatives is to make these value judgments. The role of analysts is to provide the best information possible. Recognizing that to achieve water quality goals is not without cost, sound analysis can help minimize the burdens placed on the agricultural sector and ultimately on consumers of food and fiber products.

III

Micro-level Economic Impacts of the Conservation Title

10

An Analysis of Baseline Characteristics and Economic Impacts of the Conservation Reserve Program in North Dakota

Timothy Mortensen, Jay A. Leitch, F. Larry Leistritz, Brenda L. Ekstrom, and Randal C. Coon

Retirement of cropland is an agricultural policy tool both for conservation objectives and for supply control. The Soil Bank program of the 1960s was the first large-scale, government-subsidized land retirement program. Enrollment in the Soil Bank in North Dakota peaked at about 2.7 million acres in 1960, which was nearly 10 percent of the total enrolled acres in the United States (14). During the period 1957-1970, North Dakota landowners received more than $210 million in payments from the Soil Bank, with average annual payments of about $10 per acre. U.S. enrollment in the Soil Bank also peaked in 1960 at nearly 29 million acres with an average contract rate of almost $12 per acre.

Most recently, soil conservation objectives are being sought through the Conservation Reserve Program (CRP) (P.L. 99-198). After the first five sign ups, North Dakota ranked seventh among the states in CRP sign-up, with 1.3 million contracted acres, or about 4.8 percent of the state's total cropland (5, 13). Kidder County, with nearly 25 percent of total cropland in CRP, had the largest percentage enrollment (Figure 1).

Study Procedures

We conducted a study to establish a set of baseline characteristics of CRP participants in North Dakota and to estimate the impacts of the program through the first five sign-ups. CRP has potential long-term impacts on North Dakota landowners and surrounding communities, including (1) economic impacts to retail agribusinesses, (2) environmental and water quality changes, (3) demographic impacts, (4) effects on commodity production levels, and (5) land use changes.

A review of literature dealing with the effects of the Soil Bank program suggests that enrollment in the CRP could be associated with increased off-farm work by farm operators and could speed farm consolidation and rural-to-urban migration (1, 2, 3, 6, 8, 10, 11). Taylor et al. (12) studied the effects of the Soil Bank Program in Ransom County, North Dakota, but little is known about statewide farmer or community impacts of the program. Thus, policymakers had difficulty fashioning the present program given the paucity of information on previous programs. Specific characteristics examined include landowner characteristics, CRP land characteristics, farm operator financial data, opinion questions, and economic impacts.

A mail survey of participating CRP landowners was conducted in the spring of 1988. During February 1988, a six-page questionnaire was pretested on a sample of 20 CRP participants attending the Northwest Farm Managers meeting in Fargo, North Dakota. The population of over 7,000 landowner names and addresses was stratified by pool group (Figure 1) and randomized

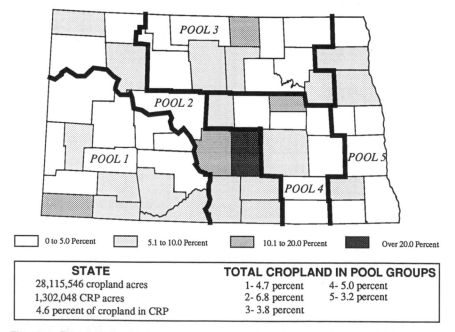

| 0 to 5.0 Percent | 5.1 to 10.0 Percent | 10.1 to 20.0 Percent | Over 20.0 Percent |

STATE	TOTAL CROPLAND IN POOL GROUPS	
28,115,546 cropland acres	1- 4.7 percent	4- 5.0 percent
1,302,048 CRP acres	2- 6.8 percent	5- 3.2 percent
4.6 percent of cropland in CRP	3- 3.8 percent	

Figure 1. Percentage of total cropland enrolled in CRP through the fifth sign-up, by category.

Table 1. Summary of survey questionnaires sent and received by pool group.

Pool	Questionnaires Sent	Questionnaires Returned	Percentage of Total Sent	Percentage of Return
			%	
1	457	199	15.6	43.5
2	805	349	27.5	43.4
3	638	274	21.8	42.9
4	479	215	16.4	44.9
5	549	252	18.8	45.9
Total	2,928	1,289	100.0	44.0

using a computerized routine. A sample of nearly 3,000 names (approximately 40 percent of the population) representing 53 North Dakota counties received questionnaires in the mail (Table 1). Follow-up mailings to nonrespondents resulted in 1,289 usable surveys, a response rate of 44 percent; we feel comfortable that the response is representative of the population and are confident in extrapolating sample characteristics to the population.

Results

Demographic Characteristics. Nearly 62 percent of CRP respondents were over age 55. The average age of CRP landowners was 57.2 years, with no significant age difference between farmers (73 percent were farmers, part- or full-time in 1987) and nonfarmers. This compares to an average age of 47.2 years for selected farmers in the state who responded to a 1988 longitudinal survey (7).

Ninety percent of the survey respondents lived in North Dakota. About 4 percent lived in the neighboring states of Montana, South Dakota, or Minnesota, and the balance lived in 22 other states.

Land/Landowner Characteristics. The average acreage owned by all respondents was about 916 acres (Table 2). Current farmers operated 1,530 total acres on average, with about 906 acres in cropland. CRP participants who farmed in 1987 owned 65.1 percent more land (1,024.2 acres) in North Dakota than did nonfarmers (620.5 acres) and had 28.6 percent more land enrolled in CRP.

Nearly 62 percent of the farms operated by CRP landowners in 1987 were classified as cash-crop farms (over 50 percent of their gross income was from sales of crops). Only 15 percent were predominantly livestock farms, and slightly over 23 percent were mixed (i.e., neither crops nor livestock accounted for more than 50 percent of their gross income).

CRP Land Characteristics. Initial Tillage. Some land entered into CRP through the fifth sign-up had been initially cultivated over 90 years ago. Although over 39 percent of the respondents were unsure when their CRP land was originally tilled, 33 percent said it was first tilled before 1921 (Figure 2). About 5 percent stated that the land was first tilled after 1960— which would include marginal land broken during the boom period that occurred in the early 1970s.

Costs and Returns. The average cost of establishing cover on CRP acres in North Dakota was $37.20 per acre (Table 3). Average annual maintenance costs were estimated to be $6.92 per acre. The annual contract payment

Table 2. Land ownership characteristics of CRP survey respondents.

Item	Farmers*	Nonfarmers†	All Respondents
		average acres	
Land owned‡	1,024.2	620.5	916.0
Land in CRP‡	213.4	165.9	200.7
Land operated	1,530.0	na	na
Total cropland	906.0	na	na

*Farmed either part time or full time during 1987.
†Did not farm in 1987.
‡Statistically significant difference between farmers and nonfarmers using the Tukey test at alpha = 0.05.

Table 3. Selected comparisons of CRP survey respondents.

Variable	Farmers	Non-Farmers	All Respondents
		$/acre	
Cover establishment costs	37.34	36.75	37.20
Annual maintenance costs	7.09	6.33	6.92
Annual contract payment	37.50*	35.44*	36.98
		%	
CRP yield compared to Non-CRP yield†	− 10.0	− 5.2	− 9.5
CRP input costs compared to Non-CRP costs†	+ 0.3	+ 1.5	+ 0.5
Planted trees for cover	7.8	12.1	9.0
More trees if cost-sharing increased	22.7	29.9	24.5
Considered water impoundments as cover	6.8	7.6	7.0

*Denotes statistical difference between groups using the Tukey test at alpha = 0.05.
†Refers to yields and costs before land was enrolled in CRP.

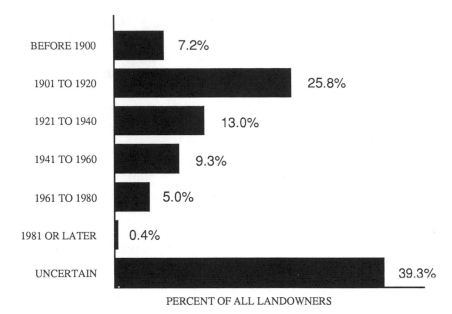

PERCENT OF ALL LANDOWNERS

Figure 2. Original tillage of CRP land, by category.

from the federal government averaged $36.98 per acre in North Dakota for land entered during the first five sign-up periods. Farmers received slightly more ($2.06 per acre) on average than did nonfarmers, possibly because farmers were more aware of bid levels being accepted in their respective counties.

Comparison to Local Cash Rent. More than one-third (37.1 percent) of the annual payments were about the same as local cash rent (Figure 3). Only about 5 percent of the respondents said the annual payment was less than the local cash rental rate. More than one-half (57.8 percent) of the respondents indicated that CRP payments were higher than local cash rent; in some cases payments were up to $20 per acre more than local cash rent. Annual CRP payments for all landowners averaged about 6.7 percent more than local cash rents.

Productivity. CRP land productivity also was explored, because CRP land is presumably more marginal with lower yields and higher relative input costs. Respondents were asked to compare yields on their CRP land to other cropland in their locale that was not enrolled in CRP. The CRP land yielded 9.5 percent less, on average, than non-CRP land (Table 3). CRP respondents indicated that input costs were slightly higher (0.5 percent) when farming CRP land compared to non-CRP land.

Cover Options. Usually, the permanent cover on CRP land consisted of grass or grass-legume mixtures, but nearly 8 percent of the farmer respondents and 12.1 percent of the nonfarmers planted trees as at least a partial cover crop (Table 3). Participants who planted trees on the CRP acreage did so only on a portion of the land, not whole tracts (5.3 percent of the tract on average). Nearly 30 percent of the nonfarmers and 22.7 percent of the farmers said they would have considered planting more trees if the cost-share percentage had been higher. Only about 7 percent of the survey respondents had considered water impoundments, such as restored wetlands, as a means of CRP cover.

Tillage Methods. Respondents were asked what seeding method they used to establish cover on CRP land and what method they intend to use after the contract expires. The four choices were: (*1*) no till, in which the landowner uses equipment that does not destroy crop residue on the soil surface; (*2*) minimum tillage, in which the operator uses a chisel plow or similar equipment designed to leave some residue for protection from soil erosion; (*3*) conventional tillage, in which a moldboard plow is used for the primary tillage operation and the soil is left virtually bare; and (*4*) other, which consisted of combinations of the previous three choices. More than

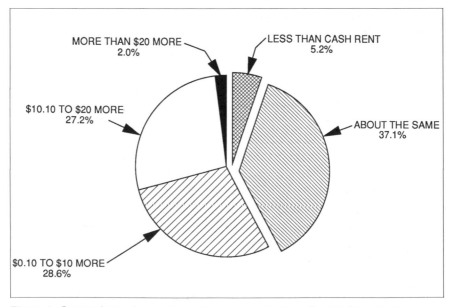

Figure 3. Comparison of annual contract payments to cash rent, by category.

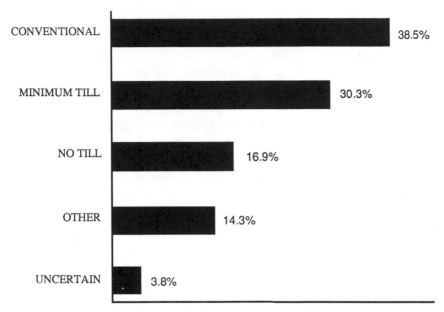

Figure 4. Tillage method for establishing cover crop on CRP land.

38 percent employed conventional methods for establishing cover, about 47 percent used either no-till or minimum tillage, and about 14 percent used other combinations (Figure 4).

Even though up to 10 years will pass before ultimate adoption of a tillage method for farming CRP land, respondents were asked their intentions regarding such tillage. More than 42 percent of all respondents indicated they will use minimum tillage; 31.4 percent, conventional tillage; and 8.7 percent, no-till (Figure 5). Only about 10 percent said they were undecided what tillage method they would use.

Intended Use. Some of the land in the CRP may ultimately fall under the "conservation compliance" provision of the 1985 Farm Bill. Although about 37 percent said they were undecided about what they will do with CRP acres after the program expires, nearly one-half (49 percent) intend to convert the land to cropland and 15.5 percent plan to leave it in permanent cover (Figure 6). In addition, more than 12 percent intend to rent it out for pasture, and nearly 14 percent will use it for pasture themselves. Slightly more than 10 percent indicated they will sell their CRP land, 4.5 percent intend to lease it for recreational purposes, and only 2 percent intend to grow trees on it.

Use of Annual Payments. The majority of survey participants (54.5 percent) will use annual CRP payments for living expenses (Figure 7). Other uses are (*1*) paying CRP land debt, 27.8 percent; (*2*) paying other debt, 24.5 percent; and (*3*) savings or investment, 21.6 percent. About 14 percent will use all or part of the annual payments to retire in North Dakota, and only about 3.5 percent plan to use payments to retire out-of-state. Likewise, about 10 percent and 3.5 percent will use their payments for leisure activities in-state and out-of-state, respectively.

Assets and Debts. Nearly 21 percent of the farmer respondents indicated that CRP was a factor that enabled them to continue their farming operation. This is manifested by the financial information supplied by respondents who were farmers in 1987. Nearly 41 percent of all CRP landowners and 36.9 percent of the CRP farmers had no debt, compared to about 16 percent of all farmers statewide having no debt, based on the 1988 farmer survey in North Dakota, which was representative of all farmers who were younger than age 65 and considered farming to be their primary occupation (*7*).

Farm Income. Farmers participating in the CRP tend to have smaller farming operations than those responding to the 1988 farmer survey; nearly

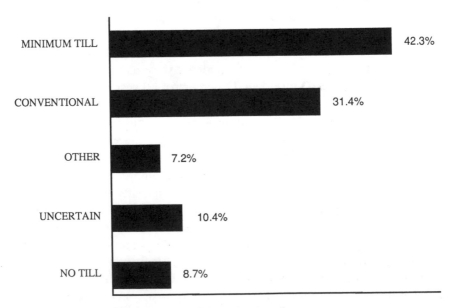

Figure 5. Intended tillage method after contract expires.

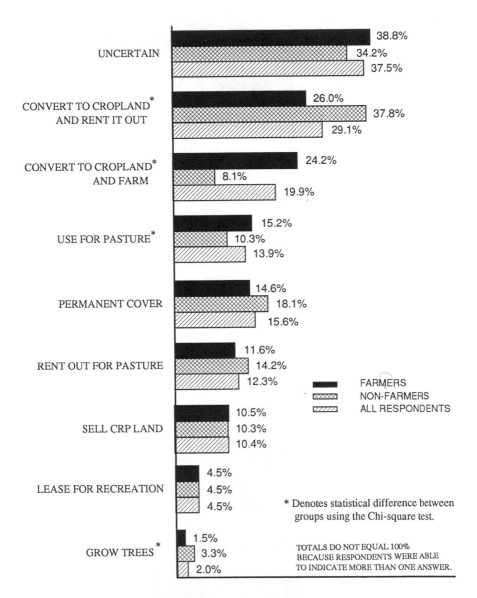

Figure 6. Intended land use after CRP contract expires.

70 percent of CRP farmers had a gross cash farm income of less than $100,000 (Figure 8), compared to 62 percent for the farmer survey. Average gross cash farm income of CRP farmers was $92,440; in comparison, participants in the 1988 North Dakota farm survey had an average gross cash farm income of $114,899.

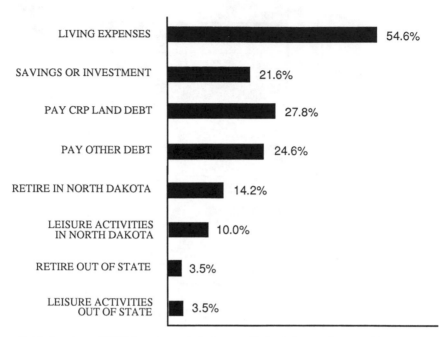

Totals do not equal 100% because respondents were able to circle more than one answer.

Figure 7. Use of CRP annual income.

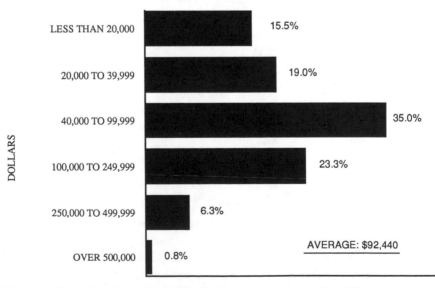

Figure 8. Gross farm income of CRP participants who farmed in 1987.

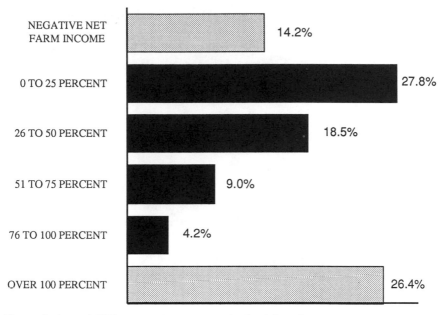

Figure 9. Annual CRP payment as a percent of net farm income.

CRP payments are a major source of income for many farmers. About 14 percent of the farmers had a negative net cash farm income (Figure 9). In addition, 26.4 percent stated the CRP payment exceeded their net cash farm income. If the two categories are added, over 40 percent of the farmers had CRP incomes greater than their pre-CRP-payment net cash farm income, indicating that CRP payments are an important source of income; and 21 percent of the farmer respondents stated that CRP payments were a major factor enabling them to continue farming.

Opinion Questions. More than 92 percent agreed that CRP provides wildlife habitat (Figure 10). In addition, nearly 90 percent believed that CRP offers protection for fragile land. About 80 percent agreed that eligibility for CRP entry should be based on soil characteristics rather than on management and tillage practices. More than 77 percent of the landowners agreed that CRP benefits them financially. A majority (71.1 percent) of the respondents also agreed that CRP reduces the sales of local agribusiness suppliers. Nearly 39 percent agreed, and over 33 percent disagreed, with the statement that land eligibility requirements should be eased. Almost an equal percentage agreed and disagreed (37.4 percent and 38.4 percent, respectively) with the statement that counties should have the option of going beyond the limit of 25 percent of total county cropland limit for enrolling CRP acreage.

About 37 percent agreed with the statement that CRP rewards poor farming practices, and about 42 percent disagreed. Reaction also was mixed to the question of raising the 45-million-acre national CRP limit; about 39 percent had a neutral response. Nearly 41 percent disagreed, and only about 27 percent agreed, with the notion that CRP is costing the federal government too much money.

Economic Impacts

In addition to providing the necessary information to establish a baseline, the survey data, when combined with other information, can be used to estimate the economic effects of CRP (9). The North Dakota Input-Output model consists of 17 sectors among which agricultural production and energy are the principal basic (export-oriented) activities (4). The model was aggregated into the five CRP pool groups. Sales for final demand were compiled for eight years (1980 to 1987) and adjusted to 1987 base dollars by economic sector.

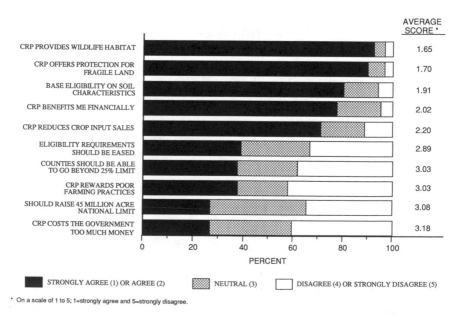

Figure 10. CRP opinions of all respondents.

Table 4. Distribution of CRP acres, CRP-related change in direct expenditures, total CRP impact, CRP impact as a percent of baseline, and CRP-related employment change.

Pool Group	CRP Acres (%)	CRP-Related Change in Direct Expenditures and Household Income (thousand $)	Total CRP Impact (million $)	CRP Impact as a Percentage of Pool Baseline (%)	CRP-Related Employment Change
1	18.8	− 8,336	− 21.2	− 0.33	− 371
2	29.3	− 12,229	− 30.0	− 0.68	− 552
3	20.0	− 10,175	− 25.5	− 0.52	− 453
4	18.5	− 12,569	− 31.6	− 0.91	− 523
5	13.4	− 12,594	− 32.2	− 0.39	− 517
Total	100.0	− 55,903	− 140.5	− 0.54	− 2,416

Direct Effects of CRP. The state total negative effect is about $56 million, with nearly 62 percent impacting the retail trade sector (Table 4). Pool groups 2, 4, and 5 have the highest net direct impact, about $12 million each. The household sector is positively impacted in pool groups 1, 2, and 3 primarily because the CRP rental payments exceed farm income and government program payments, but the net effect is negative.

Direct and Indirect Effects. The impact of $56 million in direct effects resulting from the CRP translates into about $141 million in reduced business activity for the state, or an overall multiplier of 2.56 (Table 4). This is spread among 13 sectors of the state's economy; the retail sector absorbs the greatest impact—about 40 percent of the total. Households were affected by about $34 million, or 23.9 percent of the total.

The largest net change occurred in pool group 5 in which business activity was reduced by over $32 million. While accounting for only 13.4 percent of the total CRP acres in the state (through the fifth sign-up), it had nearly 23 percent of the reduced business activity (Table 5). Pool 4 represents 22.5 percent ($31.6 million) of the CRP-associated business activity and had about 18.5 percent of the acres. Pool groups 1, 2, and 3 account for 18.2, 21.4, and 15.1 percent of the total CRP impact, respectively.

Although the net total impact of the CRP is negative for most sectors, the household sector was positively impacted for some pool groups. The gain was primarily attributable to CRP contract payments being greater than the reduction in returns from farming and commodity program payments. This was generally the case in western and northern North Dakota (pool groups 1, 2, and 3).

The overall impact on the state's economy is $141 million (based on 1987 data). In percentage terms, business activity declined statewide by about one-half of one percent (Table 4). Pool 4 had the potential for highest impact; about nine-tenths of one percent of its baseline was reduced as a result of the CRP. Pool 1 was impacted the least, at about one-third of one percent.

Secondary Job Losses. Perhaps a more poignant result shown by the analysis is the potential for secondary job loss. On a statewide basis, more than 2,400 secondary jobs may be lost over a period of years (Table 4). Although job reductions are not shown for individual industries, the retail sector certainly would be among the hardest hit, because it accounts for the largest dollar volume of CRP impact. Among the pool groups, pool 2, where 552 jobs potentially may be lost, was impacted the most.

Per-Acre Effects. An analysis of the per-acre effects of the CRP reveals that moving west to east generally increases the effect of one acre of CRP enrollment on the state's economy. The total direct effect of CRP enrollment is about $34 per acre in pool group 1 (Figure 11). Although the direct effect is slightly less for pool group 2, the effects gradually become more negative when moving eastward to pool groups 3, 4, and 5 where the direct effect of one acre is nearly $72. This is primarily because of the more intensive farming in the eastern part of the state.

Summary and Conclusions

This study was undertaken to establish baseline characteristics of CRP participants in North Dakota and to further analyze the economic impacts

Table 5. Baseline business activity associated with CRP program, percent of business activity lost, and secondary employment loss, by pool group, 1987.

Pool Group	Baseline Business Activity	CRP-Associated Business Activity	CRP Percent of Baseline (%)	Secondary Job Loss
	million $			
1	6,518	21	0.32	371
2	4,399	30	0.68	552
3	4,914	26	0.53	453
4	3,500	32	0.91	523
5	8,367	32	0.38	517
State	26,247	141	0.54	2,434

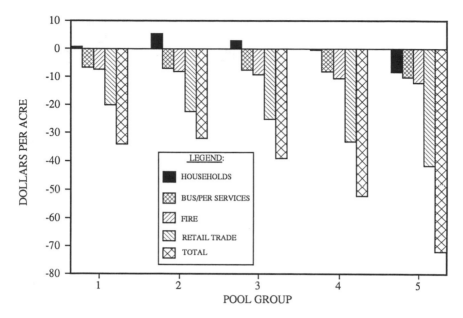

Figure 11. Net per-acre direct effect of CRP by economic sector.

of CRP on pool groups in the state. A number of observations and conclusions can be drawn from this baseline analysis:

► Some landowners planted trees as cover on CRP tracts, and about 24.5 percent indicated that they would have considered planting more if the government cost-share rate were higher.

► Many respondents (38.8 percent) indicated they did not know what their land-use intentions were after the contract expires. Up to 16 percent, however, indicated they would not use it for cropland but would keep it permanently covered, pasture it themselves, rent it out for pasture, or lease it for recreation purposes.

► About 21 percent of the farmer participants said the CRP enabled them to continue their farming operation.

► CRP income is apparently a major source of income for farmer landowners; CRP incomes of more than 40 percent of the respondents exceeded the net cash income from their farming operation.

► Injection of CRP payments into rural North Dakota was insufficient to offset reduced business activity and employment created by participation in the CRP. Net direct expenditures declined by about $56 million, and combined direct and indirect negative impacts by $141 million.

► If alternative activities do not replace changes in agricultural purchases over the long run, employment also will decline by about 2,400 jobs.

► Progress is being made toward the conservation objectives of the program, such as (1) reduced soil erosion, (2) increased wildlife habitat and cover, and (3) increased water quality.

Three policy recommendations evolve from the North Dakota study of CRP participants. First, companion programs with state or local governments or private organizations should be encouraged. These might include cost-sharing for establishing tree plantings, restoring wetlands, or otherwise enhancing wildlife habitat; supplemental payments for recreationist access; or purchase of CRP payments to provide landowners with a lump sum payment. Second, measures could be taken to mitigate the potential for negatively impacting rural communities. Possible programs might include tax credits or reduced interest loans for impacted businesses, displaced worker retraining, or business/worker relocation assistance. Finally, soil erosion objectives would be accomplished more efficiently if enrollment in future CRP-like programs were based on soil and topographical characteristics rather than on past tillage practices.

REFERENCES CITED

1. Barr, Wallace, Richard R. Newberg, and Mervin G. Smith. 1962. *Major economic impact of the conservation reserve on Ohio agriculture and rural communities.* Research Bulletin 904. Ohio Agricultural Experiment Station, Wooster.
2. Butler, Charles P., and W. J. Lanham. 1958. *An economic appraisal of the conservation reserve program in Area IIB, Upper Coastal Plain of South Carolina.* AE 135. South Carolina Agricultural Experiment Station, Clemson.
3. Christensen, Raymond P., and Edward S. Micka. 1960. *The conservation reserve program in Maine.* ARS43-123. Agricultural Research Service, U.S. Department of Agriculture, Washington, D.C.
4. Coon, Randal C., F. Larry Leistritz, Thor A. Hertsgaard, and Arlen G. Leholm. 1985. *The North Dakota input-output model: A tool for analyzing economic linkages.* Agricultural Economics Report No. 187. Department of Agricultural Economics, North Dakota State University, Fargo.
5. Dicks, Michael R., Felix L. Lacuna, and Michael Linsenbigler. 1988. *The conservation reserve program: Implementation and accomplishments, 1986-87.* Bulletin No. 763. Economic Research Service, U.S. Department of Agriculture, Washington, D.C.
6. Kaldor, Don. 1957. *Impact of the conservation reserve on resource adjustments in agriculture.* Journal of Farm Economics 39: 1,148-1,156.
7. Leistritz, F. Larry, Brenda L. Ekstrom, Janet Wanzek, and Timothy L. Mortensen. 1989. *Outlook of North Dakota farm households: Results of the 1988 longitudinal farm survey.* Agricultural Economics Report No. 246. Department of Agricultural Economics, North Dakota State University, Fargo.

8. McArthur, W. C. 1961. *The conservation reserve program in Georgia: Its effects in the Piedmont and Coastal Plain.* ERS-31. Economic Research Service, U.S. Department of Agriculture, Washington, D.C.

9. Mortensen, Timothy L., Randal C. Coon, F. Larry Leistritz, Jay A. Leitch, and Brenda L. Ekstrom. 1989. *Economic impacts of the conservation reserve program in North Dakota.* Agricultural Economics Report No. 244. Department of Agricultural Economics, North Dakota State University, Fargo.

10. Paulson, Arnold, Earl O. Heady, Walter R. Butcher, and Ross V. Baumann. 1961. *Potential effect of soil bank and corn allotment programs on income and resource use, southern Iowa.* Prod. Research Report No. 48. Agricultural Research Service, U.S. Department of Agriculture, Washington, D.C.

11. Schmid, A. Allan. 1958. *An appraisal of the soil bank in a corn and dairy area of Wisconsin.* Journal of Farm Economics 40: 148-153.

12. Taylor, Fred R., Laurel D. Loftsgard, and LeRoy W. Schaffner. 1961. *Effects of the soil bank program on a North Dakota community. Agricultural* Economics Report No. 19. Department of Agricultural Economics, North Dakota State University, Fargo.

13. U.S. Bureau of Census. 1982. *Census of agriculture—North Dakota State and county data.* Government Printing Office, Washington, D.C.

14. U.S. Department of Agriculture. Various years. *Conservation reserve program: Summary statistics.* Office of Information, Washington, D.C.

15. U.S. Department of Agriculture. Various years. *Conservation reserve program: Summary statistics.* Office of Information, Washington, D.C.

11

A Relatively Complete and Comparative Societal Accounting of the Conservation Reserve Program's Effects in a Small Watershed

Keith Kozloff and Steven J. Taff

The Conservation Reserve Program (CRP) attempts to integrate federal agricultural and environmental policy through cropland retirement. Participating landowners receive annual compensation for removing highly erodible land from crop production for 10 years and planting a soil-conserving cover on enrolled parcels. Because cropland retirement will likely be a continuing component of federal policy, evaluations of the CRP's effectiveness may help in guiding the development of future programs.

The question posed here is whether CRP land retirement in a particular watershed generates social benefits greater than costs. This study differs from national assessments of land retirement programs in that we explicitly link economic values with the physical effects associated with specific land use changes in a watershed. We adopt a societal accounting perspective for costs and benefits (in contrast to a government budgeting or participant perspective) following the approach of Ervin and Dicks (3). In our framework, the program's potential benefits include reduction of agriculturally related nonpoint-source water pollution, conservation of soil productivity for future crop use, and enhancement of wildlife habitat. The program's costs include resources used to establish permanent plant cover, foregone crop production on enrolled acres, and resources used in program administration. Government rental payments to farmers and the crop subsidies avoided are considered transfer payments and, hence, do not enter into the assessment.

Developing point estimates of net social benefits from CRP enrollments is complicated for several reasons. First, the relationship between induced land use changes and achievement of program objectives varies both spatially and over time. Second, program impacts are dispersed, so they tend to be small relative to the random noise of ecological, climatic, and anthropogenic fluctuations. Third, several outputs are not marketed, requiring that their economic values be estimated using nonmarket approaches.

Estimating a range of projected benefits and costs, however, is more straightforward. Assumptions and analytical approaches can be explicitly chosen to yield lower and upper bounds that may in turn provide sufficient direction for future land retirement policy analysis. If uncertainty regarding program effectiveness is not sufficiently low to help guide policy decisions, additional physical or socioeconomic information can be incrementally collected that will reduce, but not eliminate, the range of uncertainty.

First Order Study Area

The 7,735-acre North Branch Cascade Creek (NBCC) watershed in southeastern Minnesota was selected for analysis because its existing land use is primarily agricultural and because its CRP enrollment was thought to be large enough to generate noticeable effects while still being typical of enrollment in the region. Highly disaggregated land use and soils data are available for the watershed. In addition, the watershed has physical characteristics thought to be highly correlated with nonpoint-source pollution, its topographic characteristics make it susceptible to soil erosion, and it has potential for increases in wildlife populations of recreational importance. These presumably favorable (for CRP "success") characteristics led us to the a priori opinion that CRP societal benefits would be relatively high compared with other "less appropriate" watersheds.

Through 1987, 10 farmers in the watershed had enrolled 633 acres of land in the CRP—parcels ranging from 19 to 129 acres. In the year prior to enrollment, land use on these parcels had been as follows: corn, 290 acres (46 percent); soybeans, 133 acres (21 percent); oats, 42 acres (7 percent); hay, 56 acres (9 percent); pasture, 84 acres (13 percent); and other, 28 acres (4 percent). After CRP enrollment, 90 percent of this land was converted to a grass/legume mixture; the remainder was already in an approved cover (10).

Analytical Approach

For our purposes, total CRP enrollment in the watershed is treated as a single project, generating economic effects that may or may not extend beyond watershed borders. To measure consistently the benefits and costs, we consider the geographic scope of project benefits and costs to be national. Associated crop production changes in the watershed are too small to affect farm output or input prices. Because some benefits and costs will not be evidenced for several decades, we put a temporal boundary for program effects at 100 years.

The test of economic efficiency used here is Potential Pareto Improvement (PPI), that is, whether the sum of the gains to the gainers could hypothetically offset the sum of losses to the losers. Social benefits and costs are treated as the sum of individual benefits and costs. The test says nothing about equity among those affected by a government action, and it tends to enshrine existing property right assignments.

The PPI test ideally invokes a comparison of social welfare under without-program and with-program states of the world over the time period of program effects. This study necessarily deviates from the theoretical ideal. The without-CRP state of the world is defined as a continuation of the pattern of land uses in the watershed that prevailed in the year prior to CRP enrollment. We adjust some land uses to reflect crop rotation. Without-CRP land uses are held constant over the 100-year study period.

The with-CRP state of the world is the same as the without-CRP state for farms not participating in the program through 1987. Although some permanent plant cover may not have been established by 1987, this study treats all CRP land use changes as occurring in that year. According to ASCS program records, 97 percent of the CRP acreage in the watershed was enrolled in 1987 rather than in 1986. After 1997, two with-CRP scenarios are posited. In one, CRP parcels remain retired only for the initial 10-year contract period and then revert to preprogram land uses. In the other, CRP parcels stay out of crop production throughout the 100-year period of analysis.

Although we assume the contrary, CRP participation decisions are probably not made independently of other farm management decisions. In deciding whether to enroll land in the CRP, farmers are likely to consider interaction between the CRP provisions and other federal programs, such as conservation compliance and commodity programs. Farmers also may decide to replace CRP-enrolled land with rented land elsewhere, retire from farming, or make other management changes based on individual socioeconomic factors that can be ascertained only from knowledge of each individual decision process.

Land uses may change on some non-CRP parcels as an indirect result of CRP enrollment. USDA program records, however, do not permit a determination of which land use changes on non-CRP parcels are appropriately attributable to the CRP. As a result, the with-CRP scenario used in this analysis probably understates the total land area in the watershed that changes use as a result of CRP.

The without-CRP scenario is likewise simplified. If the CRP did not exist, pre-CRP land uses would not necessarily remain constant over the subsequent 10 years. For example, soil erosion on row-cropped land (or the advent of federal conservation compliance requirements) could induce some farmers to change to more soil-conserving uses on parcels during the time the parcels otherwise would have been enrolled in the CRP.

The societal accounting perspective dictates that changes in crop production or environmental services be valued at their real resource costs to society, given the state of the world on which the CRP is imposed. In the present analysis, both states of the world take as given the effects of all other government activities. Some analysts argue that current federal agricultural programs are partly responsible for commodity surpluses, soil erosion, water pollution, and loss of wildlife habitat (1, 7, 8). Estimated CRP benefits and costs in a world that includes these "distortions" are likely to differ from those that would be obtained in a study with no agricultural policy distortions. Because our without-CRP state consists of conditions prevailing prior to CRP enrollments, the prices and quantities used to estimate CRP benefits and costs are dependent on government policies existing at the time.

Estimation of CRP Benefits and Costs

CRP-induced land use changes affect several services, some of which are traded, albeit in imperfect markets, and some of which are not. In this study we adapt estimates of nonmarket benefits from the literature to derive lower and upper bounds for on-site and off-site recreational benefits from the CRP.

Estimation of CRP Benefits and Costs. A taxonomy of social benefit and cost categories related to erodible cropland retirement set forth by Ervin and Dicks (3) provides the basis for potential benefits and costs attributed to CRP enrollments in the watershed. Not all are directly observable.

Benefits include:

► Reduced loss of soil productivity from soil erosion and enhancement (immediately following return to cropping) of productivity. This benefit, of course, is realized only if the land returns to production.

► Increased quantity and quality of recreation in downstream water resources.

► Reduced deposition of sediment in downstream water bodies and in roadside ditches.

► Enhanced or enlarged habitat for game and nongame wildlife.

► Reduced risk of groundwater contamination from fertilizers and herbicides.

► Values for nonusers from preserving the existence of affected on-site land resources and off-site water resources in the future, above and beyond their use values.

► Reduced efficiency losses associated with variable inputs attracted to production of commodities by government support prices.

► Noncancelling secondary benefits, such as reduced negative externalities in input or processing sectors.

Costs include:

► Social value of foregone production of crops previously grown on CRP parcels, net of avoided production inputs, reduced transportation and storage requirements, and erosion-related productivity losses.

► Local program administrative resources that have opportunity uses.

► Labor, machinery, and seed needed to establish and maintain approved vegetative cover.

► Increase in costs of production on non-CRP land because of changes in field configurations and other restrictions in uses of immobile agricultural production resources.

► Noncancelling secondary costs, such as input or processing sector resource immobility.

We report bounds for each benefit category except for reduced efficiency losses and noncancelling secondary benefits. We report bounds for each cost except increased production costs stemming from immobilities and noncancelling secondary costs. Our omission of these benefits and costs reflects no presumption of their insignificance but, rather, a lack of suitable measurement techniques and appropriate scientific or economic data.

A description of the procedures used to develop economic estimates of all benefit and cost categories can be found in Kozloff (6). Here, we summarize only the principal findings.

In most cases, we estimate ranges of economic surplus values by applying CRP-induced land use changes to models that estimate physical effects (2, 10, 11). We then relate each type of physical change to one or more human activities—boating, hunting, viewing wildlife, crop production, sediment removal, and so on. Finally, we estimate economic values for the changes in human activities. Lower and upper bounds are generally calculated at each step. The cumulative difference between the bounds sometimes exceeds an order of 10, reflecting both scientific and economic measurement uncertainty.

In some cases, the relationship between the physical change and its economic value is relatively direct. For example, soil conserved over the 10 years that CRP land is retired increases crop yields over what they would have been had the land not been retired. In other cases, the relationship is indirect. For example, to obtain CRP-induced social welfare improvements associated with water-based recreation, several intermediate conceptual and empirical links must be specified. First, land retirements must be sufficient to noticeably reduce nonpoint pollution at the watershed outlet. Next, the reduction in nonpoint-source pollutants at the watershed outlet must improve objective water quality parameters in water resources further downstream. Third, those who intend to use those downstream resources for recreation must perceive the objective water quality changes. Fourth, changes in perceived water quality must result in a measurable increase in the quantity or quality of recreational experiences. Finally, recreationists must positively value this increase.

Projected physical changes and associated economic values roughly corresponding to the above taxonomy of benefits and costs are shown in table 1. For example, each CRP acre is estimated to generate downstream water recreation benefits between $0 (the lower bound) and $6 (the upper bound) per year of enrollment. On the cost side, the one-time establishment of approved plant cover is estimated to incur social costs between $83 and $105 per acre. The foregone production costs decline from the initial values shown because of the effects of erosion if CRP parcels had remained in crops.

The CRP's soil productivity benefits are not readily expressed in dollars per acre per year because differences between without-CRP and with-CRP crop yields change over several decades (Figure 1). There is expected to be both a short-term "rotation" effect from the grass/legume CRP cover (the dashed portion of the with-CRP yield path) and long-term effects from delayed soil erosion (the horizontal distance between the paths). The estimated benefits of the latter are derived from crop yield enhancements and avoided labor and machinery requirements that are multiplied by lower and upper bound estimates of the social value of crops, labor, and machinery, respectively. Because farmers may not adjust inputs for CRP-induced soil savings, the lower bound benefit for replaceable soil properties is set at $0. Because much of the CRP acreage in the study area is covered by deep topsoils, soil productivity benefits (Figure 1) are small just after CRP land re-enters production and increase over the analytical period. Estimated benefits of both long- and short-term yield effects are incorporated into the overall productivity benefits in table 2.

Because the CRP affects both foregone crop production and enhanced productivity once contracts expire, the study's results are potentially sensitive to how marginal changes in crop production are valued. Due to persistent commodity surpluses and other effects of government programs, foregone output could not have been sold at prevailing market prices and market prices themselves are unreliable guides to social values. To derive opportunity costs from foregone crop production, we first estimate a range of social values based on several approaches. We use world prices estimated from producer subsidy equivalents as upper bounds ($1.76 per bushel for

Table 1. Estimates of benefits and cost per acre (rounded to nearest 1986 dollar) (4).

Range of Physical Changes	Bounds of Benefits and Costs
Off-site environmental effects	
0%-7% increase in downstream water clarity	$0-$6/acre/year for recreation and related nonuse values
0-585 ton/year reduction in sediment delivered to downstream lake	$0-$3/acre/year for delaying the need to dredge downstream lake
15% reduction in sediment deposited in roadside ditches	$1-$2/acre/year for delaying the need to remove sediment
On-site environmental effects	
260% increase in pheasant density	$8-$36/acre/year for increase in quantity and quality of hunting
45% increase in diversity-adjusted wildlife habitat acres	$0-$3/acre/year for increase in quantity of wildlife viewing and photography and related nonuse values
Resources used in land retirement	
Foregone production initially of 48,390 bushels of corn and 8,293 bushels of soybeans	−$23-$104/acre initially for opportunity cost of foregone production
Establishment of approved plant on CRP parcels	$85-$105/acre for seed, fertilizer, labor, and machinery expenses
Local program administration	$1-$3/acre for staff time, site visits, and office supplies

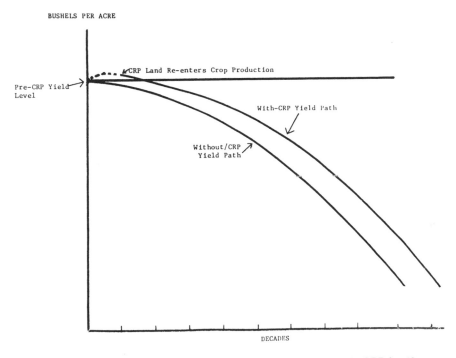

Figure 1. Crop yield paths over time showing effects of retiring land in CRP for 10 years.

corn and $5.32 per bushel for soybeans) and variable costs of production as lower bounds ($1.01 per bushel for corn and $1.73 per bushel for soybeans). (If, because of persistent surpluses, foregone output could not have eventually been sold at all, then its social value would be zero. The social value of conserved soil productivity would also be zero.) We then subtract variable production and storage costs from social values. These calculations result in lower bound net opportunity costs for corn and soybeans that are negative (meaning that marginal reductions in crop production improve social welfare) and upper bound costs that are positive. These results are also clearly sensitive to our consideration of changes on CRP parcels only; had we considered compensating changes on non-CRP parcels as well, the net amount of production foregone would likely be less.

Net Present Values. We next compare the net present values of the streams of benefits and costs over time under different discount rates and land use scenarios after initial CRP contracts expire. The upper bound of a benefit (or cost) category is always added to the upper bound of another benefit

Table 2. Summary of present values of CRP costs and benefits (1986 $ thousands).

			Discount Rate	
Category	Bound	3%	7%	11%
Benefits				
Off-site environmental				
10-year CRP	Lower	5	4	3
	Upper	53	39	30
CRP forever	Lower	20	9	5
	Upper	210	83	48
On-site environmental				
10-year CRP	Lower	42	3	27
	Upper	207	164	132
CRP forever	Lower	163	73	46
	Upper	800	356	227
Soil productivity				
10-year CRP	Lower	10	4	2
	Upper	174	64	33
Total				
10-year CRP	Lower	57	41	33
	Upper	433	267	196
CRP forever	Lower	183	81	51
	Upper	1,009	439	275

Costs

Foregone commodity production (social values less input costs, storage costs, and erosion-related productivity penalties).

10-year CRP	Lower	− 127	− 101	− 81
	Upper	534	423	342
CRP forever	Lower	− 477	− 204	− 125
	Upper	2,062	884	543
Cover establishment and maintenance				
10-year CRP	Lower	88	78	71
	Upper	114	101	91
CRP forever	Lower	193	112	88
	Upper	256	147	113
Program administration				
10-year CRP	Lower	0	0	0
	Upper	2	2	2
CRP forever	Lower	0	0	0
	Upper	2	2	2
Total				
10-year CRP	Lower	− 39	− 22	− 10
	Upper	650	526	435
CRP forever	Lower	− 283	− 91	− 37
	Upper	2,320	1,034	659

(cost) category. Four overall pairings are generated by comparing upper-bound summed benefits to lower- and upper-bound summed costs and by comparing lower-bound summed benefits to lower- and upper-bound summed costs.

Because benefits and costs arise at different times over the 100-year study period, net present values are potentially sensitive to discount rates. Analysts differ on the appropriate discount rate for benefit/cost analysis (opportunity cost of private investment or consumption, cost of borrowing to government, social time preference), so we select a broad range (3 percent to 11 percent) to span these perspectives.

Sensitivity of the net present values to the two land use scenarios also is tested. Under the first (called "10-year CRP"), all CRP acreage after the 10-year contract period reverts to crops grown prior to CRP enrollment. Under the second (called "CRP forever"), CRP acreage remains in CRP cover for the entire 100-year period of analysis. We assume that under the CRP-forever scenario, all on-site and off-site environmental benefits remain constant over time. In actuality, these benefits may vary as recreational demand shifts or resource supply changes, such as ecological succession altering wildlife habitat from the initially prescribed cover planting. Because no harvestable crops are grown on CRP land under this scenario, annual soil productivity benefits are nonexistent, but costs from foregone commodity production and CRP maintenance continue over the entire 100 years. Annual foregone production declines over this period to reflect increasing yield penalties from continuing erosive cropping practices.

Benefit and cost categories under each scenario and each discount rate are summarized in table 2, and aggregate net present values are shown in table 3. Present value benefits (for the whole project) range from $3,422 for the lower bound of soil productivity benefits at an 11 percent discount rate to $799,787 for on-site ecological benefits continuing for 100 years at a 3 percent discount rate.

The relative magnitude of different benefits and costs from land retirements in the watershed is uncertain because several lower and upper bounds overlap. However, if the values of all other benefits and costs are held constant, one can determine whether using the lower or upper bound of a given benefit or cost category changes the sign of the net present value at some discount rate. From table 2, we see that the only single benefit or cost whose difference between lower and upper bound determines the sign of the net present value at the same discount rate is the cost associated with foregone crop production.

Net present values are positive when summed lower- or upper-bound benefits are paired with summed lower-bound costs. The choice of discount rate affects the size of net present values but not their signs; in general, the absolute value of the net present values decreases with increasing discount rate. Similarly, the choice of scenario affects the size of the net present values but not their signs; both the negative and positive net present values are larger in absolute value in the CRP-forever scenario than in the crop reversion scenario. None of the net present values are close enough to zero that their signs are likely to have been affected by rounding.

Discussion

The presence of both positive and negative net present values in table 3 prevents us from reaching strong conclusions about the social welfare impacts of the CRP in the study area. It is important to note, however, that the range of net present values is only partly amenable to empirical refinement. Depending upon the perspective one takes regarding the sign of the opportunity cost of foregone production, CRP enrollments in the watershed can have either positive or negative welfare effects. If foregone crop production at the margin is taken to be substantially positive in its welfare effects, then the CRP's net welfare effects (as well as those of annual set-aside acres) are positive even if no other social benefits are generated. On the other hand, if foregone crop production has substantial negative welfare effects, then the net welfare effects of land retirement may still be negative even with significant conservation benefits. These results would hold for land retirements wherever the social value of crop production dominates the social value of conservation effects. Taking either perspec-

Table 3. Present values of CRP benefits less costs (net present values) in thousands of 1987 dollars.

	Discount Rate		
	3%	7%	11%
10-year CRP			
$B_1 - C_1$	96	64	43
$B_1 - C_u$	−592	−485	−403
$B_u - C_1$	472	290	206
$B_u - C_u$	−216	−258	−239
CRP forever			
$B_1 - C_1$	466	173	89
$B_1 - C_u$	−2,136	−952	−607
$B_u - C_1$	1,292	531	312
$B_u - C_u$	−1,310	−594	−384

tive would obviate the need to estimate the conservation benefits from land retirement if benefit/cost analysis is intended only to provide guidance on whether erodible land retirements are good social investments.

The net present values can be summarized by taking expected values over different possible outcomes. No information, however, was developed during the study that enables assigning individual probabilities to net present values. If each pairing of lower and upper bounds is assumed to be one of four equally probable states of nature, then the expected net present values are negative for both scenarios under all discount rates (and range from -$60,000 to -$422,000). Under this strong assumption, social welfare has probably declined as a result of CRP entry into the study area.

Policy Implications

The results of this study raise a note of caution about assuming a uniformly positive social welfare effect of the CRP in particular and of the long-term retirement of erodible land in general. It is inappropriate to generalize from this study to the CRP's national welfare effects; however, the study area is not unusual in its agricultural program participation or environmental traits. This raises the likelihood that projections of benefits and costs in other watersheds would also result "mixed" welfare effects, such as those found here.

More careful "targeting"—among watersheds and among parcels within a selected watershed—is one way to increase the likelihood that welfare effects of land retirement are positive. The goal of such targeting might be to increase average per acre benefits, reduce average per acre costs, or both. Particular attention must be paid to the value of foregone crop production to which aggregate net present values are quite sensitive. If the net opportunity cost of production is considered negative, then an efficient targeting scheme would try to enroll the most productive and environmentally damaging lands in a watershed to maximize net present values. If, however, one values foregone production high enough that net opportunity costs are positive, then an efficient targeting scheme would focus on the least productive lands in watershed. The extreme range of values bracketed by these perspectives suggests that researchers ought to examine the social value of crop production at the margin.

In a different vein, the government might increase welfare if it chose to rent only those rights to grow the most environmentally damaging crops, rather than renting all cropping rights. Such a program modification would tend to reduce both program costs and benefits under our analytical framework. A change from, for example, corn to oats would reduce foregone production values less than would a change from corn to an unharvestable grass/legume mixture. The reduction in social benefits would depend upon the extent to which oat production results in reduced soil loss, off-site movement of sediment and nutrients, and improvement of wildlife habitat relative to the grass/legume mixture. This modification would be an improvement over the current CRP only if lowering both per acre benefits and costs results in greater net present values than if land were totally removed from production.

In general, a more careful targeting of eligible land and a separation of cropping rights could complement each other. For example, complete crop land retirements could be targeted within a watershed to parcels both low in productivity (assuming foregone production costs are positive) and high in environmental damage potential if cropped. [For elaboration on such a scheme, see Taff and Runge (8)]. High productivity parcels that are erodible might have only their row-cropping rights acquired by the government.

Because of the large financial commitment inherent in long-term acquisition of some or all cropping rights and their uncertain impacts, any seriously considered changes should be tested in different locations before being implemented nationally.

REFERENCES CITED

1. Berner, Alfred. 1984. *Federal land retirement programs: A land management albatross.* In Transactions, 49th North American Wildlife and Natural Resources Conference. Wildlife Management Institute, Washington, D.C. pp. 118—131.
2. Berner, Alfred. 1987. *Pheasant population computer model.* Minnesota Wildlife Research Station, Department of Natural Resources, Medalia.
3. Ervin, David E., and Michael R. Dicks. 1988. *Cropland diversion for conservation and environmental improvement: An economic welfare analysis.* Land Economics 64(3): 256-268.
4. Kozloff, Keith. 1988. *An analysis of the effects of the conservation reserve program on nonpoint-source pollution in a Minnesota watershed.* A report to the U.S. Environmental Protection Agency. Department of Agricultural and Applied Economics, University of Minnesota, St. Paul.
5. Kozloff, Keith. 1989. *Benefits and costs to society from retiring erodible cropland: A case study of the Conservation Reserve Program.* Ph.D. dissertation. Department of Agricultural and Applied Economics, University of Minnesota, St. Paul.
6. Osteen, Craig D. 1985. *The impacts of farm policies on soil erosion: A problem definition paper.* ERS Staff Report No. AGES841109. Economic Research Service, U.S. Department of Agriculture, Washington, D.C.
7. Reichelderfer, Katherine, and Tim T. Phipps. 1988. *Agricultural policy and environmental quality.* National Center for Food and Agricultural Policy, Resources for the Future, Washington, D.C.

8. Taff, Steven, and C. Ford Runge. 1988. *Wanted: A leaner and meaner CRP.* Choices: 16-18.
9. U.S. Department of Agriculture, Agricultural Stabilization and Conservation Service. 1987. *Conservation Reserve Program participant contract files.* Rochester, Minnesota.
10. Winkelman, L. J., W.A.P. Graham, W. E. Larson, F. J. Pierce, and R. H. Dowdy. 1984. *GRAPHPI2: A program to display the effects of erosion on soil productivity.* Department of Soil Science, University of Minnesota, and Agricultural Research Service, St. Paul.
11. Young, Robert, et al. 1987. *AGNPS, Agricultural nonpoint-source pollution model: A watershed analysis tool.* Conservation Research Report No. 35. Agricultural Research Service, U.S. Department of Agriculture, Washington, D.C.

12

Evaluating the Economic Impact of Conservation Compliance

Colin P. Rowell, John S. Hickman,
and Jeffery R. Williams

Title XII of the Food Security Act of 1985 (1985 Farm Bill) contains provisions pertaining to soil conservation and its link with federal farm program benefits. Violation of these provisions, known as conservation compliance, sodbuster, and swampbuster, will result in the loss of most U.S. Department of Agriculture (USDA) farm program benefits for all land on which the participant receives payments.

Payments resulting from government programs have contributed substantially to the well-being of the agricultural sector in recent years and are a significant component of net returns to unpaid labor, operator's labor, equity capital, and management.

The Food Security Act of 1985 contains two provisions for highly erodible land: conservation compliance and sodbuster. Conservation compliance applies to USDA participants who continue to produce crops on highly erodible fields that were planted or considered planted to an agricultural commodity at least once during the crop years 1981 through 1985. To remain eligible for government programs, a conservation plan must be developed for the highly erodible cropland by January 1, 1990, and fully implemented by January 1, 1995. Between 1990 and 1995 and thereafter, the conservation practices must be applied according to schedule and must be properly operated and maintained.

When evaluating the effect of conservation compliance on their farm enterprise, farm program participants can consider several options, as follows:

▶ Develop and apply conservation systems on highly erodible fields, which will reduce erosion losses to soil loss tolerance, or T levels (where

T is an estimate the SCS uses for the maximum average annual rate of soil erosion that can occur without affecting crop production over a sustained period, and ranges from 2 to 5 tons per acre per year), in accordance with the Soil Conservation Service (SCS) Field Office Technical Guide, and retaining eligibility for USDA farm program benefits.

► Change the current use of highly erodible fields to nonagricultural commodities by planting to permanent vegetative cover (as in CRP) and retain eligibility for USDA farm program benefits on remaining crop acreage.

► Develop and apply alternative conservation systems (ACS) on highly erodible fields and retain eligibility for USDA farm program benefits.

► Produce agricultural commodities on highly erodible fields without appropriate conservation plans/systems and lose eligibility for USDA farm program benefits.

Most farm managers have several conservation alternatives from which to choose. In the past, they often elected not to implement soil conservation recommendations because of the perceived increase in production costs combined with little or no expected increase in returns in the short run. But the cost of losing farm program benefits by not following conservation provisions has increased the importance of evaluating which practices can be implemented economically. In addressing this issue, we selected case farms in northeast, south central, and southwest Kansas for analysis.

Review of Similar Studies

A nationwide study by Dicks (7) used annualized, per-acre, net present values to compare conservation compliance alternatives in various regions of the United States. The Northern Plains region, which includes Kansas, had an average conservation compliance cost of $11 per acre when using an 8 percent discount rate over 10 years. Net returns with program benefits were $33 per acre, compared with only $2 per acre without program benefits. With CRP, net returns were $26 per acre.

The economic impact of the conservation compliance provision (interim regulations) on cotton-producing counties in the Texas Southern High Plains was evaluated by Lippke et al. (10). Typical case farms and regional impacts were analyzed, and the findings revealed that the financial position of the farm was impacted negatively by the conservation requirements. To remain solvent, however, the producer usually had little choice but to comply with the conservation compliance provisions in order to remain eligible for USDA farm programs. Analyses of regional impacts revealed substantial economic hardship, if interim rules for meeting conservation compliance were implemented. Differences between cropping systems in that study and in Kansas are great, which make comparisons difficult. Also, alternative conservation systems (ACS) were made available by the USDA after the study by Lippke et al. (*10*) had been completed. These are evaluated in the study reported here.

Method of Analysis

The case farms selected for examination were located in three Major Land Resource Areas (MLRAs) in Kansas. The sites selected for study were Nebraska and Kansas Loess Drift Hills in northeast Kansas (MLRA 106), Central Rolling Red Prairies in south central Kansas (MLRA 80A), and the Southern High Plains in southwest Kansas (MLRA 77) (Figure 1). Farming operations in these MLRAs are vastly different in terms of cropping systems, resource problems, farm characteristics, and conservation requirements. The differences will help illustrate the relative economic

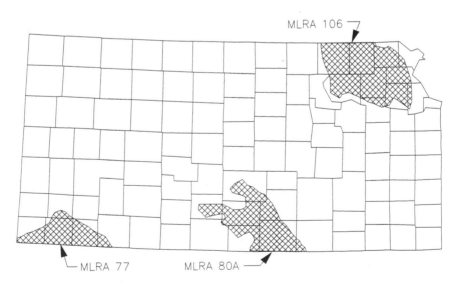

Figure 1. Major land resource areas of interest in Kansas.

impacts of conservation compliance in the three regions.

We determined farm financial characteristics and crop acreages and yields (Table 1), soil characteristics (Table 2), and yield by soil type (Table 3) for each case farm. These values represent typical characteristics of farms in each MLRA. The economic impact of conservation compliance in MLRA 80A was evaluated at both 15 percent and 50 percent highly erodible land (HEL) to determine the effect of compliance on farms with more than average highly erodible land.

Enterprise budgets were developed for each soil type and crop produced using Lotus 1-2-3 software. Single-crop budgets were determined as a weighted average over all soil types for each crop produced on the case farm, and deducted inputs paid by the landlord from the costs in the enterprise budgets. Cash expenses were entered from the budgets into FINLRB.[1] Results generated by FINLRB include gross farm income (receipts from crop production and government payments); net returns to unpaid labor, operator's labor, equity capital, and management (net returns); total percent debt (total liabilities/total assets); and potential for net worth growth (net worth change per year). FINLRB was used to compare each conservation alternative to a reference scenario—a base farm (BASE) that was not in conservation compliance and, therefore, not eligible for the government farm program.

Variable Costs. Variable costs include those expenses for machinery operation, labor, fertilizer, herbicides, insecticides, seed, crop drying, and interest on operating capital. These are costs of inputs that can be varied to change the output level of a farm (in this case, the yield per acre).

Machinery selection is a function of field workdays, acreage, equipment efficiency, and number of hours per day available for fieldwork (2). Labor requirements are based on equipment size, acreage, and field efficiency of each tillage operation. Our estimates of machinery repairs utilized an equation developed by Schrock (12). We based fuel and oil requirements for each tillage operation on data from a study by Schrock, Kramer, and Clark (13).

Kansas State University Extension agronomy personnel (11, 14) provided data on optimum fertilizer and herbicide input levels for determining

[1]FINLRB is the long-range budgeting portion of Finpack, a computerized farm and financial planning and analysis package created by University of Minnesota Extension Farm Management staff.

Table 1. Farm and financial characteristics of case farms.

Characteristics	Case Farm MLRA		
	106	80A	77
		acres	
Farm size*	640	1,000	2,000
Land owned*	225	360	560
Land rented*	415	640	1,440
		%	
Percent base†	70	100	84.3
Percent HEL‡	59	15(50)	100
		$1,000	
Value of owned cropland*	347.4	215.9	242.5
Value of machinery & buildings*	32.3	38.4	56.8
Cash reserve*	179.6	113.5	140.8
Total assets*	559.4	367.8	440.1
Long-term loans*	93.4	57.7	72.5
Intermediate loans*	20.2	23.6	26.2
Other loans*	59.8	71.9	98.9
Total liabilities*	173.5	153.2	197.6
Initial net worth	385.9	214.6	242.5
Equity ratio	0.690	0.583	0.551
Leverage ratio	0.450	0.714	0.815
Long-term debt/asset	0.269	0.267	0.299
Intermediate debt/asset	0.626	0.614	0.461
Total debt/asset	0.310	0.417	0.449
Family living expense ($1,000)	17.0	17.0	17.0
Crops produced-dryland†		acres	
Corn	190	—	—
Soybeans	195	—	—
Grain sorghum	120	—	900
Wheat	135	1,000	356
Idle	—	—	314
Crops produced-irrigated†			
Grain sorghum	—	—	300
Wheat	—	—	130
		bushels/acre	
Farm average yields-dryland			
Corn	84	—	—
Soybeans	37	—	—
Grain sorghum	83	38	35
Wheat	42	32	31
Farm average yields-irrigated			
Grain sorghum	—	—	84
Wheat	—	—	43

*(4)
†ASCS County Offices, personal communications.
‡Kansas SCS Office, personal communication.

costs. If the fertilizer or herbicide was not incorporated with tillage or applied during a planting operation, we added a charge for custom application(s) (8). The Kansas Extension Production Handbooks were the source for our estimates of seeding rates and prices for each crop (5). The Kansas Farm Management Guides (6) provided drying and miscellaneous expenses (drying charges were held constant for each crop).

With different conservation scenarios (reduced tillage, no tillage, and conservation structures), the farmability of the fields changed. The tillage system used increased or decreased field time and influenced certain variable costs. We assumed the initial farmability factor to equal 85 percent (the percentage agricultural engineers commonly use). To adjust costs associated with field time (labor, fuel and oil, crop machinery repairs, and miscellaneous expenses) input costs were multiplied by the initial farmability factor (F_o) divided by the new farmability factor (F_n), [(input usage $\times$ (F_o/F_n)].

Interest on operating capital was equal to 50 percent of the total variable costs times an interest rate of 12 percent. Cash interest on variable costs was equal to 30 percent of the variable cash costs times an interest rate of 12 percent. Interest charges for cash were less than the total to simulate the actual cash interest paid on the operating loan.

Table 2. Soil characteristics of case farms.*

MLRA	Soil	Amount (acres)		HEL	I†	K‡	Length (feet)	Slope (%)	Tons (ton/acre/year)
106	1	220		yes	48	0.37	210	5	4
	2	110		yes					
					48	0.28	175	8	5
	3	50		yes					
					48	0.32	150	14	5
	4	260		no	—	—	—	—	—
80A	15% HEL	(50% HEL)§							
	1	60	(200)	yes	48	0.28	175	5	5
	2	60	(200)	yes	86	0.20	250	1	5
	3	30	(100)	yes	134	0.17	250	1	5
	4	850	(500)	no	—	—	—	—	—
77	1	1,000		yes	134	0.17	250	2	5
	2	300		yes	86	0.24	500	1	5
	3	400		yes	48	0.32	700	2	5
	4	300		yes	48	0.20	500	1	5

*Soils chosen from county soil survey reports. Soil characteristics from SCS soil interpretation records.
†Soil erodibility factor for the wind erosion equation.
‡Soil erodibility factor for the universal soil loss equation.
§Figures in parentheses indicate characteristics for case farm with 50% HEL.

Fixed Costs. Fixed costs are defined as those for land (taxes, interest, and rent) and machinery (depreciation and interest). They accrue regardless of whether the asset is used.

We estimated real estate taxes and interest on land as a function of the value of land (*9*). Taxes equalled $0.50 per $100 of land value; interest on land was equal to 6 percent of total land value. Cash interest on land equalled 0.5896 times the total interest on land to simulate an amortized loan on land (*6*).

Land rent was equal to 40 percent of the gross returns from the rented acreage for MLRA 106 and 33 percent of gross returns from the rented acreage for MLRAs 80A and 77. These cost-share rental arrangements are typical for these MLRAs. The landlords' percentage shares of fertilizer, chemical, and drying expenses on the rented acres were equal to their percentage shares of gross returns.

We calculated depreciation on crop machinery using the straight line method. Depreciable value was equal to 85 percent of the original list price of the equipment. Assumed equipment ages were half of the expected lives: 10 years for tractors, 12 years for planters, and 14 years for tillage implements. We considered all equipment not owned on the current farms, such as no-till equipment, to be newly purchased. Salvage values came from the Cooperative Extension, Washington State University (*3*).

Table 3. Yield by soil relationships for each case farm.

		Dryland Yield*				Irrigated Yields*		Yield Relationship†	
				Grain		Grain			
MLRA	Soil	Corn	Soybeans	Sorghum	Wheat	Sorghum	Wheat	ACS	None
					bushels/acre			— % ‡ —	
106	1	79.0	34.6	78.9	39.6	—	—	98.5	97
	2	54.6	23.2	69.7	33.6	—	—	97.5	95
	3	115.9	44.9	106.2	48.7	—	—	95	90
	4	92.4	42.0	93.8	45.8	—	—	—	—
80A	1	—	—	29.6	25.6	—	—	—	97
	2	—	—	17.1	16.6	—	—	—	97
	3	—	—	28.5	29.1	—	—	—	95
	4	—	—	40.3	33.6	—	—	—	—
77	1	—	—	32.2	26.0	68.9	38.3	—	92
	2	—	—	37.8	31.3	89.0	47.7	—	96
	3	—	—	41.3	38.8	98.3	47.7	—	98
	4	—	—	33.3	36.6	109.2	47.7	—	98

*SCS soil interpretation records.
†Estimate by authors.
‡Percentage of maximum yield.

Estimates of interest on crop machinery consisted of average annual opportunity cost calculated at a 10-percent rate of interest. A 4-year amortized loan on 50 percent of the equipment value at an interest rate of 10 percent yielded the cash interest on crop machinery. All of the present machinery complement was kept even if new purchases were required, such as no-till equipment. Insurance on crop machinery equalled 1 percent of the depreciable value of the equipment.

Yields. Assumed average yield for each crop on each case farm was the same as the ASCS county average yield (Table 1), adjusted for each soil type using SCS Soil Interpretation Records (Table 3) and also adjusted depending on the conservation systems used. We adjusted yields for those systems that did not reduce erosion to tolerable T levels (Table 3) and also for soils 1 and 2 in MLRA 77, where erosion rates of 4T rather than T are allowed.

Conservation Reserve Program. We evaluated the CRP on each highly erodible soil, assuming bid rates at the maximum acceptable rental rate (pool limit) for each farm: $65, $55, and $50 for MLRAs 106, 80A, and 77, respectively. Government cost-sharing was 50 percent of the cost to establish cover, with the remainder of the established costs taken from current assets. If current assets were not enough to pay for establishment costs (options CRP1 and CRP1234 in MLRA 77), 90 percent of the costs were borrowed at a 9 percent interest rate for 10 years. On rented acreage, the producer and the landlord split the annual rental payments 50/50. The landlord paid 50 percent of the seed and herbicide costs, and the producer pays for 50 percent of the seed and herbicide costs plus 100 percent of the seeding and annual maintenance costs. Maintenance costs consisted of (1) mowing the first two years and every other year thereafter, (2) burning three times during the 10-year period, and (3) maintaining fences (*1*). Native grass was the permanent vegetative cover planted.

Government Payments and Set-aside. The producer received 100 percent of the government deficiency payments on owned land. The producer and the landlord shared deficiency payments on rented acres in the same manner as gross returns from crop production.

The cost for set-aside acres was an assumed 50 percent of the costs in a wheat enterprise for seed, herbicide and insecticide, fuel and oil, machinery repair, interest on those variable costs, and the appropriate fixed costs. Assumed program yield equalled the farm average yield. Table 4 shows long-range estimates for target prices, cash prices, and percent set aside for the time period 1990-1995.

Conservation Structure Costs. We used the SCS Field Office Technical Guide to select the various conservation alternatives for each highly erodible soil on each case farm (Tables 5, 6, and 7), and evaluated additional alternatives/scenarios, such as noncompliance, ACS, and CRP. County average costs and SCS estimates were the basis to determine conservation structure costs. The assumed government cost-sharing for conservation structures was 50 percent, with an annual limit of $3,500. We assumed that none of the structures needed for compliance had been constructed. On rented acres, the landlord paid for the terracing, while the producer paid for annual maintenance, which equalled 2 percent of the total cost. The producer paid for all terracing costs on owned acres. Annualized cash costs for terracing consisted of estimates from borrowing 90 percent of the initial structure cost, amortized at 9 percent interest over 20 years. Calculations for annualized total costs for terracing entailed the same process except that 100 percent of the initial structure cost was borrowed.

Whole-Farm Analysis. In MLRAs 106 and 80A, we evaluated different conservation scenarios for each highly erodible land. Production practices on nonhighly erodible land were constant with current cropping and tillage practices. We identified the conservation alternatives in tables 10, 12, and 13 through three-digit numbers. The first digit refers to the conservation option for soil 1, the second digit to the conservation option for soil 2, and the third digit to the conservation option for soil 3. For example, conservation option 221 in MLRA 106 refers to conservation option 2 for soil 1, conservation option 2 for soil 2, conservation option 1 for soil 3,

Table 4. Prices and percent set aside, long-range estimates, time period 1990-1995.*

Crop	Target Price	Cash Price	Percent Set-aside
	— $/bushel —		
Wheat	3.80	2.50	20
Corn	2.63	1.85	15
Grain sorghum	2.50	1.70	15
Soybeans	—	5.75	—

*Personal Communication, W.I. Tierney, Kansas State University.

and current practices (BASE) for the nonhighly erodible land. The CRP options denote which soil was enrolled in CRP, while the other soils were kept in compliance. BASE With Government denotes the current practices with government payments before conservation compliance. The BASE system denotes the use of current practices with no government payments (i.e., production in violation of conservation compliance).

For MLRA 77, crops produced were soil-specific, allowing conservation

Table 5. Conservation alternatives for MLRA 106.

Soil	Option Number*	Alternative Description
1	1	Reduced tillage (30% cover) with conventional terraces spaced 130 ft. with 11 acres of waterways. Farmed on contour. Farmability equals 0.70.
	2	No-till planting. Conventional terraces spaced 150 feet with 11 acres of waterways. Farmed on contour. Farmability equals 0.70.
	3	Reduced tillage (30% cover) with UTO terraces. Farmed on contour. Farmability equals 0.70.
	4	No-till planting. UTO terraces. Farmed on contour. Farmability equals 0.70.
	CRP 1	Soil 1 in CRP, soils 2 and 3 in option 1.
2	1	Reduced tillage (30% cover) with conventional terrace spaced 110 feet with 10 acres of waterways. Farmed on contour. Farmability equals 0.60.
	2	No-till planting. Conventional terraces spaced 130 feet with 10 acres of waterways. Farmed on contour. Farmability equals 0.60.
	3	Reduced tillage (30% cover) with UTO terraces. Farmed on contour. Farmability equals 0.60.
	4	No-till planting. UTO terraces. Farmed on contour. Farmability equals 0.60.
	CRP 2	Soil 2 in CRP, soils 1 and 3 in option 1.
3	1	No-till planting. UTO terraces. Farmed on contour. Farmability equals 0.55.
	CRP 3	Soil 3 in CRP, soils 1 and 2 in option 1.
CRP 123		Soils 1, 2, and 3 in CRP
ACS 1		Reduced tillage and contour on soils 1 and 2. No tillage and contour on soil 3.
ACS 2		All terraces were previously installed on soils 1, 2, and 3. Grain sorghum planted with reduced tillage (30% cover). All other crops conventionally tilled.
BASE		Current practices. Tillage consists of moldboard plowing, chisel plowing, disking, and field cultivating before planting. Farmability equals 0.85.

*All options utilize a corn-soybean-grain sorghum-wheat rotation in the same ratio as acreage planted on farm.

Table 6. Conservation alternatives for MLRA 80A.

Soil	Option Number	Alternative Description
1	1	Continuous wheat rotation with conventional tillage. Terraced at 130 feet spacings with 3 acres of waterways. Farmed on contour. Farmability equals 0.65.
	2	Continuous wheat rotation with reduced tillage (30 percent cover). Terraced at 130 feet spacings and 3 acres of waterways. All farming operations are on contour except planting and harvest. Farmability equals 0.70.
	3	Wheat-grain sorghum-fallow rotation. Conventional tillage wheat. Wheat residue left standing through winter. Grain sorghum planted with reduced tillage (30% cover). Sorghum stubble left standing through July. Farmability equals 0.85.
	CRP 1	Soil 1 in CRP, soils 2 and 3 in options 3 and 1.
2	1	Continuous wheat rotation. Half of field conventional tillage and other half reduced tillage (30% cover). Farmability equals 0.85.
	2	Continuous wheat rotation in 100-foot wind strips with 13.5 feet forage sorghum buffer strips. Farmability equals 0.775.
	3	Wheat-fallow rotation in 1,320 foot strips. Conventional tillage wheat. Residue left standing until July 1 during fallow period. Farmability equals 0.825.
	4	Wheat-grain sorghum rotation in 1,320 foot strips. Conventional tillage wheat. Wheat residue left standing through winter. Grain sorghum planted with reduced tillage (30% cover). Sorghum stubble left standing through July. Farmability equals 0.825.
	CRP 2	Soil 2 in CRP, soils 1 and 3 in options 2 and 1.
3	1	Continuous wheat planted with reduced tillage (30% cover). Farmability equals 0.85.
	2	Continuous wheat planted with no tillage. Wheat yield reduced 4%. Farmability equals 0.85.
	CRP 3	Soil 3 in CRP, soils 1 and 2 in options 2 and 3.
CRP 123		Soils 1, 2, and 3 in CRP.
BASE		Current practices. Tillage consists of moldboard plowing or chisel plowing, disking, field cultivating, and harrowing prior to planting. Farmability equals 0.85.

compliance options to be evaluated by soil type rather than by whole farm, such as for MLRAs 106 and 80A. Soil 2 consisted of both irrigated and dryland production, and soil 4 had two directions of furrow irrigation. We selected the conservation option with the highest net returns for each soil and production practice as the whole farm conservation plan that resulted in the highest net returns attainable. The numbering system for MLRA 77 uses only two digits. For example, option 1-2 represents conservation option 2 on soil 1 with all other soils in the BASE With Government situation. The same applies for each soil and all conservation

Table 7. Conservation alternatives for MLRA 77.

Soil	Option Number	Alternative Description
1	BASE	Continuous dryland grain sorghum. Disk, chisel, list-plant, knife-sled and cultivate. Graze 1/3 of planted acres. Farmability equals 0.85.
	1	(ACS) Continuous dryland grain sorghum. Conventional tillage, leave 1250 # small grain equivalent on until May 1, then start tillage practices. No grazing. Yields reduced 4%. Farmability equals 0.85.
	2	(ACS) Continuous dryland grai sorghum. Reduced tillage. No grazing. Yields reduced 4%. Farmability equals 0.85.
	CRP 1	Soil 1 in CRP, soils 2irr, 2dry, 3, and 4 in options 1, 1, 1, and 1, respectively.
2	Circle Irrigation	
	BASE	Continuous irrigated wheat. Burn 0.5x, disk 0.5x, sweep, chisel, disk, and plant. Graze 100% of planted acres. Farmability equals 0.85.
	1	(ACS) Same as base except replace burning with disking. Graze 100%. Yields reduced 2%. Farmability equals 0.85.
2	Dryland Production	
	BASE	Wheat-fallow. Undercut 2x, sweep,disk 2x, and plant. Graze 1/3 of planted acres. Farmability equals 0.85.
	1	(ACS) Reduce undercut 1 time, exchange field conditioner for 1 disking operation, increase herbicides charge by $7.00/acre plus custom application. Graze 1/3 of planted wheat. Yields reduced 2%. Farmability equals 0.85.
	2	(ACS) Same tillage practice as BASE but use 200-foot fallow strips. Reduce farmability to .775. No grazing. Yields reduced 2%.
	CRP 2	Soil 2 in CRP, soils 1, 3, and 4 in options 1, 1, and 1, respectively.
3	BASE	Wheat-fallow. Undercut 2x, sweep, disk 2x, and plant. Graze 1/3 of planted acres. Farmability equals 0.85.
	1	Reduce undercut 1 time, exchange field conditioner for 1 disking operation, increase herbicides charge by $7.00/acre plus custom application. Graze 1/3 of planted wheat. Farmability equals 0.85.
	2	Same tillage practice as base but use 200-foot fallow strips. Reduce farmability to 0.775. No grazing.
	CRP 3	Soil 3 in CRP, soils 1, 2irr, 2dry, and 4 in options 1, 1, 2, and 1, respectively.
4	East-West Furrows	
	BASE	Continuous grain sorghum. Disk 2x, chisel, field conditioner, ridger, rotary hoe-plant, and cultivate. Graze 100% of planted acres. Farmability equals 0.85.
	1	Same as base. Graze 100% of planted acres.
4	North-South Furrows	
	BASE	Continuous grain sorghum. Disk 2x, chisel, field conditioner, ridger, rotary hoe-plant, and cultivate. Graze 100% of planted acres. Farmability equals 0.85.
	1	Leave 1,250 pounds of small grain equivalent until May 1. Disk 1x, chisel 1x, field conditioner 1x, bed 1x, rotary hoe—plant, cultivate, and apply herbicide. Graze 100%. Farmability equals 0.85.
	CRP 4	Soil 4 in CRP, soils 1, 2irr, 2dry, and 3 in options 1, 1, 2, and 1.
CRP 1234		Soils 1, 2, 3, and 4 in CRP.

options available for each soil. The CRP and BASE scenarios are the same as in MLRA 106 and MLRA 80A.

Results and Analysis

MLRA 106—Northeast Kansas. All scenarios in conservation compliance resulted in a loss of net returns as compared to returns from current production practices including government commodity payments (BASE With Government). These options, however, were considerably better than farming in violation of conservation compliance (i.e., without USDA benefits) (BASE) (Tables 8, 9, and 10). The loss in net returns by compliance ranged from $368 to $9,509, whereas the gain over noncompliance (BASE) ranged from $3,729 to $12,870.

When in compliance, ACS1 and CRP2 had the highest net returns. Of the traditional conservation options (systems that reduced soil erosion to a tolerance level of T with conservation structures and residue management), options 111 and 331 [reduced till with conventional and underground tile outlet (UTO) terraces] had the highest net return. Options 441 and 331 reached the cost-share limit for conservation structures ($3,500 limit), but were exceeded by only $617 per year. Compliance alternatives that enrolled soils 1, 3, or all highly erodible land into CRP resulted in the lowest net returns.

The ranking of traditional conservation options from highest to lowest by net returns was 111, 331, 221, and 441 (Table 10). The range in net returns, from highest to lowest option, was only $1,613. Conservation options with

Table 8. Returns for base and alternative conservation systems, MLRA 106.

Variable	BASE	BASE With Government	ACS 1	ACS 2
Gross returns		$		
Wheat	13,669	10,935	11,035	11,081
Corn	28,436	24,171	24,509	24,670
Grain sorghum	16,993	14,444	14,633	14,699
Soybeans	39,917	39,917	40,365	36,278
Government payments	—	17,238	17,238	17,238
Gross farm income	99,105	106,704	107,779	103,965
Net return*	6,648	19,886	19,518	14,696
Total percent in debt	31.0%	31.0%	31.6%	31.0%
Net worth change per year	−11,312	−1,386	−1,631	−4,848

*Net return is defined as net return to unpaid labor, operator's labor, equity capital, and management.

Table 9. Returns for CRP alternatives, MLRA 106.

Variable	CPR 1	CRP 2	CRP 3	CRP 123
Gross returns		$		
Wheat	7,664	9,706	10,256	5,061
Corn	16,779	22,047	22,266	11,043
Grain sorghum	10,110	12,738	13,423	6,474
Soybeans	25,844	34,122	32,874	19,562
Government payments	11,705	15,049	15,496	7,647
CRP	9,654	4,827	2,194	16,674
Gross farm income	81,756	98,490	96,509	66,461
Net return	11,915	18,907	14,348	10,377
Total percent in debt	32.3%	32.3%	32.2%	31.6%
Net worth change per year	-6,897	-2,039	-5,080	-8,176

reduced tillage (options 111 and 331) resulted in a slightly higher net return than no-till options (221 and 441) because of increased production costs for the latter. Use of conventional terraces and waterways (options 111 and 221) resulted in higher net returns than their respective UTO options (331 and 441). Conventional structures reduced the income from soybean production because soybean acreage was taken out of production for waterways (but had considerably lower construction costs than UTO structures).

The type of tillage practice had a larger impact on net returns than the type of conservation structures. Reduced tillage with UTO terraces, for example, resulted in a higher net return than no tillage with conventional structures. Because the producer paid for terraces on owned land only, effects to the whole farm (i.e., both producer and landlord) would be different. When UTO structures were installed, total debt increased by 1.6 percent compared to use of conventional structures and by 3.6 percent compared to current practices (BASE). These debt loads did not take into account the possible changes in land values for being in or out of compliance. We did not determine what effect completed conservation systems would have on land values.

Placing soil 2 into the CRP (CRP2), while having the other soils in option 111, had the highest net returns of any CRP option, followed by CRP3, CRP1, and CRP123 (Table 9). Because soil 2 was low yielding and had relatively high conservation structure costs, it was the most favorable for CRP enrollment. Placing soil 1, which had low conservation structural costs and near-average farm yields, into the CRP (CRP1) resulted in the lowest net returns of all the single soil CRP options. Enrolling soil 3 into the CRP (CRP3) reduced net returns by $4,559 as compared to CRP2. Soil 3 had the highest conservation costs on the farm but also had the highest yields and consisted of only 50 acres. Net return was lowest among CRP options when all of the highly erodible land was placed into the CRP (CRP123) because of the high cost of planting 380 acres into permanent vegetative cover and the cumulative loss of crop production income. All CRP options resulted in higher net returns than producing in violation of the conservation compliance provision (BASE).

CRP options had lower debt loads than other compliance options, but they still increased debt load over current production practices (BASE with government). The cost of establishing permanent vegetative cover was less than the cost of constructing conservation structures on all highly erodible soils plus purchasing no-till equipment for soil 3. If the debt load of the farm is of major importance, placing highly erodible land into CRP is a viable alternative to constructing conservation structures. Enrolling low yielding, highly erodible land into CRP increased net return, while decreasing the total percent debt, when compared to other conservation options.

Table 8 presents the analysis of two alternative conservation systems, (ACS 1 and ACS 2). Alternative conservation system 1 had a higher farmability factor because it had no terraces, however, additional tillage operations were added to correct ephemeral and gully erosion on soil 3. Neither of these systems reduced soil erosion to T levels, therefore, they could be used only under special circumstances. Yields in both were less, compared to traditional conservation options, but still were greater than BASE because of higher soil erosion (Table 3). Alternative conservation system 1 had the highest net returns (in fact, higher net returns than any traditional or CRP options). Alternative conservation system 2 assumed that terraces already were installed and conventional tillage was used for all

Table 10. Returns for traditional conservation alternatives, MLRA 106.

Variable	111	221	331	441
Gross returns			$	
Wheat	11,286	11,286	11,240	11,240
Corn	24,999	24,999	24,837	24,837
Grain sorghum	14,892	14,892	14,826	14,826
Soybeans	36,718	36,718	40,870	40,870
Government payments	17,238	17,238	17,238	17,238
Gross farm income	105,132	105,132	109,010	109,010
Net return	16,128	15,199	15,802	14,515
Total percent in debt	33.1%	33.0%	34.6%	34.6%
Net worth change per year	– 3,893	– 4,512	– 4,110	– 4,969

crops except grain sorghum, for which reduced tillage was used. Total debt increased by 0.6 percent for system 1 because no-till equipment was purchased, whereas the total percent in debt did not change for system 2.

MLRA 80A—South Central Kansas. Because of higher yields and low conservation costs, most conservation compliance options resulted in higher net returns than current practices (BASE With Government) (Tables 11 and 12). All options had higher net returns than producing in violation of the compliance provision (BASE). The range of net returns for the conservation options was smaller for MLRA 80A than for MLRA 106, with only a $3,089 difference between the highest and lowest options. Among the conservation options, CRP options had the highest net returns. Exchanging wheat base acres for grain sorghum base acres was most profitable when it substituted for conservation structures. Otherwise, such an exchange decreased net returns because of low grain sorghum yields on highly erodible land.

Option 231 resulted in the highest net returns of the traditional conservation options, followed by 331, 211, 122, and 241 (Table 12). Option 231 was highest because this option had the highest farmability factor on each soil type and had a wheat-fallow rotation on soil 2. Fallow acres from the wheat-fallow rotation in 231 were used for set-aside acres (which increased planted acreage on the highest yielding, nonhighly erodible land). Conservation structure costs on soil 1 were modest and had little impact on net returns, even when highly erodible land changed from 15 percent to 50 percent. Options with reduced-till wheat on soil 3 had higher net returns than with no-till wheat. Yields were reduced by 4 percent for no-till continuous wheat. No-till equipment increased the total debt by 0.6 percent for 15 percent highly erodible land and 0.4 percent for 50 percent highly erodible land. Terracing for soil 1 increased total debt by 0.3 percent for 15 percent highly erodible land and by 0.9 percent for 50 percent highly erodible land.

We considered a wheat-grain sorghum base exchange for soils 1 and 2 in options 331 and 241. On soil 2, for which structures were not required, the base acre exchange on option 241 decreased net returns by $2,175 compared to option 231, because of the low grain sorghum yields. Wheat-grain sorghum base exchanges were more profitable when the exchange replaced conservation structures. For example, option 331 reduced net returns by only $548 as compared to option 231, which does not have a wheat-grain sorghum base exchange, but was $1,627 greater than option 241. Option 331 had the highest net returns with a wheat-grain sorghum base exchange.

With 15 percent highly erodible land, all CRP options except CRP3 resulted in higher net returns than the best traditional conservation option (231). When highly erodible land was increased to 50 percent, CRP123 and CRP3 had lower net returns than option 231. CRP options ranked slightly higher with 15 percent highly erodible land because few acres were in CRP. CRP2 was the best CRP option because the yields in soil 2 were lowest for any of the soils. Conversely, soil 3, with the highest yields, was the lowest-ranked CRP option. With 15 percent highly erodible land, the largest increase in total debt with any CRP option was 0.3 percent (CRP123).

Table 11. Results for BASE and CRP systems, MLRA 80A.

Variable	BASE	BASE with Government	CRP 1	CRP 2	CRP 3	CRP 123
15% HEL			$			
Gross returns						
Wheat	79,750	63,800	61,833	61,736	62,942	57,120
Grain sorghum	0	0	0	0	0	0
Grazing	10,000	10,000	10,000	10,000	10,000	10,000
Government						
payments	0	26,169	25,362	25,424	25,918	23,429
CRP	0	0	2,244	2,244	1,122	5,610
Gross farm						
income	89,750	99,969	99,439	99,404	99,981	96,159
Net returns	2,432	21,621	23,311	23,427	22,724	23,280
Total percent in						
debt	41.7%	41.7%	41.9%	42.2%	42.1%	42.3%
Net worth						
change						
per year	− 15,017	− 245	865	942	480	845
50% HEL						
Gross returns						
Wheat	69,375	55,500	48,848	48,998	52,398	33,600
Grain sorghum	0	0	0	0	0	0
Grazing	10,000	10,000	10,000	10,000	10,000	10,000
Government						
payments	0	22,765	20,036	20,417	21,795	13,782
CRP	0	0	7,480	7,480	3,740	18,700
Gross farm						
income	79,375	88,265	86,364	86,896	87,933	76,082
Net returns	− 5,773	11,653	17,307	18,245	15,238	16,354
Total percent						
in debt	41.7%	41.7%	42.5%	43.5%	43.1%	46.5%
Net worth change						
per year	− 23,173	− 7,115	− 3,106	− 2,481	− 4,487	− 3,742

Table 12. Returns for traditional conservation alternatives, MLRA 80A.

Variable	122	211	231	241	331
Gross returns			$		
Wheat	63,880	63,720	64,677	62,388	63,922
Grain sorghum	0	0	0	1,046	1,006
Grazing	10,000	10,000	10,000	10,000	10,000
Government payments	26,300	26,235	26,628	25,829	26,138
Gross farm income	100,180	99,955	101,305	99,263	101,066
Net returns	20,338	22,375	23,076	20,901	22,528
Total percent in debt	42.6%	42.0%	42.0%	42.0%	41.7%
Net worth change per year	−1,088	250	−711	−718	351
50% HEL					
Gross returns					
Wheat	55,952	55,655	58,223	51,288	55,474
Grain sorghum	0	0	0	3,485	3,356
Grazing	10,000	10,000	10,000	10,000	10,000
Government payments	23,240	23,117	24,184	21,399	22,756
Gross farm income	89,192	88,773	92,407	86,112	91,587
Net return	10,077	13,951	16,495	9,518	14,671
Total percent in debt	43.3%	42.6%	42.6%	42.6%	41.7%
Net worth change per year	−8,426	−5,345	−3,648	−8,895	−4,865

At 50 percent highly erodible land, the total debt increased 3.9 percent for CRP123.

MLRA 77—Southwest Kansas. The case farm in MLRA 77 required only residue management (reduced or no tillage) and a decreased amount of grazing to control erosion. CRP1 had the highest net returns, because of the lower yields on soil 1 and reduction of grazing income for soil 1 to be in compliance (Tables 13 and 14). Combination 11211 was determined to have the highest net returns for the traditional conservation options. BASE With Government had higher net returns than the best traditional option, but CRP1 was $2,958 higher. All options had higher net returns than producing in violation of the conservation compliance provision (BASE).

Among the traditional conservation options, total percent debt did not change with the different conservation options, because no extra tillage equipment or conservation structures were necessary to comply (Table 13). The differences among the traditional options were very small.

Among the CRP options, CRP1 had the highest net returns but also the second highest total debt: 12.9 percent higher than BASE or traditional

Table 13. Returns for base and traditional conservation alternatives, MLRA 77.

Variable	BASE	BASE with Government	1-1*	1-2	2irr-1†	2dry-1†	2dry-2	3-1	3-2	4-1ns‡	11211§
Gross returns					$						
Grain sorghum	100,8?5	85,702	87,379	87,379	85,702	85,702	85,702	85,702	85,702	85,859	87,537
Wheat	40,581	37,541	37,541	37,541	37,541	37,672	37,672	37,926	37,926	37,541	38,057
Grazing	5,200	4,093	3,710	3,710	4,093	4,093	3,809	4,093	3,426	4,093	3,427
Government payments	0	45,630	46,233	46,233	46,233	45,682	45,682	45,783	45,783	45,688	46,494
Gross farm income	146,607	172,965	174,862	174,862	173,568	173,149	172,865	173,502	172,836	173,180	175,515
Net return	-31,226	38,153	36,906	35,514	38,263	37,724	37,860	37,934	37,550	37,748	35,899
Total percent in debt	44.9%	44.9%	44.9%	44.9%	44.9%	44.9%	44.9%	44.9%	44.9%	44.9%	44.9%
Net worth change per year	-48,626	10,616	9,797	8,883	10,689	10,335	10,424	10,473	10,220	10,350	9,136

*First digit is soil. Second digit is conservation option. All other soils are in current production (BASE with government).
†Irrigated and dryland production denoted by irr and dry, respectively.
‡North-south furrow irrigation.
§Conservation option 11211 had the highest net returns of all traditional conservation options.

conservation options (Table 14). Because soil 1 had the lowest yields and
the lowest income from grazing, it was more profitable to take this soil
out of production and enroll it in CRP. Ranking of the other CRP options,
with respect to net returns, was CRP2, CRP3, CRP4, and CRP1234. The
CRP1234 option exceeded the $50,000-per-year payment limit (CRP has
a separate payment limit of $50,000 per year from deficiency payments),
which caused this option's net returns to be $14,000 less than if no yearly
limit were applied.

Summary

Conservation compliance had the largest impact in Northeast Kansas (Major Land Resource Area 106), where conservation structures and no-till
equipment were necessary. Production in violation of conservation provisions had the lowest net returns for all MLRAs. The conservation options
with the highest net returns were those using reduced tillage and enrolling
low-yielding, highly erodible land in the CRP.

To make a generalized conclusion about the economic impact of conservation compliance would be difficult because of the vast differences in erosion problems across the state. The impact depends a great deal on whether
structures are necessary, because structures decrease net returns to unpaid
labor, operator's labor, equity capital, and management. Second, it depends
on the farm manager's ability to adopt reduced- or no-till production prac-

Table 14. Returns for CRP systems, MLRA 77.

Variable	CRP 1	CRP 2	CRP 3	CRP 4	CRP 1234
Gross returns			$		
Grain sorghum	47,338	87,537	87,537	40,198	0
Wheat	38,057	19,375	18,682	38,057	0
Grazing	3,427	3,143	2,760	2,747	0
Government payments	32,072	39,057	38,813	29,510	0
CRP	32,000	9,600	12,800	9,600	50,000
Gross farm income	152,894	158,742	160,592	120,113	50,000
Net return	41,111	30,752	29,081	11,166	-13,439
Total percent in debt	51.4%	45.9%	46.3%	45.6%	57.8%
Net worth change per year	12,728	5,754	4,656	-7,520	-16,850

tices and the impact these new production practices have on farm yields. Depending on the type of erosion, sheet and rill or wind, conservation compliance could have a positive or a negative impact on the financial condition of a farm.

ACKNOWLEDGEMENTS

Funding for this research was provided by the Kansas Soil Conservation Service, Salina, Kansas, in cooperation with Kansas State University. The authors thank Jayson Harper for editing an earlier version of this manuscript and Larry C. Bonczkowski, Dale L. Fjell, and Dwight G. Mosier for technical assistance.

REFERENCES CITED

1. Agricultural Stabilization and Conservation Service. 1988. *Estimated annual costs of maintaining CRP land.* KS Notice CRP-123. Manhattan, Kansas.
2. Buller, O. H., L. N. Langemeier, J. L. Kasper, and L. R. Stone. 1976. *Field workdays in Kansas.* Agricultural Experiment Station Bulletin 596. Kansas State University, Manhattan.
3. Cooperative Extension. 1982. *The costs of owning and operating farm machinery in Washington.* Extension Bulletin 1055. College of Agriculture and Home Economics, Washington State University, Pullman.
4. Cooperative Extension Service. 1988. *The county report, 1987, management information, Kansas Farm Management Associations.* Department of Agricultural Economics, Kansas State University, Manhattan.
5. Cooperative Extension Service. 1986, 1987. *Crop production handbooks.* Department of Agronomy, Kansas State University, Manhattan.
6. Cooperative Extension Service. 1987. *KSU farm management guides.* Department of Agricultural Economics, Kansas State University, Manhattan.
7. Dicks, Michael R. 1986. *What will it cost farmers to comply with conservation provisions.* Agricultural Outlook. (October). pp. 27-30.
8. Kansas Crop and Livestock Reporting Service. 1985. *Kansas custom rates.* Kansas State Board of Agriculture, Topeka..
9. Langemeier, L. N. 1986. *Land prices.* Unpublished. Department of Agricultural Economics, Kansas State University, Manhattan.
10. Lippke, Lawrence A., James W. Richardson, Edward G. Smith, Bill L. Harris, Lonnie L. Jones, and John G. Lee. 1986. *Impact of the conservation compliance provisions of the Food Security Act of 1985—interim rules on the Texas Southern High Plains.* Texas Agricultural and Food Policy Center, College Station.
11. Nilson, E. B., D. L. Regehr, O. G. Russ, W. H. Fick, D. W. Morishita, P. W. Stahlman, P. D. Ohlenbusch, and D. K. Kuhlman. 1988. *Chemical weed control for field crops, pastures, rangeland, and noncropland 1988.* Agricultural Experiment Station Bulletin 530. Kansas State University, Manhattan.
12. Schrock, M. D. 1976. *Avoiding machinery bottlenecks.* Cooperative Extension Bulletin C-563. Kansas State University, Manhattan.
13. Schrock, M. D., J. A Kramer, and S. J. Clark. 1985. *Fuel requirements for field operations in Kansas.* Transaction, American Society of Agricultural Engineers 28(3): 669-674.
14. Whitney, D. A. 1987. *Soil test interpretations and fertilizer recommendations.* Cooperative Extension Bulletin C-509. Kansas State University, Manhattan.

13

Farmers' Willingness to Supply Land as Filter Strips: Evidence from a Michigan Survey

Amy Purvis, John P. Hoehn, and Vernon Sorenson

Filter strips represent a significant change in the design of farm conservation practices. Filter strips are bands of cropland adjacent to streams or drainage ditches. Filter strips are set aside from crop production and planted in permanent vegetative cover. They act as buffers to stop sediment from being washed downstream. Agronomists estimate that filter strips can reduce off-farm damages from sediment movement caused by cropland erosion from 25 to 50 percent (*3, 17*). In February 1988, the secretary of agriculture announced that landowners could enter into 10-year contracts to set aside filter strips in the Conservation Reserve Program (CRP). The CRP is the first experiment using a nationwide conservation program as a policy instrument for controlling nonpoint water pollution caused by cropland erosion.

Through the 1970s and early 1980s, farm conservation programs emphasized technical assistance and cost-sharing to support farmers' decision-making about adopting conservation practices to control on-farm erosion damages. The advent of a filter strip program forges a new direction in conservation policy.

Making a contract to set aside filter strips is different from deciding to adopt a conservation practice for two primary reasons. First, adopting conservation practices involves changing farm management strategies to control erosion. Conservation is expected to pay off in either sustained or improved net production revenues over time. On the other hand, entering a 10-year contract to set aside filter strips means exchanging revenues from crop production for a yearly payment. Second, the objective for installing filter strips is to stop displaced sediment from moving off the farm where it can affect downstream water users. Other conservation practices are designed primarily to address the on-farm effects of cropland erosion and to prevent productivity losses.

The conceptual framework for our research acknowledges these differences and then builds on the empirically-based literature regarding the adoption and diffusion of conservation practices. The purpose of previous studies was to identify the socioeconomic characteristics of landowners and their farms correlated with decisions to adopt conservation practices.

Financial and economic factors, including current and expected farm income levels, farm size, debt load, real interest rates, and access to credit or cost-sharing, have been shown to play a significant role in determining whether farmers adopt conservation practices (6, 12, 13). Farmers' values and attitudes are also important in directing their conservation behavior (9). In our research, farmers' willingness to participate in a 10-year program to set aside filter strips is understood within a utility-maximization framework. Farmers maximize utility subject to economic constraints, including opportunity costs, transaction costs, and expectations about the future. To explore the relative importance of these economic decision criteria, farmers' responsiveness to yearly payments in return for setting aside filter strips is analyzed using contingent valuation methods.

Supply and Demand for Cropland Erosion Control

The demand for erosion control on cropland is determined by the marginal benefits, both on and off the farm, from using conservation practices. Farmers are concerned with on-farm benefits and costs of conservation as they are experienced on the farm, whereas public decisions consider both on-farm and off-farm benefits and costs. Analysis of on-farm and off-farm benefits and costs, from both the farmers' and the public's perspectives, provides some insights into the divergence between private and public conservation decisions. Graphically, this can be shown using marginal benefit and marginal cost curves (Figure 1).

Farmers who invest in conservation practices do so to achieve higher levels of erosion control. Those who take land out of production for conservation purposes face higher opportunity costs as they set aside more acreage, and as they set aside more productive acreage. Farmers' willingness to enter land into conservation practices depends on an upward-sloping marginal cost function.

The demand for conservation practices relates to the benefits associated

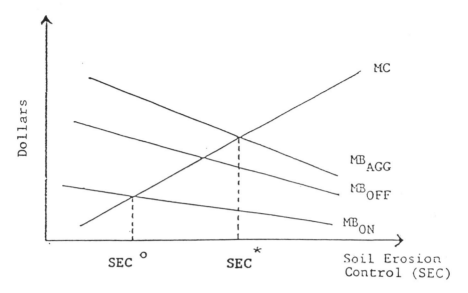

Figure 1. Supply and demand for conservation.

with controlling cropland erosion, depicted graphically with a downward sloping marginal benefit function. On the farm, landowners perceive the need to prevent cropland erosion to avoid productivity losses that could result in lower yields now and in the future. Off the farm, the demand for conservation comes from downstream water-users who are concerned about sediment displaced by erosion entering streams, rivers, and lakes.

From a farmer's perspective, the benefits from erosion control are derived largely from preventing productivity losses. Yield reductions lower production revenues and reduce the capacity of cropland to produce food and fiber. Market mechanisms tend to reward farmers who use conservation and punish those who erode. Eroded cropland commands a lower price in the land market. Commodity and land prices offer farmers incentives to control cropland erosion, with pay-offs in higher net farm incomes over time. Nonmonetary benefits also play an important role in determining farmers' willingness to conserve. Improved wildlife habitat, increased recreational uses of cropland, and the ethical satisfaction derived from good land stewardship have intrinsic value to farmers and make a difference in their decisions about investing in conservation practices.

To maximize the benefits from using a conservation practice, farmers normally try to achieve a level of soil erosion control (SEC°) at which the marginal on-farm benefits (MB_{on}) equal the marginal costs (MC) of conservation. From a farmer's point-of-view, investing in higher levels of erosion control is inefficient; the costs are more than additional improvements are worth on the farm.

The on-farm decision regarding conservation tends to ignore the off-farm erosion effects of sediment movement, which muddies streams, rivers, and lakes. Even so, when farmers use conservation practices to control erosion, these off-farm effects can be reduced, and water quality improved, benefitting downstream water-users. But because the direct incentives to farmers for preventing off-farm erosion damages are small, these considerations play a minor role in their decisions about using conservation practices.

In contrast, from a public perspective, interest in conservation practices arises because of benefits that result from curtailing several types of damages caused by displaced sediment. Reduced sedimentation may prevent flooding, reduce the costs of dredging inland waterways and drainage systems, and lower water prices for those who rely on surface water to supply residential or commercial water needs. Improved water quality also benefits boaters, swimmers, anglers, and other recreators. Graphically, in figure 1, the marginal off-farm benefits from erosion control are drawn separate from the on-farm benefits to acknowledge different beneficiaries and different motives for conservation on and off the farm.

The estimated dollar value of off-farm benefits is larger than the estimated on-farm benefits from erosion control. Clark and associates (3) estimate the total benefits of eliminating off-farm effects of cropland erosion to be approximately $2.2 billion per year. In considering on-farm benefits, Crosson (4) estimates that benefits from eliminating cropland erosion amount to approximately $500 to $600 million per year on the farm.

From a public perspective, on-farm benefits and off-farm benefits are both important. Decisions about public support for conservation represent downstream water-users who are concerned about off-farm effects of cropland erosion, and also the more general social goal of saving enough soil on farms to meet the food production demands of future generations. To provide a level of erosion control that will satisfy public demands for both on- and off-farm benefits, ideally farmers would choose to use conservation practices in which the benefits from reducing damages both on and off the farm equal the marginal costs of erosion control. From the public's point of view, it would be desirable for farmers to use conservation toward the level SEC*, to the extent that the aggregate marginal benefits (MB_{AGG}) exceed the marginal costs. But bearing the costs of these higher levels of erosion control would be difficult for farmers to justify because the costs are greater than the benefits that accrue on the farm.

The discrepancy between the on- and off-farm benefits from erosion control is significant; the magnitude of potential benefits to off-farm water-users supports farm conservation efforts to reduce sediment delivery to streams and ditches. But farmers themselves are motivated to use conservation practices in response to the on-farm benefits; without policy interventions, farmers aim to invest in conservation to the extent that the on-farm benefits exceed the marginal costs. Therefore, if farmers are offered financial incentives to bear the additional costs incurred from conservation practices, especially for practices designed to counter the off-farm effects from cropland erosion, they may be willing to provide more erosion control.

Offering public support to farmers who conserve is a way to narrow the divergence between the farmers' and the public's desired levels of erosion control. Farmers' willingness to supply land for conservation uses is measured by the marginal costs of controlling erosion. Graphically, the size of the divergence between farmers' chosen levels of erosion control (SEC$^\circ$) and the socially desirable level of erosion control (SEC*) depends on the slope of the marginal cost curve. An argument can be developed in favor of policy intervention, to offer farmers funding to help offset the costs of controlling erosion and increase their investments in conservation above SEC$^\circ$ toward SEC*.

Baseline estimates of the on- and off-farm benefits from conservation are available. Although several researchers are working to assess the extent of off-farm damages from cropland erosion (8, 15), empirical data required to begin estimating the marginal costs associated with increasing farmers' use of conservation practices is lacking. Without an idea of the these costs, it is impossible to judge the amount of divergence between the level of conservation farmers would choose and the level of conservation the public is prepared to support. If the marginal cost curve is inelastic, the expected difference between farmers' conservation decisions and the levels of erosion control the public deserves would be relatively small. A more elastic marginal cost function would increase the importance of the role of incentives to farmers, to encourage more use of conservation practices than they would otherwise choose.

Study Design

Recognizing the limited benefits to be gained from investing in conservation to reduce off-farm damages, even farmers with strong preferences for environmental quality make their decisions about filter strips subject to economic constraints. Setting aside filter strips means taking land out of production and losing revenues, as well as incurring the costs associated with establishing and maintaining permanent vegetative cover on filter strips. Entering a 10-year contract means agreeing to refrain from economic uses of the enrolled cropland, even if commodity prices or incentives from other farm programs go up. Offering financial incentives to farmers who set aside filter strips is a way to compensate for these costs. Each individual has a threshold at which the benefits from receiving a yearly payment will make up for lost production revenues, the costs of establishing and maintaining filter strips, and the risk of committing to a conservation program for 10 years.

To model these influences, the farmer, in deciding whether to enroll in a filter strip program, was viewed as seeking to maximize well-being. A farmer's preferences and attitudes are central to a utility-maximizing decision, but maximization is subject to economic constraints such as the level of direct payments, foregone sources of incomes, and expected market conditions. With filter strips, we expected the relationship between payment and participation to be contingent upon four categories of economic constraints: (1) opportunity costs, (2) transaction costs, (3) expectations about the future, and (4) farmer preferences or attitudes.

To measure the payment-participation relationship and to test the importance of economic constraints, we conducted a case study among individuals who own cropland in Newaygo County, Michigan. Three considerations were important in selecting the site. First, surface water is plentiful, with 4 rivers, 234 lakes, and 356 miles of streams in Newaygo County, and many landowners using tiled farm drainage systems. Second, estimates from the 1982 National Resource Inventory (NRI) indicate that approximately 20 percent of the cropland in the county is highly erodible. Third, the agricultural economy in Newaygo County is diverse. Approximately 40 percent of the cropland is in row crops, and another 40 percent in forage crops. Both dairy and livestock production are significant; an estimated 20 percent of the farms in the county have dairy operations, and 36 percent have livestock enterprises. Orchards and high-value specialty vegetable crops are important in the county. On cropland with rich organic muck soil, which is used to grow carrots and onions, annual land rental rates range from $200 to $500 per acre. In contrast, acreage used for corn and hay is rented for $30 to $70 per acre.

This research used contingent valuation (CV) methods (11) to measure the relationship between payment and participation in a filter strip program. Respondents reacted to a hypothetical situation—an option to accept or reject a yearly payment in return for putting land into filter strips in a 10-year conservation program. To adequately assess landowners' responsiveness to financial incentives, the levels of yearly payments offered across the sample were varied.

To identify the population for the survey, we developed a sampling frame of 925 landowners by merging mailing lists from local offices of the Soil Conservation Service (SCS), the Agricultural Stabilization and Conservation Service (ASCS), and the Cooperative Extension Service (CES). Approximately one-third of the sampling frame is composed of individuals who are not currently participating in USDA farm programs. Questionnaires were mailed to a random sample of 600 landowners in August, 1988. The mail survey, administered using the total design method (5), produced a response rate of 72 percent. Forty-one percent of the respondents who participated in the study (167 landowners) identified cropland on their farms adjacent to streams or drainage ditches that could be set aside as filter strips. We analyzed data from 93 returned questionnaires to assess how yearly payment offers influence landowners' willingness to participate in a 10-year conservation program.[1]

The questionnaire was comprised of two parts—a contingency, followed by a valuation question. Respondents were to read a scenario describing an opportunity to set aside filter strips, and the following information: First, a description of the filter strips—bands of cropland 66 to 99 feet wide next to creeks or ditches, planted in permanent vegetative cover that acts as a buffer to help stop topsoil and fertilizer from being washed into ditches and creeks; second, an outline of the eligibility requirements for participation in a 10-year program to set aside filter strips and a simple formula for respondents to use in calculating how many acres they could set aside as filter strips; and third, the rules for participating in the program—entering a 10-year contract and receiving a yearly payment for each acre in filter strips, no haying or grazing allowed on filter strip acreage, and cost-sharing available for 50 percent of the costs to establish permanent vegetative cover.

The valuation question offered respondents a yearly payment to enter a 10-year contract and asked whether they would enroll any land in the filter strip program at the stated payment level. Respondents who accepted the payment were asked to indicate how many of their eligible acres they would enroll. A different payment was offered to each of 12 subsets of respondents within the overall sample; payment levels ranged from $20 to $550 per year. The selected payment levels were chosen based on cash rental rates and on bids submitted for CRP contracts in 1986.

[1]The other 74 respondents did not provide complete answers to the questionnaire.

After answering the valuation question, respondents identified reasons for deciding whether to set aside filter strips. In the final section, landowners described themselves and characteristics of their farms. We used these descriptive data to test hypotheses about economic factors associated with responsiveness to financial incentives for setting aside filter strips.

Results

We estimated the payment-participation relationship using a two-limit Tobit econometric analysis (16). Tobit analysis results in a participation index analogous to a regression equation. The dependent variable is the proportion of eligible acreage enrolled in the filter strip program. The independent variables are payment level and the four sets of economic constraints—opportunity costs, transaction costs, expectations about the future, and preferences. Tobit analysis is appropriate because, unlike a case with ordinary regression, the range of the dependent variable is limited or censored. Landowners cannot enroll anything less than zero acres and no more than their total eligible acreage, thus, the dependent variable is limited to an inclusive range between 0 and 1.

Rather than analyzing the statistical significance of the independent variables one at a time, we conducted hypothesis tests to determine whether adding any of the four sets of variables contributed to the explanatory power of the participation index. Then we performed likelihood ratio tests to evaluate the statistical significance of each of the four sets of variables.

Table 1 lists the four categories of economic variables thought to be important to the payment-participation relationship. Within each category are the empirical variables selected as proxies for the underlying concept. For instance, farm income (FINCOME) provided one measure of the economic productivity of farm activities and may indirectly represent the opportunity cost of setting aside acreage in a filter strip program (14). The relationship between any one proxy and the underlying economic concept is not entirely unambiguous. Nevertheless, the significance of the overall set of proxies within a category should provide insight into the factors that condition the payment-participation relationship.

Table 2 lists the estimated payment-participation relationships. Index A gives the simple payment-participation equation with no conditioning variables. Proportion of eligible acreage enrolled (participation) is the dependent variable, and PAYMENT is the only independent variable. Notably, the coefficient on PAYMENT is positive and statistically significant. As economic theory would suggest, farmers are price responsive: annual pay-

Table 1. Groups of variables for hypothesis-testing.

Categories and Variables	Conceptual Descriptions	Expected Relationship
Payment	Yearly payment for participation	Positive
Opportunity costs		
Yield	Average yield on filter strip acreage	Negative
Rent	Cash rent on most productive acreage	Negative
Income	Household income	Positive
Farm income	Percentage of income from farming	Negative
Transaction costs		
ASCS	Contact with ASCS in the past 3 years	Positive
SCS	Contact with SCS in the past 3 years	Positive
Tenure	Over 50 percent of cropland is rented	Negative
Proportion of eligibility	Proportion of cropland on the farm eligible for filter strips	Positive
Future expectations		
Too long	Ten-year contract is too long	Negative
Price expectations	Price expectations for the next 10 years	Positive
Preferences		
Soil conservation ethic	Concern about conserving soil on the farm	Positive
Environmental ethic	Concern about the environment	Positive

ment for participation in the filter strip program is positively and significantly related to enrollment of eligible acreage.

Index B is the payment-participation equation conditioned on the three categories of economic constraints that were statistically significant. As in the simple equation, the coefficient PAYMENT was positive and statistically significant. We tested the statistical significance of each economic constraint, one at a time, by adding each set of variables to the simple payment-participation index (Index A). Then we carried out four likelihood ratio tests to measure the significance of each additional set of independent variables.

The likelihood ratio tests indicated that the sets of opportunity cost, future expectations, and preference variables had a statistically significant impact on participation. Thus, the equation given in table 1 includes only opportunity cost, future expectations, and preference variables.

In the equation, the opportunity cost variables YIELD and INCOME are statistically significant. A negative coefficient on the yield variable indicates that farmers who can get higher yields on their cropland are less likely to set aside filter strips. The positive coefficient on the variable representing household income shows that well-to-do farmers are more likely to set aside filter strips than are low-income farmers. Neither the rental price of farm land (RENT) nor the proportion of family income from farming (FINCOME) are statistically significant.

One of the expectations variables, TOOLONG, is statistically significant, indicating that the 10-year contract period was an important deterrent to participation. The price expectations variable (PEXPECT) is not statistically significant. It was included to test the hypothesis that those who believe farm prices will rise more slowly than inflation over the next 10 years are more likely to participate in a 10-year program than those who think prices will rise more rapidly or at the same rate as inflation.

The preference variables represent how farmers may order outcomes and weigh money and nonmonetary benefits. Values and attitudes held are essential to a utility-maximizing trade-off between economic alternatives (2). Landowners who expressed concern about environmental quality (ENVETHIC) and about conserving soil on their farms (SCETHIC) were more likely to set aside filter strips than those who did not cite these as

Table 2. Estimated payment-participation relationships.

	Variables	Participation Index A	Participation Index B
	Payment*	138,629†	123.785†
		(58.08)§	(47.59)
	Intercept	− 602.610	− 399.401
		(266.76)	(810.79)
Opportunity Costs	Yield*	—	− 188.318‡
			(131.80)
	Rent*	—	− 47.917
			(55.73)
	Income*	—	87.437†
			(62.46)
	Farm income*	—	− 11.499
			(14.07)
Future expectations	Too long	—	− 124.585‡
			(71.82)
	Price expectations	—	60.580
			(59.97)
Preferences	Soil conservation ethic	—	52.041
			(76.97)
	Environmental ethic	—	102.152†
			(67.12)
Log-likelihood value		− 148.11	− 135.46

*Continuous variables are logged.
†Significance within a 90 percent confidence interval.
‡Significance within a 95 percent confidence interval.
§Standard error is in parentheses.

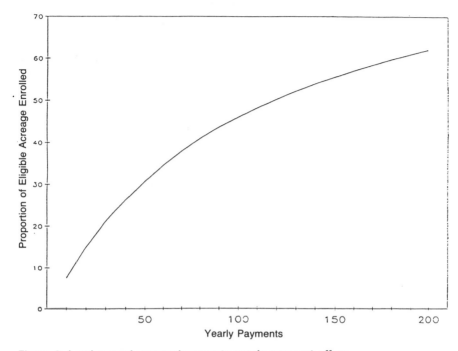

Figure 2. Landowners' responsiveness to yearly payment offers.

reasons for setting aside filter strips. Concern about environmental quality was positively correlated with participation and was statistically significant.

The group of variables selected to represent transaction costs was not statistically significant in explaining decisions about setting aside filter strips. However, this lack of significance does not indicate that transaction costs should be generally ignored as a category. Additional research is needed to better understand and characterize the empirical proxies for transaction costs.

The estimated Tobit equation can be used to show the relationship between payment and farmers' willingness to participate in filter strips.[2] A positive functional relationship exists between the proportion of eligible acreage they would enroll in filter strips and the yearly payment offers

[2]The estimated payment-participation index is conditioned on the information provided in the survey format. It included a description of filter strips, a simple worksheet to determine eligibility, and a clear statement of how much the farmer would be paid to participate. If this information were changed or not included, the payment-participation also would change.

(Figure 2). Because the Tobit model uses a limited dependent variable, the normalized coefficients from the estimated participation index are adjusted for censoring in the error term (*10*).

The estimated equation indicates that the Newaygo County respondents would be willing to set aside 26 percent of their eligible acreage in filter strips for a yearly payment of $40 per acre. These respondents would enroll 41 percent of their eligible acreage in the proposed program if the payment was doubled. As the level of yearly payments increases, the participation index function becomes more inelastic.

These survey results indicate the importance of a program that offers the general farm population clear, concise information about the filter strip program. Currently, the CRP bid cap in Newaygo County is $40 per acre; yet the amount of acreage enrolled in filter strips is negligible. One may argue that this difference between actual and survey behavior simply represents the difference between actual and hypothetical behavior. Previous research, however, suggests that the willingness-to-accept-payment questions used in the survey should understate rather than overstate actual behavior (*1*).

The difference between the survey predictions and actual enrollment appears to be related to information. Information about filter strips, the type of land that is eligible, and the payment level has not reached the general farm population in Newaygo County. Both in the mail survey and in follow-up personal interviews, farmers had virtually no knowledge of the filter strip program available through the CRP. Indeed, 24 percent of Newaygo County farmers claimed to have had no contact with any conservation agency in the past three years. Without knowledge of the program, their own eligibility, and the payment level, farmers have no opportunity to make the decision, much less the opportunity to participate.

Policy Implications

The analysis suggests three considerations in designing more effective farm conservation programs. First, the results indicate that farmers' enrollment decisions are consistent with economic principles. An increase in payments results in an increase in acreage enrolled. Opportunity costs, future expectations, and individual preferences are statistically important in explaining farmers' participation decisions.

A second policy implication from these research results is that farmers must be informed about filter strips if they are going to participate. Farmers need to know what filter strips are, what land is eligible, and the level of payment. Without clear knowledge of eligibility and payment levels, they cannot make an informed decision. Ambiguity about the relationships between bid caps, payments, and acceptance of a contract weakens the payment-participation relationship. Program design must recognize that filter strips are not likely to be a large source of income.[3] Thus, farmers are unlikely to make a large investment of their time just to find out if they are eligible or if their contract is accepted. For a filter strip program that is easy to understand and straightforward in implementation, the survey results suggest that Newaygo County farmers would put up to 26 percent of their eligible land into filter strips for a payment of $40 per year.

Finally, farmers need decision support tools to help them overcome uncertainty about participating in conservation programs. Our mail survey questionnaire appeared to provide a helpful framework.

Future Research

Further research is needed to investigate contingent valuation as a method for predicting farmer behavior. Results from this case study in Newaygo County are preliminary and represent the behavior of a sample of farmers in one place at one point in time. To test the validity of these results, conducting similar CV studies across the state or the nation as a whole would be useful. Also, conducting experiments in which farmers are actually offered lower and higher yearly payments for signing contracts to set aside filter strips would be helpful. An experiment of this type could compare what people say they would do in a CV survey setting with their actual behavior in response to a binding agreement.

An experiment could be designed wherein landowners are offered various types of information to assist them in deciding about accepting financial incentives to set aside filter strips. For example, one group of respondents might be presented with statistics about the effectiveness of filter strips in reducing erosion damages in various on-farm situations. A second group might visit on-farm demonstrations of filter strips in use. A third group might work through a budgeting routine presenting dollar estimates of the costs and benefits associated with filter strips, contrasted with several other conservation alternatives. Farmers who invest more decision resources, time, and thought would be expected to make better decisions about participating in a conservation program.

[3]Among Newaygo County respondents, the average acreage reported eligible for filter strips was 12 acres.

Analysis of this experiment would indicate how the payment-participation relationship is conditioned on the information a given decision support tool provides. Comparative analysis would show how information influences individuals' choices among conservation alternatives and would help to identify which kinds of information are most helpful to landowners in their decision-making processes. These comparisons also would indicate whether having better information and investing more decision resources influences farmers to accept lower or higher yearly payments. This type of systematic evaluation of decision support tools would provide guidelines for those concerned about the content of conservation education programs and about strategies for marketing conservation programs.

REFERENCES CITED

1. Bishop, Richard C., and Thomas A. Heberlein. 1979. *Measuring values of extramarket goods: Are indirect measures biased?* American Journal of Agricultural Economics 61: 926-930.
2. Brown, Thomas C. 1984. *The concept of value in resource allocation.* Land Economics 60: 231-246.
3. Clark, Edwin H., Jennifer A. Haverkamp, and William Chapman. 1985. *Eroding soils: The off-farm impacts.* The Conservation Foundation, Washington, D.C.
4. Crosson, Pierre. 1986. *Soil erosion and policy issues.* In Tim T. Phipps, Pierre R. Crosson, and Kent A. Price [editors] *Agriculture and the Environment.* Resources for the Future, Washington, D.C.
5. Dillman, Don A. 1978. *Mail and telephone surveys: The total design method.* John Wiley and Sons, New York, New York.
6. Ervin, C. A., and D. E. Ervin. 1982. *Factors affecting the use of soil conservation practices: Hypotheses, evidence and policy implications.* Land Economics 58, 3(1982): 277-292.
7. Esseks, J. Dixon, and Steven E. Kraft. 1988. *Why eligible landowners did not participate in the first four sign-ups of the Conservation Reserve Program.* Journal of Soil and Water Conservation 41(3): 251-256.
8. Giannessi, Leonard P., Henry M. Peskin, Pierre Crosson, and Cyndi Puffer. 1986. *Nonpoint-source pollution: Are cropland controls the answer?* Journal of Soil and Water Conservation 41(4): 215-218.
9. Lynne, Gary D., J. S. Shonkwiler, and Leandro R. Rola. 1988. *Attitudes and farmer conservation behavior.* American Journal of Agricultural Economics 70: 12-19.
10. McDonald, J. F., and R. A. Moffitt. 1980. *The uses of Tobit analysis.* Review of Economics and Statistics 60: 318-321.
11. Mitchell, Robert Cameron, and Robert T. Carson. 1986. *Using surveys to value public goods: The contingent valuation method.* Resources for the Future, Washington, D.C.
12. Nielsen, Elizabeth G., John A. Miranowski, and Mitchell J. Norehart. 1989. *Investments in soil conservation and land improvements: Factors explaining farmers' decisions.* Economic Report No. 601. Economic Research Service, Washington, D.C.
13. Norris, Patricia E., and Sandra S. Batie. 1987. *Virginia farmers' soil conservation decisions: An application of Tobit analysis.* Southern Journal of Agricultural Economics 19: 79-90.
14. Purvis, Amy. 1989. *An economic analysis of landowners' willingness to enroll filter*

   strips in a conservation program: A case study in Newaygo County, Michigan. M.S.
   thesis. Michigan State University, East Lansing.
15. Ribaudo, Marc O. 1986. *Consideration of off-site impacts in targeting soil conservation programs.* Land Economics 62: 402-411.
16. Rossett, Richard N., and Forrest D. Nelson. 1975. *Estimation of the two-limit Tobit
   regression model.* Econometrica 43: 141-146.
17. Walter, John. 1989. *Filter strips: A little land with a big bang.* Successful Farming
   2: 36-37.

IV

Barriers and Facilitators to Implementation of the Conservation Title at the Farm Level

14

Factors Affecting Knowledge of and Participation in the Conservation Reserve Program in in a Microtargeted Area of Ohio

Silvana M. Camboni, Ted L. Napier,
and Stephen B. Lovejoy

Soil erosion has contributed to environmental degradation and social problems in the U.S. for several decades (7, 8, 10, 15, 17). Soil loss from agricultural sources emerged as a serious socioenvironmental problem during the 1920s and 1930s, when dust storms significantly reduced the productivity of many Midwestern farms. Wind erosion removed topsoil from large tracts of farmland in the Midwest to the extent that food and fiber production was impossible. Farm owners were forced to leave the eroded land and many were never able to return to agricultural production. The deterioration of land resources and the dislocation of farmers exacerbated effects of the depression.

Public concern for loss of productivity of agricultural land generated political support for the creation of government programs to halt erosion of valuable land resources. Educational programs, soil conservation agencies, and economic subsidies were implemented on a national basis (13). Millions of dollars of federal monies and extensive human resources were devoted to soil conservation programs, and the rate of soil loss from wind erosion was significantly reduced. Unfortunately, government-sponsored programs have not reduced soil erosion to socially acceptable levels, so potential solutions continue to be explored.

One recent attempt to resolve erosion problems is the Conservation Title of the Food Security Act of 1985. Proponents of this legislation argue that program participation by owners of highly erodible land will result in significant soil erosion reduction. However, few of the program objectives can be achieved without extensive participation by landowners.

One of the most important Conservation Title programs is the Conservation Reserve Program (CRP). This program is substantially different from previous soil conservation efforts because of the elements of coercion included. Previous government-sponsored soil conservation programs relied heavily on voluntary compliance and land operators could withdraw from them without penalty. Such is not the case with the CRP. Participation necessitates compliance with contractual agreements, and violation can result in penalties. Further, CRP contracts are long-term (10 years).

Because the CRP is substantially different from past conservation programs, we selected theoretical modeling previously used to predict adoption of innovations to guide the investigation. Participation in the CRP was viewed as being analogous to adoption of an innovation, inasmuch as participation is the behavioral manifestation of land operators' acceptance of the program.

Because voluntary adoption of soil conservation practices and participation in government-sponsored soil conservation programs have many similarities, we examined literature focused on the voluntary adoption of soil conservation practices (4, 7, 8, 10, 11, 17, 18, 19, 23, 24). This literature was useful in identifying factors to predict participation in the CRP, and also in identifying alternative theoretical perspectives to expand the traditional diffusion model.

An Eclectic Model of Adoption

The Traditional Diffusion Model. We selected components of the traditional diffusion model (1, 22) and the farm structure-institutional constraints perspective (2, 3, 4, 9, 23) to guide our investigation. The traditional diffusion model argues that adoption of any innovation is a function of awareness that a problem exists, recognition that options for problem resolution are available, personal characteristics of the adopter, perceptions of profitability associated with adoption, and psychosocial orientations of potential adopters (1, 3, 14, 16, 18, 19, 22). The diffusion model states that people will not consider adopting an innovation unless they are aware that a problem exists and that a socially acceptable solution is available. Individuals are not motivated to change their behaviors unless they perceive existing methods of problem resolution as being less appropriate than innovations.

The diffusion model posits that people learn about innovations through information systems; thus, access to information systems is critical to adoption. The model further suggests that personal characteristics of potential adopters can affect access to communication systems; therefore, personal factors that impede access to information systems can act as barriers to adoption of innovations.

An important element of the diffusion model is the perception of profitability. The model asserts that people will not consider adopting an innovation unless they perceive it to be profitable for them. People have little motivation to change existing behaviors if the innovation does not generate benefits in excess of what they are presently receiving for using existing behaviors.

The model further asserts that people will not be motivated to change existing behaviors unless they develop positive attitudes toward the innovation. Certain types of attitudes facilitate adoption. Individuals who develop attitudes that are favorable toward the innovation will have a higher probability of adopting the innovation.

The Farm Structure-Institutional Constraints Perspective. The second theoretical orientation used to examine adoption behaviors is the farm structure-institutional constraints perspective. This model basically argues that characteristics of the farm enterprise and the structure of the agricultural system in which farmers operate their businesses affect adoption decisions. This perspective suggests that the farmer's ability to act is a partial function of the constraints imposed by the farming system in which the individual operates. The individual is assumed to have relatively little influence on macro-level systems, but constraints imposed by the larger system influence everyday decision-making at the farm level.

The farm structure-institutional constraints model states that an individual's ability to act is extremely important in the adoption decision-making process. An individual may be prevented from adopting an innovation because of factors such as lack of access to economic resources, type of farming operation, and institutional barriers.

If adopting an innovation requires extensive expenditures of economic resources, the lack of access to money is an important barrier to adoption. Individuals who do not have necessary capital will be effectively barred from adoption even though they may wish to do so.

An important component of the farm structure-institutional constraint model (and the traditional diffusion model) is relevance of the innovation. Innovations must be relevant to the needs of the potential adopter or motivation to change existing practices will be low. Relevance is particularly important to the farm structure-institutional constraint model, because the present agricultural system strongly encourages product specialization. Some innovations will not be useful to certain types of agricultural producers.

Adoption decisions are always made in the context of institutional constraints. Institutions such as government agencies implement programs that influence the behaviors of individuals who participate in them. Federal programs designed to maintain high levels of food and fiber production are strongly affecting the present U.S. agricultural system. Rewards received for program participation are predicated on compliance with rules and regulations governing program implementation.

Participation in agricultural programs can affect adoption of innovations at the farm level. Government programs may establish conditions for participation that do not permit farmers to participate unless they adopt specific innovations. Conversely, requirements for program participation may make adoption of some types of innovations impossible because the innovations may be inconsistent with the goals of the government program.

Several types of variables will affect participation in the CRP. The modeling suggests that traditional diffusion-type variables combined with farm structure indicators will be a better explanatory model than either alone.

Methodology

Selection of Study Area. In late spring of 1988 we collected data from 84 landowners in a small watershed in central Ohio to examine the merits of the theoretical perspective just outlined. We purposefully selected the study area to satisfy the following criteria: (*1*) a large proportion of highly erodible land that would be eligible for inclusion in the CRP, (*2*) a population that had received extensive information by SCS field staff to enhance awareness of existing soil conservation programs, and (*3*) a study population that was heterogenous in terms of farm specialization.

The selected group satisfied each of these requirements. Farmland within the study area is on rolling hills and is subject to extensive erosion when cultivated. Thus, a large portion of the land is eligible for inclusion in the CRP and will be subject to other provisions of the Conservation Title.

The SCS field staff has devoted considerable effort to inform local farmers of government-sponsored soil conservation programs. Special education programs and economic incentives have been introduced in the area to motivate landowners to participate in soil conservation programs.

Data Collection. From the local SCS agent we secured a list of names and addresses of all landowners within the study area. We then mailed a questionnaire, a self-addressed, stamped return envelope, and a letter explaining the purpose of the study. Nonrespondents received a follow-up telephone call and two additional questionnaires by mail.

Questionnaires were mailed to 229 people, and 163 were returned, for a response rate of 71.2 percent. Of these, only 84 were sufficiently completed for use in the statistical analyses. Forty-five questionnaires were returned because the landowner had died or because the land was not in

Table 1. Sample characteristics (N = 84).

Characteristic	Mean	Standard Deviation
Age	55.1 years	14.5 years
Education	12.5 years	2.7 years
Acres cultivated	181.1 acres	299.5 acres
Acres owned	152.0 acres	170.4 acres
Acres rented	92.4 acres	180.6 acres
Acres owned but not cultivated	34.1 acres	53.7 acres
Days worked off farm per year	87.7 days	114.2 days
Source of farm income	Corn	42.3 percent
	Soybeans	10.9 percent
	Wheat	5.3 percent
	Hay	4.1 percent
	Vegetables	0.0 percent
	Beef	13.1 percent
	Swine	2.8 percent
	Poultry	0.1 percent
	Sheep	0.3 percent
	Dairy	3.8 percent
	Fruit	0.0 percent
	Other Crop	0.2 percent
Gross farm income	Less than $ 5,000	37.0 percent
	$ 5,000 to 9,999	7.1 percent
	$ 10,000 to 14,999	6.0 percent
	$ 15,000 to 19,999	7.1 percent
	$ 20,000 to 24,999	3.6 percent
	$ 25,000 to 29,999	2.4 percent
	$ 30,000 to 34,999	4.8 percent
	$ 35,000 to 39,999	1.2 percent
	$ 40,000 to 44,999	1.2 percent
	$ 45,000 to 49,999	1.2 percent
	$ 50,000 to 59,999	1.2 percent
	$ 60,000 to 69,999	3.6 percent
	$ 70,000 to 79,999	0.0 percent
	$ 80,000 to 89,999	1.2 percent
	$ 90,000 to 99,999	0.0 percent
	$100,000 and above	11.9 percent
	Missing data	10.7 percent

agriculture production. An additional 34 landowners said they were renting their land to farmers who had completed questionnaires and did not believe they should participate in the study.

Although the 84 study respondents constitute only a third of the landowners in the study area, they control the decision-making on approximately 18,077 acres of land. SCS data indicate that the total acreage in the study area is approximately 19,103. Therefore, the respondents control the decision-making in almost the entire watershed (18,077/19,103 = 94.6 percent of all land in watershed). Given that these respondents control nearly all of the land in the study area and that a large percentage of the original sample can be accounted for by the sampling procedure used to collect the data, the sample does represent the study area in terms of land use decision-making.

Characteristics of Study Sample. Characteristics of the study population (Table 1) show that the respondents as a whole are older people who have completed high school. Respondents tend to specialize in producing corn and soybeans (53.2 percent of gross farm income during the last three years), and a large minority earned less than $5,000 from farming during the previous crop year. Approximately 41.7 percent of the respondents indicated that they usually work at off-farm jobs (mean number of days worked off-farm was = 87.7).

Measurement of Study Variables. The study variables, chosen to represent elements of the theoretical perspective outlined were: farm structure factors, personal characteristics, psychosocial attitudes, past investments in soil conservation practices, and institutional constraints.

Farm structure factors examined in the study were farm specialization, acres farmed, ownership status, farm income, and days worked off-farm.

We measured farm specialization by asking the respondents to state the percentage of gross farm income derived from 13 different types of farm products during the past three years. We summed the percentages reported for corn, soybeans, wheat, and oats to form Percent Grain Farmers; the percentages reported for beef, swine, poultry, sheep, and dairy were summed to form the Percent Animal Farmer. The percentages reported for hay, vegetables, fruit, and other to form the Percent Other Farmer.

Other farm structure factors measured were:

► Acres farmed, as the number of acres the respondent usually had under cultivation each year.

► Ownership status, in terms of the number of acres the respondent owned at the time of the study.

► Farm income, according to total gross farm income for the 1987 crop year. (The categories used to collect the data ranged from less than $5,000 to more than $50,000); these were weighted from 1 to 11 with higher values representing higher income.)

► Days worked off-farm, in terms of the number of days the landowner usually worked off the farm each year.

Personal characteristics we examined were:

► Age, as years at last birthday.

► Education, as the number of years of formal education that the land-owner had completed.

► Knowledge of CRP, asking landowners to select a number on a scale of 1 to 10 that best represented their knowledge of the CRP. (A value of 0 represented No Knowledge, whereas a value of 10 represented Complete Knowledge.)

► Awareness of eligibility for the CRP, asking landowners to indicate if they owned land that was eligible for the CRP. (Persons who said they owned land eligible for inclusion in the CRP received a 0, and persons who were unaware of eligibility received a 1.)

Psychosocial attitudes assessed were efficiency-profitability criteria used in decision-making, attitudes toward government involvement in farming, awareness of erosion on own land, and attitude toward profitability of soil conservation programs. We measured the efficiency-profitability criteria scale in terms of the importance given to 13 criteria that could be used to make decisions about adopting soil conservation practices. Landowners were to circle a number, along a continuum of 0 to 9, that best represented the importance attached to each criterion. Item analyses (5) produced an alpha of .96, which means that the items are highly intercorrelated and that the weighting values can be legitimately summed into a composite scale score. Items composing the scale are presented in table 2.

We measured attitudes toward government involvement in farming using three Likert-type items (6, 20) that assessed government investment to increase production, government involvement in soil conservation programs, and attitude toward commodity programs. The possible responses ranged from "strongly agree" to "strongly disagree," with weighting values of 1 to 5 representing the responses. Higher values indicated more positive attitudes toward government involvement in agriculture. Item analysis produced an alpha of .67; thus, the items are sufficiently intercorrelated to justify summation of the weighting values to form a composite scale.

Table 2. Importance placed on factors affecting adoption of soil conservation practices (N = 84).

	Not Important		Slightly Important		Important			Very Important			MD*	X̄	SD
	0	1	2	3	4	5	6	7	8	9			
Awareness that soil erosion control practices are needed on your land	10 (11.9)	2 (2.4)	2 (2.4)	0 (0.0)	4 (4.8)	8 (9.5)	15 (17.9)	12 (14.3)	12 (14.3)	17 (20.2)	2 (2.4)	5.9	2.9
Savings on production input costs	10 (11.9)	6 (7.1)	0 (0.0)	1 (1.2)	7 (8.3)	10 (11.9)	15 (17.9)	10 (11.9)	10 (11.9)	13 (15.5)	2 (2.4)	5.4	2.9
Demonstrated profitability of the conservation practice	9 (10.7)	4 (4.8)	4 (4.8)	5 (6.0)	4 (4.8)	8 (9.5)	18 (21.4)	8 (9.5)	11 (13.1)	12 (14.3)	1 (1.2)	5.3	2.9
Necessity of buying new farm equipment to effectively use the conservation practice	12 (14.3)	7 (8.3)	2 (2.4)	2 (2.4)	8 (9.5)	6 (7.1)	10 (11.9)	6 (7.1)	12 (14.3)	17 (20.2)	2 (2.4)	5.2	3.2
Access to information about the conservation practice	11 (13.1)	5 (6.0)	0 (0.0)	1 (1.2)	7 (8.3)	10 (11.9)	20 (23.8)	9 (10.7)	8 (9.5)	10 (11.9)	3 (3.6)	5.2	2.8
Potential loss of production associated with adopting conservation practice	14 (16.7)	3 (3.6)	3 (3.6)	5 (6.0)	8 (9.5)	9 (10.7)	12 (14.3)	8 (9.5)	7 (8.3)	13 (15.5)	2 (2.4)	4.9	3.0

Factor												Mean	SD
Size of investment to adopt conservation practice	10 (11.9)	6 (7.1)	2 (2.4)	5 (6.0)	8 (9.5)	8 (9.5)	21 (25.0)	8 (9.5)	6 (7.1)	9 (10.7)	1 (1.2)	4.9	2.8
Disruption in the farm production system in order to use the conservation practice	12 (14.3)	5 (6.0)	2 (2.4)	6 (7.1)	7 (8.3)	11 (13.1)	16 (19.0)	6 (7.1)	9 (10.7)	9 (10.7)	1 (1.2)	4.8	2.9
Anticipated saving of your time due to adoption of the conservation practice	12 (14.3)	6 (7.1)	3 (3.6)	4 (4.8)	7 (8.3)	9 (10.7)	20 (23.8)	6 (7.1)	7 (8.3)	9 (10.7)	1 (1.2)	4.8	2.9
Availability of government subsidies to help pay the costs of adopting soil conservation practice	14 (16.7)	4 (4.8)	3 (3.6)	2 (2.4)	10 (11.9)	14 (16.7)	10 (11.9)	4 (4.8)	11 (13.1)	11 (13.1)	1 (1.2)	4.8	3.0
Cost to maintain conservation practice	11 (13.1)	8 (9.5)	2 (2.4)	3 (3.6)	7 (8.3)	12 (14.3)	20 (23.8)	5 (6.0)	6 (7.1)	9 (10.7)	1 (1.2)	4.7	2.8
Return on investment within 2 years for using the conservation practice	13 (15.5)	6 (7.1)	4 (4.8)	5 (6.0)	7 (8.3)	10 (11.9)	16 (19.0)	11 (13.1)	4 (4.8)	7 (8.3)	1 (1.2)	4.5	2.8
Necessity to acquire new farming skills to effectively use the conservation practice	15 (17.9)	5 (6.0)	1 (1.2)	3 (3.6)	8 (9.5)	14 (16.7)	18 (21.4)	5 (6.0)	7 (8.3)	6 (7.1)	2 (2.4)	4.5	2.8

*Missing data.

To measure awareness of soil erosion, we used a single, Likert-type item that assessed perception of soil erosion on the landowner's property. Higher values indicated greater awareness of soil erosion. We evaluated attitude toward profitability using a single Likert-type item that assessed perceived profitability associated with adopting soil conservation practices. Higher values indicated higher levels of perceived profitability.

Past investments in soil conservation practices were assessed in terms of the types of soil conservation practices used. We assessed Percent of Land Protected by Filter Strips according to the percent of cultivated fields protected by grass filter strips and evaluated Percent of Waterways Protected in of the percent of waterways protected by grass.

Institutional constraints were assessed with a single indicator called Participation in Government Programs. The variable was the number of government farm programs in which the landowner had participated during the past three years. Programs assessed were: low interest loans to purchase farm inputs, government corn program, wheat program, soybean program, dairy buyout program, loan storage program, and FmHA programs. We summed the number of farm programs to form a composite index of participation.

Study Findings

Descriptive and multivariate statistics were used to examine this data. Descriptive statistics were used to examine general trends in the data, while multivariate statistics assessed the merits of the theoretical perspective created to explain knowledge of and participation in soil conservation programs.

Descriptive Findings. The descriptive findings for Knowledge of the CRP (Table 3) show that more than 20 percent of the respondents had little knowledge of the program. This is surprising given the effort that the local SCS field staff had expended to inform landowners of existing soil conservation programs. The percentage reporting no knowledge of the CRP and other conservation programs would have been much higher had retired landowners responded to the questionnaire. During the course of data collection, we made telephone contact with nonrespondents. Many of these people were retired and indicated they were no longer involved in decisions about practices used on their land and did not know anything about new government conservation programs. Conventional methods of diffusing information apparently are inappropriate for retired landowners in the study area.

Findings for the Efficiency-Profitability Criteria Scale presented in table 2 demonstrate that the respondents place considerable importance on efficiency and profitability when making decisions about adopting soil conservation practices. The respondents perceived all of the criteria to be important.

The most important reason for adopting soil conservation practices was the awareness that erosion control practices were needed on the land. The least important consideration was the necessity to acquire new farming skills. Apparently, farmers are willing to develop new skills, if the reward for doing so is perceived to be sufficiently great.

Although many respondents indicated that awareness of a need for erosion control practices on the land was the most important reason for adopting conservation practices, only 28.6 percent of them stated that soil erosion was a problem on their farm. Approximately 14.3 percent of the respondents said productivity was being lost on some of the land they owned. These findings suggest that awareness of a need to use soil conservation practices will act as a motivator for a small minority of respondents, and only for a small portion of land owned by these farmers.

In the descriptive findings for Attitudes Toward Government Involvement in Farming (Table 4) the respondents were slightly favorable to the issues assessed. They were most favorable to government participation in soil conservation programs and least favorable to government investment in new ways to increase crop yields. The respondents were basically undecided about government commodity programs being a waste of money.

The respondents agreed slightly with the statement that soil erosion was problematic on their own land. They also indicated that adopting soil erosion control practices was profitable for people who use them.

Multivariate Findings. We used multiple regression and discriminant analyses to examine merits of the theoretical perspective when considering all variables simultaneously. Regression modelling was used to examine the data for perceived knowledge of the CRP. Discriminant analysis was used to predict participation in the CRP.

Table 3. Perceived knowledge of the Conservation Reserve Program (N = 84).

No Knowledge		Some Knowledge			Considerable Knowledge			Complete Knowledge				
0	1	2	3	4	5	6	7	8	9	10	$\overline{X}$	SD
10	8	1	24	10	6	7	3	7	1	7	4.2	2.9
(11.9)	(9.5)	(1.2)	(28.6)	(11.9)	(7.1)	(8.3)	(3.6)	(8.3)	(1.2)	(8.3)		

Table 4. Attitudes toward soil conservation and involvement of government in agriculture (N = 84).

Attitude Statement	Possible Response					MD	$\overline{X}$	SD
	Strongly Agree 1	Agree 2	Undecided 3	Disagree 4	Strongly Disagree 5			
1. Soil erosion is not a problem on my farm	8 (9.5)	23 (27.4)	26 (31.0)	21 (25.0)	3 (3.6)	3 (3.6)	2.9	1.0
2. Most soil erosion control practices do not increase farm profits for farmers who use them	3 (3.6)	18 (21.4)	16 (19.0)	40 (47.6)	6 (7.1)	1 (1.2)	3.3	1.0
*3. The federal government should not invest more money in the development of new ways to increase crop yields	5 (6.0)	26 (31.0)	20 (23.8)	24 (28.6)	8 (9.5)	1 (1.2)	3.0	1.1
*4. The government should not be involved in soil conservation programs	5 (6.0)	7 (8.3)	20 (23.8)	34 (40.5)	17 (20.2)	1 (1.2)	3.6	1.1
*5. Commodity programs are a waste of taxpayer money	7 (8.3)	18 (21.4)	22 (26.2)	25 (29.8)	9 (10.7)	3 (3.6)	3.1	1.1

*Attitude toward government involvement in agriculture produced an alpha of .67.

Factors Affecting Perceived Knowledge of the CRP. Knowledge of the Conservation Reserve Program was designated as the dependent variable and regressed against the independent variables discussed. The findings are presented in standardized regression coefficient form. All beta coefficients are significant at the .05 level.

$$Y = .934X_1 + .646X_2 - .364X_3$$

where Y is the perceived knowledge of CRP, X_2 is the participation in government programs index, X_2 is the percentage other farmer, and X_3 is the percentage of waterways protected by grass.

The regression findings revealed that the three-variable model explained approximately 64.7 percent of the variance in perceived knowledge of the CRP. The best explanatory variable was Participation in Government Farm Programs.

Respondents who perceived they were better informed about the CRP had the following characteristics: (1) participated in more government programs, (2) derived a higher percentage of their farm income from sources other than grain and animal production, and (3) had a smaller percentage of their waterways protected by grass cover.

The Participation in Government Programs Index findings suggest that more effort should be directed toward providing soil conservation information through governmental agencies that administer farm programs. When farmers contact agencies for information about commodity programs or low-interest loans for agricultural purposes, information about soil conservation programs should also be provided. Conservation information could also be included with program payments.

Farmers who derived a higher percentage of their gross farm income from hay, vegetables, fruits, and other crops tended to perceive themselves as being more knowledgeable of the CRP. Possibly these land operators have access to sources of information that are not readily available to grain and animal farmers. These types of farmers may be more aggressive in seeking information about government programs to help them survive in the competitive market economy.

One disconcerting finding is that farmers who reported more knowledge about the CRP had a smaller percentage of waterways protected by grass cover. These people either do not have a perceived need to protect waterways by grass cover or they are not motivated to retire waterways to permanent grass.

Factors Affecting Participation in the CRP. We asked the respondents to indicate whether they participated in the CRP. A positive response received a value of 1, and a negative response, a 0. Twenty-four respondents (28.6 percent) said they had enrolled land in the CRP.

Given the dichotomous nature of the dependent variable, we used discriminant modeling to examine the factors that differentiate CRP participants from nonparticipants. The discriminant analysis findings (Table 5) show that Awareness of Eligibility for CRP and the Efficiency Criteria Index were significant at the .05 level.

We assessed strength of association by squaring the canonical correlation, which gives an approximation of the amount of variance explained in the discriminant function scores by Participation in the CRP. The data presented in table 5 show that approximately 21.2 percent of the variance can be explained by participation in the CRP. The discriminant model correctly classified 76.2 percent of the respondents.

The discriminant findings revealed that awareness of eligibility on the part of farmers affected participation in the CRP. Farmers who were aware of owning land that was eligible for enrollment in the CRP tended to participate. This strongly suggests that information provided to landowners should include specifics about the number of acres that qualify for the CRP. General information about existence of the program is a necessary but not sufficient condition for participation. This could explain why perceived knowledge of the CRP did not enter the discriminant model.

Farmers with greater concern for efficiency and profitability tended to participate in the CRP. These farmers may very well believe they will receive a better return on the land via rental fees from the government than from agricultural production. This suggests that landowners should receive information about the economic benefits associated with CRP participation compared to expected returns from farming the land. If participation in the CRP can be shown to be profitable in the short-run, this information

Table 5. Disciminant analysis for participation in the Conservation Reserve Program and selected predictive variables (N = 84).

Variables in the Model	Standardized Disciminant Coefficients	Canonical Correlation Coefficient	Wilks' Lambda	Chi-Square	Significance Level	Percent Correctly Classified
Awareness of eligibility for CRP	.949	.460	.788	19.3	.000	76.2
Efficiency criteria scale	−.584					

could be a significant factor that would motivate them to enroll highly erodible land in the CRP.

Summary and Conclusions

The study findings revealed that a significant number of respondents were uninformed about the CRP, which means that conventional methods for diffusing information about new soil conservation programs are inadequate for the study group. Landowners will not likely be motivated to participate in conservation programs unless they receive sufficient information to make an informed decision.

The findings also showed that a significant number of the respondents were unaware of how many of the acres they owned qualified for inclusion in the CRP. Without specific information about eligibility, landowners cannot be expected to participate.

The regression analysis indicated that participation in government farm programs was significantly related to perceived knowledge of the CRP. This suggests that information provided through agencies commissioned to administer farm programs may increase knowledge of new soil conservation programs. But increased knowledge of the CRP will not necessarily increase participation in the CRP. Perceived knowledge of the CRP did not enter the discriminant model to predict participation in the CRP.

Type of farm speciality was shown to influence perceived knowledge of the CRP. This finding suggests that farming is not a homogenous occupation and implies that specific information may have to be developed for certain subgroups of farmers to make them knowledgeable of the CRP. Grain farmers most likely are different from animal farmers, and both speciality groups are different from farmers with "other" product specialties. If this interpretation is correct, designing information for specific farm interest groups probably will be necessary. Different methods to diffuse information to specific farm specialty groups may also be useful.

The discriminant modeling for "participation in the CRP" revealed that awareness of eligibility was the best discriminator of participation. Landowners with greater awareness of CRP eligibility tended to participate more often. This finding is consistent with the traditional diffusion model which argues that people will not adopt anything unless they become informed about the innovation being considered for adoption and clearly understand how they will benefit from adopting it.

The discriminant modeling also showed that perceptions of efficiency and profitability were important predictors of participation in the CRP. Landowners who used efficiency-profitability criteria in making decisions regarding the adoption of soil conservation practices tended to participate in the CRP. This suggests that some of the study respondents perceived participation in the CRP to be an efficient and profitable use of their highly erodible land resources. Information programs designed to "sell" participation in the CRP should stress the efficiency-profitability aspects of the program.

In summary, the study findings partially supported the theoretical perspective we developed to guide the study. Diffusion-type variables were the best predictors of participation in the CRP. This is contrary to much of the existing literature focusing on the voluntary adoption of soil erosion control practices, but the apparent inconsistencies can be explained.

Participation in the CRP is potentially profitable and entails little risk for the landowner once the contract is initiated. In contrast, voluntary adoption of many soil conservation practices without substantial subsidy from the federal government is seldom without risk. Many soil conservation practices are not profitable in the short-run and may not be profitable even in the long-run (12, 21). The diffusion model can be effectively applied only to situations in which the innovation being considered for adoption will generate extensive benefits for the adopter (1, 22, 24).

Educational programs combined with existing economic incentives should motivate farmers to participate in the CRP and other subsidized soil conservation programs. This assumes, of course, that landowners will be adequately informed of eligibility requirements and will be made aware of the relevance of the programs to their specific type of farming operation. Greater targeting of information to specific farm specialty groups may be required to meet this goal.

REFERENCES CITED

1. Brown, Lawrence A. 1981. *Innovation diffusion: A new perspective.* Methuen Press, New York, New York.
2. Buttel, F. H., and Louis E. Swanson. 1986. *Soil and water conservation: A farm structural and public policy context.* In Stephen B. Lovejoy and Ted L. Napier [editors] *Conserving Soil: Insights from Socioeconomic Research.* Soil Conservation Society of America, Ankeny, Iowa. pp. 26-39.
3. Camboni, Silvana M. 1984. *The adoption and continued use of consumer farm technologies: A test of a diffusion-farm structure model.* Doctoral Dissertation. Department of Agricultural Economics and Rural Sociology, Ohio State University, Columbus.
4. Carlson, John E., and Donald Dillman. 1983. *Influence of kinship arrangements on farmer innovativeness.* Rural Sociology 48(2): 183-200.
5. Cronbach, L. J. 1951. *Coefficient alpha and the internal structure of tests.*

Psychometrika 16: 297-334.
6. Edwards, Allen. 1957. *Techniques of attitude scale construction.* Appleton-Century-Crofts, New York, New York.
7. Ervin, David E., and Robert Washburn. 1981. *Profitability of soil conservation practices in Missouri.* Journal of Soil and Water Conservation 36(2): 107-111.
8. Halcrow, Harold G., Earl O. Heady, and Melvin L. Cotner, editors. 1982. *Soil conservation policies, institutions, and incentives.* Soil Conservation Society of America, Ankeny, Iowa.
9. Hooks, Gregory M., Ted L. Napier, and Michael V. Carter. 1983. *The correlates of adoption behaviors: The case of farm technologies.* Rural Sociology 48(2): 309-324.
10. Lovejoy, Stephen B., and Ted L. Napier, editors. 1986. *Conserving soil: Insights from socioeconomic research.* Soil Conservation Society of America, Ankeny, Iowa.
11. Lovejoy, Stephen B., and Ted L. Napier. 1988. Institutional constraints to soil conservation on steep slopes. In W. C. Moldenhauer and M. W. Hudson [editors] *Conservation Farming on Steep Lands.* Soil and Water Conservation Society, Ankeny, Iowa. pp. 107-114.
12. Mueller, D. H., R. M. Klemme, and T. C. Daniel. 1985. *Short- and long-term cost comparisons of conventional and conservation tillage systems in corn production.* Journal of Soil and Water Conservation 40(5): 466-470.
13. Napier, Ted L. 1987. *Farmers and soil erosion: A question of motivation.* The Forum for Applied Research and Public Policy 2(2): 85-94.
14. Napier, Ted L., Cameron S. Thraen, Akia Gore, and W. Richard Goe. 1984. *Factors affecting adoption of conventional and conservation tillage practices in Ohio.* Journal of Soil and Water Conservation 39(3): 205-209.
15. Napier, Ted L., Cameron S. Thraen, and Silvana M. Camboni. 1988. *Willingness of land operators to participate in government sponsored soil erosion control programs.* Journal of Rural Studies 4(4): 339-347.
16. Napier, Ted L., Cameron S. Thraen, and Stephen L. McClaskie. 1988. *Adoption of soil conservation practices by farmers in erosion prone areas of Ohio: The application of Logit modeling.* Society and Natural Resources 1(2): 109-129.
17. Napier, Ted L., and D. Lynn Forster. 1982. *Farmer attitudes and behavior associated with soil erosion control.* In H. G. Halcrow, E. O. Heady, and M. L. Cotner [editors] *Soil Conservation Policies, Institutions and Incentives.* Soil Conservation Society of America, Ankeny, Iowa. pp. 137-150.
18. Napier, Ted L., and Silvana M. Camboni. 1988. *A social science perspective of conservation of soil resources.* In H. A. Henderson and Tim K. Meeks [editors] *Alternative Uses of Highly Erodible Agricultural Land.* Tennessee Valley Authority, Muscles Shoales, Alabama. pp. 165-177.
19. Napier, Ted L., and Silvana M. Camboni. 1988. *Attitudes toward a proposed government-sponsored soil conservation program.* Journal of Soil and Water Conservation 43(2): 186-191.
20. Nunnally, James C. 1978. *Psychometric theory.* McGraw-Hill Book Co., New York, New York.
21. Putman, John, and Klaus Alt. 1988. *Erosion control: How does it change farm income?* Journal of Soil and Water Conservation 42(4): 265-267.
22. Rogers, Everett M. 1983. *Diffusion of innovations.* The Free Press, New York, New York.
23. Swanson, Louis E., Silvana M. Camboni, and Ted L. Napier. 1986. *Barriers to the adoption of soil conservation practices on farms.* In Stephen B. Lovejoy and Ted L. Napier [editors] *Conserving Soil: Insights from Socioeconomic Research.* Soil Conservation Society of America, Ankeny, Iowa. pp. 108-120.

24. van Es, John C. 1983. *The diffusion adoption tradition applied to resource conservation: Inappropriate use of existing knowledge.* The Rural Sociologist 3(4): 26-32.

15

Participation of Eligible Landowners in the Conservation Reserve Program: Results and Implications of Survey Research, 1986-1988

J. Dixon Esseks and Steven Kraft

The first sign-up for the Conservation Reserve Program (CRP) took place in March, 1986 (*7, 8, 9, 10, 11, 12, 13*); subsequent sign-ups occurred in May and August of 1986, February and July of 1987, and February and July-August 1988. After seven sign-ups, approximately 28 million acres of the 45 million authorized under the law were entered into the program (*19*). Approximately 34 percent of this total came in the fourth sign-up period (February, 1987), when a special incentive payment was offered in addition to the annual per-acre rent.

During a sign-up period, a landowner or operator can submit a sealed bid indicating the minimum annual payment the bidder is willing to accept from the federal government in return for converting the land from crop production to vegetative cover or trees. The bid must be low enough to be acceptable to the Agricultural Stabilization and Conservation Service (ASCS), and the land must meet size, cropping history, and erodibility requirements.

As the Conservation Reserve Program has evolved, a number of public policy issues have emerged, including incentives to encourage more bidding, implications of conservation compliance for the CRP, use of the program as a supply management tool, its implications for trade negotiations, benefits and costs of increasing the target size of the program, the possibility of using different criteria for determining land eligibility, and the relationship of the CRP to concerns about the quality of surface and groundwater supplies (*18*).

Since its initiation in early 1986, the Conservation Reserve Program has undergone significant changes (7, 8, 9, 10, 11, 12, 13). Eligibility has been liberalized with regard to erodibility and entering land being planted to trees. In addition, eligibility has been extended to filter strips, wetlands, and erosion-prone floodplains. Maximum acceptable rental rates have increased in many counties, and 1987 appropriations legislation requires local ASCS committees to not accept bids that exceed the going cash rental rates for the same quality land.

Local implementation practices have led to modification of some of the regulations. For example, local ASCS officials have permitted landowners without cropping histories from commodity programs to establish histories by using receipts from grain elevators and similar documents. Additional incentives encourage landowners to bid land into the program; e.g., during the February 1987 sign-up period, farmers received an incentive payment figured on the number of corn base acres entered into the CRP (20). These changes mean that to be successful in bidding land into the program, landowners must be well-informed about the program and cognizant of program modifications. If the CRP is to reach its 1990 goal of keeping 45 million acres of highly erodible acres of cropland out of production, many more landowners must participate in the program. Here, we explore some of the economic and institutional factors that are likely to determine the ease of enrolling the remaining 17 million acres. Insights gained from analyzing the reserve should be useful for effectively designing and implementating similar programs based on voluntary incentives to protect groundwater from agricultural contamination—part of the planning process incorporated in section 319 of the 1987 amendments to the Clean Water Act (18).

Data Collection Methods

We collected survey data from a number of sites in 1986, 1987, and 1988. Based on the quantity of land eligible for inclusion in the CRP or participation during the first three sign-up periods for the reserve, two survey sites were selected. For one study, the survey sites encompassed 59 counties throughout the country (4, 5) that had either 100,000 acres of eligible land or 20,000 to 99,999 acres of eligible land comprising at least 20 percent of the county's total cropland. Working with the district conservationists in these counties, we identified townships with high concentrations of CRP-eligible land. The study sample consisted of randomly selected owners of land within those townships, currently registered with the county offices of the Agricultural Stabilization and Conservation Service (ASCS). In the summer of 1986, 1,173 landowners were interviewed using a telephone survey with an overall response rate of 79 percent.

For the second study (5) we used the level of previous participation in the reserve to identify four counties in the midwest as study sites. we measured previous participation based on the proportion of eligible land successfully enrolled in the CRP during the first three sign-up periods. Data collected were from counties in Illinois, Iowa, Minnesota, Missouri, and Wisconsin having either 100,000 acres of eligible land or 20,000 to 99,999 acres of eligible land comprising at least 20 percent of the county's total cropland. From these counties we determined the average level of participation during the first three sign-ups, and the standard deviation. We added or subtracted one-half of one standard deviation unit from the mean. Counties having a level of participation less than the mean minus the one-half standard deviation unit or more than the mean plus one-half standard deviation unit became potential counties for study.

Actual county selection from the candidate counties was based on location, (not close to a large urban area), agroecological considerations (to achieve a mix of farm types based on dominant enterprises), and administrative unit (state boundaries). We selected four counties for study: Grant County, Wisconsin; Pike County, Missouri; Richard County, Illinois; and Wayne County, Iowa. Working closely with the district conservationist of the Soil Conservation Service (SCS) in three of the counties, we identified watersheds characterized by high levels of soil loss and land eligible for the CRP. In the fourth county we identified as our study area two adjoining townships with high levels of land eligible for the reserve. Using soil maps and tract maps in conjunction with data on farm units from the ASCS, we identified the owners within each area who were eligible for the CRP according to the criteria in force as of the first three sign-ups. In March-April, 1987, we initiated a census of all these landowners through telephone interviewing. The 99 to 160 respondents per site reflected response rates of 80 percent to 89 percent. Through local ASCS records, we verified landowners' responses regarding their bids on land to be entered in the CRP.

In the fall of 1988, after the seventh CRP sign-up, we resurveyed, by telephone, landowners surveyed in the two preceding studies. Across the various sites, from 77 percent to 92.4 percent of the original interviewees or their successors participated.

Findings of the 1986, 1987, and 1988 Studies

Data collected during the 1986 and 1987 studies revealed that large proportions of the landowners surveyed who had not participated in the CRP lacked accurate information about eligibility criteria regarding erodibility and use for land entering the reserve, prevailing rental rates for land entering the reserve during the most recent previous sign-up, complementarity between the CRP and conservation compliance, and the bonus paid for acres of corn base retired through the program during the fourth sign-up. In short, these eligible nonparticipants lacked information essential to make informed decisions about participating in the reserve.

In an analysis of information gaps among potential participants in the CRP,[1] we tested landowners with eligible land who had not participated in the fourth sign-up for information gaps that might help explain their nonparticipation. The data included the nonparticipants' knowledge about eligibility, prevailing CRP rents, the corn bonus inducement for the reserve, and conservation compliance (a complementary portion of the Conservation Title). Although we went to great lengths to interview only eligible landowners across the four sites of the 1987 study, 27 percent to 39 percent of the nonbidders did not perceive themselves as eligible for the reserve, 21 percent to 77 percent underestimated or had no idea of the prevailing reserve rental rate, 15 percent to 46 percent had not heard of the corn bonus, and 24 percent to 39 percent were ignorant of conservation compliance. From 57 percent to 79 percent displayed at least one of these four information gaps, and 22 to 56 percent had at least two gaps.

Results from stepwise, logistic regression analysis indicated that, other things being equal, landowners who were knowledgeable about one feature of the program tended to be also informed about the others. These associations suggest that the information network between the USDA agencies and the farming community somehow systematically excludes certain landowners. If landowners are not part of the network through which the USDA disseminates policy information, they are at a disadvantage in terms of assessing the relevance of policy initiatives vis-a-vis their own situations.

Given that the CRP has existed since 1985 and that seven sign-up periods have passed, we anticipated, in the 1988 study, that nonparticipating eligible landowners would be better informed about the program than they had been in the earlier studies. Data in table 1 report the reasons eligible landowners gave for never participating in the CRP by submitting a bid. The five survey areas consist of the 59 counties surveyed in the 1986 study and the four single-county sites of the 1987 study. Respectively, across these five study areas, 27 percent, 41 percent, 43 percent, 60 percent, and

[1]Esseks, J. Dixon, and Steven E. Kraft. "Information Gaps Among Potential Participants in the Conservation Reserve Program." Paper presented at the 43rd annual meeting of the Soil and Water Conservation Society of America, Columbus, Ohio, July 31-August 3, 1988.

Table 1. Reasons given by owners for never bidding on CRP lands, by survey areas.

Reasons	59 Counties	Grant County (WI)	Pike County (MO)	Richland County (IL)	Wayne County (IA)
			Survey Areas*		
			%		
Since 1986, did not have any eligible land	18	14	14	12	12
(Percent of nonbidders who gave this reason in the previous survey)	(47)	(50)	(44)	(40)	(33)
Land that is or might be eligible for CRP is unlikely to earn more in CRP than in crops.	56	53	53	55	50
(Percent of respondents giving reason who reported a cash rent that was actually less than the most recent maximum USDA paid-for CRP land in county)	(27)	(46)	(37)	(44)	(20)
Ten-year contract too long	11	6	8	14	4
Need land for livestock operation	7	24	8	4	14
Want to farm, like to farm, not ready to retire, this land should be farmed	10	4	5	0	6
Land will or might be sold	1	4	0	2	4
Opposed to this kind of program on principle	6	8	3	6	4
Number in subsample	250	49	36	49	50

*The 59 counties correspond to the 1986 study. The survey areas of Grant, Pike, Richard, and Wayne Counties correspond to the 1987 study.

38 percent of the landowners resurveyed in 1988 had never submitted a bid to include land in the CRP. The data in table 1 show that relatively few of these nonparticipants viewed their land as being ineligible because of erosion. The second row of figures in the table represents the number of nonparticipants who reported that their land was ineligible when they were interviewed the first time in either 1986 or 1987; the decrease is significant—ranging from 21 to 36 percentage points.

Across all the columns, half or more of the eligible nonparticipants surveyed in 1988 stated that their land could earn more in crop production than in the CRP. Of the nonparticipants, however, 20 to 46 percent said that cash rents that they could obtain from CRP rents was actually less than the most recent maximum the USDA paid for reserve land in their counties. In most cases, this contradiction is explained by the landowners' not knowing the most recent maximum rental rate the USDA paid for land placed in the CRP. Among all owners eligible to participate in future sign-ups for the reserve, 28 to 66 percent could not accurately state the maximum rental rate, plus or minus $5. These data indicate that a large pool of potential participants in the CRP lack basic information about one of the prime financial motivations for entering the program.

Similarly, the 1988 study revealed that only 42 to 61 percent knew about filter strip eligibility for the reserve, and only 20 to 31 percent were aware that the portion of reserve land planted to trees need be only one-third highly erodible land rather than the usual two-thirds required for other land. Fewer than 30 percent of the surveyed landowners knew that the local ASCS committees were obliged to pay less than the maximum acceptable rental rate if the parcels had low productivity. Owners did not know that land placed in the CRP could be used for dual purposes—growing trees for future sale or charging fees for hunting or recreational uses of the reserve land. It was noted that recent contact (since the previous Christmas) with a USDA agency significantly increased the likelihood of a landowner's having knowledge about these aspects of the program.

These findings from the 1988 study support the results from the early studies that landowners eligible to participate in the CRP often lack accurate information about the program to use in making informed decisions about participation. This is especially the case for rental rates the USDA pays for reserve land. We do not necessarily support an offer system for the CRP in which the USDA would announce in advance the rental rates they would be paying and landowners would decide to participate in the reserve based on this rate. Rather, we support making information about past maximum rental rates readily available to all potential participants.

CRP Hypotheses and Methodology

In previous writings (1, 4, 6), we adopted the interpersonal interpretation of random utility maximization underlying discrete choice theory (14, 22) to study economic and institutional factors influencing participation in the CRP through bidding. We estimated a discrete choice model using logistic regression. From survey data, we studied owners who had land eligible and analyzed their participation in the bidding activity to place land in the CRP.

In the earlier analyses based on data collected in 1986 and 1987, we hypothesized that a number of variables would be important in predicting the likelihood of landowners with eligible land offering a bid to place the land in the CRP. First, we hypothesized that landowners' knowledge of the maximum bid level in an area would be a useful proxy for the extent of their involvement in the network disseminating information about USDA programs and their knowledge of eligibility criteria; their involvement in the network would positively affect their likelihood of bidding.

We further hypothesized that income from farming would negatively affect their likelihood of bidding; as farming increased in importance to the family, the value of maintaining crop bases for commodity programs would increase correspondingly, along with maintaining flexibility to respond to changes in commodity prices. For the same reason, we expected that as the percentage of a landowner's tillable land in annual crops increased, the likelihood of the owner's bidding land into the CRP would decrease. We hypothesized, however, that, other things being equal, as the percent of agricultural sales from annual crops increased, the likelihood of a landowner's bidding land into the program would increase. As the landowner derived more income from annual crops, alternative uses in which marginal agricultural land could be employed, i.e., supporting livestock would be fewer. Consequently, if the land was not very productive for crops, it could be "retired" in the CRP and still earn a return.

Landowner's age also would seem to be important in predicting the likelihood of their bidding land into the reserve—with no strong a priori reason to expect either a positive or a negative sign. We expected that education also would be related positively to the likelihood of landowners' trying to place land in the CRP. Given the different eligibility criteria and the bidding process, we projected that individuals who had more education would be better able to make informed judgments about the reserve and arrive at a competitive bid than would individuals with less education.

We further expected that with landowners' increasing belief that erosion was a problem on their farm, they would tend to place land in the reserve; we measured this using the percentage of the landowner's land that he or she believed had an erosion problem. We hypothesized that if a landowner had problems getting credit, he or she would be more likely to bid land into a program that offered guaranteed revenues over a 10-year period. Finally, we expected that previous contact with USDA agencies for conservation assistance would increase the likelihood of participating in the CRP.

Probability of a landowner offering land for the reserve through a bid was estimated using a nonlinear maximum likelihood estimation of the cumulative logistic probability function of the form, as follows:

(1) $P = [1/1 + \exp(-BX)]$

where P equals the odds that a particular choice—offering land for inclusion in the reserve—will be made. For estimation purposes, P takes the value of 1 if the landowner has offered land, and 0 otherwise; B's equal estimated coefficient; and X's equal explanatory variables just described.

Results from the Estimation

Table 2 presents results from the estimation. The pseudo R-squares of Cragg-Uhler (*3, 16*) and McFadden (*14, 16*) indicate that, with the exception of Richland County in Illinois, the model was reasonably successful in explaining the likelihood of landowners' offering land for inclusion in the CRP. For the Cragg-Uhler R^2, values range from a high of 0.46 for Grant County, Wisconsin, to a low of 0.21 for Richland County. All the hypothesized explanatory variables are statistically significant in the expected direction in at least one of the study sites.

The variables that are significant at each site differ in the four study areas, reflecting differences in the underlying nature of the agricultural economy. For example, in comparison to the other sites, Wayne County had one of the highest participation levels during the first three sign-ups, in which more than 30 percent of the eligible land was offered to the reserve. The area was also extremely depressed economically as a result of the agricultural financial crisis. As a result, the variable CREDIT (difficulty in getting credit) showed more variation in Wayne County than in the other three study sites. It follows that this is the only site where CREDIT is a significant variable.

Similarly, the relatively greater role of cattle-based livestock enterprises is reflected in the variable INCANP (percent of agricultural revenue from annual crops) for the sites in Grant, Pike, and Wayne counties. The only variable significant in all the sites is ERPRO (percent of land with erosion problems). This variable indicates that as landowners' appreciation of erosion on their land increases, the likelihood increases for their offering land for inclusion in the CRP.

The policy question addressed in this study is: How is more participation in the CRP achieved by landowners with eligible land? Findings presented in table 2 provide insight to this question. Following Kohn, Manski, and Mundel (*15*), the results reported in table 2 were used to calculate change in the likelihood of owners' offering land for the reserve

Table 2. Results of logistic regression explaining the probability of eligible landowners' bidding land into the CRP*.

Variable	Expected Sign	Grant County (WI)	Pike County (MO)	Richland County (IL)	Wayne County (IA)
EXPAND Landowner's knowledge of maximum bid	+	0.017†	—	0.017‡	—
INC Income from farming	−	− 0.009‡	—	− 0.005	− 0.005
ANNERP Percentage of tillable land in annual crops	−	− 0.026†	—	—	− 0.037‡
AGE	+/−	− 0.776§	0.675	—	—
EDUC	+	0.113§	—	—	—
INCANP	+	0.014§	0.023†	—	0.017‡
ERPRO Percent land with erosion problems	+	0.016‡	0.020†	0.024†	0.010§
CREDIT Difficulty in getting credit	+	—	2.115†	—	0.346§
USDAAG Contact with USDA agency for conservation assistance	+	—	2.115†	—	0.904‡
Constant		0.947	− 1.790†	0.011	− 0.167
Cragg-Uhler (R²)		0.42	0.38	0.18	0.33
McFadden (R²)		0.27	0.25	0.12	0.21

*Models with variables having coefficients significant at at least the 0.15 level.
†Significant at 1 percent level.
‡Significant at 5 percent level.
§Significant at 10 percent level.
Note: All statistical tests are one-sided except for age.

in response to changes in the independent variables that can be influenced by conservationists. In terms of the CRP, conservationists, through agencies such as the Soil Conservation Service, the Agricultural Stabilization and Conservation Service, Soil and Water Conservation Districts, and Cooperative Extension, have the capability to influence the variables in the model: EXPAND (landowner's knowledge of program features),

ERPRO (landowner's knowledge of erosion on his/her land), and USDAAG (recent contact with a USDA agency for conservation assistance). We call these "program" variables.

Table 3 reports changes in the likelihood of offering land when these program variables are changed while the other variables are held at their mean values. To evaluate the effect of changing EXPAND, it was first set at the level of no information about the maximum reserve rent ceiling and then adjusted to "perfect" information—accurately knowing the ceiling. With the level of all other variables held at their means, this shift resulted in a change in the likelihood of offering land, ranging from 5.4 percentage points in Grant County to 24.6 percentage points in Richland County. A change in USDAAG from no contact to contact resulted in a change in the likelihood of offering land, ranging from 21.9 percentage points in Wayne County to 36.2 percentage points in Pike County. Similar results exist when landowners' appreciation of erosion on their land increases. A change from the lowest quartile to the highest quartile results in an increase in the likelihood of offering land, ranging from a low of 7 percentage points in Grant County to a high of 36.1 percentage points in Richland County.

Regression results on bid information are supported by data collected during the 1988 study. We asked landowners still eligible to offer land for inclusion in the CRP to specify the annual per-acre rent that would attract them to place land in the CRP. Across the five-study areas, 14 to 25 percent of eligible landowners selected rental rates no higher than the most recent maximum acceptable rental rates for their counties. Results also indicated that a substantial number of eligible landowners would offer land

Table 3. Percentage-point changes in the likelihood of landowners with eligible land offering it for inclusion in the CRP in response to variation in program variables.

	Site			
Program Variable	Grant County (WI)	Pike County (MO)	Richland County (IL)	Wayne County (IA)
EXPAND	5.4	—	24.6	—
EXPRO	7.0	26.9	36.1	16.0
EXPAND + EXPRO	19.0	—	55.8	—
USDAAG	—	36.2	—	21.9
EXPRO + USDAAG	—	55.5	—	36.1

Changes were calculated using regression results reported in table 2, and independent variables not changing set at their mean values.
Program variables are defined in table 2.

to the CRP at rental rates no more than $10 above the most recent maximum. From 32 to 55 percent of the eligible landowners reported such rental levels.

These changes are substantial and can be brought about by conservation agencies taking a more proactive stance in terms of informing landowners about bidding activity in their counties—passing on information about the potential level of erosion on the landowner's land and the extent of the erosion; explaining how the reserve is implemented; specifying the various eligibility options under which land can enter the reserve (potential erosion, filter strips, tree planting, wetlands, and scour erosion); and clearly presenting the options for using land placed in the CRP in terms of cover and possibilities of allowed remunerative uses for enrolled land (planting trees and renting out recreational opportunities).

The Industrial Marketing Approach

The approach advocated corresponds to what is commonly referred to as industrial marketing: the marketing of goods and services to business and industrial firms, commercial enterprises, nonprofit institutions, and governmental agencies for use in the production of goods and services or for resale (2, 21). Essentially, agencies such as the Cooperative Extension Service, the Soil Conservation Service, soil and water conservation districts, the Agricultural Stabilization and Conservation Service, and the Forest Service are marketing conservation practices to farm owners/operators in the hopes the practices will be adopted resulting in reduced erosion and enhanced water quality. The CRP embodies a set of such practices implemented through a voluntary program authorized by public policy. Given its voluntary nature, the approach of industrial marketing is appropriate. Usefulness of this approach changes when conservation policy shifts from being voluntary, as in the CRP, to being mandatory/regulatory as with conservation compliance. In the first instance, agency personnel responsible for marketing the conservation practices or the program must demonstrate their efficacy with regard to the owner's/operator's goals and extant operation. In the second instance, the police power of the state establishes the efficacy of the practices or program and the focus of agency personnel shifts from demonstrating appropriateness of the practices to an owner/operator to one of monitoring the extent of compliance the owner/operator achieves.

Industrial marketing is different from the marketing of consumer goods. The role of "sellers" in industrial marketing is to demonstrate that the marketed products or services directly support the goals of their potential clients. For many businesses the prime goal is to make a profit. In industrial marketing the sellers must be able to show that their products and services are compatible with the buyer's existing production processes or business activities. Consequently, this type of marketing frequently rests on the direct personal involvement of sellers with buyers, sellers' knowledge of buyers' production constraints, sellers' willingness to redesign their products or services to conform to buyers' needs, and an understanding of buyers' business goals. An important aspect of industrial marketing is market segmentation—separating potential buyers into subgroups that have similar characteristics in terms of goals, product needs, nature of buying decisions, and business characteristics. As a result, different marketing strategies can be designed and implemented for distinct market segments.

In terms of soil conservation, the industrial marketing perspective points to agencies such as the Soil Conservation Service "marketing" voluntary soil conservation practices by emphasizing how the practices will complement farmers' efforts to attain their goals. This entails adequately informing landowners about conservation policy, changes in conservation policy, and the mechanics of policy implementation. To this end, conservationists must have data available to demonstrate that conservation policies and practices are compatible with existing enterprises on the farm and the level of technology embodied in these enterprises.

If conservation policies and practices can ever change existing production technologies or on-farm enterprises, then conservationists must be able to predict the consequences for the farm operation and attainment of the owner's/operator's goals. Conservationists also must be able to redesign conservation strategies to render them compatible with the particular needs of the individual farm. Finally, conservationists must be able to segment their market of farm operators and farmland owners into groups that have similar characteristics in terms of their goals, the nature of their farm businesses, adoption decisions, existing conservation practices, and views on soil conservation. Although some conservation agencies have started to adopt this approach, the business environment conditioning the reactions of farmers and landowners must be accorded much greater recognization. Agency personnel must clearly demonstrate how conservation policies and practices affect the overall structure of the farm business.

Summary and Conclusions

Data from the three studies and the bidding model point out that many landowners lack adequate information to make informed decisions about participating in the CRP. The nature and extent of these informational gaps have changed over the course of CRP implementation. Nonetheless, serious barriers to successful implementation of the CRP still exist. The bidding model suggests that eligible nonparticipants will respond favorably to improved information about program incentives, agency contact, and information about soil loss on their land. Data also show that direct agency contact results in more precise information about the program that should be translated into better informed active bidders. Industrial marketing may be a useful guide in developing marketing strategies for conservation practices and voluntary conservation programs. The informational problems identified and the marketing strategy proposed are not unique to the CRP; they have parallels with other policies based on voluntary adoption of conservation practices to protect the environment. If the agencies involved take a proactive position vis-a-vis their "clientele," industrial marketing can provide a mechanism for translating that proactive position into actual programs.

REFERENCES CITED

1. Aly, Hassan, J. Dixon Esseks, and Steven E. Kraft. 1989. *Conservation programs of the 1985 Food Security Act: Lessons from implementation and implications for the future.* In A. H. Nielsen and A. Dubgaard [editors] *Economic Aspects of Environmental Regulations in Agriculture.* Kiel: Wissenschafts-Verlag Vauk pp. 85-98.
2. Corey, E. Raymond. 1983. *Industrial marketing: Cases and concepts.* Prentice Hall, Englewood Cliffs, New Jersey.
3. Cragg, J. G., and R. S. Uhler. 1970. *The demand for automobiles.* Canadian Journal of Economics 3: 386-406.
4. Esseks, J. Dixon, and Steven E. Kraft. 1986. *A national survey of farmer attitudes about the Conservation Reserve Program.* The American Farmland Trust, Washington, D.C.
5. Esseks, J. Dixon, and Steven E. Kraft. 1986. *Landowner views of obstacles to wider participation in the Conservation Reserve Program.* Journal of Soil and Water Conservation 41(6): 410-414.
6. Esseks, J. Dixon, and Steven E. Kraft. 1988. *Why eligible landowners did not participate in the first four sign ups of the Conservation Reserve Program.* Journal of Soil and Water Conservation 43: 251-256.
7. Federal Register. 1986. *Conservation Reserve Program, Interim Rule.* 51:8,780-8,787.
8. Federal Register. 1986. *Conservation operations, reconsideration and appeal procedures.* 51:12,826-12,829.
9. Federal Register. 1986. *Conservation Reserve Program amendments.* 51:17,167-17,169.
10. Federal Register. 1986. *Highly erodible land and wetland conservation.* 51:23,496-23,514.
11. Federal Register. 1986. *Conservation operation reconsiderations and appeal procedures.* 51:26,535-26,538.

12. Federal Register. 1987. *Conservation Reserve Program—final rule.* 52:4,265-4,275.
13. Federal Register. 1989. *Conservation Reserve Program—interim rule.* 54:801-803.
14. Hensher, David A., and Lester W. Johnson. 1981. *Applied discrete-choice modelling.* Croom Helm, London.
15. Kohn, M. G., C. F. Manski, and D. S. Mundel. 1974. *An empirical investigation of factors which influence college going behavior.* Report R1470NSF. Rand Corporation, Santa Monica, California.
16. Maddala, G. S. 1983. *Limited-dependent and qualitative variables in econometrics.* Cambridge University Press, Cambridge, Massachusetts.
17. U.S. Congress, House of Representatives. 1985. *H.R. 2100: The Food Security Act of 1985.* 99th Congress, 1st Session, Washington, D.C.
18. U.S. Congress, House of Representatives. 1986. *Conference report: Amending the Clean Water Act.* Report 99-1004. 99th Congress, 2nd Session, Washington, D.C.
19. U.S. Department of Agriculture. 1989. *Conservation Reserve Program: Includes seventh sign-up results.* Agricultural Stabilization and Conservation Service, U.S. Department of Agriculture, Washington, D.C..
20. U.S. Department of Agriculture. 1987. *Secretary of Agriculture Lyng has announced a fourth CRP sign-up.* Notice CRP-54. U.S. Department of Agriculture, Washington, D.C.
21. Webster, Frederick E., Jr. 1984. *Industrial marketing strategy.* John Wiley and Sons, New York, New York.
22. Wrigley, Neil. 1985. *Categorical data analysis for geographers and environmental scientists.* Longman, London.

16

Participation and Perceived Impacts of the Conservation Reserve Program in Iowa

Gordon Bultena, Paul Lasley, and Eric Hoiberg

Excessive soil erosion on cropland has reached "crisis" proportions in American society (2). Especially troublesome is the recent finding that many of this nation's farmers with highly erodible cropland display little or no inclination to implement needed erosion-control measures (4). This neglect may diminish, given the conservation provisions of the Food Security Act of 1985 (sodbuster, swampbuster, conservation compliance, and Conservation Reserve Program). These programs have introduced a more coercive element into decision-making. Farmers must now either implement needed erosion-control measures on their highly erodible cropland or lose important financial benefits provided by the USDA (commodity payments and loans).

The 1985 conservation provisions have drawn mixed reviews, characterized by some as forward-looking, ambitious, much-needed, and far-reaching in their implications, and by others as diminishing farmers' property rights. In any case, the provisions substantially transform the conservation challenge in this country—perhaps not eliminating soil erosion but at least bringing it under better control (3). At the same time, the long-term effectiveness of these provisions has been questioned (5, 9, 17).

Perspective and Hypotheses

Patterns of Participation in the Conservation Reserve Program (CRP). The importance of various social and economic factors for farmers' decisions to take part in the CRP is unclear. The distribution of CRP acreage between regions and within states suggests that the program has proven most appealing in marginal cropping areas. The Mountain states and Northern Plains have comparatively high rates of CRP participation, whereas the Corn Belt has lower rates. Rental payments for CRP land tend to be highest, relative to land values, in the poorer farming areas, suggesting that farmers are making rational decisions about the best (most profitable) uses of their land.

Surveys of officials in public agencies administering the CRP (12, 13) reveal the pervasive view that nonparticipation of eligible farmers is a result of inadequate rental payments relative to the production values of the land. A recent study of farm operators in several Midwestern states (6) found that financial considerations were important to CRP decision-making.

Social factors also have been shown to be important to CRP participation. For example, perceived severity of soil erosion and awareness of the CRP provisions can affect participation (6, 11, 12). Also, farmers' hostility to the imposition of more governmental regulations, as well as skepticism about the government's eventual enforcement of the conservation provisions, may shape their decisions about such participation (12, 16).

Past research has shown that farm scale is often an important determinant of farmers' orientations and behavior. Farmers on the larger, more capital-intensive operations tend most often to acknowledge soil erosion problems on their farms, are usually the most supportive of conservation ideology and government programs, and are the most likely to implement needed conservation measures. However, the utility of these findings in predicting farmers' participation in the CRP is unclear.

On the one hand, persons on the larger, more capital-intensive operations may be the best informed about the CRP, the most ideologically inclined to support governmental intervention in soil conservation (8) and the most amenable to adopting new approaches (15). These arguments suggest that, for farmers with highly erodible land, it is the larger-scale operators who should be the most attracted to the CRP. On the other hand, by providing increased income security and more time to pursue off-farm employment, the CRP may hold special appeal to farmers on the smaller-than-average operations (7), partly because it offers a convenient mechanism for early retirement or withdrawal from agriculture.

We tested these alternative arguments by correlating some farm enterprise characteristics of Iowa farm operators with their CRP participation. We also examined the importance of selected attitudinal orientations for CRP participation—namely, personal familiarity with the program, assumed governmental intent to ultimately enforce the new conservation initiatives, and perceived governmental propriety of forcing farmers to adopt conservation practices.

Impacts of the CRP. Although the CRP is expected to help reduce soil erosion, improve water quality, and stabilize farm incomes, it also portends some adverse socioeconomic impacts. Predicting these impacts is complicated, however, by the uncertainty of farmers' use of their CRP lands after completing the 10-year contracts.

Several types of impacts are anticipated from the CRP. Some claim that the program will principally benefit persons on the smaller, less viable operations by providing them income stability and more time to pursue off-farm employment (7). Others see the program as accelerating the trend toward larger operations by providing a convenient vehicle for farmers on the smaller operations to leave agriculture (18, 19).

Some tenants probably will experience pressure to relinquish claims to CRP land (18). Also, inflation in land prices may occur as investors compete to acquire CRP acreage, and as some farmers with added income from CRP payments expand their operations (10, 14, 18). Because of resentment of the coercive nature of the program, "wildcat farming" outside of governmental programs also could increase, resulting in further natural resource exploitation (19).

The CRP is expected to have some important impacts on farm families. Securing a more stable income from CRP participation should enhance the ability of some farmers to remain in agriculture by stabilizing land values and permitting expansion of their operations. The program also may promote greater residential and family stability and contribute to an improved level of living. But it could bring demographic upheaval in some areas as older operators use the program to leave agriculture. Thus, the CRP is likely to have both positive and negative impacts upon farm communities.

The amount of land enrolled in the CRP will be a major determinant of the nature and severity of these impacts. Increased or more secure incomes of CRP participants should be beneficial to businesses offering consumer goods but disadvantageous to persons selling farm inputs, especially seed, fertilizer, pesticides, and machinery (1, 7, 14, 19).

Sample and Procedures

Sample. Our data are from a 1988 survey of Iowa farm operators, in which we sent questionnaires, including items about the CRP, to a statewide representative sample of 3,624 farmers. Of these, 2,276 questionnaires were returned. After adjusting for persons who were ineligible (had left farming or were deceased), this represented a 64 percent response rate.

CRP Participation. We asked several questions to measure respondents' participation in the CRP. First, they reported the number of acres, if any, of "highly erodible" cropland in their farming operations. Nearly half (46 percent) had such cropland, which ranged from 1 to 1,500 acres. Of those with erodible cropland, the average was 147 acres. In total, there was nearly 140,000 acres of highly erodible cropland on the respondents' farms.

Second, respondents with highly erodible cropland reported the number of acres, if any, they had enrolled in the CRP as of January 1, 1988. This enrollment ranged from 0 to 600 acres, with the average being 23 acres. For the subgroup of respondents participating in the CRP, enrollment averaged 83 acres. The respondents had over 23,000 acres enrolled in the CRP.

Two variables were derived from the acreage information. First, the number of acres enrolled in the CRP provided a measure of the magnitude of each respondent's CRP participation. However, this measure introduces a possible bias in that some farmers, especially large operators, are likely to have more erodible land and, thus, greater opportunity for participation. To overcome this problem, we calculated a second measure of participation—the proportion of a farmer's highly erodible farmland enrolled in the CRP. This measure provides a better indicator of commitment to the program than the actual number of acres enrolled. Both measures of participation are used in the data analysis.

Perceived Impacts from the CRP Program. We used seven items to measure respondents' perceptions of the likelihood of some environmental, economic, and social impacts that have been projected for the CRP. A five-item response format permitted answers of "very likely," "somewhat likely," "uncertain," "somewhat unlikely," and "very unlikely."

Farm-Enterprise Characteristics and Attitudes. Farm-Enterprise Characteristics. We examined five structural characteristics. Total Farm Acreage ranged from 2,000 to 9,000 with a median of 360 acres. Acres Owned ranged from 0 to 9,000 with a median of 194 acres. Acres Rented ranged from 0 to 3,100, with a median of 228 acres. Gross Farm Sales, which had fixed response categories, ranged from less than $2,500 to more than $500,000. Total Farm Assets, the estimated current market value of all farm assets (land, buildings, machinery, livestock), ranged from less than $10,000 to more than $5,000,000.

Anticipated Enforcement of the CRP. Respondents rated the likelihood of the government carrying out and enforcing the conservation provisions of the 1985 farm bill. Responses were on a five-point scale ranging from "very likely" to "very unlikely." A majority of the farmers (56 percent) anticipated that enforcement was likely, only 16 percent foresaw it as unlikely, and 28 percent were undecided.

Propriety of Governmental Intervention. We measured respondents' perceptions about the propriety of governmental action in controlling soil erosion using the item: "The government should be able to force farmers to adopt soil conservation practices if they have erosion problems." Responses were on a 5-point scale ranging from "strongly agree" to "strongly disagree." Responses were almost equally split: 43 percent agreed, 42 percent disagreed, and 15 percent were undecided.

Awareness of the CRP. Respondents indicated their familiarity with the CRP on a four-point scale that ranged from "not at all informed" to "very well informed." Most (79 percent) perceived themselves as being informed, but only 30 percent believed they were very well informed.

Plans for Highly Erodible Cropland. In the query about future plans for highly erodible cropland not protected by the CRP, respondents could select from four possible actions: (*1*) eventually enrolling all of this land in the CRP (selected by 4 percent of those with highly erodible cropland), (*2*) obtaining an approved conservation plan and protecting some or all of this land through conservation compliance (69 percent), (*3*) not taking any action and thus losing eligibility to participate in USDA programs (7 percent), and (*4*) uncertainty about their eventual actions (20 percent).

Statistical Procedures. The data were analyzed using Pearsonian correlation and one-way analysis of variance. Relationships and differences between subgroups are considered statistically significant if they are at or beyond the .05 level of probability.

Findings

Highly Erodible Cropland. Nearly half of the respondents (46 percent) reported having "highly erodible" cropland. The amount of this cropland differed widely, ranging from 1 to 1,500 acres. About one-third (31 percent) of those with highly erodible land had over 160 acres in this category, and 10 percent had over 320 acres.

The proportion of highly erodible cropland within farmers' overall operations also varied widely, ranging from none to 100 percent. Of those with such land, the average erodible land to total acres was 35 percent, and the median was 24 percent. One-fourth (27 percent) of those with highly erodible land had half or more of their total acres in this category. About 44 percent had a third or more.

To determine how highly erodible cropland was distributed among certain types of farm operations, we examined two measures of the amount of erodible land: (1) number of highly erodible acres, and (2) the proportion of these erodible acres comprised of all land in the farming operation. As shown in table 1, conclusions about the socioeconomic correlates of erosion problems are highly contingent upon the measure used. On the average, the larger operations had the greater number of erodible acres. But erosion problems were the most prominent relative to total acreage in the smaller operations.

CRP Participation. Persons with highly erodible cropland were asked how many acres, if any, they had enrolled, as of January 1988, in the CRP. Only a fourth (26 percent) of those eligible were participating in the program. Furthermore, most (90 percent) had no plans to bid acres into this program in the future.

Of respondents participating in the CRP, 80 percent had enrolled half or more and 43 percent all of their highly erodible cropland. Thus, for persons participating in the program, the amount of enrolled acreage is substantial.

Table 1. Relationships of farm-enterprise characteristics to amount of highly erodible cropland.

Farm-enterprise Characteristics	Measure of Erodible Cropland*	
	Number of Acres	Percent of Total Acreage
	Correlation†	
Total acres	.33‡	−.22‡
Acres owned	.25‡	−.07§
Acres rented	.23‡	−.21‡
Gross farm sales	.28‡	−.22‡
Total farm assets	.25‡	−.17‡

*Analysis includes all respondents.
†Pearsonian correlation.
‡Statistically significant at .01 level.
§Statistically significant at .05 level.

Table 2. Relationships of farm-enterprise characteristics to level of participation in the Conservation Reserve Program.

Farm-enterprise Characteristics	Measure of CRP Participation*	
	Number of Acres Enrolled	Percent of Erodible Acreage Enrolled
	——— Correlation† ———	
Total acres	.29‡	.00
Acres owned	.33‡	.03
Acres rented	.13§	−.05
Gross farm sales	.13§	−.09
Total farm assets	.06	−.01

*Analysis includes only persons with one or more acres enrolled in the CRP.
†Pearsonian correlation.
‡Statistically significant at .01 level.
§Statistically significant at .05 level.

Correlates of CRP Participation. In our analysis of the relationships of farm-enterprise characteristics to CRP participation, we examined both the absolute and the relative numbers of eligible acres enrolled in the program. Whereas several of the farm-enterprise variables were significantly associated with enrolled acres, these relationships were negligible when examined in the context of the proportion of erodible land enrolled (Table 2).

Our findings point up the importance, when testing for socioeconomic correlates of CRP participation, of considering how participation is measured (whether as acres enrolled or as proportion of eligible acres enrolled). When using total acres, we found the larger, more capital-intensive farm operators disproportionately enrolled in the CRP. But when measuring participation as the proportion of eligible acres enrolled, no significant relationships were found with the farm-scale variables.

We also analyzed the importance of selected attitudinal orientations for CRP participation. Contrary to expectations, no differences were found in enrollment levels (using percentage of erodible acreage enrolled) between persons with divergent views about the likelihood of the government enforcing the conservation provisions of the 1985 Farm Bill (Table 3). But we did find differences in CRP enrollment between persons with opposing views about the propriety of the government forcing farmers to adopt soil conservation practices. As expected, those who most adamantly opposed governmental intervention in agriculture had lesser involvement (percent of erodible acres enrolled) than those who approved this intervention (Table 4).

Farmers who said they were very well informed about the CRP program were more active in this program than those rating themselves as less well-informed, or uninformed (Table 5). But these data do not clearly show whether well-informed persons were disproportionately attracted to the program, or if their participation was responsible for their becoming more knowledgeable than others.

Finally, we examined the effects on CRP participation of respondents' future plans for their highly erodible cropland. As expected, farmers anticipating the eventual placement of all of their erodible land in the CRP program had substantially higher levels of participation than those contemplating other actions, or inaction (Table 6).

Table 3. CRP participation, by perceived likelihood of the government enforcing the conservation provisions of the 1985 farm bill.

Perceived Likelihood of the Government Enforcing the Conservation Provisions	Measure of CRP Participation*	
	Number of Acres Enrolled	Percent of Erodible Acreage Enrolled
Very likely	23	18
Somewhat likely	26	19
Undecided	24	17
Somewhat unlikely	14	10
Very unlikely	12	7
Group differences†	None	None

*Analysis includes only persons with highly erodible cropland.
†Differences were tested using one-way analysis of variance (Scheffe procedure).

Table 4. CRP participation, by perceived propriety of the government forcing farmers to adopt soil conservation practices.

Propriety of Government Action	Measure of CRP Participation*	
	Number of Acres Enrolled	Percent of Erodible Acreage Enrolled
Strongly support	35	24
Somewhat support	22	18
Uncertain	22	19
Somewhat opposed	21	18
Strongly oppose	19	9
Group differences†	None	1>5

*Analysis includes only persons with highly erodible cropland.
†Differences were tested using one-way analysis of variance (Scheffe procedure).

Table 5. Participation in the Conservation Reserve Program, by awareness of the program.

Awareness of CRP	Measure of CRP Participation*	
	Number of Acres Enrolled	Percent of Erodible Acreage Enrolled
Not at all informed	12	4
Relatively uninformed	23	10
Somewhat informed	12	11
Very well informed	38	27
Group differences†	4>3	4>1, 2, 3

*Analysis includes only persons with highly erodible cropland.
†Differences were tested using one-way analysis of variance (Scheffe procedure).

Table 6. CRP participation, by plan for highly erodible cropland.

Plan for Highly Erodible Cropland	Measure of CRP Participation*	
	Number of Acres Enrolled	Percent of Erodible Acreage Enrolled
Place it all in the CRP	52	56
Put some or all under conservation compliance	22	12
Take no action: Lose USDA commodity price supports	8	3
Uncertain	20	14
Group differences†	1>2, 3, 4	1>2, 3, 4

*Analysis includes only persons with highly erodible cropland.
†Differences were tested using one-way analysis of variance (Scheffe procedure).

A subgroup of farmers (7 percent of those with erodible land) said they were planning no conservation actions on their highly erodible land and did not intend to place it in the CRP or under a conservation plan. By their inaction, they are knowingly jeopardizing their eligibility to participate in or preventing themselves from becoming enrolled in USDA programs.

Those planning no actions were differentiated from others by their smaller scale of operation. Collectively, they farmed fewer acres and had smaller gross farm incomes and financial assets. They also reported the greatest amount of erodible land, as measured by the proportion these acres comprised of their total land base. Despite the comparative prominence of their erosion problems, they were less likely than others to have ever had an approved conservation plan. Not surprisingly, they were the most adamant in their opposition to governmental intervention in soil conservation and were united in rejecting the notion that farmers should be required to implement an approved conservation plan.

Anticipated Impacts of the CRP. Respondents rated the likely occurrence of each of seven environmental, economic, and social impacts that have been projected for the CRP. They were the most optimistic about environmental benefits from the program. Over four-fifths (85 percent) believe the CRP will reduce soil erosion, and 67 percent predict lessened chemical contamination of groundwater (Table 7).

Respondents had lesser expectations for economic benefits from the CRP. About half (48 percent) felt the CRP will reduce commodity surpluses, but 28 percent saw this as an unlikely outcome. Only two-fifths (38 percent) saw the program as bringing improvements in farmers' financial well-being. Three-fifths were concerned that the program will likely place added financial burdens on local agribusinesses (Table 7).

The most pervasive concerns about the CRP were for its potentially adverse impacts on rural communities. Respondents perceived the CRP as having deleterious effects on local agribusinesses. Also, over half (54 percent) saw the program as leading to increased off-farm migration. The respondents, however, were sharply divided in their judgments about whether or not the quality of life in rural areas would decline as a result of the program (Table 7).

We predicted that CRP participants would hold more favorable impressions of the program's impacts than would nonparticipants. To test this, we analyzed responses to the individual impact items and calculated an "impact scale score" for all seven items.

The data only partially support the argument that CRP participation would influence judgments about impacts of the program (Table 8). We found differences by participation for four of the seven impact items and for the overall scale score. In explaining the respondents' impact assessments, the distinction between participation and nonparticipation in the program was shown to be more important than the actual extent of participation. Nonparticipants consistently were the most critical of the program.

Summary and Conclusions

Our findings on farmers' CRP participation reveal that the way participation is measured is vital to the conclusions that can be drawn. When participation is defined according to total acreage enrolled, larger operations are over represented. But if participation is defined as the proportion of

Table 7. Perceived likelihood of environmental, economic, and social impacts from the Conservation Reserve Program.

Impact	Perceived Likelihood of Impact Occurrence					
	Very Likely	Somewhat Likely	Uncertain	Somewhat Unlikely	Very Unlikely	Total
Environmental						
Substantial reduction of soil loss on highly erodible land	47	38	8	4	3	100
Fewer farm chemicals in the groundwater	20	47	17	11	5	100
Economic						
Improvement of the financial well-being of farmers	9	29	36	17	9	100
Increased financial stress on local agribusiness	18	41	23	14	4	100
Substantial reduction in the surpluses of farm commodities	10	38	24	22	6	100
Social						
Decline in the quality of life in rural communities	6	20	37	27	10	100
Increased number of people leaving their farms	18	36	22	18	6	100

Table 8. Impact assessment, by level of CRP participation.

Impact Item	Level of CRP Participation*				Significant Differences Between Groups‡
	None†	Low‡	Medium§	High	
		Average Item Score†			
Environmental					
A—Reduced soil loss	4.2	4.5	4.6	4.5	1<2, 3
B—Less chemical contamination	3.6	3.9	3.9	3.8	ND
Economic					
C—Improved financial well-being of farmers	3.0	3.3	3.3	3.4	1<2, 4
D—Increased financial stress on agribusinesses	3.7	3.3	3.8	3.7	2<3, 4
E—Reduced commodity surpluses	3.2	3.3	3.2	3.4	ND
Social					
F—Decline in quality of life	2.9	2.5	2.6	2.8	ND
G—Increased displacement of farmers	3.5	3.0	3.4	3.3	1>2
Impact scale score§	21.8	23.1	23.3	24.1	1<2, 3, 4

*Analysis includes only persons with highly erodible cropland. The four participation categories are based upon the number of acres enrolled in the CRP: None is 0 acres, Low is 1-36 acres, Medium is 37-90 acres, and High is 91 or more acres.
†Item scores were obtained by assigning the five response categories a score of 1 (very unlikely) to 5 (very likely).
‡Differences between subgroups were tested for statistical significance using one-way analysis of variance (Scheffe procedure).
§The impact scale score measures respondents' overall perceptions of favorability impacts from the CRP. In calculating this score, responses were scored from 1 (very likely) to 5 (very likely), except for items D, F, and G, in which this scoring was reversed. The scale scores ranged from 7 (anticipates undesirable impacts) to 35 (anticipates desirable impacts).

highly erodible land enrolled, no particular socioeconomic group predominates in the CRP.

Persons with lower levels of CRP awareness were the least often enrolled. Also, those who were opposed to the government forcing farmers to adopt conservation practices tend to reject the program.

Farmers who were not planning to protect their highly erodible cropland through either the CRP or conservation compliance were distinguished from those anticipating such action by their smaller farming operations and financial assets, larger amount (proportionate to all land) of highly erodible acreage, frequent absence of approved conservation strategies for protecting erodible cropland, and adamanant opposition to the government being able to force farmers to practice erosion control. As a group, these persons constitute a fringe element that is prepared to operate outside the confines of governmental regulations despite the likely penalties to be incurred by this action.

We examined respondents' perceptions of the likelihood of various benefits and costs accruing from the CRP. The greatest anticipation was for environmental benefits from reduced soil loss and less chemical contamination of water. Opinion was divided about economic benefits to be realized from the program, with many perceiving these benefits would be negligible. Of greatest concern were some potentially adverse impacts of the CRP on rural communities, specifically in boosting off-farm migration and in imposing greater financial stress on local agribusinesses. As predicted, participants felt more positive about CRP impacts than did nonparticipants.

Enrollment in the CRP in Iowa has fallen short of desired levels, but many of the acres not now enrolled will eventually be brought under conservation compliance. Because of the high productivity of Iowa cropland, retaining erodible land in commodity production has obviously proven more appealing to many farmers than placing it in the CRP.

ACKNOWLEDGEMENT

Journal Paper No. J-13482 of the Iowa Agriculture and Home Economics Experiment Station, Ames; Projects No. 2726 and 2550.

REFERENCES CITED

1. Bartlett, E. T. 1988. *Social and economic impacts of the Conservation Reserve Program*. In *Impacts of the Conservation Reserve Program in the Great Plains*. General Technical Report RM-158. U.S Forest Service, Fort Collins, Colorado. pp. 52-54.

2. Batie, Sandra S. 1983. *Soil erosion: Crisis on America's croplands?* The Conservation Foundation, Washington, D.C.
3. Benbrook, Charles M. 1986. *The science and art of conservation policy.* Journal of Soil and Water Conservation 41: 285-291.
4. Bultena, Gordon L., and Eric O. Hoiberg. 1988. *Preserving topsoil: A study of U.S. farmers' commitments to resource conservation.* Society and Natural Resources 1: 159-165.
5. Durban, Clarence. 1987. *Meeting the challenge.* Journal of Soil and Water Conservation 42: 70-71.
6. Esseks, Dixon J., and Steven E. Kraft. 1988. *Why eligible landlords did not participate in the first four sign-ups of the Conservation Reserve Program.* Journal of Soil and Water Conservation 43: 251-256.
7. Flora, Jan L., and Cornelia Butler Flora. 1988. *The effects of different production systems, technology mixes, and farming practices on farm size and communities: Implications for the Conservation Reserve Program.* In Impacts of the Conservation Reserve Program in the Great Plains. General Technical Report RM-158. U.S. Forest Service, Fort Collins, Colorado. pp. 75-83.
8. Hoiberg, Eric O., and Gordon L. Bultena. 1981. *Farm operator attitudes toward governmental involvement in agriculture.* Rural Sociology 46: 381-390.
9. Lovejoy, Stephen B. 1988. *The unfulfilled promise of the 1985 Food Security Act.* Journal of Soil and Water Conservation 43: 85.
10. Napier, Ted L. 1988. *Anticipated changes in rural communities due to financial stress in agriculture: Implications for conservation programs.* In Impacts of the Conservation Reserve Program in the Great Plains. General Technical Report RM-158. U.S. Forest Service, Fort Collins, Colorado. pp. 84-90.
11. Napier, Ted L., and Silvana M. Camboni. 1988. *Attitudes toward a proposed soil conservation program.* Journal of Soil and Water Conservation 43: 186-191.
12. Nowak, Pete, and Max Schnepf. 1987. *Implementation of the conservation provisions in the 1985 Farm Bill: A survey of county-level U.S. Department of Agriculture agency personnel.* Journal of Soil and Water Conservation 42: 285-290.
13. Purvis, Amy K., and Vernon L. Sorenson. 1987. *A survey of Michigan CES county extension directors, ASCS county executive directors, and SCS district conservationists.* Staff Paper 87-50. Department of Agricultural Economics, Michigan State University, East Lansing.
14. Reichenberger, Larry. 1987. *Reeling from the reserve.* Farm Journal (2): 16-19.
15. Rogers, Everett. 1983. *Diffusion of innovations.* The Free Press, New York, New York.
16. Sand, Duane. 1988. *Where are the conservationists?* Journal of Soil and Water Conservation 43: 278.
17. Stoddard, Glenn M. 1987. *Implementing the Conservation Title of the Food Security Act: The unfinished agenda.* Journal of Soil and Water Conservation 42: 93-94.
18. Strange, Marty. 1988. *Social impacts of the Conservation Title.* Journal of Soil and Water Conservation 43: 73-74.
19. Woods, Mike D., and Larry Sander. 1988. *The economic impact of farm policy changes on rural communities: Conservation provisions—a case in point In Impacts of the Conservation Reserve Program in the Great Plains.* General Technical Report RM-158. U.S. Forest Service, Fort Collins, Colorado. pp. 60-65.

17

Participation in the Conservation Reserve Program In Kentucky: Implications for Public Policy

Louis E. Swanson, Kurt Stephenson, and Jerry R. Skees

The conservation provisions of the 1985 Food Security Act (FSA) represent a qualitative change in agricultural policy. This is especially the case for Conservation Compliance (CC), sodbuster, and swampbuster which introduced quasi-regulatory provisions. Each of these policies relies upon negative incentives to encourage participation. In contrast, FSA's most encompassing and expensive conservation initiative, the Conservation Reserve Program (CRP), is better categorized as continuing within the tradition of multi-objective voluntary agricultural conservation policies.

The Policy Contest

The New Deal conservation provisions were based upon at least three assumptions: (*1*) that conservation programs were to be voluntary, (*2*) that the primary economic concern was the loss of soil productivity attributable to soil erosion, and (*3*) that the primary cause of soil erosion was a depressed farm economy (*1, 6, 9*). During the intervening 55 years, these primary assumptions have been discarded or substantially modified.

The third assumption was the first to be critiqued. In the early 1950s, Heady and Allen (*3*) set forth the now widely accepted alternative assumption that most conservation techniques are not profitable in the short-run, even with relatively higher farm prices. Therefore, though the previous assumption was acceptable for a very depressed farm economy, the implied ancillary assumption that good times would be accompanied by an expansion of conservation measures was not acceptable. Those authors proposed that conservation policy should not assume that conservation practices will be adopted—even during periods of higher farm prices—given the short-term planning horizons of most farmers. They concluded that conservation policy should continue to be voluntary and that a mutually beneficial partnership between the profit goals of farmers and the ecological goals of larger society be forged based upon some type of cost-sharing formula.

The second assumption proved to be more resilient. Not until this decade did research suggest that the greatest economic costs of soil erosion were off the farm and not from loss of soil productivity (2). These studies did not deny that highly erodible land experienced serious losses in productivity; rather, they pointed out that only about 10 percent of the land was subject to this type of erosion. The policy conclusion was that conservation programs should be targeted to highly erodible land. Moreover, off-site costs of soil erosion and other forms of environmental pollution from production agriculture—such as chemical contamination of groundwater—were estimated to be vastly greater than previously thought (4). Burgeoning public concern over ecological and human health degradation brought traditionally nonagricultural interest groups into the farm policy process with important results for the 1985 FSA.

Thigpen (11) discussed the emergence of the conservation dimension of what Don Paarlberg has referred to as the New Agenda in agricultural policy. He argued that the beginnings of the qualitative changes witnessed in the 1985 FSA can be traced to the implicit historical policy of permitting the externalization of productivity, ecological, and health costs of soil erosion. Thigpen pointed out that in the years since the 1933 Agricultural Adjustment Act, farmers' relative political clout has diminished as the farm population has declined, while the political influence of urban-based environmental and public health interest groups has expanded.

By the late 1970s, soil erosion was increasing as marginal land was brought into production. Farmers at that time were responding to higher farm prices resulting primarily from favorable international trade conditions. The silting of rivers and waterways, nitrogen poisoning of rivers and lakes, and growing evidence of groundwater chemical pollution were just three of many factors that encouraged nonfarm groups to enter the agricultural policy debate. They no longer were convinced that traditional voluntary conservation programs were viable policies for reducing the adverse off-site consequences of soil erosion. Many also believed that the Soil Conservation Service (SCS) had not received the resources necessary for voluntary programs to succeed, especially during the 1980s, when cost-sharing programs were cut back rather than expanded. Unlike the traditional agricultural interest groups, nonfarm people were not against direct environmental regulation of production agriculture.

During the 1980s the farm policy process has been complicated further by the fiscal crisis of the federal government. Deficit reduction has become a primary congressional and administration goal. As a result, cost-sharing conservation programs, such as Heady and Allen advocate as being the best means of promoting voluntary conservation practices (3), were perceived to be politically unattractive.

The first and cornerstone assumption of traditional agricultural policy— uncoerced voluntarism—was at best gravely bent with the CC, sodbuster, and swampbuster provisions. Although direct regulation has not occurred, these cross-compliance provisions certainly cannot be construed as a continuation of voluntarism—unless the lexicon includes a term for negative voluntarism when given a choice between two undesirable outcomes. Provisions of the CRP, on the other hand, are clearly voluntary, relying on positive economic incentives.

The CRP is similar to the Soil Bank, but differs significantly because it is targeted to highly erodible land whereas the Soil Bank was open to all farmland owners. Like the Soil Bank, however, CRP is a multi-goal conservation program. What makes CRP so interesting from a policy perspective is the politically diverse coalition that produced it.

The Multiple Goals of CRP

We can identify at least six general goals for the CRP, either in the legislation or from the literature: (1) supply control of particular agricultural commodities through acreage reduction, (2) reduction of soil erosion on highly erodible land, (3) improvement of groundwater quality, (4) reduction of the federal deficit, (5) increased farm family income during a period of farm recession, and (6) enhancement of wildlife habitat.

As with any multi-goal policy, emphasis on any one dimension will likely dilute the effectiveness of others. As might be expected, CRP has been criticized for trying to do too much and thereby not doing anything well (5, 7, 8, 10). For instance, the goals of reducing erosion on highly erodible land and improving water quality would seem to be highly compatible. However, Phipps (5) has noted that by not sharply distinguishing between wind erosion in a state like Colorado and sheet and rill erosion in Tennessee, the program is less targeted upon the latter types of erosion, which most directly affect groundwater. Moreover, a multi-goal conservation policy also might conflict with other goals of the 1985 FSA, such as improving international trade. Robert Paarlberg has critiqued the CRP, and other acreage reduction programs, as a form of unilateral disarmament in the current trade war with the European Economic Community.

Sample and Research Methodology

The data reported here come from a panel analysis of Kentucky farmers. A panel design involves two or more points in time for the same units of analysis—in our case, farmers. In this way, we can infer economic and social change for Kentucky farmers.

We surveyed the same farmers at two points in time: spring of 1986 and spring of 1988 (for the production years 1985 and 1987, respectively). At both points, we asked questions about conservation, with specific queries about CRP in the second survey (1988). For our study of CRP, these two points in time are significant: the first contains data prior to the first sign-up period, and the second encompasses information on CRP up to the spring 1988 sign-up.

The sampling frame is the Agricultural Stabilization Conservation Service (ASCS) state list, which in Kentucky includes almost all of its farmers. We used a five percent sample of this list. As would be expected with an ASCS list, it included quite a few farmland owners who do not produce agricultural products. Therefore, we sent out two survey instruments in 1986—one for farmers and one for nonfarmers. The response rate was 65 percent; 1,074 farmers responded. In addition, we conducted a random sample of the nonrespondents to assess if they had any systematic biases toward key individual and farm structural variables. We did not detect any systematic error.

For the second point in time (1988), we sent surveys only to farmers who had responded to the 1986 survey. Again, we mailed two surveys, one to those who have continued farming and one to those who have left farming. The response rate for the 1988 follow-up survey was 84 percent.

Our data analysis sought to determine on which factors CRP participants differed from non-CRP participants. The analysis involved a relatively straightforward and simple comparison of means for statistically significant differences. We included only farmers with class 3 land or worse, on the assumption that they might be qualified to participate in the CRP.

Table 1 presents data for farmers enrolled through the first seven Kentucky sign-ups (through February 1, 1989). Therefore, ASCS data for Kentucky contain the most recent sign-up information, though the survey goes only through the spring 1988 sign-up. Also, the survey data can be

Table 1. CRP program in Kentucky.*

	Kentucky	Sample
Average contract size	55-60 acres	38 acres
		(Standard deviation = 34)
Average bid level	$50-$70	$54.7
Participation rate	7%	11%
Acres eligible	1.5 million	
Acres enrolled	380,000	
Distribution of enrolled acres		
Pool 1	90%-96%	
Pool 2	4%-10%	
Pool 3	<1%	

*Kentucky data from the state ASCS office, Lexington, Kentucky.

generalized only to the state level; therefore, no estimates from the survey are made for the three pools.

Two conclusions are evident from table 1. First, the survey data set is comparable to the actual state sign-up performance and bid levels. Second, a small proportion of Kentucky's farmers have enrolled land in the program even though land in all regions of this state are eligible.

Findings

The findings are presented in two steps. The first step examines factors in which CRP participants and nonparticipants do not differ (Table 2). The second step reviews factors that have statistical significance (Table 3). Within each step the factors are divided into three characteristic categories: individual farmer, farm structure, and attitudinal/behavior intention. Although this format does not fit the usual scientific style, we think it more succinctly and clearly presents the results.

Item 2A from table 2 lists individual-level characteristics that were not significant. Several of these are of particular interest given the adoption and diffusion literature on conservation. Many studies have identified education and family income as important determinants in conservation behavior, with higher educated and wealthier farmers more likely to use conservation techniques (4).

Item 2B lists nonsignificant farm structural factors. Of interest here is the absence of influence for land-rental variables, and the lack of influence of total government payments, suggesting that dependence on government program payments has not directly influenced who signs up for the CRP. But most interesting is the absence of any association between debt-asset ratios and whether a Kentucky farmer signed up for CRP, which suggests that the farmer's financial condition did not influence participation.

Indicators of scale, measured in gross sales and total acres in production, also were not significantly different for CRP participants and non-participants. This suggests that there may be little impact on supply.

Among the attitudinal and behavioral intention factors (Item 2C) none of the conservation attitudinal questions were significant. The behavioral

Table 2. Similarities between CRP and non-CRP participants by:

(2A) Individual characteristics
Number of years worked off farm
Household income
Education level

(2B) Farm structure characteristics
Acres of pasture owned
Acres of land rented from others
Total acres (owned and rented in)
Gross sales
Debt/asset ratios
Land values
Total government payments
Use of minimum tillage planting

(2C) Attitudes and behavioral intentions
Extension office helpful in farm success
Attending county extension meetings
Planning to quit farming

Table 3. Significant differences between CRP and non-CRP participants by:

(3A) Individual characteristics
Age of man
Age of woman
Years farming as an adult
Number of days worked off farm

(3B) Farm structure characteristics
1987 conservation payments
Ratio of cropland to pasture (owned)
Farm type according to SIC code
Total acres owned
Acres of cropland owned
Distribution of land

(3C) Attitudes and behavioral intentions
Planning to participate in acreage set aside
Planning to retire

Table 4. Significant differences in individual characteristics.

Variable	Participants	Nonparticipants
Age (man)*	60	54
Age (woman)*	59	52
Years farming (as an adult)*	35	27
Number of days worked off the farm†	203	242

*Significant at the 1 percent level.
†Significant at the 5 percent level.

intention questions also were of interest. Use of no-till—the most widely adopted conservation technique—did not differentiate participants from nonparticipants.

Table 3 lists the factors that did differentiate participants and nonparticipants, under the same three categories as table 2. The most interesting of these is age (Table 4). As with income and education, age has been a relatively reliable predictor of conservation behavior (4). Unlike the other two, however, age is significant here—but in the nontraditional direction. In Kentucky, older farmers are most likely to sign up for the CRP, whereas the literature on conservation behavior, indicates that younger farmers are more likely to take advantage of the benefits of conservation techniques and programs.

Item 3B presents the farm structure characteristics that were significantly associated. First, and somewhat surprisingly, farmers with a larger proportion of their cropland in pasture (measured as the proportion of their land in Class IV or greater) were much less likely to participate in the program (Figure 1). We would have hypothesized that these farmers who were more likely to participate. Possibly these farmers did not meet the CRP requirement that row crops must have been planted on this land during two of the past five years.

Another distinct pattern of program nonparticipation related to the principal agricultural commodity was identified (Figure 2). Dairy farmers were least likely to have enrolled in the program, and grain farmers were most likely. Tobacco farmers were considerably less likely to participate, which may account for the seemingly low participation rate (11 percent) by Kentucky farmers.

Maybe one of the most interesting significant associations was not evident in the means significance tests but, rather, in terms of its uneven distribution (Figure 3). Farmers most likely to participate in CRP appear to be the so-called medium-sized farms, measured in acres. Farmers having about 100 acres to 400 acres were the most likely to participate. Smaller

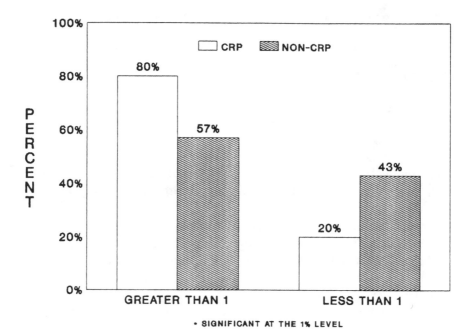

Figure 1. Ratio of cropland to pasture (significant at the 1 percent level).

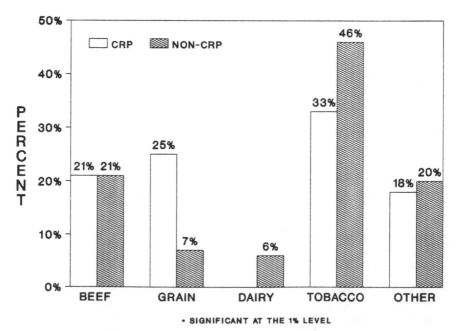

Figure 2. CRP participation by farm type (significant at the 1 percent level).

farms were less likely to participate, and the largest farm category showed no apparent difference.

Farmers with higher conservation payments in 1987—most likely inflated by their first CRP payments—were more likely to have participated in the program. We expected this outcome.

Although the structural factors shed some light on which farmers are most likely to participate in the program, the attitudinal/behavioral intention factors in item 3C perhaps provide a more complete picture. No attitudinal factors distinguished CRP participants from nonparticipants, but two behavioral intention factors did so. CRP participants were more likely to have participated in or intended to participate in a set-aside program (Figure 4), and they were more likely to have retired or plan to retire by 1991 (Figure 5). These two factors show little overlap among CRP participants. Farmers planning to retire were not necessarily the same as those participating in a set-aside program.

We draw two conclusions from this information. First, farmers with some familiarity with acreage reduction programs were more likely to participate. Thus, experience in similar programs seems to promote participation in

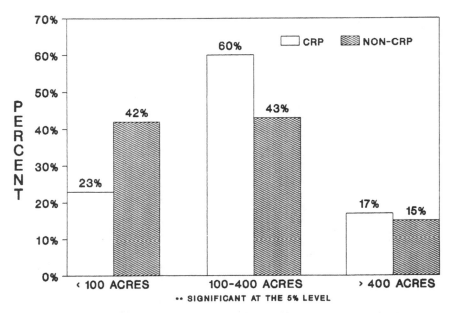

Figure 3. Distribution of total acres (owned and rented in) (significant at the 5 percent level.

CRP. Second, participation in CRP is possibly a retirement strategy for some Kentucky farmers. This observation is buttressed by the fact that fully 35 percent of all CRP participants either had retired from farming or planned to do so by 1991. On the other hand, CRP does not appear to be a strategy to quit farming (Item 2C). Of the farmers who were farming in 1986 but had left farming by 1988, those who left for reasons other than retirement did not show a propensity to participate in the CRP.

Policy Implications

The data do not lend themselves to assessment of all the policy goals claimed for CRP, or even a full assessment of those it can address. For instance, little can be said of whether the program is qualitatively improving the groundwater supply or local wildlife habitat. Some very tentative conclusions can be presented.

In terms of reducing soil erosion in Kentucky, the low number of acres presently enrolled in CRP and the seemingly low farmer participation rate suggest that the program is having some success because some highly erodible land is being taken out of production, though not at the levels hoped.

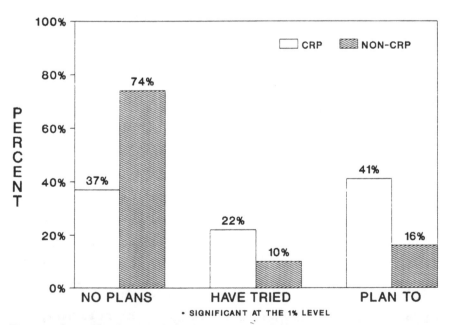

Figure 4. Set aside plans in 1985 (significant at the 1 percent level).

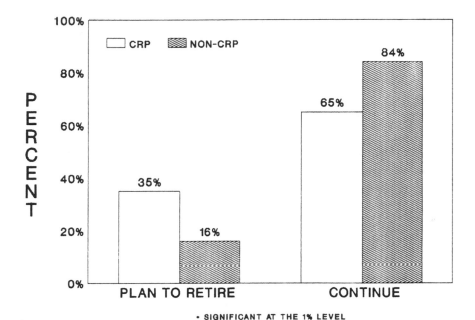

Figure 5. Retirement plans in 1987 (significant at the 1 percent level).

Of possible concern is the tendency of farmers with a high ratio of pasture to cropland to not participate in the program.

As a supply control program, our data do not indicate a substantial drop among CRP participants in acreage under production or in gross sales. But our data analysis to this point cannot state with any certainty that some impact on supply has not occurred.

In terms of the goal for deficit reduction, our data once again are not definitive but they do reveal an interesting pattern. In 1988, CRP participants had a significantly larger payment for conservation programs than did nonparticipants. There was no difference between these in terms of total payments from the government. This would indicate that the effect on deficit reduction has been negligible. It should be noted that CCC payments were the highest ever in history during 1987.

Assessing whether the program improved farm income is also difficult. Two groups showed no difference in gross sales or in family income. This would indicate little, if any, effect.

Our study also suggests that one type of Kentucky farmer may hold a seventh, and unanticipated, goal for CRP. Farmers close to retirement may see CRP as a retirement strategy.

These are only tentative observations based upon data for a comparison between 1986 and 1988 and therefore cannot be considered conclusive. But two concerns are apparent. First, in Kentucky, only a relatively small number of farms are participating. Second, no strong indications pointed to the program's success in achieving any of its goals. Though it is too early to say with certainty, the results suggest that at this time the CRP's multiple objectives may be hindering the overwhelming success of any one of the objectives. If so, we might conclude that the muddling-through process of compromise in putting together this multi-goal program also may have doomed it to only muddling successes.

REFERENCES CITED

1. Buttel, Frederick H., and Louis E. Swanson. 1986. *Soil and water conservation: A farm structural and public policy context.* In Stephen B. Lovejoy and Ted L. Napier [editors] *Conserving Soil: Insights from Socioeconomic Research.* Soil Conservation Society of America, Ankeny, Iowa. pp. 26-39.
2. Crosson, Pierre R. 1982. *The long-term adequacy of agricultural land in the United States.* In P. R. Crosson [editor] *The Cropland Crisis: Myth or Reality?* Johns Hopkins University Press, Baltimore, Maryland. pp. 1-22.
3. Heady, Earl, and Carl Allen. 1951. *Returns from capital required for soil conservation farming systems.* Research Bulletin No. 381. Experiment Station, College of Agriculture, Iowa State University, Ames.
4. Lovejoy, Stephen B., and Ted L. Napier. 1986. *Conserving soil: Insights from socioeconomic research.* Soil Conservation Society of America, Ankeny, Iowa.
5. Phipps, Tim T. 1988. *The conservation reserve and water quality.* Paper presented at the annual meeting of NCR-111, Alexandria, Virginia, March 2.
6. Rasmussen, Wayne D. 1982. *History of soil conservation, institutions and incentives.* In Harold G. Halcrow, Earl O. Heady, and Melvin L. Cotner [editors] *Soil Conservation Policies, Institutions and Incentives.* Soil Conservation Society of America, Ankeny, Iowa. pp. 3-18.
7. Reichelderfer, Katherine. 1989. *Policy issues arising from implementation of the 1985 farm bill conservation provisions.* In *Increasing Understanding of Public Problems and Policies—1988.* Farm Foundation, Oak Brook, Illinois.
8. Reichelderfer, Katherine, and William G. Boggess. 1988. *Government decision-making and program performance: The case of the Conservation Reserve Program.* American Journal of Agricultural Economics 70: 1-14.
9. Swanson, Louis E. 1987. *A century of periodic research on soil conservation.* In Lawrance Busch and William B. Lacy [editors] *The Agricultural Scientific Enterprise: A System in Transition.* Westview Press, Boulder, Colorado. pp. 134-147.
10. Taft, Steven J., and C. Ford Runge. 1988. *Wanted: A leaner and meaner CRP.* CHOICES (first quarter): 16-18.
11. Thigpen, John F. III. 1988. *The sociology of soil conservation.* Unpublished dissertation. Department of Sociology, University of Kentucky, Lexington.

18

Conservation Practices and Government Programs: Solving Personal Troubles or Social Problems

Stephen B. Lovejoy and Ted L. Napier

The 1980s have seen a distinct change in attitudes toward soil erosion. Although the long-run economic viability of individual farm operators or small geographic areas is still debated, concerns about aggregate levels of production have been largely stilled by overproduction and surplus commodities generated by the American agricultural sector. In addition, information concerning the productivity impacts of erosion suggests that loss of productive potential is much less significant than previously indicated. Citizens have begun to express more concern about nonfarm impacts of soil erosion and more generally about agricultural production practices.

Estimates of the offsite costs of agricultural production have ranged up to several billion dollars per year (2). This is manifested in the increased importance attached to water quality in agricultural policy, and the importance attached to agriculture in water quality and environmental policy. USDA's latest National Conservation Plan (NCP) has elevated water quality as a goal, and several USDA agencies are formulating water quality programs. The Water Quality Act of 1987 obviously recognizes the role of agriculture in water quality—and clearly says we must reduce agricultural nonpoint-source (NPS) pollution to meet water quality goals. Further, dozens of bills were introduced in the 100th Congress to help alleviate groundwater problems. Most of these bills mentioned agriculture, and several were introduced specifically to help agriculture meet water quality goals (e.g., Nunn-Cochrane, Dole's ECRP, and Fowler's Bill).

Although none of this legislation was enacted, the 101st Congress will again be grappling with these issues as well as debating a new farm bill.

We hope that scientific discussions of soil erosion problems can provide Congress with the necessary inputs for relevant and useful legislation and can supply administrative agencies with sufficient information to be able to construct effective programs.

A great many public policy issues are associated with instituting a program to control erosion and sedimentation, particularly when the objective is to alleviate off-farm impacts. The variety of available tools include targeting, cost-sharing, cross-compliance, and regulation. Each of these alternative policies has both positive and negative aspects, and each has different groups of beneficiaries and payees (4). Questions related to equity, fairness, and political clout muddy what is already an extremely complex process. Many observers suggest that solutions to agricultural NPS water pollution problems will be quite difficult and that solutions will require some or all of the following:

► Authorization and use of regulatory powers.

► More accurate targeting on both national and local levels.

► New production techniques that reduce the amounts of nutrients and pesticides used in agriculture.

► Programs to permanently retire the most erodible land or land most environmentally damaging from row-crop production.

Several agricultural analysts and interest groups suggest that some of these techniques and regulations are "draconian" and will shut down agricultural production in the United States. Others suggest that farmers will not and cannot live with restrictive farm practices, such as those suggested by some conservationists and environmentalists. Members of several agricultural interest groups are adamantly opposed to any further restrictions of the private rights of landowners and operators. To the extent that these statements correctly reflect the views of farmers and environmentalists, the potential for conflict is obvious.

Personal Troubles-Social Problems: Definitions

Frameworks helpful for understanding the issue of soil and water conservation come from economics, market and nonmarket goods, and sociological analyses of personal troubles-social problems. As C. Wright Mills (5) has defined them, personal troubles are those that occur within the range of an individual's immediate relations; they are limited to areas of which the individual is directly and personally aware. Therefore, resolution of personal troubles lies within the individual. A personal trouble is a private matter that the individual has to endure or solve. A social problem, on the other hand, transcends individuals and their local environments. Social problems result from the broader organization and structure of society or the manner in which various milieus overlap and interact to form the larger societal structure. Social problems are public matters that occur because institutional, technological, or environmental changes result in patterns that are incongruous with public values. Whereas personal troubles are mutable by the individual, social issues or problems are solved only by changes in the larger body politic.

In years past, the interests of farm operators and the general public converged because both groups were significantly interested in preserving the productive potential of American agricultural lands. Beginning with the Dust Bowl of the 1930s, the general public came to believe that the agricultural sector cannot be expected to resolve soil conservation problems on its own. Public input and technical and financial assistance are essential to maintain the nation's ability to produce the necessary agricultural commodities. But as the general public has become better fed and wealthier, it also has become less concerned about the problem. Also, our losses in productivity as a result of erosion seem to be much smaller than previously believed, leading some to argue that additional incentives are not needed to persuade landowners to conserve the socially optimal amount of soil productivity.

Concurrently, the general public has become more concerned about adverse impacts of agricultural production upon environmental resources such as rivers and lakes, wildlife habitat, and drinking water supplies. Because many of these represent generalized public benefits, farmers often have no more interest than any other citizen in achieving them. However, farmers and rural landowners may have to incur significant costs to attain improved environmental quality. Of course, this lack of mutual interests forms the potential for conflict. The seeming divergence between private and public incentives also may result in increased calls for government intervention and regulation.

Soil Conservation Issues

Citizens increasingly view soil conservation differently than they view other types of environmental protection. Protection of soil resources is actually a vehicle for protecting our ability to produce food and fiber products for our own consumption as well as for export. Most Americans appear not to be overly concerned about our ability to produce food and fiber as needed. Although they seem to be somewhat aware that not all consumers, domestic and foreign, can afford adequate foodstuffs, they perceive that our agricultural sector has the ability to produce sufficient quantities. In fact, surpluses have been the topic of major news stories several times during the past decade. Recent predictions suggest that current levels of erosion will reduce our productive capacity only slightly during the next 100 years.

Therefore, the issue of soil productivity is primarily a private trouble facing a small number of landowners and having only slight ramifications for society in general. But the issue of off-site costs of erosion, or more generally the negative externalities of the agricultural production process, may potentially affect large numbers of citizens. Because the causes are concentrated but affect millions of citizens, off-site erosion impacts can justifiably be classified as a social problem. We cannot reasonably expect farm firms to make private decisions to achieve public objectives. On the other hand, to blindly enact regulations may not achieve the public water quality objectives and may unnecessarily burden producers and consumers.

Study Parameters and Findings

As perpetual skeptics (i.e., social scientists), we decided that investigation of the social structure surrounding farm firm conservation decisions would be appropriate. Therefore, we selected a small, highly erodible watershed in central Ohio and conducted interviews among local farmers (*1*).

Over the years many observers have agreed that loss of productive potential is a serious problem for society, but the preceding information suggests that for our nation as a whole, the problem is minor, although it may be extremely serious for some landowners. In the study watershed, which the Soil Conservation Service (SCS) identified as a relatively erodible watershed, 77 percent of the respondents believed they were not losing any productivity from soil erosion. From their responses, only 587 acres (of nearly 20,000 acres) were losing productivity, and the average productivity loss was only 1.5 percent per year. From this, we infer that the producers in the study watershed do not view soil erosion as a private trouble. Part of this reaction may be related to past expenditures that may have alleviated much of the erosion problem, although SCS believes that several thousand acres are not adequately protected.

When questioned about why they have adopted or would adopt soil conservation practices, 52 percent of the respondents indicated future productivity as the reason and 14 percent indicated government financial assistance. However, 20 percent said they have adopted or plan to adopt practices

Table 1. Attitudes toward soil and water conservation (N = 84).

	Agree	Undecided	Disagree	Mean*
		%		
Farmers who wish to adopt soil erosion control practices should have to pay for them from their own resources	25	33	42	3.2
No one has the right to tell farmers what practices they should use on their own land	49	27	24	2.6
Agricultural pollution caused by soil erosion is a serious threat to fish and wildlife in Ohio	49	33	18	2.6
Farmers should be forced to use soil conservation practices on highly erosive land they farm	29	24	47	3.4
Land operators do not have the right to farm land in a manner that will cause damage to the resource	51	27	22	2.6
Farmers who ignore soil erosion on their land should not be permitted to continue farming	17	45	38	3.2
Agricultural pollution resulting from soil erosion should be stopped even if some farmers are forced to stop farming highly erosive land	32	40	28	3.0
Most soil erosion control practices do not increase farm profits for farmers who use them	25	20	55	3.3
Water pollution caused by soil erosion does not pose a health problem to people in the U.S.	18	37	45	3.4
Soil erosion from farm land often makes rivers and lakes unusable for recreation purposes	52	31	17	2.6

*Weighting values ranged from 1 to 5 with higher values indicating disagreement with the statement.

designed to protect the environment and improve wildlife habitat; thus, a minority of respondents appear to be altruists or place a higher value on certain environmental amenities than their neighbors.

Considerable ambivalence is apparent among farmers concerning their rights and responsibilities as landowners—especially in relation to the broader public interest in protecting and enhancing environmental quality.

Less than 20 percent disagreed with the statement that agricultural pollution is a threat to fish and wildlife, while nearly half agreed that agricultural operations threaten wildlife (Table 1). Over half said they believe soil erosion from farmland often makes rivers and lakes unusable for recreational purposes. Although these responses suggest that some of the respondents perceive the off-site costs of agricultural production practices, most are not certain that these pollutants (while causing damage) constitute a threat to public health.

Thus, respondents tend to agree about some aspects of the problem, but they show significantly less agreement about solution(s) for the problem. In response to a series of questions about alternative actions, one-fourth of the respondents indicated that farmers should have to pay for soil and water conservation practices, about two-fifths did not agree, and one-third were undecided (Table 1). About half of the respondents stated that no one has the right to tell farmers what practices they should use on their land and another fourth were undecided. More than a fourth of the respondents said that farmers with highly erodible land should be forced to use soil conservation practices.

When asked whether farmers who ignore soil erosion on their lands should be allowed to continue farming, 17 percent said they should not continue farming and 45 percent were undecided. But when asked whether agricultural pollution resulting from farming highly erodible land should be stopped even if some farmers were forced to stop farming, 32 percent said yes. This implies that some of the farmers are making a distinction between impacts upon the individual decision-maker (e.g., productivity losses) and impacts felt by others (e.g., water quality). The respondents seemed to be more amenable to restrictions on production practices when the damage is being imposed on the general public or on other individuals.

These findings also are illustrated by respondents' attitudes toward government involvement in agriculture (Table 2). Only a third indicated that the role of government was to maintain farm income, and over a fourth were undecided. Thirty percent stated that commodity programs are a waste of taxpayer dollars, 40 percent indicated they are not. More than 65 percent did not think the government should control the amount of food and fiber produced. But nearly half believed the government has the primary responsibility for protecting the environment from agricultural pollution (only 25 percent disagreed); and only 14 percent believed that soil conservation programs were not the legitimate concern of government. More than 60 percent believed that the federal government should continue to be involved in pesticide control programs.

Table 2. Attitudes toward government involvement in agriculture (N = 84).

	Agree	Undecided	Disagree	Mean*
		%		
The most important reason for having government involvement in agriculture is to maintain farm income	33	26	41	3.1
The government should not be involved in soil conservation programs	14	25	61	3.6
The federal government should continue to be involved in pesticide control programs	64	24	12	2.3
Commodity programs are a waste of tax-payer money	30	30	40	3.1
The government should control the amount of food and fiber produced at the farm level	11	24	65	3.8
The government has primary responsibility for protecting the environment from agricultural pollution	45	30	25	2.8

*Weighting values ranged from 1 to 5 with higher values indicating disagreement with the statement.

These findings suggest that a minority of the study farmers see the government as legitimately performing income support and supply control functions, but a majority think that the government has a major role in environmental quality protection. Although these farmers suggest that they have certain responsibilities as landowners and guardians of a public trust (land), the government has some obligations to protect land and water resources for future generations. Many respondents indicated that the government should fulfill its obligation to citizens even if this means limiting production on some acres, but many respondents also expressed uncertainty about those ideas. Most seem to appreciate that agricultural production activities are imposing negative externalities. And only a minority is definitely opposed to the government using some type of police powers to fulfill its obligations to protect environmental quality.

One method the government is utilizing to fulfill its responsibility is the Conservation Reserve Program (CRP). Although programs such as this have proved to be relatively popular with farmers, increasing concern is being voiced about the long-run impacts. Specifically, what will happen at the end of the 10-year contract? Even though the goal of preserving productivity may be served by temporarily taking highly erodible acres out of production, environmental goals may not be well served. If agricultural production on certain acres is creating water quality problems or if society is desiring increased wildlife habitat, idling those acres probably has to be a long-term or permanent commitment. Some analysts have proposed permanently purchasing the rights to row-crop those acres as an appropriate solution (3). But many farmers seem to resist permanently retiring crop acres.

Response to Conservation Easements

More recently, the concept of 50-year conservation easements has been advanced as a method for long-term land retirement for environmental enhancement. Like traditional easements used for road and utility access, a conservation easement secures a defined set of property rights to the easement manager while allowing the landowner to retain title. Under a Farmers Home Administration program, initiated by the Food Security Act of 1985, easements may be established for conservation, recreation, and wildlife purposes on some farmland that is wetland, upland, highly erodible land, or wildlife habitat. It must have been row-cropped each year of the three years prior to December 23, 1985. Natural resources that are eligible include:

► One-hundred-year floodplains.

► Aquatic life or wildlife habitat or endangered species habitat.

► Aquifer recharge areas.

► Areas of high water quality or scenic value.

► Buffer zones for wetlands.

► Areas adjacent to federal or state-owned lands used for conservation or recreational purposes.

► Areas adjacent to federal or state wild or scenic rivers.

► Areas with soils that are unsuitable for agriculture.

Although conservationists and environmentalists have shown substantial interest in this concept, the willingness of farmers to utilize such a program has been largely ignored.

We asked the farmers in our central Ohio watershed to rate, on a 10-point scale from "completely unwilling" to "completely willing," their willingness to participate in such a program. Specifically, we presented the following statement to each respondent:

"The federal government recently introduced a new soil conservation program called the Conservation Easement Program (CEP), which is designed to retire highly erosive farmland from crop production for a period of 50 years. We would like to ask you a few questions about your potential involvement in this."

Table 3. Willingness to participate in a 50-year conservation easement program.

Completely unwilling (0)	37	44%
Somewhat unwilling (1-4)	25	26%
Neither willing nor unwilling (5)	14	17%
Somewhat willing (6-9)	11	13%

$\bar{x}$ Response = 2.4.

Forty-four percent said they would be completely unwilling, and an additional 26 percent indicated they would be somewhat unwilling (Table 3). The finding that 70 percent of the respondents would be unwilling to participate may be disheartening to some, but most new concepts and changes are accepted slowly. More important, 30 percent of the respondents did not rule out the possibility of participating in a 50-year conservation easement program.

To understand the mechanisms by which such a new program becomes acceptable, we examined the extent to which willingness to participate in a conservation easement program was correlated with a variety of socioeconomic, attitudinal, and farm firm characteristics. For analytical purposes, we separated respondents by those completely unwilling to participate, and all others. This provides for a clear demarcation, in which those who have not totally formed their opinion against the concept may have different characteristics. But the simple correlation analysis suggests that the respondents' answer to the question is related to only one other characteristic. Farmers who stated that they are not completely unwilling were more likely to have cropland acres that are losing productivity. This suggests that farmers who think they have a problem are more receptive to this alternative than other farmers are. But even this relationship was not strong; the correlation coefficient was 0.3168. As a result of this analysis, we know that more than 40 percent of the respondents were completely unwilling to consider a 50-year conservation easement program, and these same respondents did not have any cropland losing productivity.

Willingness to participate in a conservation easement program is not related to any of the following:

► Knowledge of or participation in CRP.

► Tillage system.

► Present use of filter strips, grassed waterways, gully plugs, or terraces.

► Use of grass or small grains in rotation with field crops.

► Importance attached to financial factors as reason for use or nonuse of conservation practices.

▶ Attitudes toward the government's role in soil and water conservation.

▶ Opinions on the role of erosion in water pollution and habitat degradation.

▶ Off-farm employment.

▶ Age.

▶ Education.

▶ Size of farm firm.

▶ Participation in other government programs.

▶ Farm income.

This lack of correlation suggests that no set of characteristics would identify a priori willingness to participate in a conservation easement program. On the positive side, however, the analysis suggests that those who think they are having productivity losses are more receptive.

We asked those who were not completely unwilling to participate, what they would require in terms of a per-acre rental rate. The average response, $124 per acre per year, is a relatively high rental rate for cropland in this area, but it was significantly influenced by a few high outliers. More important, might be their responses to the amount needed in terms of a one-time payment; that average was $1,122 per acre. Although this is higher than the present market value for much of the land in the watershed, it does indicate a window of opportunity. These figures suggest that opportunities for conservation easements that offer more incentives up front may be greater than for a long-term cash flow. And examining the net present value of the $124 income stream for 50 years, society could save considerable resources with one-time payments because these farmers apparently have a much higher discount rate ($\sim$11 percent) than normally used for society (4 to 6 percent).

Summary and Discussion

New structures and new innovative ways of thinking are required to jointly pursue the goals of agricultural productivity and environmental quality. The old structure to assist producers in pursuing personal goals and avoiding private troubles is inadequate for pursuing public goals of water quality protection.

Farm firm operators in this study were ambivalent about the respective roles and responsibilities of landowners, operators, and government. Also, many said they would be unwilling to participate in a 50-year conservation easement program. Those who were willing were not easily identified by any sociodemographic or structural characteristic used in the analysis, although those who were more willing were more likely to be cropping land that was losing productivity. To the extent that those lands overlap the lands creating water quality problems, we may have a situation in which, on a limited scale, private troubles and social problems can be ameliorated simultaneously.

When public and private objectives and goals are incongruent, other types of programs will be needed. Development of new technologies may offer partial solutions in the long-run, but they will likely have small short-run impacts. We will, in general, be left with the dilemma of offering a bigger carrot or using a bigger stick.

REFERENCES CITED

1. Camboni, Silvana M., Ted L. Napier, and Stephen B. Lovejoy. 1989. *Factors affecting knowledge of and participation in the Conservation Reserve Program in a Micro-Targeted Area of Ohio.* In Ted L. Napier [editor] *Implementing the Conservation Title of the Food Security Act of 1985.* Soil and Water Conservation Society, Ankeny, Iowa. pp. 205-222.
2. Clark, Edwin, Jennifer A. Havercamp, and William Chapman. 1985. *Eroding soils, the off-farm impacts.* The Conservation Foundation, Washington, D.C.
3. Lee, John, Stephen B. Lovejoy, and D. Beasley. 1985. *Soil loss reduction in Finley Creek: An economic analysis of alternative policies.* Journal of Soil and Water Conservation 40(1): 132-135.
4. Lovejoy, Stephen B., and Harry Potter. 1986. *Changing agricultural property rights in the environmental era.* In *Water Resources Law: Proceedings of the National Symposium on Water Resources Law.* American Society of Agricultural Engineers, St. Joseph, Michigan. pp. 160-170.
5. Mills, C. Wright. 1959. *The sociological imagination.* Oxford University Press, New York, New York.

19

Farmers' Response to Conservation Compliance

Thomas J. Hoban

Problems of soil erosion and related nonpoint-source water pollution remain very serious in many parts of the United States—which is particularly frustrating given that the federal government has spent more than $20 billion in soil conservation efforts during the past 50 years (22). State and local governments also have spent considerable sums attempting to control soil erosion. Disincentives for farmers under previous USDA agricultural programs and policies, such as increasing USDA program benefits by plowing up marginal land for annual crops, represent one reason for the limited success of past soil conservation efforts (2, 19).

Most observers agree that the conservation provisions of the 1985 Farm Bill represent the most fundamental changes in conservation programs and policies during the past 50 years (3, 10, 18). Under conservation compliance, farmers' continued eligibility for many USDA assistance programs will depend on their developing and implementing an approved conservation farm plan. Most USDA farm programs are affected, including price and income supports, crop insurance, Farmers' Home Administration loans, Commodity Credit Corporation, storage payments, and other USDA programs. Farmers who violate the provisions will no longer be eligible to receive benefits from these programs.

Model of Farmers' Response to Conservation Compliance

My research tries to determine if the main findings from the considerable research on conservation practice adoption also apply to farmers' adoption of a conservation plan in response to conservation compliance. I developed and tested a theoretical model of factors that may be related to farmers' adopting conservation plans (Figure 1).

Personal Characteristics of Individual Farmers. Most studies have found that farmers who practice conservation tend to have more formal education than farmers who do not apply conservation (6, 7, 24). This probably reflects these farmers' management ability to handle the additional complexity associated with conservation (20). Bultena and Hoiberg (4) found that farmers using USDA information sources were better educated.

Age of farm operators has an unclear influence on their decision to use conservation. Carlson and Dillman (6) found that no-till users tended to be either somewhat younger or older than average. Swanson et al. (24) hypothesized that younger farmers with greater exposure to information sources were more likely to adopt conservation practices but they found that age was relatively unimportant as a predictive variable. Bultena and Hoiberg (4) found that farmers who used USDA sources tended to be younger than farmers who had never used USDA sources of assistance.

Although off-farm employment is becoming increasingly important for many smaller-scale farm operators, research has not yet specifically ex-

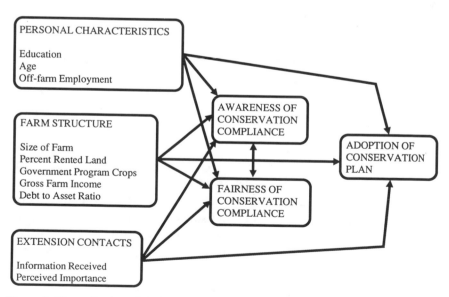

Figure 1. Theoretical model of influences on adoption of a conservation plan.

amined the influence of off-farm employment on conservation adoption. Farmers who work off-farm probably have a different orientation toward farming and conservation because they are more integrated into nonfarm communication networks and may make less use of farm-related information sources.

Farm Structural Characteristics. Research has established that farmers with larger operations are more likely to practice conservation (*7, 17, 23*). Farm size tends to be directly related to greater availability of resources, more flexibility in decision-making, higher status in the local community, and better ability to deal with risk. Heffernan and Green (*12*) found that larger farms had lower soil loss than did smaller farms, primarily because the land had lower erosion potential. Farm firm characteristics also may influence their use of conservation information sources; farmers with the largest operations are most likely to use public agencies for farm information (*3*).

Another frequent finding is that rented land usually receives less conservation attention than land a farmer owns. Ervin (*8*), however, argues that the question of whether rented land receives less, more, or the same amount of erosion control than owner-operated land is not clear. Carlson and Dillman (*6*) found that farmers who used no-till tended to farm more rented land. Using actual field measurements, Korsching and Nowak (*16*) determined that the more rental land included in a farmer's operation, the more erosive were the tillage practices and crop rotation.

Economic conditions are highly influential in farmers' willingness and ability to adopt conservation practices (*2, 5*). Farm income is an indicator of farm scale and farmers' ability to pay for conservation investments. Money available for investment probably is even more important than gross farm income. Many farmers have incurred high debt levels during the past decade, and at the same time, the value of their farm assets has been reduced. This suggests that farmers with higher debt-to-asset ratios would be less willing and able to invest in conservation practices.

Finally, type(s) of crop grown can influence adoption of conservation practices. Certain crops (e.g., corn and soybeans) contribute more to soil erosion problems than do other crops (e.g., hay). Conservation compliance adds a new dimension to the relationship between type of crop and conservation. Government financial assistance programs support only certain crops (corn, tobacco, peanuts, and small grains). Farmers who rely most on these crops have the most to lose if they do not comply with the 1985 farm bill provisions. In contrast, farmers who raise mainly livestock or nonprogram crops (e.g., soybeans, fruits, or vegetables) have less to lose if they are not in compliance.

Contacts with the Extension Service. Various studies have found that the number of contacts that farmers have with sources of information and assistance is positively related to adoption of conservation practices (*4, 7, 16, 17*). Nowak (*20*) argues that farmers need education to recognize erosion problems and learn how using available conservation technologies can reduce the severity of problems. Napier et al. (*19*) found that farmers who used more institutional sources of information, on a more frequent basis, tended to be more concerned about environmental issues in their decision-making. To adopt a conservation plan, all farmers must have some contact with the Soil Conservation Service, so I did not include it in this theoretical model. Contact with the Extension Service, on the other hand, indicates a more general inclination to seek information about farm management and technological innovation. Extension contact also points toward integration into institutional assistance and information networks.

Awareness and Perceived Fairness of Conservation Compliance. Government policies and programs have an important influence on adoption of conservation practices (*2, 5*). Awareness and perceptions of government conservation programs can influence farmers' willingness to adopt conservation practices (*17, 20*). The intent of conservation compliance is, in fact, to greatly increase the adoption and implementation of farm conservation plans. Conservation compliance will be an empty threat if farmers are not aware of its potential impact on their USDA program eligibility. Farmers' awareness of and support for cross compliance, therefore, should be positively related to adoption of a conservation plan.

Research Methods and Results

Results of the study are based on telephone interviews with 595 North Carolina farmers from across the state after selecting phone numbers at random from lists maintained by the Crop and Livestock Reporting Service. The February, 1988, survey was the second wave of a panel study begun in 1987.

Personal Characteristics of Individual Farmers. Responses for the educational level of participants were: less than high school, 17 percent; some high school, 15 percent; high school graduate, 43 percent; some college,

13 percent; college graduate, 10 percent; completed post-graduate degree, 2 percent. The mean age of respondents was 55 years old; ages ranged from 21 years to 86 years. Many (40 percent) of the respondents worked off the farm for pay during 1987.

Farm Structural Characteristics. Farm size was measured as total acres (both owned and rented) farmed in 1987. Mean farm size was 186 acres, with a range of 1 to 4,574 acres. Amount of rental land ranged from zero to 100 percent, with a mean of 35 percent. To determine whether a farmer relied on government program crops, the question was: "Of the crops or livestock that you raised in 1987, which was the most important for your gross farm income?" Government program crops were defined to include tobacco, corn, peanuts, cotton, and wheat or other grains. Farmers who relied most on soybeans, fruits, vegetables, or livestock were assumed to be less reliant on government programs affected by conservation compliance.

The nine categories of gross farm income covered the range of "less than $5,000 to over $200,000." The mean income category, on the 9-category scale, suggested a mean farm income of about $30,000. Debt-to-asset ratio was computed from categorical measures using the same scale as for gross farm income. To determine assets and debts, the questions posed were: "About how much would you be willing to pay for your present farm if it was on the market and you were looking to buy a farm?" and "What is the total amount of your debt?"

Contacts with the Extension Service. I measured the extent of respondents' contacts with the Cooperative Extension Service in two ways: information received from Extension and perceived importance of Extension. The amount of information received was calculated by adding responses to two questions: "During the past two years has an Extension agent visited your farm?" and "During the past two years have you read any Extension publications or attended any Extension sponsored meetings?" Perceived importance of Extension was measured by the following question: "How important do you feel your contacts with Extension are to your farming operation? (Very important, somewhat important, or not important). Respondents rated the importance of their Extension contacts as follows: very important, 46 percent; somewhat important, 37 percent; not important, 17 percent.

Awareness and Perceived Fairness of Conservation Compliance. To measure awareness of conservation compliance, the question was: "Have you heard that farmers who do not have a conservation plan by 1990 for their erodible land will not be eligible for some USDA program benefits?" Despite fairly extensive publicity during the previous year, almost 30 percent of the respondents had not heard of conservation compliance. When asked, "Do you think this policy (conservation compliance) is fair?" responses were evenly divided: 46 percent said it was fair and 46 percent thought it was not fair; 8 percent had no opinion.

Adoption of a Conservation Plan. In response to the question, "Do you have a conservation plan prepared by the Soil Conservation Service for the farm that you operate?" only 214 (36 percent) of the respondents said they had a conservation plan. Of all farmers, about one-quarter (24 percent) said they had considered developing a conservation plan. Therefore, in the whole sample, 238 farmers (40 percent) did not have a conservation plan and had not considered developing one.

Most of these conservation plans were relatively new; 84 (39 percent of those with plans) had developed a plan in the last four years. Respondents reported considerable variation in implementing their plans. Of the 214 farmers with a conservation plan, only one-third (35 percent) claimed to have implemented 100 percent of the plan's recommendations. This means that only 12 percent of all farmers in the sample would now be ready for the 1995 deadline. Over one-third of the farmers with plans had implemented 50 percent or less of the plan's recommendations. Analysis of factors possibly related to farmers' implementation of their conservation plans and the year the plans were developed showed few significant results.

Research Results

Table 1 presents the bivariate correlation coefficients for the relationships between independent and dependent variables. Adoption of a conservation plan is positively related to education but negatively related to age (younger farmers were more likely to have adopted a plan). Farm size, gross farm income, and debt-to-asset ratio also are positively related to adoption. Farmers who rely most on government program crops also were more likely to have adopted a plan. Contact with Extension has a relatively strong positive relationship to adoption of a conservation plan. Farmers who were aware of conservation compliance and those who thought it was fair also were more likely to have a conservation plan.

Farmers who are aware of conservation compliance also tend to have more formal education and are slightly younger than those who are not aware. Awareness is greater among farmers who have larger operations, rely more on government program crops, have higher farm incomes, and have higher debt-to-asset ratios. Farmers who were aware of cross-compliance also have much greater contact with Extension, and they were more likely to see conservation compliance as fair.

Farmers with more education were more likely to perceive conservation compliance as being fair. Farmers who rely more on government program crops were less likely to see conservation compliance as being fair. Contact with Extension tends to promote the perception that conservation compliance is fair; and those who believe conservation compliance to be fair also were more likely to be aware of it.

Table 2 presents the results of multiple regression analysis. Because some of the independent variables in the model are themselves interrelated, this analysis controls for such relationships. In the model, contact with Extension has the most important positive influence on adoption of a conservation plan. Awareness of conservation compliance also is positively related to adoption. Farmers with larger operations and those who rely more on government program crops also are more likely to have adopted a conservation plan. In this analysis, off-farm employment now shows a weak, negative relation to adoption of a conservation plan.

Farmers who received more information from Extension were more likely

Table 1. Zero-order correlation coefficients.

	Adoption of Plan	Awareness of Compliance	Fairness of Compliance
Personal characteristics			
Education	.19‡	14‡	.15‡
Age	−.14‡	−.08*	−.05
Off-farm employment	.05	.00	.01
Farm structure			
Size of farm	.20‡	.16‡	−.01
Percent rented land	.06	.06	−.05
Government program crops	.12†	.16‡	−.13†
Gross farm income	.20‡	.18‡	−.01
Debt-to-asset ratio	.12†	.10†	.01
Extension contacts			
Information received	.41‡	.31‡	.11†
Perceived importance	.33‡	.19‡	.13†
Awareness of compliance	.33‡	n/a	.11†
Fairness of compliance	.12†	.11†	n/a

* r significant at .05.
† r significant at .01.
‡ r significant at .001.

Table 2. Beta coefficients for multiple regression models.

	Adoption of Plan	Awareness of Compliance	Fairness of Compliance
Personal characteristics			
Education	.05	.06	.09
Age	−.08	.02	−.05
Off-farm employment	−.10*	−.03	−.10*
Farm structure			
Size of farm	.12†	.09	−.03
Percent rented land	−.06	−.02	−.03
Government program crops	.09*	.16‡	−.13†
Gross farm income	−.08	.02	.01
Debt-to-asset ratio	.01	.01	.00
Extension contacts			
Information received	.24‡	.24‡	.03
Perceived importance	.15†	.02	.09
Awareness of compliance	.19‡	n/a	.10*
Fairness of compliance	.05	.10*	n/a
R-square for model	.26	.13	.07

* t significant at .05.
† t significant at .01.
‡ t significant at .001.

to be aware of conservation compliance. Farmers who rely more on government program crops also were more likely to be aware of conservation compliance. Perceived fairness of conservation compliance was still weakly related to awareness in the multiple regression model. Perceived fairness of conservation compliance was negatively related to off-farm employment; farmers who relied more on government program crops were also less likely to consider conservation compliance fair.

Summary, Recommendations, and Conclusions

At the time of the survey, many North Carolina farmers were not in compliance with the conservation provisions of the 1985 farm bill. But considerable progress on conservation planning probably has taken place since this survey was conducted in February 1988. Results should provide some guidance to help ensure that most farmers are in compliance by January 1, 1990.

Research has shown that farmers who are more likely to adopt conservation practices tend to have larger scale operations, more education, and greater contact with agencies and they are better off financially. Some of these same relationships appear to hold for adoption of conservation plans. But some important differences are apparent. When considering the multiple regression analysis, some variables identified as important for the adoption of conservation practices are not related to adoption of a conservation plan. Individual demographic variables appear to be relatively unimportant. Economic factors (gross farm income and debt-to-asset ratio) also were unrelated to conservation plan adoption. And rental land does not appear to present a barrier to adoption of a conservation plan.

Variables that are important for adoption of a conservation plan point out the importance of education for promoting conservation compliance. Contact with Extension showed the strongest relationship with adoption of a conservation plan. Awareness of the conservation compliance provision also was important in adopting a conservation plan. Awareness is accomplished through education. Farmers who perceive that compliance is in their own interests will also be more likely to adopt plans. (This is suggested by the relationship between reliance on government program crops and awareness of conservation compliance and adoption of a conservation plan.)

Certain groups of farmers were more likely to be aware of conservation compliance, as well as more likely to have adopted a conservation plan. Farmers may not be concerned with government assistance programs if they depend more on off-farm income. Farmers who raise crops that are most dependent on federal financial assistance programs have the most to lose if they are not in compliance; therefore, they are more likely to be in compliance. To avoid negative social impacts, educational efforts must be targeted to farmers who are least likely to have a conservation plan or be aware of conservation compliance.

Implementation Challenges. Conservation compliance appears to be a well-designed and logical response to chronic natural resource problems. Just because policies are adopted, however, does not ensure that their goals will be met. Program development and implementation represent formidable challenges (*1*). Innovative policies require related innovations in program implementation. The 1985 Farm Bill did not adequately reform the long-standing institutional structure for implementing soil and water conservation.

Farmer participation in various conservation programs historically has been on a "first come, first served" basis. The U.S. Government Accounting Office (*9*) was critical of the widespread practice of this approach. Successfully implementing the conservation provisions will depend on aggressive, proactive approaches. Organizations must actively promote the provisions to farmers who may be difficult to reach and resistant to change. Local organizations might not be up to the challenges, as they have not implemented these types of programs before (21). Therefore, local conservation district leaders and USDA program managers will need enhanced communication skills and leadership ability, as well as support and clear policy direction from state and federal agencies.

Cooperation and coordination among organizations are vital for success. A division of labor exists among the USDA agencies, the conservation districts, and the Extension Service, each of which has an important role in implementing the conservation provisions of the 1985 farm bill. Organization roles for financial and technical assistance are clearly spelled out. Overlap and gaps in program delivery, however, present potential problems for conservation education programs (13, 14). The Cooperative Extension Service traditionally has been a significant organization for providing information and education for farmers. The SCS and the local conservation districts also have a mandate for conservation education. The result in some counties may be that conservation education falls through the cracks between agencies.

Many farmers may be confused and uncertain about the conservation provisions of the farm bill. They may not realize how the provisions will affect their own operations. Because the conservation provisions of the 1985 farm bill are complex and have far-reaching implications, farmers need unbiased, timely, and locally relevant information. Because no single conservation practice is required for all land, farmers must have options. They will need help in identifying and incorporating conservation systems that are compatible with their existing farm business and enterprise mix.

Extension Challenges and Opportunities. My research supports a more prominent role for the Cooperative Extension Service in conservation policies and programs. As one of the educational arms of the USDA and land grant universities, the Extension Service is in good position to provide education on farming systems. The Extension Service traditionally has been a source of agricultural information; county agents work with farmers to help them identify, evaluate, and implement a host of agricultural technologies, including those aimed at conserving soil and water. In some areas, however, Extension has not been able to assume a major role in educational programs relative to the 1985 farm bill.

Extension's educational mandate is broad, involving all areas of farm management as well as many other areas (e.g., community development, home economics). Official pronouncements argue that Extension has a major role in conducting educational efforts (*11, 15*), and the 1985 farm bill called for renewed emphasis on conservation education. The Extension Service was charged with developing and conducting educational programs to help implement the conservation provisions. Although Extension is working closely with other organizations to educate farmers, it generally has not been given additional resources to carry out the educational role.

Extension can make important contributions in a team approach to conservation. It can serve as a clearinghouse for agricultural information, including conservation information. It can educate farmers to evaluate their own alternatives. Extension programs focus on total farm management, and soil and water conservation is viewed as one part of the larger farm decision process. Extension interprets information and applies technology for different types of farmers, based on their enterprise mix, scale of operation, and financial situation. Extension recommendations consider farmers' individual educational backgrounds and level of management skill. The fact that Extension's conservation efforts often merge with total farm management is desirable in that conservation is seen as part of total farm management, but it also can be undesirable if attention deviates from conservation to an overemphasis on production.

In any case, Extension is an important link in the technology transfer system, ensuring that information flows in two directions. Farmers can find out about the latest research and technology, and Extension specialists can educate university researchers about farmers' needs and problems. At the local level, Extension agents can provide general educational expertise to support the efforts of more narrowly focused agencies (SCS and ASCS). Extension agents generally have good working relationships with local mass media, helping to target messages that reach specific audiences with relevant information, using multiple channels of communication.

If a vacuum exists in conservation education, some organization must step in to fill the gap. The question remains as to what extent Extension can and should become involved in promoting conservation and offering farmers advice on technical aspects of conservation. Technical conservation assistance should remain the primary responsibility of the SCS and local conservation districts. Extension's comparative strength is in providing research-based education on all aspects of farming. Conservation should be considered in the light of the total farming system. Off-site impacts also deserve greater attention, which Extension may be in a good position to provide. The general public and decisionmakers need education about causes and consequences of natural resource problems. These all represent challenges and opportunities for the Extension Service.

Research Needs. Policymakers, resource managers, and academic researchers still do not completely understand farmers' motivations to practice conservation. We cannot predict what factors will be most important in their decisions. Research has not yet discovered what types of farmers are most likely to be in compliance with the 1985 farm bill provisions. Without such knowledge, our educational programs and policy intentions will miss their mark. Not all farmers participate in USDA programs tied to conservation, and if those who have the most erosive land do not participate in the affected USDA programs, conservation compliance could become an empty threat that may backfire. Some farmers may even decide to quit participating in USDA programs rather than comply with provisions of 1985 farm bill. We have not been able to consider these and other important issues through social science research because of lack of funding.

Equity concerns and impacts on the structure of American agriculture rarely have been raised in relation to conservation provisions of the 1985 farm bill. Farmers who rely most on USDA programs will be most adversely affected by the provisions; these tend to be mid-size, full-time grain farmers, who already are at greater financial risk than the smaller or larger classes of farm operators. Those with more diversified operations are in better financial shape and may be less affected by the provisions. Regional impacts also will result from the conservation provisions. Social impact assessment studies must be designed and conducted to identify potential problems and develop strategies for mitigating hardships.

Design and implementation of the conservation provisions have tended to ignore important differences among farmers and their operations. Therefore, the politically safe philosophy of first-come, first-served continues to prevail. Effective policies must explicitly consider socioeconomic factors that constrain farmers from adopting soil and water conservation practices. Certain groups of farm operators (e.g., those with small operations or those who do not have contact with government organizations) may be unable or unwilling to practice conservation adequately to comply with conservation compliance.

Conclusions

Most experts agree that the voluntary approach to conservation has not been adequate to resolve soil erosion problems (*2, 5, 18 24*). The conservation provisions of the 1985 Farm Bill show a clear belief that legislation is the ultimate way to solve a problem, which is a questionable assumption. Adequate resources, proactive education, and innovation are required to implement even simple, noncontroversial policies. In the case of a controversial policy such as conservation compliance, more resources and creativity will be required than have been committed to this point.

Educational efforts will continue to be important. Farmers and other land users will need to understand their options and the implications of their decisions. To successfully implement the provisions, government agency personnel and conservation district leaders will need in-service education. Training in areas such as policy analysis, public education, conflict management, and interorganizational coordination would be helpful. Extension must receive adequate resources to develop innovative educational programs for diverse audiences.

We have to be realistic about how much the conservation provisions will accomplish. As with any government program, danger lies in expecting too much. Different groups have different expectations and possibly competing goals. Not all interest groups will be equally satisfied. The conservation provisions certainly will have important impacts on farmers and future conservation programs. Whether they will reach their full potential, however, will depend on the creativity and resolve shown in implementing these innovative provisions.

ACKNOWLEDGEMENTS

Data collected for this research are part of the North Carolina Farm and Rural Life Study (1988), a project of the Department of Sociology, Anthropology, and Social Work, North Carolina State University, Raleigh, North Carolina. The North Carolina Farm and Rural Life Study is supported by the North Carolina Agricultural Research Service and the North Carolina Agricultural Extension Service. The opinions expressed are those of the author.

REFERENCES CITED

1. Bardach, Eugene. 1977. *The implementation game: What happens after a bill becomes law.* The MIT Press, Cambridge, Massachusetts.
2. Batie, Sandra S. 1983. *Soil erosion: Crisis in America's croplands?* The Conservation Foundation, Washington, D.C.
3. Berg, Norman A. 1987. *Making the most of the new soil conservation initiatives.* Journal of Soil and Water Conservation 42: 6-7.
4. Bultena, Gordon L., and Eric O. Hoiberg. 1986. *Sources of information and technical assistance for farmers in controlling soil erosion.* In Stephen B. Lovejoy and Ted L. Napier [editors] *Conserving Soil: Insights from Socioeconomic Research.* Soil Conservation Society of America, Ankeny, Iowa. pp. 71-82
5. Buttel, Frederick H., and Louis E. Swanson. 1986. *Soil and water conservation: A farm structural and public policy perspective.* In Stephen B. Lovejoy and Ted L. Napier [editors] *Conserving Soil: Insights from Socioeconomic Research.* Soil Conservation Society of America, Ankeny, Iowa. pp. 26-39.
6. Carlson, John E., and Don A. Dillman. 1986. *Early adopters and nonusers of no-till*

in the Pacific Northwest: A comparison. In Stephen B. Lovejoy and Ted L. Napier [editors] *Conserving Soil: Insights from Socioeconomic Research.* Soil Conservation Society of America, Ankeny, Iowa. pp. 83-92.

7. Choi, Hyup, and C. M. Coughnour. 1979. *Socioeconomic aspects of no-tillage agriculture: A case study of farmers in Christian County, Kentucky.* Department of Sociology, University of Kentucky, Lexington.

8. Ervin, David E. 1986. *Constraints to practicing soil conservation: Land tenure relationships.* In Stephen B. Lovejoy and Ted L. Napier [editors] *Conserving Soil: Insights from Socioeconomic Research.* Soil Conservation Society of America, Ankeny, Iowa. pp. 95-107.

9. General Accounting Office. 1977. *To protect tomorrow's food supply soil conservation needs priority attention.* U.S. Government Printing Office, Washington, D.C.

10. Gray, Robert J. 1986. *Proving out: On implementing the Conservation Title of the 1985 Farm Bill.* Journal of Soil and Water Conservation 41: 31-32.

11. Greenwood, Mary Nell. 1986. *Extension's role in promoting soil and water conservation.* Journal of Soil and Water Conservation 41(1): 1

12. Heffernan, William D., and Gary P. Green. 1986. *Farm size and soil loss: Prospects for a sustainable agriculture.* Rural Sociology 51: 31-42.

13. Hoag, Dana, Stephen Lilley, Mike Smolen, Maurice Cook, and Joan Wright. 1988. *Extension's role in soil and water conservation.* Journal of Soil and Water Conservation 43(2): 126-129.

14. Hoban, Thomas J., and Maurice G. Cook. 1988. *Challenge of conservation.* Forum for Applied Research and Public Policy (Summer): 100-102.

15. Johnsrud, Myron D. 1988. *Meeting the information and education challenge.* Journal of Soil and Water Conservation 43(1): 49-50.

16. Korsching, Peter F., and Peter J. Nowak. 1983. *Social and institutional factors affecting the adoption and maintenance of agricultural BMPs.* In F. Schaller and G. Bailey [editors] *Agricultural Management and Water Quality.* Iowa State University Press, Ames. pp. 349-373.

17. Korsching, Peter F., Thomas J. Hoban, and Jane Maestro-Scherer. 1985. *The selling of soil conservation: A test of the voluntary approach Volume 1: Farmer survey.* Sociology Report 157. Iowa State University, Ames.

18. Napier, Ted L. 1987. *Farmers and soil erosion: A question of motivation.* Forum for Applied Research and Public Policy (Summer): 85-94.

19. Napier, Ted L., Silvana M. Camboni, and Cameron S. Thraen. 1986. *Environmental concern and the adoption of farm technologies.* Journal of Soil and Water Conservation 41: 109-113.

20. Nowak, Peter J. 1984. *Adoption and diffusion of soil and water conservation practices.* In Burton C. English, James A. Maetzold, Brian R. Holding, and Earl O. Heady [editors] *Future Agricultural Technology and Resource Conservation.* Iowa State University Press, Ames. pp. 214-237.

21. Nowak, Peter J. 1986. *New challenges for conservation partners.* Journal of Soil and Water Conservation 41: 278-284.

22. Office of Technology Assessment. 1982. *Impacts of technology on U.S. cropland and rangeland productivity.* U.S. Government Printing Office, Washington, D.C.

23. Pampel, Fred, and J. C. van Es. 1977. *Environmental quality and issues of adoption research.* Rural Sociology 42: 57-71.

24. Swanson, Louis E., Silvana M. Camboni, and Ted L. Napier. 1986. *Barriers to the adoption of soil conservation practices on farms.* In Stephen B. Lovejoy and Ted L. Napier [editors] *Conserving Soil: Insights from Socioeconomic Research.* Soil Conservation Society of America, Ankeny, Iowa. pp. 108-120.

V

Wildlife Impacts of the Conservation Title

20

Effects of the Conservation Reserve Program on Wildlife Habitat

Mark Reeff

The wildlife habitat benefit of the Conservation Reserve Program (CRP), originally seen as a secondary benefit, may be one of its most important aspects. The amount of habitat created by the CRP is staggering. The first seven sign-up periods under the program enrolled over 28 million of the 45-million-acre reserve authorized by Congress—which means that 28 million more acres of additional wildlife habitat have been created. Prior to enrollment, much of the CRP-enrolled land had been cropped, grazed, or harvested for hay.

Wildlife conservationists, along with agricultural interests, worked strenuously for the CRP because they saw the potential positive benefits of acreage left in permanent groundcover. They also recognized the necessity of quantifying the wildlife aspects of the CRP because Congress and the farm community demanded evidence to justify continuing the program. To be able to speak to this issue, a study of the wildlife impacts of the CRP was clearly needed. In 1987, the International Association of Fish and Wildlife Agencies, in conjunction with the U.S. Fish and Wildlife Service, undertook a landmark study. The study's objectives were (1) to describe the establishment of permanent cover and the characteristics of vegetation on CRP lands, (2) to describe trends in wildlife habitat resulting from the CRP, and (3) to summarize the results for congressional deliberations of Farm Bills in 1990 and 1995.

The Association acts as study coordinator, the individual states gather data, and the Service analyzes the data using sophisticated habitat modeling techniques. This study is an example of state and federal governments working together toward a common goal, determining the efforts of a major program on wildlife.

Methods

Four regions were chosen for study. For each region, three indicator species (pheasant, cottontail, and eastern meadowlark) were chosen after consulting with state and federal wildlife experts. Key habitat variables, such as height of vegetation, were identified for each of the species. The habitat quality for each species then was determined. Habitat quality is estimated from that data using a Habitat Suitability Index (HSI) model for each species.

HSIs are models based on professional judgment, expressed in a quantifiable form. For example, the HSI model for ringnecked pheasants pinpoints nesting cover (amount of vegetation) as the factor that limits pheasant production. In the case of birds, an important variable in determining the HSI is the amount of nesting cover available. The greater the amount of vegetation, the more likely a species, such as pheasant, is able to successfully nest. The HSI's are calculated and range between 0.0 (no value) and 1.0 (optimal habitat conditions). The contribution that the CRP makes to wildlife will be determined by comparing the HSI on CRP fields with the HSI calculated for the field prior to being put into the CRP.

During 1988, state fish and wildlife personnel gathered data in 27 states, which included all the study regions (Figure 1).

Information on CRP contracts, which the Agricultural Stabilization and Conservation Service (ASCS) provided, was added to the computer database. A random sample was drawn that represented all contracts in a region. In the Midwest region, a variety of conservation practices (CP) were compared, including tame grass (CP 1), native grass (CP 2), trees (CP 3), wildlife plantings (CP 4), shelterbelts (CP 5), and land already in grass (CP 10). CRP contracts were divided into 28 sampling populations on the basis of the conservation practices, the year the contract took effect, and by type of grasses (tame and native) in which base crop was retired. For each population, the researchers randomly selected 30 contracts, and sampled at least one CRP field for each contract. If more than one field was included in the contract, two fields were sampled.

Establishment of Permanent Cover

Establishment of permanent cover was considered a key indicator of wildlife habitat improvement. Most of the land surveyed had permanent

☒ AREA SAMPLED

Figure 1. The study regions.

cover, as required under the landowner's CRP contract. The cover was largely composed of young plantings of grasses with open stands of herbs rich in weedy species. Most of the vegetation was on older native grass (CP 2) fields.

Habitat Quality

To accomplish the research objective of investigating general habitat quality on CRP lands it was necessary to assess the contributions of CRP-enrolled land to habitat for the three indicator species in the Midwest (pheasant, meadowlark, and cottontail). Further, differences between conservation practices in providing habitat were examined.

Until the USDA authorized emergency haying because of drought, in June 1988, mowing was allowed only for weed suppression or as part of the planting process for permanent cover. Although emergency haying was extensive in many states in the Midwest, most of the data for this study were collected before the haying began. In Minnesota, haying was concurrent with data collection. Uncertainty exists relative to how haying or grazing impacts wildlife. Unfortunately, our data do not allow determination of the impacts of haying on habitat during 1988, but some educated guesses can be ventured. In some states, pheasants and meadowlarks that nested near "greenup" may have still been on the nest when haying occurred, with direct mortality or nest destruction likely.

Conclusions

Conclusions drawn from the findings at this point are as follows:

► Establishment of vegetation is progressing on CRP fields—which is important in improving the habitat quality for the species studied. Most of the fields sampled are in early establishment stages. The various conservation practices described differ from one another, with the highest amount of cover being native grasses (CP 2).

► Even using preliminary data, the CRP clearly is already providing nesting habitat for pheasants, and for meadowlarks in the Midwest, with further improvement likely. This should result in an increased population of both species. Unlike the success for the bird populations, habitat for the cottontail rabbit does not seem to be improving. This will be examined in more detail as the study progresses.

► Pheasant populations may be limited significantly by winter food supply and winter cover rather than by nesting cover on many CRP fields. For wildlife managers, this may necessitate introducing woody plants, herb species with persistent residues, and food plots as possible means to improve pheasant populations.

► Mowing and haying during the drought of 1988 probably affected pheasants and meadowlarks and will most certainly impact pheasant nesting in 1989. The amount of damage, however, is not known and will require more data to quantify the impacts.

Policy Implications. This study is attempting to quantify what common sense has told many working on farm bill legislation: more habitat will likely result in increased populations of game and nongame species. As data bases are developed and analyzed, evidence that the CRP is not only reducing the loss of our nation's soil resource but is also improving the habitat quality of our wildlife resources. Some obvious and not so obvious implications for future agricultural are:

► Mechanisms and programs should be developed to ensure CRP-enrolled land that provides quality habitat for game and nongame species is protected even after the contracts expire. This is particularly important with the realization that habitat quality is enormously better than at initial enrollment and will continue to improve. To permit CRP enrolled land to return to agricultural production not only would allow highly erodible land to be cultivated, but it also would destroy the habitat that has been developed on those lands and waste tax dollars.

▶ Greater attention should be directed toward the development of shelterbelts, food plots, and attendant areas, since they would provide food and winter cover. These factors limit pheasant populations as much as nesting cover. Agricultural policy and regulations that facilitate development of such areas should be encouraged.

▶ At present the study is not addressing the impacts on wildlife and fish in riverine and stream environments. Nonpoint-source pollution reduction is a major result of the CRP and will in all likelihood greatly improve habitat for fish and water-dependent wildlife. Without quantifing these aspects of the program, it is difficult to say to what extent the aquatic environment is being improved. However, it is probably significant in certain areas of the country. The study also does not address the reduction of pesticide runoff, which would contribute to overall improvement of the aquatic environment.

The various conservation practices used to achieve the goals of soil conservation in the U.S. may affect different species in different ways. Agricultural commodity producers and managers must be aware of the differing impacts of the various practices on each species.

REFERENCES CITED

1. Hayes, R. L., R. P. Webb, and A. H. Farmer. 1989. *Effects of the Conservation Reserve Program on wildlife habitat: Results of the 1988 monitoring.* Translations, 54th North American Wildlife and Natural Resources Conference. Wildlife Management Institute, Washington, D.C.
2. Robel, R. J., J. N. Briggs, A. D. Dayton, and L. C. Hulbert. 1970. *Relationships between visual obstruction measurements and weight of grassland vegetation.* Journal of Range Management 23: 295-297.

21

Implementing the Conservation Title: Effects on Wildlife

Ann Robinson and Alfred Berner

When the Conservation Title of the Food Security Act of 1985 became law, conservationists told the country that its provisions, if rigorously implemented, represented the opportunity to reduce soil erosion and improve water quality and wildlife populations (34). As implementation proceeds, the promise pales. The Title still deserves praise, but politics force compromise and reduce big improvements to small incremental steps.

To make definitive statements about the effects of conservation provisions on wildlife is premature. The Conservation Reserve Program (CRP) will be one of the most researched agricultural programs in history, but studies around the country are only beginning to provide data to indicate the program's actual influence. Impacts of the other provisions on wildlife are much more difficult to document and may never be thoroughly understood. Nevertheless, as the country enters the decision-making phase for the next farm bill, we must make some educated guesses about effects of the conservation provisions based on the best available knowledge.

Changes in the Conservation Reserve Program

As interest in CRP sign-ups has waned, the eligibility requirements have been modified in several ways to encourage participation. Erosion criteria have been reduced for tree planting contracts, and eliminated for planting filter strips along waterways or around wetlands. Cropped wetlands became eligible for the CRP in January 1989, in time for the eighth sign-up period, February 6-24. Through 1988, about 28.1 million acres had been approved after seven sign-ups, with estimated annual soil savings of 574 million tons (45).

The federal government pays half the cost of establishing cover, and some states, notably Minnesota, Missouri, Maryland, and Ohio, fund additional cost-sharing, at least for some cover practices (CPs) in targeted areas. Participants can use 13 approved cover options, though not all may be available in every county (Table 1). Although the impact on wildlife varies by CP, wildlife use in all cases will be enhanced by conversion from annual crops to less disturbed perennial habitats (Table 2). Despite the availability of a wide variety of CPs, a high percentage of CRP acres is in tame grasses and legumes (CP 1), which are easy and inexpensive to establish. Although the resulting grasslands have high wildlife values, the potential for harvesting during hay emergencies is also high, and haying these lands considerably reduces their benefits to wildlife (8, 9).

Table 1. Cover practices allowed and established on Conservation Reserve Program acres through the seventh sign-up (45).

Cover Practice Number	Cover Practice Description	Acreage Affected
CP 1	Tame grasses and/or legumes	16,523,027
CP 2	Native grasses	7,205,398*
CP 3	Trees (forestry)	1,680,700
CP 4	Wildlife plantings (any combination of trees, shrubs, forbs, grasses, legumes, or other vegetative cover)	1,136,183
CP 5	Field windbreaks	5,531
CP 6	Diversion	80,640
CP 7	Erosion control structures	37,446
CP 8	Grass waterways	14,273
CP 9	Shallow water areas for wildlife	2,570
CP 10	Existing grass and/or legumes	1,457,594
CP 11	Existing tree and/or shrub planting	74,858
CP 12	Annual wildlife food plot	8,948
CP 13	Filter strips	29,650
SL 5	Diversions (ACP)	1
WP 1	Structures (ACP)	1,606
WP 3	Waterways (ACP)	557
Total		28,258,982†

*Reports from the field indicate that a number of native grass contracts have been changed to tame grasses.

†The total acres affected are 129,072 more than contracted because acres for CP 6, CP 7, CP 8, CP 9, SL 5, WP 1, and WP 3 are, in some cases, also being counted under the other CPs.

Note: USDA statistics.

Native grass seedings (CP 2) are less popular because establishment costs are 2 to 3 times higher than for CP 1, and stands are more difficult to establish. Native seedings, however, are more likely to remain than are the cheaper CP 1 mixtures after the 10-year contract expires.

Planting trees and shrubs for cover and field windbreaks (CP 3, 4, and 5) provides many potential long-term benefits for erosion control and wildlife. This category also offers substantial benefits for landowners as investment in timber and as protection of crop productivity. But interest has been low because: (1) these practices are more costly and the cover is difficult to establish; (2) the landowner has to have a greater degree of commitment to permanence; and (3) landowners do not understand well the benefits of windbreaks for crop production[1].

Planting filter strips along waterways and around wetlands (CP 13) has great potential for improving water quality and fisheries. Streamside (riparian zone) management has been identified as one of the most effective methods of controlling land use impacts on water quality (*31, 32*). Unfortunately, this option has not been popular (even though land does not have to be highly erodible to qualify), in part because the number of actual acres that can be signed up is low—which means the payment is low.

[1]Brandle, J., B. Johnson, and T. Akeson. 1988. "Field Windbreaks: Are They Effective?" Paper presented at the 43rd Annual Meeting, Soil and Water Conservation Society, Columbus, Ohio, 16 pp.

Table 2. Mean number of breeding birds and bird species per 100 acres observed using various farmland habitats in Illinois, 1957-1958 (17).

Cover Types	Breeding Birds		All Birds
	Species	Per 100 Acres	Per 100 Acres
Corn	3	no data	66
Soybeans	3	no data	53
Fallow (plowed)	0	0	86
Fallow with volunteer	13	105	219
Oats	10	113	178
Wheat	5	30	100
Pasture (grazed)	17	113	219
Pasture (ungrazed)	7	no data	228
Mixed hay	14	328	408
Red clover	10	210	371
Sweet clover	4	no data	381
Alfalfa	9	138	294
Marshland	18	no data	595
Shrubland	17	no data	401
Forest with understory	no data	no data	215
Forest without understory	no data	no data	397

To recruit substantially more acres for cover practices that provide increased benefits to society, federal or state agencies are going to have to increase incentives (30).[2] But even without increased incentives, wildlife advocates' and foresters' personal contacts with landowners have proven effective in increasing landowners' willingness to plant trees or restore wetlands on CRP land (personal communication, Helbig, 1987; personal communication, Lange, 1987). Private organizations interested in preserving wildlife (e.g., Pheasants Forever, Quail Unlimited) should utilize this type of salesmanship more extensively.

Distribution of land enrolled in the CRP also has an important effect on the program's wildlife impacts. Sign-ups have been most numerous in the Great Plains states, in areas where land prices are depressed, and where planting pines is compatible with existing timber industry (Table 3). This is not necessarily the best distribution for wildlife or other resource enhancements (8). Once again, to balance the distribution and thereby improve the resource benefits of the programs, increased incentives are needed, especially if grain prices continue to improve. The farm bill implementation study being coordinated by the Conservation Foundation and the Soil and Water Conservation Society (SWCS) promises to shed light on many of these issues.

The decision to release CRP lands for haying during the drought in 1988 and again in 1989 represented a considerable setback for wildlife. The extent of the damage is difficult to ascertain, though wildlifers around the country put in extra time last summer attempting to document the losses. This information eventually will be reported in the results of a survey of CRP acres from 32 states in five geographic regions, coordinated by the National Ecology Center in Colorado (15). In addition, research projects are underway in a number of states, including Iowa, Minnesota, Missouri, and Texas, to measure the direct impacts of CRP acreages and cover management on wildlife.

Figures are not available on the number of CRP acres nationwide that were hayed. According to the Agricultural Stabilization and Conservation Service (ASCS), 2,236 counties in 43 states were declared drought counties and offered the opportunity to hay commodity set-aside and CRP acres. (Water Bank acres in 191 counties in 11 states, as well as some state conservation lands, also were opened.) Based on verbal reports, the ASCS expects that the data will show haying on CRP acres to be most active in

---

[2]Jahn, L. R. "Responses Needed to Address New Opportunities in Agriculture/Wildlife Programs." Paper presented at the National Farm Bill Workshop, November 1-3, 1988. Harpers Ferry, West Virginia, 7 pp.

the northern plains states, including the Dakotas and Minnesota (personal communication, Wright, 1989).

To justify raids on our few wildlife lands, better protective mechanisms must be written into law and not left to administrative discretion. Under any justified hay emergency, the land retired under commodity control programs must be utilized first. Only as a last resort should CRP acres be opened to haying or grazing. In these extreme cases, guidelines for cutting dates and procedures that are fair to farmers and to wildlife must be established. In 1988, every rule to protect wildlife was relaxed or rescinded. Ironically, the destroyed habitat provided costly low-quality forage (48), which in some cases was unusable because of pesticide residues (4).

Prior to opening up CRP, USDA had opened up annual commodity-control acres in the Acreage Reserve Program (ARP) for haying and grazing, as has happened in all or part of the nation since 1984. Even though

Table 3. Total acres enrolled in the Conservation Reserve Program in the United States by state through the seventh sign-up (45).

State	Acres Enrolled	State	Acres Enrolled
Alabama	469,429	Montana	2,264,770
Alaska	24,701	Nebraska	1,159,688
Arizona	0	Nevada	2,343
Arkansas	174,490	New Hampshire	0
California	170,479	New Jersey	364
Colorado	1,748,117	New Mexico	468,309
Connecticut	10	New York	47,174
Delaware	724	North Carolina	115,999
Florida	105,157	North Dakota	2,175,123
Georgia	570,801	Ohio	179,950
Hawaii	85	Oklahoma	1,017,301
Idaho	714,307	Oregon	497,622
Illinois	464,768	Pennsylvania	71,205
Indiana	259,700	Rhode Island	0
Iowa	1,635,516	South Carolina	227,289
Kansas	2,385,453	South Dakota	1,222,860
Kentucky	383,504	Tennessee	379,468
Louisiana	87,809	Texas	3,457,007
Maine	32,221	Utah	227,359
Maryland	9,668	Vermont	187
Massachusetts	25	Virginia	58,518
Michigan	152,752	Washington	870,230
Minnesota	1,644,159	West Virginia	553
Mississippi	583,445	Wisconsin	464,749
Missouri	1,381,896	Wyoming	222,606
		Total	28,129,910

between 40 and 50 million ARP acres were available, cover on the ARP (though usually required) was so scanty or nonexistent that it provided little value as forage. As a result, CRP acres were compromised. The decision to allow haying longer than the originally allotted 30 days undoubtedly magnified the negative impact on wildlife and also increased the potential negative impact on some cost-shared cover plantings (8, 9).

This series of events has recharged the call for a multiyear set-aside under ARP (20, 36, 42, 49). The grass-legume seedings required under such a program would yield multiple benefits—commodity control, better conservation, and a strategic forage reserve for emergencies. The relatively inexpensive seeding of legumes or grass-legume mixes also would help farmers control weeds and insects, reduce the need for chemical pesticides, improve soil tilth, and add nitrogen and organic matter to depleted soils.

Sodbuster and Conservation Compliance

Sodbuster does not allow commodity crop farming on previously undisturbed highly erodible soils unless the land is farmed in such a way as to keep the erosion rate at or below the soil loss tolerance or T level. Conservation compliance, on the other hand, encourages conservation by requiring that farmers have a fully implemented conservation plan on their highly erodible croplands by 1995. In both cases farmers can lose their federal farm program benefits if they do not comply.

Sodbuster's purpose is to discourage landowners from plowing up highly erodible land to produce commodity crops; it applies to lands not planted to annually tilled crops in 1981-1985. If producers plow up grassland or woodland on highly erodible soils (with an exception for legumes in a rotation), they must have, and be implementing, a rigorous conservation plan on that land, designed to keep erosion at or below T. Estimates indicate that sodbuster has the potential to protect as many as 146 million acres of grasslands and 74 million acres of forests (43).

Conservation compliance requires that farmers who produce commodity crops on highly erodible cropland must develop and start to implement an approved conservation plan by 1990 to remain eligible for most USDA farm program benefits; the plan must be fully operational by 1995. This provision affects about 118 to 144 million acres of cropland that are most subject to wind and water erosion (40, 43).

Regulations that once required reducing soil loss to less than 2T now allow widespread use of SCS-approved plans for "alternative conservation systems" (ACSs) intended to "substantially" reduce soil loss. Permitted soil loss has no ceiling. Under the original regulations, some lands with severe erosion would have had to be converted to pasture or other uses. Presently, however, these acres still will be cropped using primarily conservation tillage to reduce erosion. Many of the acres will continue to erode at rates greater than 2T and still be eligible for farm program benefits (personal communication, Daigle, 1988; *19, 47*).

Sodbuster probably will have a more positive impact than compliance on wildlife, because of more acreage and stricter requirements. Stringent rules for sodbuster should prevent land use changes to row crops in some areas, and even when the land is converted, should encourage good erosion control practices, which will help prevent nonpoint-source pollution.

Considering the weakened rules, compliance by itself will provide few benefits for terrestrial wildlife species. By 1990, the Conservation Foundation/SWCS farm bill study, referred to earlier, should provide some valuable insight into actual erosion reductions resulting from compliance. If terrestrial wildlife does benefit from compliance, it probably will result from the minor habitat enhancement offered by conservation tillage and other conserving practices.

Conservation tillage (CT) includes a range of techniques that leave crop residue on the land to protect soil from the forces of wind and water. These practices have been gaining popularity since the late 1970s, and conservation compliance is providing a strong impetus for more widespread adoption. Some problems with no-till—the most extreme variation of conservation tillage—during the 1988 drought may discourage adoption, at least in the short run (*14*). In general, CT provides few advantages for terrestrial wildlife, especially if it allows farmers to bring some marginal land (steeper slopes) into row crop production. But studies have shown that no-till has the potential for reducing or eliminating bird nest disturbances in small grains and row crops (*37*). Warburton and Klimstra (*46*) found that no-till cornfields offer more food and cover than do conventionally tilled corn fields, leading to a greater diversity of invertebrate species and a more stable population of small mammals.

Researchers in Iowa have questioned some of these findings. Best (*10*) suggests that some conservation tillage fields actually can be ecological death traps—areas that attract nesting birds because of good early cover in crop residue, but where breeding success would be lower than in alternative available habitats because of factors such as planting operations or high herbicide use. Another study found that no-till environments did not increase arthropod availability (*3*).

The minimal disturbance of cover that accompanies no-till farming probably will benefit wildlife to some extent, but the increased use of herbicides that often accompanies CT practices poses added risks to terrestrial and aquatic species (*1, 46*). Careful management can help. Chemical contamination can be decreased in several ways—by "knifing" the pesticide into the soil, splitting applications, timing pre-emergence herbicides prior to nesting, and selecting less toxic chemicals (*1, 37*). Some row crop farmers use little or no pesticides, with a low-input CT variation known as ridge-till, which depends on cultivation between rows to control weeds. The trade-offs between reduced chemical use and increased disturbance of potential nest sites require investigation.

Some other soil conservation measures also can improve wildlife habitat on cropped acres (*25, 28*), but the positive impacts of soil conservation practices on wildlife are for the most part secondary and highly dependent on the resulting vegetative composition, structure, and location of cover (*20*). Again, careful management can improve the wildlife benefits possible from erosion control structures and practices. If farmers are aware of opportunities for improving terrestrial wildlife habitat, some will select conservation practices for the dual purpose of controlling erosion and providing habitat (*11*).

Overall, changes in land use (e.g., row crops to grassland) have a far greater impact on habitat quality than do changes in management practices (*28*). Illinois data support this contention; between 1967 and 1982, farmland game harvest declined 46 percent, while cropland "adequately treated" to control erosion increased 48 percent (*11*). Another Illinois study showed that eight grassland bird species in the state declined by 80 to 98 percent between 1958 and 1978 (*18*). The deciding factor for this decline in wildlife was land use change; the proportion of cropland used for row crops increased almost 80 percent during the 20-year period.

If widespread use of ACSs is allowed to stand, compliance will result in a negligible amount of actual land-use change to perennial cover, except in the few instances in which compliance still encourages participation in the CRP. In fact, USDA's express purpose in weakening the requirements for conservation plans was to avoid forcing farmers to change land use, regardless of the environmental implications (*35*).

Compliance probably will contribute to wildlife habitat primarily through improving water quality. Conservation compliance will reduce sediments and associated pollutants that are washed or blown off cropland, thus improving water quality and habitat for fish and other aquatic species. USDA originally estimated that conservation compliance could prevent about 1.2 billion tons of soil from eroding off farmlands each year after 1995. Under present rules, however, erosion reductions in the range of half to three-fourths of original predictions are probably more realistic.

It is impossible to calculate how much the amount of sediment being dumped into streams, lakes, potholes, and rivers will be reduced as a result of compliance. But these measures, along with erosion reductions resulting from the CRP, should bring much needed improvements in water quality and aquatic ecosystems. Soil particles degrade aquatic habitat while they are suspended in water and after settling out of it; in both cases, sediment harms aquatic life all along the food chain, from microscopic algae to valuable game fish (6, 12, 31, 39). For example, a study of fish population changes in Illinois identified excessive siltation as a principal cause for the disappearance of native fish species (39). Siltation and turbidity have been major causes in reducing the abundance and diversity of clam species, including fingernail clams, a widely distributed, important food source for ducks and fish (13, 24).

Sediments that are blown or washed off land frequently carry along nutrients such as nitrogen and phosphorus that otherwise are limited in aquatic systems. These nutrients cause one of the most serious water quality problems, eutrophication—excessive nutrient enrichment of a body of water, stimulating high rates of biological productivity. Besides conveying nutrients, cropland runoff also carries pesticides and other contaminants to waterways and lakes.

Reducing these inputs to already damaged streams or lakes may not immediately result in improved fishing. Many factors are involved, making the link between erosion reduction and fisheries difficult to pinpoint (31). One still must conclude, however, that policies that reduce erosion have great potential for improving fish habitat. A study of Black Creek, in Indiana, found that erosion control measures had measurable benefits for fish (29). Terraces or retention basins, designed to hold water on the land and direct it through a subsurface draining system, were quite effective in reducing sediment and phosphorus to the waterway. Conservation tillage was somewhat less effective, but still of significant benefit. Grassed waterways reduced the sediment and phosphorus entering the stream but, because of their small total area, were not as effective as either terraces or conservation tillage in improving water quality.

Swampbuster

Under swampbuster, producers who drain wetlands to grow agricultural commodities after December 23, 1985, are not eligible for farm program benefits. The loss of benefits applies not just to crops grown on the converted wetland, but on all land they farm. There is no minimum size for wetlands protected under this measure—one of swampbuster's prime benefits to wildlife but also a prime reason why it is so hotly contested. Swampbuster protects as much as 5.1 million acres of wetlands that have a potential for being converted to cropland (44). Unlike sodbuster and compliance, a conservation plan in no way affects eligibility for farm programs under swampbuster.

Previously, farmers could include converted wetlands as part of their base acreage for USDA price support programs, which effectively provided a subsidy for converting wetlands to cropland. In fact, under USDA's agricultural conservation programs, drainage was cost-shared well into the 1970s. Nearly 90 percent of all wetland drainage can be attributed to agriculture, and many remaining marshes are slowly being filled in by farm run-off (41).

Wetlands play a vital role in maintaining good surface and groundwater quality (2), thus improving fish habitat. Some fish species, including northern pike (*Esox lucius*), either depend on or use shallow, marshy wetlands for spawning (27). In Minnesota, where recreational fishing is an important industry, most of the state's minnow harvest, worth $30 million, comes from natural ponds and wetlands (personal communication, Hennagir, 1988) (33). Wetlands provide valuable habitat for many terrestrial species, most notably waterfowl, grassland birds, and muskrats (*Ondatra zibethicus*). The wetland environment—marshes dominated by grasses, sedges, and cattails— is one of the most productive for wildlife (38). These areas typically have breeding densities up to 13 times greater than grain crop fields (17).

Swampbuster helps protect shallow, seasonal wetlands, sometimes called potholes, that provide an environment for high-protein foods for migrating waterfowl (23). The Prairie Pothole region, which has lost about half its wetlands, once produced an estimated 15 million ducks annually but now produces only one-third that number, with drainage being the major reason for the decline (5). The continental populations of several duck species that nest in this region are at record low levels (personal communication, Hansen, 1989).

Despite the obvious potential for saving wildlife habitat, enforcement of swampbuster remained largely nonexistent two years after passage by Congress (16, 22). By late 1987, only two producers in the entire United States were denied benefits for violating swampbuster provisions notwithstanding widespread reports that drainage was extensive and may actually have increased as a result of this measure. The U.S. Fish and Wildlife

Service (FWS) reported 346 potential swampbuster violations in North Dakota, South Dakota, and Minnesota during 1987 and 1988, but only three farmers in those states lost their agricultural subsidies. According to its own figures, ASCS granted over 80 percent of the 810 requests for commenced conversion exemptions in these three states during the same time period[3].

This situation has improved somewhat as a result of intensive interagency training on wetlands and swampbuster and increasing familiarity with the law. Also, wildlife agencies and the National Wildlife Federation's Prairie Wetlands Resource Center have pursued some of the most blatant violations through informal appeals.

Opposition continues to be fierce, especially in North Dakota. Many angry landowners, encouraged by drainage concerns (who have even supplied signs and run advertisements), have posted their land as off-limits to hunters until swampbuster is repealed. Several congressional hearings have been held to review swampbuster implementation and the need for the provision. Requested changes in the law include: (1) small wetlands and "nuisance spots" should be exempted; (2) the penalties should be graduated depending on the amount of acres drained, or the intent of the violation; and (3) the law should be repealed in favor of a "no-net-loss" policy. As of January 1989, the law has not been repealed or weakened though, as mentioned earlier, plans were finalized to allow cropped wetlands into the CRP.

Conservationists and wildlife proponents throughout the country also would like to see changes in swampbuster (*16*). The final rules, which came out September 17, 1987, in the *Federal Register,* were considered generally good for conservation. One regulatory provision of particular concern, however, is the "third party exemption" that waives sanctions if the wetland conversion was carried out by someone other than the landowner or his or her agent. Wildlifers would like to see this exception eliminated or modified because it provides continued opportunities for drainage districts and other public or quasi-public entities to drain, sometimes on farmers' behalf (*8*). Possibly the most controversial of the proposed changes would transfer primary responsibility for enforcing the law to the FWS. Currently FWS is the principal investigator of violations and consults with both ASCS and SCS concerning wetlands. Thus, FWS has the expertise to implement swampbuster without the political and pro-

---

[3]Turrini, A. N., W. Baron, and D. Nomsen. "Swampbuster Implementation in North Dakota, South Dakota and Minnesota." Paper presented at the 50th Midwest Fish and Wildlife Conference, Columbus, Ohio, 1988. 12 pp.

fessional entanglements that plague ASCS. If the FWS were to establish the existence of a swampbuster violation, it would simply notify the ASCS county committee to withhold benefits from the violator.

Two other proposed modifications that would make the law more effective are to make the act of conversion itself the violation and to provide an appeals process for third parties. Under current law, a violation occurs not when land is drained but when the converted wetland is planted to a commodity crop—defined as any crop that requires annual tilling of the soil. This diminishes the law's effectiveness in a number of ways. For example, a farmer can convert wetlands and then plant crops in only those years when commodity prices are high, or when he or she does not intend to apply for agricultural subsidies. In other years, the farmer can hay converted wetlands without jeopardizing benefits. Also, the additional hayland this provides allows other haylands that are not covered under swampbuster or sodbuster to be converted to commodity crops without losing hay production and allows an increase in acres planted to commodities. The cropping requirement creates an administrative nightmare for those who are charged with monitoring the planting status of wetlands converted after the 1985 deadline.

An informal administrative appeals process for nonproducers is needed as well. A producer has the right to appeal if he or she is denied benefits under the law. But no channel exists whereby a third party can request reconsideration of a decision allowing drainage. Informal appeals have been made to USDA, resulting in the reversal of several decisions made by county and state ASCS committees. The agency, however, is not obligated to consider informal appeals of this nature. Moreover, attendant to this problem, third parties cannot be present at appeal hearings unless the landowner consents.

Conclusions

Preserving our wildlife heritage was a goal that Congress specifically mandated in the Food Security Act of 1985. Outdoor enthusiasts, particularly wildlifers, are aware of the impacts that agriculture has had on natural resources. As a result, this constituency will continue to be involved in the farm policy debate, along with those whose primary concerns are to maintain productive soils and drinkable water.

The Conservation Title was designed primarily to make agricultural programs more consistent with the need for a quality environment. Its provisions are an important first step in solving many serious resource problems in the nation's countryside. Reform is inevitably slow and will require continuing public support to provide incentives for stewardship, education about the reasons for change, and training in new techniques and approaches.

The ultimate responsibility for implementing the conservation provisions rests with farmers. Unfortunately, an integral link to the farmer, and thus to implementing reforms—state and local-level ASCS committees—is often forgotten.

Congress passes laws and top administrators in the agencies within USDA make the rules, in consultation with many interests, but much of the day-to-day administration of programs is left to ASCS committees. As with all farm acts since 1947, the only voting members of these committees are landowners and producers who are eligible to participate in commodity programs. The secretary of agriculture appoints a three-member committee for each state. In each county, the eligible producers elect a maximum of three local committees of three members each. Members of the elected local committees then select county committees.

These farmers make many decisions that affect the distribution of large amounts of money provided by the taxpaying public. Usually, ASCS committees have been so concerned with issues such as weed control and convenience for their farmer constituents that they have completely neglected the "conservation" portion of their charge (7, 21). Committee members receive little or no training, and the mechanisms to hold them accountable to the public are weak.

Despite the large sums of money involved and the enormous impacts that USDA programs have on natural resources, the 1985 farm bill has no provision for voting input from natural resource professionals (soil, water, and wildlife) and other interested parties. Though committees may "consult" with such interests, the committees are not obligated to use the information.

Steps must be taken to include biologists, soil conservationists, or other conservation-oriented persons as voting members on ASCS committees. In addition, ASCS should take more responsibility for educating its agents at every level about the impacts of agricultural practices on soils, water quality, and wildlife. These committees also must be made more accountable for their decisions.

The conservation provisions represent a significant improvement in farm policy in relation to natural resources, but the detrimental aspects of some ongoing farm programs and the way they are administered still work against conservation. Much of the Conservation Title's potential is being lost, along with a great deal of soil and wildlife, as well as goodwill from conservationists and nonfarm taxpayers. As we look to the next farm bill, we must work together to preserve and build on the gains represented by CRP, sodbuster, conservation compliance, and swampbuster.

REFERENCES CITED

1. Baker, J. L., and J. M. Laflen. 1983. *Water quality consequences of conservation tillage.* Journal of Soil and Water Conservation 38(3): 186-193.
2. Bardecki, M. 1984. *What value wetlands?* Journal of Soil and Water Conservation 39(3): 166-169.
3. Basore, N. S., L. B. Best, and J. B. Wooley, Jr. 1987. *Arthropod availability in no-tillage fields.* Wildlife Society Bulletin 15: 229-233.
4. Becker, R. L., B. R. Durgan, and J. L. Gunsolus. 1988. *Grazing a hay harvest on herbicide treated CRP or set aside acres released in response to drought.* University of Minnesota Extension, St. Paul. 2 pp.
5. Bellrose, F. 1980. *Ducks, geese, and swans of North America.* Wildlife Management Institute, Washington, D.C. 495 pp.
6. Berkman, H. E., and C. R. Rabeni. 1987. *Effects of siltation on stream fish communities.* Environmental Biology of Fishes 18(4): 285-294.
7. Berner, A. H. 1984. *Federal land retirement programs: A land management albatross.* Transactions, North American Wildlife Natural Resources Conference 49: 118-131.
8. Berner, A. H. 1988a. *The 1985 farm act and its implications for wildlife.* In W. J. Chandler and L. Labate [editors] *Audubon Wildlife Report 1988/1989.* The National Audubon Society, New York, New York. pp. 437-465.
9. Berner, A. H. 1988b. *Federal pheasants—impact of federal agricultural programs on pheasant habitat, 1934-1985.* In D. L. Hallett, W. R. Edwards, and G. V. Burger [editors] *Pheasants: Symptoms of Wildlife Problems on Agricultural Lands.* North Central Section of the Wildlife Society, Bloomington, Indiana. pp. 45-93.
10. Best, L. B. 1986. *Conservation tillage: Ecological traps for nesting birds?* Wildlife Society Bulletin 14: 308-317.
11. Brady, S. J., and R. Hamilton. 1988. *Wildlife opportunities within federal agricultural programs.* In D. L. Hallett, W. R. Edwards, and G. V. Burger [editors] *Pheasants: Symptoms of Wildlife Problems on Agricultural Lands.* North Central Section of the Wildlife Society, Bloomington, Indiana. pp. 95-109.
12. Clark, E. H., J. A. Haverkamp, and W. Chapman. 1985. *Eroding soils: The off-farm impacts.* The Conservation Foundation, Washington, D.C. 241 pp.
13. Ellis, M. M. 1936. *Erosion silt as a factor in aquatic environments.* Ecology 17(1): 29-41.
14. Fee, R. 1988. *Don't count no-till corn out.* Successful Farming 86(14): 46.
15. Farmer, A. H., R. L. Hays, and R. P. Webb. 1988. *Effects of the Conservation Reserve Program on wildlife habitat: A cooperative monitoring study.* Transactions, North American Wildlife Natural Resource Conference 53: 232-238.
16. Goldman-Carter, J. L. 1988. *Effects of swampbuster implementation on soil, water and wildlife resources.* Transactions, North American Wildlife Natural Resource Conference 53: 249-262.
17. Graber, R. R., and J. W. Graber. 1963. *A comparative study of bird populations in Illinois—1906 and 1956-1958.* Illinois Natural History Survey Bulletin 28(3): 383-528.
18. Graber, J. W., and R. R. Graber. 1983. *The declining grassland birds.* Illinois Natural History Survey No. 227. Champaign, Illinois. 4 pp.

19. Gulliford, J. B. 1988. *Statement of Iowa Department of Agriculture and Land Steward-ship before Senate Subcommittee on Conservation, Credit and Rural Development, August 9.* U.S. Senate, Washington, D.C. 4 pp.
20. Harmon, K. W. 1974. *Do incentives to protect soil and water benefit fish and wildlife?* Soil Conservation Society of America, Syracuse, New York. 10 pp.
21. Harmon, K. W., and M. M. Nelson. 1973. *Wildlife and soil conservation in land retirement programs.* Wildlife Society Bulletin 1: 28-38.
22. Jones, L. A. 1988. *Implementing swampbuster: A view.* Journal of Soil and Water Conservation 43(1): 30.
23. Lambertson, R. E. 1988. *Testimony of Assistant Director for Fish and Wildlife Enhance-ment, U.S. Fish and Wildlife Service, before Senate Committee on Agriculture, Sub-committee on Conservation and Forestry, concerning the 1985 Food Security Act, March 24.* U.S. Senate, Washington, D.C. 6 pp.
24. Lewis, J. B. 1984. *The effect of substrate on burrowing in freshwater mussels (Unionidae).* Canadian Journal of Zoology 62: 2,023-2,025.
25. Lines, I. L., and C. J. Perry. 1978. *A numerical wildlife habitat evaluation procedure.* Transactions, North American Wildlife Natural Resources Conference 43: 284-301.
26. McSweeny, W. T., and R. A. Kramer. 1986. *The integration of farm programs for achieving soil conservation and nonpoint pollution control objectives.* Land Economics 62(2): 159-173.
27. Minnesota Department of Natural Resources. 1988. *Muskie and northern pike: Min-nesota's big-game fish.* Division of Fish and Wildlife, Section of Fisheries, St. Paul, Minnesota. 15 pp.
28. Miranowski, R. J., and R. Bender. 1982. *Impact of erosion control policies on wildlife habitat on private lands.* Journal of Soil and Water Conservation 37(5): 228-291.
29. Morrison, J. 1982. *Environmental impact of land use on water quality: Black Creek Project—executive summary.* Allen County Soil and Water Conservation District, Indiana, 22 pp.
30. Moss, S. 1988. *Statement of President of National Association of Foresters, before Subcommittee on Agricultural Research and Forestry and General Legislation of the Senate Agriculture Committee, March 24.* U.S. Senate, Washington, D.C. 8 pp.
31. Pajak, P. 1988. *Fisheries management: Developing a strategy for the Milwaukee River Basin.* Wisconsin Department of Natural Resources Report, Milwaukee. 19 pp.
32. Perry, J., N. H. Troelstrup, Jr., W. Bartodziej, and T. Wilton. 1988. *Risks to sur-face water quality in the Lanesboro watershed: Southeastern Minnesota.* Staff Paper. Department of Forest Resources, University of Minnesota, St. Paul. 112 pp.
33. Peterson, D. L., and F. A. Hennagir. 1980. *Minnesota live bait industry assessment study.* Investigation Report No. 367. Minnesota Department of Natural Resources, Division of Fish and Wildlife, Section of Fisheries, St. Paul. 75 pp.
34. Robinson, A. Y. 1987. *Saving soil and wildlife: The promise of the Farm Act's con-servation title.* Izaak Walton League of America, Minneapolis, Minnesota. 57 pp.
35. Robinson, A. Y. 1988. *Implementation of conservation compliance: Implications for soil, water and wildlife.* Transactions, North American Wildlife Natural Resources Conference 53: 210-221.
36. Robinson, A. Y. 1988. *U.S. needs better forage reserve.* News-Gazette, Champaign, Illinois 137(17): 2A.
37. Rodgers, R. D., and J. B. Wooley. 1983. *Conservation tillage impacts on wildlife.* Journal of Soil and Water Conservation 38(3): 212-213.

38. Schitoskey, F., Jr., and R. L. Linder. 1978. *Use of wetlands by upland wildlife.* In P. R. Greson, J. R. Clark, and J. E. Clark [editors] *Wetland Functions and Values: The State of Our Understanding.* American Water Resources Association, Minneapolis, Minnesota. pp. 307-311.
39. Smith, P. W. 1971. *Illinois streams: A classification based on their fishes and an analysis of factors responsible for disappearance of native species.* Biological Notes No. 76. Illinois Natural History Survey, Springfield. 14 pp.
40. Soil and Water Conservation Society. 1988. *Conservation tillage on the rise.* Journal of Soil and Water Conservation 43(6): 47.
41. Stanley, G. 1987. *The good old days are coming back.* Outdoor America 52(2): 8-11.
42. U.S. Congressional Record. 1988. *Farm Conservation and Water Protection Act.* 134(146).
43. U.S. Department of Agriculture. 1987. *Environmental assessment for highly erodible land conservation provisions of the Food Security Act of 1985.* Washington, D.C. 46 pp.
44. U.S. Department of Agriculture. 1987. *Environmental assessment and final regulatory impact and flexibility analyses for the wetland conservation provisions of the Food Security Act of 1985.* Soil Conservation Service, Washington, D.C. 62 pp.
45. U.S. Department of Agriculture. 1989. *Conservation Reserve Program statistics.* Conservation and Environmental Protection Division, Agriculture Stabilization and Conservation Service, Washington, D.C. 10 pp.
46. Warburton, D. B., and W. D. Klimstra. 1984. *Wildlife uses of no-till and conventionally tilled corn fields.* Journal of Soil and Water Conservation 39(5): 327-330.
47. Ward, J., and T. Kuhnle. 1988. *USDA policies undercut conservation aims.* Statement of Natural Resources Defense Council before the Senate Committee on Agriculture, Nutrition and Forestry, Subcommittee on Nutrition and Investigations. U.S. Senate, Washington, D.C. 8 pp.
48. Webb Publishing. 1988. *CRP hay tests show poor quality results.* The Farmer 106(13): 12.
49. Wildlife Management Institute. 1988. *Establishing a strategic forage reserve fact sheet.* Washington, D.C. 2 pp.

VI

Future Policy Needs After the Conservation Title of the Food Security Act of 1985

22

Future Policy Needs for Soil Conservation: The Soil Conservation Service Perspective

R. Mack Gray

In 1985 the Soil Conservation Service (SCS) celebrated its 50th birthday. The 1930s had set the philosophical tone that would guide conservation efforts for half a century. President Franklin Roosevelt endorsed changes that would "broaden present adjustment operations so as to give farmers increasing incentives for conservation and efficient use of the nation's soil resources" (3).

The primary impetus for increased emphasis on soil conservation was to be focused not in Washington but at state and local levels. Indeed, the Soil Conservation Act of 1935 required SCS to confine its work to "states that passed laws of their own establishing a suitable soil conservation policy" (3). Thus the stage was set for formation of the conservation districts and the foundation of 50 years of conservation policy in the U.S.

Quoting Kirkendall: "[It was] assumed that a program to modify land use practices could be made effective only if farmers cooperated voluntarily. Thus, the suggested statute was drawn in such a way that it provided machinery which could be used by the farmers after they had been educated in the need to act. Little compulsion was to be involved" (3).

Treatment of the conservation districts, too, exhibited this "helping hand" philosophy. Historically, the SCS "has been most reluctant to use coercive measures either in establishing the original framework of specific district obligations or in keeping the districts to their commitments" (4).

Early on, the type of assistance SCS rendered was in the form of demonstration projects on individual farms. SCS provided necessary resources, including labor from SCS-operated CCC camps, Emergency Conservation Work camps, and "laborers recruited from local relief rolls" (5). With the formation of the districts beginning in 1937, demonstration projects were phased out and were totally eliminated by 1945.

Our current form of conservation technical assistance (CTA) replaced the demonstration projects. SCS's basic tenets which remained unchanged for five decades were (a) to assist individuals directly via trained technicians, (b) to depend on the land user to make sound conservation decisions, (c) to maintain high technical standards, and (d) to have comprehensive approaches to conservation planning (7). Although CTA has shrunk in relative importance in SCS, because of the addition of other programs, it remains the foundation of USDA's conservation activities. CTA expenditures in 1985 were $365 million.

In sum, the voluntary philosophy embraced in 1935 was firmly entrenched by 1985. Resource owners were exhorted by reason other than decree. Reliance on moral suasion and information dissemination campaigns formed the cornerstone of CTA, aided by ACP cost-sharing.

Was it effective? As in every public program, CTA has its admirers and detractors. Proponents of the system within the conservation community point to estimates of reduced erosion, while critics point to estimates of erosion remaining.

The debate over whether the cup is half empty or half full was exacerbated by the Malthusian "scarcity scare" of the 1970s. This debate resulted in passage of the Resources Conservation Act (RCA) in 1977. The term "cross-compliance" began to emerge in the debates surrounding RCA. Cross-compliance—requiring those receiving USDA farm program benefits to practice conservation management—was considered in the first National Conservation Program (NCP) but was discarded, despite the fact that a 1979 RCA public opinion poll showed that 75 percent of those surveyed thought cross-compliance should be required (6).

Cross-compliance was not considered in the second NCP either because the 1985 FSA made it redundant. In the 1985 farm bill, cross-compliance—now called conservation compliance—became a major issue and a major FSA provision. An unusual coalition of environmental, conservation, and other groups fashioned the idea of conservation compliance into law, along with sodbuster, swampbuster, and the conservation reserve.

To illustrate the clarity of my crystal ball in those days (and probably nowadays, too), I have been correctly quoted as saying that if anyone had told me on New Year's day, 1985, that we'd have cross-compliance by Christmas, I would have said that they had lost their mind!

In three short years, FSA already has changed the way we do business in SCS. Conservation compliance called for about 800,000 conservation plans to be written by January 1, 1990. Wetland determinations were needed on an unknown number of acres. Highly erodible land (HEL) determinations already have been made on about 94 percent of the highly erodible acres. The new workload was undertaken, however, with the program delivery and institutional structure that existed prior to FSA. Our success in meeting the FSA workload stems from the viability of that structure (the districts playing a key role aided by the SCS staff in the field).

There are some reasons for concern, however, as we look down the road. FSA has been hailed as the most significant expression of conservation policy since Pinchot and Muir—and particularly since the establishment of SCS in 1935. But is it appropriate? Is it too much? Is it too little? Are modifications needed?

The Context of Conservation Policy

Conservation policy must be viewed as part of a system—a system of agricultural policy; a system of national economic, social, and environmental policy; and a system of foreign policy. These systems themselves exist at the pleasure of an overall system of law and custom. Conservation policy does not drive, but is driven by these systems. We need, then, to look at conservation programs not because it is intrinsically "good" (though conservationists think it is) but because it has a positive supporting role in the larger scheme.

Why conservation? Ciriacy-Wantrup wrote that conservation is a redirection of resource use toward the future (*1*). Conservationists and students of conservation policy are, by necessity, future oriented. To be viable, conservation policy must be compatible with other policy objectives and do one of two things. It must show immediate results, or it must show congress that voters are happy with long-term results. The nature of natural resource use precludes the former. The swift debate attending FSA is evidence that conservation policy is perceived to be popular with the voters. That popularity stems from a notion of context—how policy fits the total system.

Discussion on future policy needs stems from our interpretation of systemic conditions. Policy, after all, is the bridge between what is and what should be. Conservation policy either influences or is influenced by the resource base, trade policy, structure of the agricultural sector, and technology.

Resources. In 1982, SCS estimated that the private land base included 394 million acres of forest land, 405 million acres of rangeland, and 133 million acres of pastureland. Of these, an estimated 153 million acres could reasonably be converted to cropland should the need arise. Existing cropland was tagged at 421 million acres, making 574 million acres available (*8*).

Cropland use in 1988 was about 328 million acres (*9*). The most pessimistic scenario developed for the second RCA appraisal indicates a need for only 345 million cropland acres in 50 years. The probable need may be fewer than 300 million acres, possibly under 250 million (*13*). Although these figures are arguable, the relative magnitudes can lead to only one conclusion: we are not about to run out of land.

Physical surplus aside, economic oversupply may be a different matter. If the need arises, the last acre of the 560 million that goes into production will be an expensive one indeed—the point being that significant increases in demand must occur given current supply conditions before any of the excess cropland base need be tilled.

Therefore, in the context of resource availability, a shortfall in the cropland base will not be of overriding concern in forming future conservation policies. This is a reversal of the "fencerow-to-fencerow" attitudes of the 1970s that accelerated public interest in conservation and resulted in the RCA in 1977.

Larry Libby, chairman of the Department of Food and Resource Economics, University of Florida, says that conservation is, and should be, a national concern because the cost of being wrong about our estimates of resource needs is exceedingly high. His criterion is—and I agree—that spending a fraction of national income to protect resource productivity is worthwhile as long as there is a chance of running out of productive capacity, irrespective of how small that probability may be. He sees conservation as a sort of national insurance policy. I think this is a sound and reasonable way to look at the question of conservation as a basis for maintaining future productive capacity.

Farm Income. The 1985 Food Security Act continued the half-century tradition of income transfer to the farm sector. Most likely, transfers will continue, though possibly in different form and magnitude than today. As we near the opening debates on the 1990 farm bill, we hear more and more about "decoupling," along with a stated policy of eliminating those subsidies that "distort" global trade. Conservation policy must be established in the context of basic agricultural policies that are likely to be in place at the time the conservation policies are introduced.

For example, with the present system, the size of the transfer payment depends on maintaining farmers' bases for program crops. In 1996, the first CRP contracts will expire. Under present rules a farmer must break out this land and plant it to a program crop to protect his or her base. The implications for conservation policy are significant. Obviously, a producer will not leave the land out of production if it causes a loss in base.

Technology. One reason many are blase about resources is our implied reliance on technology to forestall the limits of scarcity. Good arguments are made on both sides, however, I lean toward the high tech future. There is technology awaiting adoption that could increase yields significantly by the year 2000 (2). My view of technical advance stems from public perception of a loss of our competitive edge in the global marketplace. The desire to regain that edge will foster a public policy environment conducive to rapid technological advance.

In this context, future conservation policies will have to be flexible enough to deal with rapidly changing physical and biological production processes. Policy itself will have to be high tech.

Trade and Budget Policy. Today's conservation policy operates in the arena of trade and budget deficits. Because these issues are of major concern, the issue at hand for conservation policy will be the means that policymakers use to ameliorate the deficits. The Export Enhancement Program (EEP) is one such tool.

Currently, EEP is drawing down stocks and may become unpopular with consumers as stocks diminish and consumer prices increase. Conceivably, trade deficits could become so alarmingly high as to promote production enhancement policies. A hypothetical example with serious consequences for conservation policy would be to release CRP land into production. But some serious implications of trade deficits for conservation policy can be hypothesized, even without going to such extremes.

The budget deficit and associated policies will affect conservation policy. One method may be to decrease federal conservation spending. More subtle and ultimately more important may be federal monetary policies and their effects on capital and interest. Conservation policy resides in the environment created by the capital available to agricultural production and infrastructure and the industries that support them.

Structure of the Production Sector. Farm size and tenure likely will continue to influence conservation policy. Despite 50 years of income transfers into the agricultural sector and recurring images of the disappearing family farm, farms continue to become fewer and larger. This trend will likely continue, which has real implications for the use of inputs and any possible move toward a low-input, sustainable agriculture.

These structural changes in agriculture imply some change in the behavioral aspects of farm management. Manager incentives on a large corporate farm are different from those of an owner/operator of a small farm. The conservation ethic may be meaningless to a manager unless "conservation" somehow is woven into profits.

Farm size will play a role in future conservation policy. The economic efficiency implications of economies of size and scale, land-labor-capital-management ratios, and variability of landscapes under single decision-maker control, should be considered when designing and implementing policies and policy instruments. A firm that controls large amounts of land and capital will respond to a given set of policy instruments differently than, say, a small farm operating in a limited financial environment. For effective results, policies have to be tailored to firms' economic and natural resource settings.

Environment. Some say that John Muir was one of the first environmentalists and Gifford Pinchot was the first conservationist, but the two concepts have always been cousins. Over the years each idea has expanded to include some aspects of the other. The FSA debates saw environmentalists and conservationists forming coalitions that in large part are responsible for its passage. Conservationists and environmentalists found bases for cooperation in one law.

In discussing conservation policy in the future, we must remember that it will be virtually inseparable from agricultural and environmental policy. After all, the vast majority of the landscape is composed of nonfederal, privately owned rural land. Conservation policy that impacts the land will have environmental and economic implications, some of which may well be unintended.

Some of the key environmental issues that will affect future conservation policy include water quality (particularly groundwater), erosion's off-site effects, wildlife habitat, global warming, and energy. Those of us in the conservation/extension/research/policy arena find these issues familiar. Some of them already have been integrated into conservation policy, and some are waiting in the wings for public perception to grow.

The issue of water quality is here and will be around a long time. It will be one of the major issues impacting the conservation title of the 1990 farm bill. Press exposure on the rudimentary knowledge we have of water quality has served to make additional legislative response very likely. In fact, the USDA already has made a policy response. The second national conservation program has raised the water quality objective to the co-equal of erosion control (12).

The impact of actual and potential contamination of groundwater by agricultural pollutants may well be one of the most discussed and debated elements of conservation policy in the 1990 farm bill. The public associates groundwater with drinking water and is afraid of the potential health effects that are discussed, almost daily, in the media. The electorate responds to fear, and the elected respond to the electorate, irrespective of science.

Off-Site Effects. A major portion of the water quality problem is sediment—which is also a large part of the off-site problem. Other potential off-site effects include chemicals, animal waste, salts (salinity), and air pollution (dust). Future policy and policy instruments will be developed with an eye toward these types of impacts.

Habitat. Of the many environmental benefits produced by wetlands, the most significant are their wildlife habitat features. Congress recognized this, and it resulted in the swampbuster provision of the FSA. CRP also resulted in habitat improvement. Interactions between conservation activities and habitat will continue to impact policy formation.

Energy. Sooner or later, the issue of energy will become problematic once again. What it means for conservation is not clear. One land-related aspect of energy scarcity may be land used in the production of biomass or grain for ethanol. But production of grain and production of ethanol are themselves energy-intensive processes.

Fossil fuel scarcity should stimulate more land-intensive production from both the demand side and the supply side because such scarcity would increase ethanol demand. On the supply side, fuel price increases would favor grain production that leans toward being more land-intensive and less energy-intensive. This result runs counter to the excess capacity arguments presented earlier. We may be arguing a future that requires more, not less, cropland. In this case, Libby's national insurance concept may be of particular importance.

Policy Context in Summary. Because policy is the tool intended to turn the current situation into the desired situation, we must consider that desired situation—social objectives. First, where are we now?

The food security issue in the U.S. is not a major concern today. This is, of course, not true worldwide, but food shortage, in most places, is a problem of distribution rather than production. Future trends seem to be like the present, which is excess capacity.

The food security issue that Libby raises remains, however. Positive risk is associated with the trend projections. The issue becomes whether resources unneeded now should be reserved for the future, and the opportunity cost of that preservation. As a society we have a responsibility to provide insurance for future generations. What is a reasonable amount of insurance to carry?

During the same period that concern for food security has been on the decline, concern for the environmental conditions associated with agriculture has been on the rise. In fact, future farm bills will distinguish less and less among income, conservation, and environmental instruments. They will (or should) be integrated to meet the multiple objectives of society.

The launch platform for future conservation policy appears to be excess capacity, environmental concern, and income transfer to the farm sector. Given this context, some speculations may be made on the path of future conservation policy.

Future Policy Needs

If I had been talking about future conservation policy needs in 1984 (and I probably was), I would like to think that my conclusions would have looked a lot like Title XII of FSA. My plea would have been, "Give us these new tools, and we can move a long way toward solving our problems." I do believe that FSA will go a long way toward that end. Since FSA became law, it has undergone continual interpretation as we have developed the regulations and implemented the act. Even now, several bills relating to Title XII are being considered. Most relate to amending the conservation reserve provision. Some are concerned about extending the authority to include more acres, while others are designed to broaden the intent of the program beyond highly erodible land.

Carrots and Sticks. Our 50-year tradition of voluntary compliance remains firmly entrenched. Voluntary compliance remains our only tool on eroding land that does not meet the highly erodible land (HEL) criteria for conservation compliance. Voluntarism has its roots in the ethical dimensions of the conservation movement's early days. But one weakness of this approach is its failure to address the questions of who benefits and who pays. The individual landowner can't capture many of the tangible benefits society reaps from erosion reduction. To the extent that voluntarism works, society gains while the farmer pays the bill. To the extent that voluntarism fails, society's loss may be the farmer's gain, if the foregone erosion reduction would otherwise have entailed real cost to the farmer.

Conservation compliance, too, has its roots in ethics and social values. The 1979 RCA public opinion poll showed an overwhelming majority of respondents thought that subsidizing erosive production practices was "wrong." This idea permeated the system to emerge as conservation compliance. We now have a policy that ties farm program benefits to stewardship of the land. The stick is the threat of program benefit denial. It applies to annual crops grown on HEL, a large but not total subset of the national erosion problem.

As we move into the next decade we face several problems with compliance. Two concerns threaten the viability of this instrument of policy—one economic, one political. First, many analysts are predicting that market prices and target prices eventually will converge, thereby eliminating deficiency payments. This would eliminate a major source of USDA program benefits. Target prices ratchet downward each year. Second, a major trade policy objective is to eliminate all farm subsidies by the year 2000. Should this happen, incentives will have to be developed for the compliance concept to be effective, even though FmHA loans, crop insurance, and disaster payments are still covered. Voluntarism will continue to play a major role in conservation policy.

Barring these two events, an additional threat to conservation efforts could be another short cycle of high prices and "fencerow-to-fencerow" farming. During the 1970s, land in production (cropland used for crops) expanded by 50 million acres. It is now on the decline—328 million acres in 1988, the least since 1910. Tying conservation benefits to the existence and viability of farm programs will not assure achievement of FSA's conservation objectives.

If the cycle of high prices coincides with completion of CRP contracts, conservation gains may be lost. CRP acres will be under pressure from the plow rather than under cover. During the mid-1970s, excess capacity varied from 10 to 30 million acres (*11*). Capacity of physical plant was much greater.

What, then, can replace the farm program incentive? We can replace it with another carrot, or with a stick, or, perhaps, with a combination of the two. On the carrot side, some sort of payment—either direct conservation payments or perhaps tax reductions—might provide the required incentive. An RCA pilot study in Wisconsin offered reduced property taxes to farmers in exchange for installation of approved conservation practices.

This seemed to be amazingly successful given that the only incentive was a $3-per-acre tax break. We will have a better idea of its success when USDA funding expires and the county has to pick up the bill.

Anyone who has watched TV or read a newspaper in the last few years is aware of the concern for the federal deficit. Additional federal funding for soil and water conservation programs in the foreseeable future is unlikely. The conservation reserve program has been extremely effective in practically eliminating erosion on the highly erodible acres enrolled in the CRP. President Reagan's 1990 budget proposed full funding for up to 40 million acres, but it was not an inexpensive program. Payments exceed $1.4 billion annually.

What about disincentives? These could be in the form of erosion taxes or direct regulation by some empowered authority. My guess is that USDA will not support this type of approach. For one thing, these types of disincentives would be an administrative and bureaucratic nightmare. They are administratively unworkable. In addition, someone would have to play the part of policeman in this scenario—a job that no agency wants. The administrative expense of policing would be prohibitive.

Policy Integration. The major need for conservation policy is to integrate with other governmental policies, with the regulatory and programmatic responsibilities among federal agencies, and with the policies and programs of states and other jurisdictions, including the conservation districts. We also need improved administrative integration within and among the conservation agencies for efficient program delivery. Finally, we need integrated policy analysis and analytical systems.

By integration, I mean reduction in the inefficiencies resulting from two or more policies or institutions working at cross-purposes. Federal and state policies must be coordinated, particularly in environmental regulation. Many of the policies for water quality will be formulated at the state level. For this to be successful, careful state-federal coordination is required. Likewise, the district-state-federal relationships have to be examined. A plea for better working relationships among the various natural resource jurisdictions has for years been a standard in any conservation policy discussion. It never has been more important.

Summary

Future conservation policy must be viewed within the context of the current situation versus the desired future situation. Possibly the incentives and disincentives included in FSA for the installation of conservation practices on HEL may be ineffective, as the decade of the 1990s progresses, if agricultural prices improve or federal farm benefits decline. Incentives would be more effective, easier to administer, and probably cheaper than disincentives.

The second policy need is for integration of policies, program delivery administrative procedures, and policy analysis and analytic systems. Program delivery techniques must be designed to balance improved efficiency with political viability. Policy analysts must provide the analyses so that policymakers operate with as much information as possible.

The 1985 Food Security Act changed the way we view conservation policy. The voluntary approach has been augmented by carrot and stick alternatives. We cannot, however, throw away the tools of voluntarism, as they continue to be important to successful conservation policy.

REFERENCES CITED

1. Ciriacy-Wantrup, S. V. 1963. *Resource conservation economics and policies.* University of California Press, Berkeley.
2. English, Burton C., James A. Maetzold, Brian R. Holding, and Earl O. Heady, editors. 1984. *Future agricultural technology and resource conservation.* Iowa State University Press, Ames.
3. Kirkendall, Richard S. 1966. *Social scientists and farm politics in the age of Roosevelt.* University of Missouri Press, Columbia.
4. Parks, W. Robert. 1952. *Soil conservation districts in action.* Iowa State College Press, Ames.
5. Simms, D. Harper. 1970. *The Soil Conservation Service.* Praeger, New York, New York.
6. U.S. Department of Agriculture. 1982. *A national program for soil and water conservation.* Soil Conservation Service, Washington, D.C.
7. U.S. Department of Agriculture. 1985. *Evaluation of conservation technical assistance.* Soil Conservation Service, Washington, D.C.
8. U.S. Department of Agriculture. 1987. *Basic statistics: 1982 national resources inventory.* Statistical Bulletin No. 756. Soil Conservation Service, Washington, D.C.
9. U.S. Department of Agriculture. 1988. *Agricultural resources: Cropland, water, and conservation situation and outlook report.* AR-12. Economic Research Service, Washington, D.C.
10. U.S. Department of Agriculture. 1988. *Ethanol: Economic and policy tradeoffs.* Agricultural Economic Report No. 585. Economic Research Service, Washington, D.C.
11. U.S. Department of Agriculture. 1988. *Excess capacity in U.S. agriculture: An economic approach to measurement.* Agricultural Economic Report No. 580. Economic Research Service, Washington, D.C.
12. U.S. Department of Agriculture. 1989. *A national program for soil and water conservation.* Washington, D.C.
13. U.S. Department of Agriculture. 1989. *The second RCA appraisal: Soil, water, and related resources on nonfederal land in the United States.* Washington, D.C.

23

Future Policy Options for Natural Resource Management: An Agricultural Stabilization and Conservation Service View

Paul Harte and Michael Linsenbigler

The Food Security Act of 1985 (FSA) linked two of the major features of farm policy—conservation and commodity objectives. The Conservation Reserve Program (CRP) linked production adjustment and income support objectives to a conservation program. The compliance features of the FSA linked conservation objectives to production adjustment, income support, and other farm programs. These linkages allow the federal government to achieve many objectives with each program, so they generally are viewed as worthwhile tools. However, implementation of these initiatives has provided a challenge to the Agricultural Stabilization and Conservation Service (ASCS), Soil Conservation Service (SCS), Forest Service (FS), conservation districts, and other groups, and has encouraged more communication and interaction between and among these groups.

ASCS is looking ahead to the tasks that remain. Without even considering CRP and compliance features, ASCS farm programs have greatly increased in number and complexity in recent years that have strained the current resources and capabilities of field offices. County ASCS offices that ordinarily have 1 to 10 people per office receive more than 50,000 pages of detailed farm program instruction each year. ASCS has so many national handbooks that we even need a handbook for handbooks. Analyses prepared for the possible implementation of modified and new farm policies should include administrative ramifications, such as basic practicality, administrative feasibility, program complexity, and current agency resources, in addition to the usual macroeconomic and natural resource concerns. An important related issue is time. The minimum amount of time needed to implement any major new program is 90 days, and 120 days is preferred. Experience has shown that use of 60-day restrictions potentially results in faulty operating provisions and other administrative problems.

The 1988 national program for Soil and Water Conservation directs ASCS to follow two high-priority goals when managing its conservation programs: (1) to reduce excessive soil erosion on crop, pasture, range, forest, and other rural land; and (2) to protect the quality of surface water and groundwater against harmful contamination from nonpoint sources of pollution. ASCS is committed to cost-effective and equitable erosion control and water quality measures. The general direction of future natural resource policy has already been set, and the remaining need is to develop rational, workable laws that balance budgetary concerns and property rights with natural resource, income support, and production adjustment goals.

"Cost-effective" and "equitable" imply a sound balance of incentives and disincentives that seek to solve real problems on a local level. Combinations of cost-share programs and compliance features attached to the current voluntary annual programs can meet this criteria. Many believe that expansion or modification of these current programs and provisions should be the primary thrust of future natural resource policy.

Current Activity

ASCS currently is managing a variety of worthwhile water quality efforts. These programs and policies include the Rural Clean Water Program (RCWP) research projects, the Agricultural Conservation Program (ACP) special water quality projects, the Colorado River Salinity Control Program, the Water Bank Program, the swampbuster provision, and the Wetland and Scour CRP Eligibility. Most of the other conservation efforts managed by ASCS also have positive water quality impacts.

The soil conservation priority, too, has been served well. By 1995, up to 90 million acres of highly erodible cropland will be covered by conservation plans under conservation compliance and sodbuster. Although some of the resulting soil conservation measures may not reduce erosion to the levels originally intended, compliance will require a huge soil conservation effort. Some producers are using federal and state cost-sharing to help bear the costs. Base-exchange also has been made available where closely-grown crops provide the best solution to erosion problems. However, most of the affected producers probably will change production practices on their own, using the more cost-effective measures available, such as conservation tillage, contouring, and crop rotations.

As a result of the CRP, another 40-45 million acres of highly erodible cropland will be covered by conservation and forestry plans. On September 30, 1995, 21,000 CRP contracts will expire, reestablishing the cultivation rights on 2 million acres of highly erodible cropland. Roughly 1.2 million acres of crop acreage base also will be reestablished on this acreage. By the year 2000, roughly another 400,000 CRP contracts will have expired, opening the legal door to continued cropping on the entire 40-45 million acres of highly erodible cropland. In cost-share outlays alone, the federal government will have paid over $1.6 billion to convert this acreage to permanent vegetative cover.

Effective encouragement of environmentally sound land use practices is the objective. CRP cover permanency is, and will be, one of the key issues. Although program administrators desire to keep as much of the expired contract acreage out of production as long as possible, high crop prices or lucrative annual farm programs may pull most of this acreage back into crop production. The Soil Bank Program, followed by the grain crisis of the early 1970s, demonstrated how these pressures can come about. Although many old Soil Bank tree-stands still exist, total cultivated acreage trends throughout the 1970s clearly show large increases in acres farmed, some of which are believed to have been on previously enrolled Soil Bank fields.

The general belief is that under chronic surplus conditions much of the marginal/fragile acreage in the country should not be used for intensive crop production. Benefits from the annual price and income support programs undoubtedly encouraged some of this cultivation. On the other hand, by keeping net returns generally within a confined corridor, these programs also work to minimize boom and bust cycles in agriculture, which could possibly be even more damaging to the environment.

Options for Current Initiatives

Measures that encourage producers to maintain permanent vegetative cover and similar land uses on their expired CRP acreage fall into two categories: (1) those that may be needed under most circumstances and (2) those that may be needed if certain circumstances develop. Examples of the first category are tailored cost-share practices that encourage producers to maintain CRP cover. These include wildlife habitat improvements, livestock measures such as fencing and well water assistance, and other general range and pasture improvements such as forage and hay assistance. In some parts of the country, the larger CRP tracts should be appealing to hunting and sportsmen clubs, providing producers with an opportunity to earn incomes while maintaining conservation uses.

A number of transition schemes have been proposed, allowing and encouraging producers to begin conserving land uses on expired CRP acreage before their contracts expire. This approach is potentially worthwhile, with caution against the use of stringent national goals. Any proposals that allow grazing, haying, or other conserving land uses during the contract period should be designed in ways that avoid inequitable gain or market disruption. Payment reductions similar to those implemented for the emergency CRP haying provisions or other offsetting devices should be part of any transition scheme to help avoid such circumstances.

The second category covers decisions to use measures depending on the future economic and environmental situation. Examples are to offer extensions upon contract expiration if land retirement programs are needed in the future, or to selectively target desirable commodity or cover patterns for future actions. Large tracts of highly erodible marginal cropland in the Southern Plains or other areas could be targeted for continued retirement through contract extensions or easements.

The use of easements to keep land in conserving uses is one of the more drastic remedies proposed. Although easements can be effective long-term measures, they are expensive and in effect represent a form of government ownership. Thus, some do not view them favorably.

Another potentially worthwhile effort related to a current initiative would be full-scale implementation of the experimental RCWP. Testing results from the approximately 21 projects nationwide are beginning to show which practices and projects represent effective water quality measures. This program could be implemented to target site-specific water quality problems throughout the country.

Conservation compliance often has been viewed as a tool that encourages participation in the CRP. It also will encourage desirable stewardship on expired CRP acreage. The highly erodible land standard under conservation compliance, however, currently is considerably narrower than it is for CRP eligibility. This means that a portion of the acreage determined to be highly erodible and enrolled in the CRP will not require future conservation plans for USDA program benefit eligibility upon contract expiration and future crop planting. A review of the 1982 National Resource Inventory (NRI) shows that roughly 18 percent of the 101 million acres eligible for the CRP are "safe from compliance," largely because of their land capability class eligibility. An easy way to handle this peculiar situation is to define all CRP acreage (except perhaps filter strips and similar acreage) as highly erodible for conservation compliance purposes. Thus, when CRP contracts expire, any future program participants would be required to revise conservation plans they needed under CRP to incorporate practices that complement their new cropping patterns.

Unlike the old Soil Bank fields, almost all land enrolled in the CRP has the potential to seriously erode. Land retired under the CRP is considered planted for purposes of crop acreage base maintenance and highly erodible land conservation provision determinations. Hence, this acreage will come under the conservation compliance provision and not the sodbuster provision. The distinction is important because, as a result of recent changes, sodbuster conservation plans are much more stringent and, thus, likely to be more costly and effective. Changing future contracts to bring this acreage under sodbuster would put teeth back into those plans that cover expired CRP acreage. Such a change would cause more of the marginal ex-CRP acreage to be abandoned or at least stay out of crop production, and would enhance the erosion control measures that will be implemented on the ex-CRP acreage that is farmed.

Producers who do not enter the CRP and then fall under conservation compliance by producing on highly erodible acreage after January 1, 1990, will have five years to fully implement the measures called for in their conservation plans. CRP participants who fall under conservation compliance when their contracts expire will have to fully implement the needed measures as soon as they begin to farm those fields. Some producers have shown enough reluctance to be in this latter situation (in which they may be forced to rapidly implement unfamiliar conservation practices) that they are less willing to participate in the CRP. Changes in compliance rules for CRP contract holders have been recommended to give producers more time to comply. Ten years of idle cropland and annual rental payments should provide plenty of time and money well in advance of any needed compliance dates. But early reminders or notifications to USDA contract holders may be needed to help ensure that compliance problems do not develop.

Options for New Initiatives

Long-term land retirement provides for better conservation because terminal contracts permit highly erodible land to be returned to crop production. Annual land retirement programs are even less desirable because requirements change from year to year. One means to improve annual retirement programs would be to require retirement of the same site-specific plots each year for the acreage reduction to the extent mandated for the program that year. The ASCS administrator currently recommends that states and counties encourage this approach. Some believe that many participants already retire the same hard-to-plow fields on their farm each year. Also, some producers meet the acreage reduction requirements by using skip-row patterns and sub-sectional farming arrangements. These practices would complicate administration of this provision and would reduce its wildlife benefits. In addition to site-specific land retirement rules, weed control requirements on retired acreage as necessitated by state and local laws, can be revised in ways to minimize habitat disruption.

A related "stick approach" would require or strongly encourage future annual program participants to always retire any ex-CRP acreage as part of their annual set-aside requirements when the CRP contracts expire. This would maintain some of the conservation benefits of the program from the long-term land retirement.

ASCS also might implement a voluntary three-year land retirement option in conjunction with the annual programs. A scheme such as this would qualify participants for price and income support programs by retiring a constant percentage of participants' farm acreage base each year on the same site-specific plots regardless of the annual program requirements. Ten percent of the base on enrolled farm is proposed for discussion purposes. Payment generally equal to the projected 0-92 paid land diversion program payment rates would be provided for any acreage retired in excess of the annual requirement for a given year. During years when the annual requirement is greater than the new program level, additional land retirement would be required. The three-year set-aside would require a producer to maintain a permanent cover that would reduce erosion below the soil loss tolerance level or enhance wildlife, on acreage designated by a conservation district representative. Participants could receive cost-sharing for cover establishment, and eligibility could be restricted to needed areas. The three-year set-aside could be renewed continuously until the USDA or the participants deem it inappropriate. ASCS also would still have annual land retirement through which it could influence supply/use trends.

A third approach would be to require or strongly encourage annual program participants to develop and implement plans for both planted and retired acreage that seek to conserve soil, enhance water quality, and contribute to wildlife habitat. Under this comprehensive compliance scenario, conservation district representatives would have the authority, under state and federal guidelines, to design tailored resource management plans for annual program participants.

This holistic approach to natural resource management would entail a great deal of government intervention, but it could be an effective incentive for widespread land use change. Some redundancy would occur because of the current compliance requirements, and many farms would likely have no need for land use changes. Nevertheless, holistic approach provisions managed properly at the local level, and combined with aggressive cost-sharing, should be flexible enough to accommodate the diverse resource needs that exist. Watershed troubles and other large-scale problems, for example, could be attacked collectively. This proposal would provide incentives in the form of increased annual benefits for "good stewardship" producers who volunteer to implement locally recommended measures.

Another incentive proposal could be called the "Environment Preservation Program" (EPP), the first component of which would be a 1-million-acre reserve designed to retire irrigated acreage. Review of the Conservation Reporting and Evaluation System data indicates that only 16,000 irrigated acres are in CRP, of the total 11,000,000 irrigated acres in existence. EPP could achieve significant environmental and production adjustment benefits by taking irrigated land out of production. The producer would enter into a five-year contract during which time he or she would be required not to irrigate any additional acreage or existing acreage or sell water rights. Irrigation throughout much of the West is causing the build-up of salts and toxic metals in both surface and groundwater supplies. This component would cost an estimated $75 million per year for a 1-million-acre program.

The second component would be a 2-million-acre tree planting initiative. Trees would be established for conservation and commercial uses under 15-year contracts on both cropland and pasture land. Eligibility would be targeted broadly to include both critical and noncritical areas. This component would cost roughly $90 million per year.

The third and final component would be a sensitive area reserve. Croplands that are environmentally sensitive as wildlife habitat, groundwater recharge areas, regions of excessive eutrophication, and the like, could enter this program. Areas surrounding endangered species habitat also could enter the program. This component would allow a producer to enter into a 10-year conservation contract only if substantial environmental needs are present. This component would cost an estimated $50 million for a 1-million-acre program per year.

Other Thoughts

If program yields remain frozen at their current levels, incentives to achieve large and sometimes unrealistic yields in order to increase subsidy payments (and land values) would be reduced. During an era of general surplus conditions, encouraging less-intensive though profitable methods of production that are more environmentally sound makes sense. These include minimal-till, and reduced fertilizer and pesticide applications. The "high yield is a good yield" mindset is still pervasive in U.S. agriculture. Although the net returns of many program participants may still increase when actual yields rise, frozen program yields encourage farmers to increase profitability through other avenues—which in many cases will be less intensive use of pesticides and fertilizers.

Another suggestion is to link the ACP to conservation compliance by offering tailored ACP cost-share practices that help producers meet compliance erosion requirements in ways that enhance water quality. These practices might include integrated pest management assistance for those who incorporate minimal tillage to reduce chemical applications, the use of filter strips along with onfield erosion control measures, and the use of legumes in rotation crops.

Some modification of ASCS's traditional cost-sharing approaches may be needed to help meet conservation priorities. The current funding allocation method used to provide ACP cost-share monies to states has to be adjusted to target regions that have more conservation compliance needs, and regions where erosion and water quality problems are most severe. The current ACP allocation should be updated, using the 1987 NRI and all other available resource data bases, to better allocate cost-share funds.

The current assortment of practices for which cost-sharing is available should be revised to encourage more environmentally sound farm management practices. Research and demonstration projects have shown that improving producers' management can dramatically reduce erosion, as well as off-farm loadings of pesticides and nutrients. Cost-sharing could be enhanced to encourage producers to adopt integrated pest management, pesticide sprayer calibration, nutrient management, wellhead sampling and protection efforts, and other water quality/conservation projects. These practices would be applied in areas identified as having a high potential for either surface water or groundwater problems.

24

Conservation Beyond the 1985 Food Security Act: Linking the Water Quality Act Section 319 with the 1990 Farm Bill

Peter J. Kuch, James J. Jones, and Robert Wolcott

Seventeen years after passage of the Clean Water Act in 1972, nonpoint sources of water pollution remain largely unaddressed. In 1986, states reported that nonpoint sources accounted for 45 percent of the pollution in estuaries with impaired uses (5). The relative contribution of nonpoint-source pollution was 76 percent for lakes and 65 percent for rivers and streams. Of all nonpoint sources, agriculture is by far the greatest contributor. States have identified agriculture as the source of the problem in 64 percent of impaired rivers and 57 percent of impaired lakes (4). Contamination of groundwater with agricultural chemicals is an increasing source of public concern. The 1990 farm bill will provide a major opportunity to address agricultural nonpoint sources of pollution with voluntary programs.

Evaluation of the Conservation Title

The success or failure of the Conservation Title of the Food Security Act (FSA) of 1985 continues to be debated. Most agree, however, that the Conservation Reserve Program (CRP) has been successful in removing from production a considerable proportion of the most highly erodible cropland in the United States. Through the seventh sign-up, cropland erosion has been reduced by 574 million tons per year. Conservation compliance (CC) has yet to prove itself in terms of its ability to control erosion on highly erodible cropland. In June 1988, the Soil Conservation Service (SCS) abandoned its proposed T/2T standard in favor of less stringent Alternative Conservation Systems (ACS).

The SCS has estimated erosion reductions in 10 midwestern states that would result from adoption of Alternative Conservation Systems. The analysis showed that ACSs would reduce erosion on highly erodible land in the study area from 956 million tons per year to 545 million tons per year, or from 14.8 tons per acre per year to 8.5 tons per acre per year. The CRP (assuming a 40-million-acre reserve) would further reduce erosion on highly erodible cropland to 424 million tons per year. If these projections hold true, the combination of CRP and CC will prove to have been successful in reducing erosion on highly erodible cropland.

But few, if any, conservationists would limit the definition of conservation solely to protecting highly erodible cropland. Webster's Dictionary defines conservation as "controlled use and systematic protection of natural resources." The Conservation Title of FSA, however, really focused only on soil conservation (with the exception of swampbuster). Although USDA made water quality an objective of the CRP, the principal aim of the program was to control soil erosion.

A move toward conservation of water resources is by now well underway. The SCS recently made the protection of surface water and groundwater against harmful contamination by nonpoint sources the number two priority of its conservation activities. Reducing soil erosion on rural lands remains its first priority. In addition to protecting soil and water, conservation in agriculture should include protecting valuable natural resources, such as wetlands and other habitats. The swampbuster provision and the recent inclusion of cropped wetlands in the CRP represent a major step in protecting wetlands. Farmers Home Administration (FmHA) conservation easements offer some potential for improving wildlife habitat.

Water Quality Problems Related to Public Conservation

Although the argument can be made that water quality should be the number one public conservation priority, as yet it seems to be an afterthought for most agricultural policymakers. On-site erosion effects should be a concern primarily of the farm operator. The farmer will address soil erosion when the marginal benefits of investing in erosion control exceed the marginal costs of lost production. The farmer is the one who will capture the benefits of that investment. The profit-maximizing producer will not address the off-site effects, particularly water quality, so the government is left to deal with these effects.

In 1984, 6 of the 10 U.S. Environmental Protection Agency (EPA) regions reported that nonpoint-source pollution was their principal remaining cause of water quality problems. Agricultural runoff was reported to be the most common nonpoint-source pollutant. Resources for the Future (2) has estimated that cropland erosion is responsible for over one-third of the sediment, 30 percent of the phosphorus, and 40 percent of the nitrogen entering the nation's waterways (pasture and range lands account for another 13 percent and 17 percent, respectively, of these pollutants).

In terms of groundwater, EPA has verified that 46 pesticides have been found in the groundwater of 26 states, attributable to normal agricultural use (6). Seventy-four pesticides have been found in the groundwater of 38 states; this includes point-source discharges and misuse (6).

The U.S. Geological Survey (USGS) reported in 1984 that more than 20 percent of the 124,000 wells it had sampled had nitrate levels in excess of health standards (3). In Iowa, state officials have cautioned that as many as half of the state's 800 public water supplies may be contaminated with pesticides and other organic compounds.

Section 319 Provisions

The 1987 Water Quality Act Amendments to the Clean Water Act include Section 319 dealing with nonpoint-source water pollution. Section 319 required states to prepare assessment reports and management plans. Assessment reports must "describe the nature, extent and effect of nonpoint-source water pollution, the causes of such pollution, and methods used for controlling this pollution." The management plan provision requires states to provide "an overview of a state's nonpoint-source program as well as a summary of what the state intends to accomplish in the next four fiscal years" toward addressing nonpoint-source problems identified in its assessment. Unfortunately, the $400 million authorized for state implementation of management plans never has been appropriated. Despite this lack of funding, Section 319 assessments provide the best picture at present of the extent and location of agriculture's impact on water quality. A well-done 319 assessment provides the policymaker with information on where and to what extent agriculture impacts surface water quality (some states have included groundwater in their assessments). These assessments also differentiate among cropland, pasture, range, and dairy-related problems.

Limited Usefulness of Title XII

If one accepts water quality as the largest conservation public policy issue facing the agricultural sector, addressing this shortcoming in the Conservation Title is appropriate. Proposals are being set forth for a CRP aimed at water quality enhancement and for more strict conservation compliance in priority watersheds (as defined in Section 319 assessments). But the current tools designed to deal with highly erodible cropland may not be useful or available, for technical, political, and efficiency reasons, for dealing with water quality. These current tools include the CRP and conservation compliance in general and the soil loss tolerance level (T) and erodibility index (EI) in particular. Therefore, reviewing the weaknesses of these conservation tools in dealing with agricultural water quality problems might be useful.

Identification Problems. To target lands that contribute most to water quality degradation is an expensive undertaking. A water quality analog of USLE or the soil loss tolerance (T) has not been developed. A number of effective models (e.g., AGNPS, CREAMS) are available for water quality targeting, but they are designed for application to small watersheds and the cost of using them at the national level is prohibitive. For groundwater the only accurate existing tool is monitoring for the presence of pollutants. The usefulness of indices such as DRASTIC is being debated.

Expense of CRP for Water Quality. Even if one would like to see a CRP for water quality, it would prove to be much more expensive than the current program. Lands that contribute to nonpoint-source problems are generally more expensive to "rent," on average, than lands the current CRP has retired. These lands typically are east of the 96th meridian of longitude and are either tremendously productive (the heart of the Corn Belt) or close to urban areas. CARD has estimated that the average rental rate would have to be increased by 25 percent, and annual set-asides (ARP) would have to be significantly reduced for wheat and feed grains just to meet the goal of 40 million acres (*1*).

Limits on Linking Conservation to Program Participation. As commodity prices rise and target prices fall, farmers will be more inclined to avoid costly compliance-type programs (programs tied to commodity programs) by ceasing to participate in government programs. Although the direction that commodity prices will take over the next several years is not clear, they are expected to strengthen significantly during this period. In addition, the new administration is likely to continue the thrust of the Reagan administration toward weaning farmers from price supports, by continuing to lower target prices. This is likely to have much support in Congress, particularly in view of the intractable budget deficit.

Budget Constraints. Budget constraints render a CRP-type program aimed at water quality unlikely, and they limit the amount of money available for bribing farmers to adopt conservation practices. Although several studies (including ones done for EPA by CARD in 1988) have shown that the CRP is revenue-neutral because of off-setting reductions in deficiency payments, this line of argument does not appeal to Congress. During the budget debate that will take place over the next few years, it is unlikely that anyone will be able to sell the CRP as being revenue neutral, especially if target prices are reduced further.

Existence of a Coalition. SCS' inability to impose stringent erosion controls on producers under conservation compliance, or to completely halt wetland drainage under swampbuster, demonstrates the ability of the agricultural sector to resist costly conservation requirements. Farmers' resistance to voluntary conservation may lead agriculture's former environmental allies in 1985 to seek more regulatory solutions to agricultural nonpoint-source pollution in the future. In 1987, Congress demonstrated its concern for nonpoint-sources of pollution in Section 319 of the Water Quality Act Amendments, and gave the states primary authority to deal with the nonpoint-source problem. If water quality improvements do not appear to be achievable with a state-directed voluntary approach, reauthorization of the Clean Water Act in 1992 probably will emphasize more federal regulation.

Guiding Principles for the 1990 Conservation Title

We suggest several principles for efficiently addressing agricultural off-site impacts on water quality, which we believe would be helpful in designing the Conservation Title of the next farm bill:

Targeting. For budget and efficiency reasons, we must move to a targeted approach in implementing conservation programs. Because resources are limited, we as a nation should focus available resources on the areas of greatest priority. Efficiency indicates that the croplands for which the ratio of benefits (from pollution prevention) to costs is greatest should be targeted first. USDA's Water Quality Initiative in the 1990 budget proposes to target research, education, and demonstration projects at Section 319 watersheds.

Permanence. Long-term arrangements—easements and other management agreements for buying out farmers' rights to certain activities on critical land—should be emphasized. Short-term programs, such as the CRP, offer limited benefits for water quality and wildlife habitat. In some areas the benefits of reduced pollutant loadings may not occur for several years, or they may disappear at the end of the contracts. FAPRI/CARD projections assume that one-half of the CRP land will return to crop production when leases expire. If targeting is accurate and permanent easements are obtained, the amount of land necessary to positively affect environmental quality would be much less than with short-term, nontargeted programs.

State-Specific Identification. Identification of problem areas should be made at state and local levels (using the 319 assessment). Washington cannot effectively assess state and local water quality/habitat problems. State priorities may be different from federal priorities. For example, EPA may think that sedimentation is the major water quality impairment, and a state may consider groundwater protection as a higher priority. States should be able to make those decisions. Conservation compliance could be a more effective water quality program if state conservationists, in conjunction with state water quality officials and state agriculture officials, were to jointly determine the desired level of erosion control. A need exists for strengthening institutional bridges between state water quality agencies and state SCS offices (state conservationist). Farmers are more likely to be responsive to local concerns than to those of the federal government.

Inclusion of All Agriculture. Future conservation programs should go beyond cropland to dairy, livestock, range, specialty crops, and so on. We will not be able to fully address the nonpoint-source pollution problem if conservation policy ignores several of the important contributing activities. For example, the proclivity of dairy cattle to wander into and defecate in streams appears to be a significant source of surface water turbidity and nutrient loadings. This relates to the fact that the Conservation Title deals only with soil erosion (and wetland preservation) on cropland. Preserving the natural resource base by controlling solely for cropland erosion is not adequate. Nutrient loadings from dairy and poultry operations are identified as leading contributors to water quality impairment in several state 319 assessments. Poorly maintained rangeland is another area in which substantial conservation gains can be made. Consequently, any effective conservation program must include all of agriculture.

State/Federal Roles. States must be active partners in any attempt to deal with nonpoint-source pollution. Some states have accepted their respon-

sibilities in this area. One legacy of the Reagan era has been to shift responsibility for environmental quality to the states. The states have to recognize
that successfully dealing with their agricultural and environmental problems
will require additional resources. Future conservation titles should recognize
this fact and cost-share or leverage as many programs as possible to make
federal dollars go farther. States that show they are serious about dealing
with the environmental impacts of agricultural production should be
rewarded.

Residual Economic Use. Arrangements that leave the farmer with some
economic use reduce the costs of such programs. Conservation and land
retirement are not synonymous. Effective conservation programs could include: mandatory soil conservation practices (such as conservation compliance), planting perennial crops rather than annual crops, required fencing of livestock, and allowing grazing or haying on CRP lands after hay
covers have been permanently established. These provisions would reduce
the required rents, keep land out of cropping longer, and ultimately encourage more diversified agricultural enterprises. This in turn might make
farmers more interested in rotations involving hay crops. Low-input systems
might be entirely appropriate for critical groundwater recharge areas.

Taken together, targeting, leveraging state funds, and allowing residual
economic use make permanent nonpoint-source pollution abatement more
economically feasible.

The First Step

A first step in the direction of addressing water quality in agriculture
conservation programs would be to formally link the conservation provisions of the 1990 farm bill to the Section 319 provisions of the Water Quality
Act Amendments of 1987. Resources and programs should be targeted to
watersheds that states have identified as not achieving water quality standards
because of agricultural nonpoint-source contamination. Within selected
watersheds, participation and money should be targeted to land having the
greatest relative impact on water quality. Targeting should be done at the
state or local level (conservation district). Because some states will be unable
to accurately identify priority watersheds because of poorly implemented
319 assessments, providing a substantive use for such information should
encourage states to improve their assessments.

This may appear to be an attempt to "fund" EPA's Section 319 program.
In some respects, it is. But that does not diminish the appropriateness of

the approach. Solving water quality problems, like soil erosion problems, requires targeting. States know where their most important water quality problems are located, and they understand the nature of the problems better than EPA or USDA. The Water Quality Act of 1987 recognized the need to do something about nonpoint-source pollution, but it required the states to identify the sources of pollution. The 1990 farm bill provides an opportunity to bring together the water quality objectives of the agricultural sector and of the environmental movement. If we are unable to deal effectively with these problems in 1990, reauthorization of the Clean Water Act in 1992 undoubtedly will address agricultural water quality degradation in a more direct manner.

Research Needs

To get the job done most effectively, additional support from the research community will be required. Field level, developmental research, policy research, and socioeconomic research are needed. The greatest research needs relate to development of tools for predicting where agricultural chemicals are concentrated and where they will contaminate groundwater. Cost-effective, alternative cultural practices that would reduce groundwater contamination also must be identified. Contamination of groundwater by agricultural chemicals is the water quality issue of greatest concern in rural America, and it is also the problem we are most poorly equipped to address.

Another high priority research need is to develop a tool that would allow field-level personnel to target lands and agricultural activities that contribute most to nonpoint-source loadings of surface waters. A tool analogous to T (the soil loss tolerance level) is needed. This would permit policymakers to devise efficient water quality programs they were able to do in the area of soil erosion with conservation compliance and CRP. Presently, the lack of models beyond those designed for small watersheds constrains regional and national water quality targeting.

REFERENCES CITED

1. Food and Agricultural Policy Research Institute. 1989. *FAPRI U.S. and world agricultural outlook summary and tables, February 1989.* Columbia, Missouri.
2. Resources for the Future. 1985. *A national data base of nonurban nonpoint source discharges and their effect on the nation's water quality.* Washington, D.C.
3. U.S. Department of the Interior. 1985. *National water summary, 1984.* Water Supply Paper 2275. U.S. Geological Survey, Washington, D.C.

4. U.S. Environmental Protection Agency. 1985. *America's clean water: The state's evalua-tion of progress.* Washington, D.C.
5. U.S. Environmental Protection Agency. 1987. *National water quality inventory 1986 report to Congress.* Washington, D.C.
6. Williams, W. M., et al. 1988. *Pesticides in ground water data base 1988 interim report.* U.S. Environmental Protection Agency, Washington, D.C.

VII
Summary and Conclusions

25

Implementing the Conservation Title: Outcomes and Potentials

Ted L. Napier, James A. Maetzold, and
Stephen B. Lovejoy

The issues discussed in this book can be categorized into five broad areas:
(1) potential economic impacts of Conservation Title (Conservation Title)
programs, (2) barriers and facilitators to participation in Conservation Title
programs, (3) wildlife impacts of Conservation Title set-aside programs,
(4) future directions of Conservation Title program initiatives from the
perspective of natural resource development agencies, and (5) future research
needs and policy implications.

Economic Impacts of the Conservation Title

Sophisticated statistical modeling of data collected to monitor Conservation Title program performance, synthesis of existing economic theory
and assessments of other land diversion efforts provided the means for several
contributors to predict a number of economic outcomes of Conservation
Title programs. Some of the identified economic impacts of Conservation
Title programs are as follows:

▶ Conservation Title programs will result in lower production of certain commodities, which will contribute to price increases. Consumer prices
are expected to increase gradually over time as changes in commodity stocks
are reflected in market prices for processed agricultural products.

▶ The demand for agricultural production inputs will decrease as land
is taken out of crop production. This suggests that Conservation Title programs will adversely affect agricultural input industries.

▶ Conservation Title land diversion programs will negatively affect the economic and service infrastructures of states and communities that are heavily dependent on agriculture for economic survival, because of the loss of direct and indirect revenues generated by crop production.

▶ Higher levels of unemployment in agriculturally dependent regions should be expected as Conservation Title programs are implemented. The decrease in commodity acreage will reduce the demand for hired farm labor. The expected decline in demand for agricultural inputs because of land diversion programs also should result in reduced demand for labor in agricultural input industries. Without alternative employment options, agriculturally dependent areas will suffer increased unemployment.

▶ Impacts of the Conservation Title on the U.S. Treasury will be partially mitigated by withdrawal of ARP-enrolled land, reduced storage costs of commodity stocks, reduced administrative costs of traditional commodity programs, and reduced commodity payments. The net cost of Conservation Title set-aside programs to the U.S. Treasury should be relatively small for a 45-million-acre diversion program.

▶ Expanding Conservation Title set-aside programs from 45 million acres to 65 million acres will increase U.S. Treasury costs substantially. Commodity prices also will increase significantly. Expected increases in government costs stem from increasing rents to ensure enrollment of land in the Conservation Title set-aside programs and the inability to achieve further saving through ARP withdrawals.

▶ Regional variation in the economic impacts of the Conservation Title should be expected. Community groups in the more arid regions of the West, probably will experience the greatest initial economic impacts, because much of the initial enrollment of highly erodible land was in this region. Local economic activity in several regions in western states has declined substantially because these groups traditionally have depended heavily on agriculture as the primary source of employment.

▶ The criteria used to implement Conservation Title programs will affect the economic impacts of the programs. If maintenance of farm income is emphasized over environmental concerns, landowners should receive greater benefits from Conservation Title programs.

▶ The Conservation Title should tighten local land markets and increase land values as commodity stocks are drawn down. Unencumbered land available for crop production will be in greater demand as commodity prices increase. Land values and rents should be bid upward.

▶ The economic impacts of individual landowners' violating Conservation Title regulations are significant. Loss of government payments because of violations of Conservation Title regulations will significantly reduce net farm income. The result will be that farming will be unprofitable in many instances.

► Farm income losses attributable to participation in Conservation Title set-aside programs usually are compensated adequately by government rental payments. In many instances, Conservation Title payments exceed local rents or expected revenues generated from production of commodities on enrolled land. Evidence suggests that Conservation Title set-aside programs will enhance farm income in all regions of the U.S.

► Net farm income for landowners in certain areas of the country will be significantly reduced by Conservation Title programs that do not generate rental payments for land operators. Conservation compliance provisions, for example, will make crop production unprofitable in geographical areas that require implementation of conservation structures to meet expectations of the legislation.

► Set-aside programs will generate little economic loss for the agricultural processing sector, because landowners will continue to consume processed agricultural products with rents received from enrolled land.

► Implementation procedures used to achieve the goals of Conservation Title will significantly influence the economic costs and benefits of Conservation Title. For example, alternative options for implementing targeted set-aside provisions, such as land for filter strips, will affect the economic impacts of the Conservation Title. Some regions will benefit more than others, depending on the procedures used to implement specific aspects of the program.

► The level of Conservation Title rental payments affects the distribution of economic benefits among various commodity producers. Corn and soybean producers will receive fewer benefits from Conservation Title programs than will other commodity producers until the caps are elevated to a level that makes enrollment of corn and soybean land profitable.

► Conservation Title programs will adversely affect livestock producers, because of increases in feed grain prices. Consequently, livestock prices will increase slightly over time, resulting in higher consumer costs.

► Conservation Title set-aside programs have made it possible for some landowners to continue farming when they otherwise would have been forced to leave production agriculture as a result of debt and cash-flow problems. This is because those farmers have been assured revenues from government rent of set-aside land.

► Conservation Title set-aside programs can produce economic benefits to society in general in the form of increased on-site and off-site recreational opportunities. Participation in Conservation Title set-aside programs frequently enhances hunting and fishing, and these opportunities have economic value.

Barriers and Facilitators to Participation

One of the most important factors contributing to the success or failure of soil and water conservation initiatives is whether landowners participate in the programs. Unless they enroll highly erodible land in Conservation Title programs, there can be no economic or environmental benefits to evaluate. Therefore, one of the most important aspects of Conservation Title assessment is to examine the barriers to and facilitators of participation.

The preceding chapters presented research findings from several studies organized to isolate the barriers and facilitators to participation in Conservation Title programs. The major findings of these studies are as follows:

► One of the greatest barriers to participation in and compliance with Conservation Title programs is lack of awareness of the regulations governing the programs. Landowners cannot be expected to participate in or comply with conservation programs they do not understand.

► The 10-year enrollment period of the Conservation Title set-aside program acts as a barrier to participation. Landowners are not able to respond quickly to market opportunities when their land is encumbered by long-term land diversion contracts. They also cannot sell their land unless the proposed owners accept existing leasing arrangements.

► The bid price of eligible land significantly affects participation in Conservation Title set-aside programs. Higher bid prices facilitate enrollment of eligible land.

► The expected economic returns from crop production can affect participation in Conservation Title set-aside programs. If land operators believe they can improve their income by enrolling land in Conservation Title programs, they are more likely to do so.

► Contact with extension and conservation agency personnel influences participation in Conservation Title set-aside programs. This contact also should affect compliance with other components of the Conservation Title, because landowners must be aware of regulations before they can be expected to conform to program expectations.

► Involvement in government farm programs can facilitate participation in Conservation Title efforts because involvement in these programs can increase awareness of the regulations governing eligibility for participation in the Conservation Title. The involvement also would enhance knowledge of the penalties associated with noncompliance.

► Age of the farm operator can act as a barrier to participation in Conservation Title programs. Older landowners may be motivated to enroll eligible land in Conservation Title set-aside programs so they can retire earlier with no loss of income.

► Negative attitudes toward government involvement in agriculture can act as a barrier to participation in Conservation Title programs. Landowners who believe that government should be involved in agriculture tend to participate more often in Conservation Title programs.

► Perceptions that personally owned and operated land resources require soil and water conservation efforts to maintain future productivity facilitate participation in Conservation Title set-aside programs. Landowners tend to be motivated to participate in conservation efforts that produce rewards for themselves.

► Farm size is a factor in participation in Conservation Title set-aside programs. Owners of intermediate-size landholdings tend to participate more often in Conservation Title programs; owners of small landholdings tend to participate least often.

► Awareness of the benefits to be derived from Conservation Title programs can facilitate participation. Potential participants must be made aware of how the Conservation Title programs will aid them in achieving their personal goals.

Environmental Impacts of Conservation Title Programs

One of the primary goals of the Conservation Title is to improve environmental quality by reducing soil erosion, improving water quality, and improving wildlife habitat. Research reported in this book indicates that Conservation Title programs have partially accomplished these objectives. The major conclusions derived from the information presented are as follows:

► The introduction of Conservation Title programs has substantially reduced soil erosion. Soil loss most likely will be reduced even further as additional acreage is enrolled in Conservation Title set-aside programs and as landowners implement approved farm plans required by conservation compliance provisions.

► Filter strips contribute to improved water quality by preventing sediments and farm chemicals from reaching waterways. But filter strips must be maintained constantly to achieve environmental benefits.

► Conservation Title programs tend to enhance sport fisheries. Improved water quality resulting from participation in Conservation Title programs increases the probability that sport fishes, such as trout and pike, will survive and flourish.

► Pheasant populations tend to increase on Conservation Title set-aside lands, because of improved habitat. Some upland game species, such as rabbits, may not benefit greatly from Conservation Title set-aside programs.

► Sodbuster probably will contribute more to maintaining wildlife habitat than will any other Conservation Title provision. Sodbuster prevents land from being converted to crop production without complete implementation of an approved farm plan. Maintenance of established habitat is the preferred strategy for benefiting wildlife.

► Conservation tillage probably will do little for improving wildlife habitat. Conservation tillage practices reduce soil erosion by slowing runoff, but they provide practically no cover for game animals and contribute little to food supplies.

► Swampbuster will protect existing wildlife habitat for ducks, fishes, and many nongame species. This component of the Conservation Title also will improve surface water quality.

► Swampbuster will protect some fragile aquatic ecosystems from damage. These have significant nonmarket value to society.

► The type and quality of groundcover applied significantly affect the wildlife impacts of Conservation Title programs. Development of food plots and shelterbelts to provide better feed and cover for animals is needed.

► The type of mowing and maintenance programs used on set-aside lands influence the impacts of Conservation Title programs on wildlife. Timing of mowing and spraying for pests is critical for increasing wildlife production on enrolled land.

► Although Conservation Title-enrolled land may be used for recreation purposes, markets for user rights have not been extensively developed. Improved environmental quality that has potential economic benefits should be explored.

► Permanent retirement of Conservation Title-enrolled land and maintenance of good groundcover on set-aside land are essential for maintaining the advances made in wildlife habitat since introduction of Conservation Title legislation.

Future Directions: The Agency Perspective

Implementation of national soil and water conservation programs necessitates an elaborate system of service infrastructures to diffuse conservation information to potential clients, to provide technical assistance to landowners, and to give administrative support to conservation field staff. The problems in integrating the efforts of such a complex service system are compounded by the fact that several agencies are frequently involved.

Implementation of the Conservation Title has been an evolutionary process that has required interpretation and experimentation by agency personnel commissioned to implement broad policy statements with little precedent. Experiences acquired from daily contact with the problems associated with implementing such a complex policy as the Conservation Title should prove useful in developing new initiatives for the next farm bill. Members of three agencies examined future directions in conservation programs from the perspective of their respective agencies. The issues they perceive to be important for future soil and water conservation policy are as follows:

► SCS and ASCS personnel predict that future soil and water conservation programs will continue to emphasize technical and economic incentives combined with voluntary participation. EPA, however, appears to perceive a role for regulation to ensure compliance with environmental standards when the changes required to achieve environmental goals at the farm level are not profitable for the landowner.

► The ability of Conservation Title programs to influence future behaviors of landowners is substantially dependent on the continuation of government farm programs. Removal of penalties associated with violation of Conservation Title programs probably would render the legislation ineffective.

► Long-term prosperity in the agricultural sector could doom Conservation Title programs because landowners would not find government rents acceptable and they would view the penalties imposed on them for violation of Conservation Title programs as being less costly than foregone returns from crop production.

► Some agency people believe that multiple objectives can be achieved via the Conservation Title. They believe that maintenance of farm income, reduction of soil erosion, reduction of commodity stocks, increased commodity prices, and enhancement of wildlife habitat can be accomplished with a single program.

► Greater targeting of limited conservation resources on highly erodible land areas is needed. Particular attention should be directed to microtargeted areas that contribute disproportionately to off-site damages.

► Environmentally sensitive areas, such as recharge areas of significant aquifers, should be protected. One approach would be to permanently retire these land resources to grass and tree cover.

► One of the major problems associated with the coercive elements of the Conservation Title is that none of the environmental agencies wants to function in the role of enforcer. Some agency should be commissioned to assume the role of enforcer and should be provided the human and economic resources to effectively fulfill its task.

► Existing regulations require landowners to return Conservation Title set-aside enrolled land to crop production in the first year following expiration of contracts or they will lose their base. Therefore, landowners are under considerable pressure to do so. This incentive to return set-aside land to crop production should be examined.

► There is a perceived need in all conservation agencies to permanently retire highly erodible land enrolled in Conservation Title set-aside programs.

► Implementation of a land diversion program designed primarily to enhance water quality would be much more expensive than existing soil conservation programs. Cropland that would have to be retired to significantly affect water quality is very productive, which means that the rents required to lease the land would be quite high.

► Future soil and water conservation policies should encompass all agricultural activities. The Conservation Title primarily focuses on commodity producers, but additional farm specialties contribute to pollution. For example, livestock operations generate considerable waste materials that can significantly reduce water quality if they are permitted to enter waterways.

► Future soil and water conservation programs should consider options other than complete retirement of set-aside land. Permission to use set-aside land to produce nonerosive agricultural products could significantly reduce the rents necessary to retire highly erodible land from commodity production.

Policy Issues and Research Needs

Policy Issues. The preceding chapters identified a number of significant policy issues. The soil and water conservation issues raised ranged from objectives to be accomplished by Conservation Title programs to the procedures employed to implement specific components of the legislation. Several of the policy issues noted are as follows:

► The relative importance of soil and water conservation efforts should be prioritized in the context of competing societal objectives.

► The legitimacy of targeting conservation resources on problem land areas should be established by policymakers.

► The operation of existing conservation agencies should be examined in the context of their ability to implement soil and water conservation policies efficiently and equitably.

► The criteria used to evaluate success and failure of soil conservation efforts should be articulated by policymakers in the context of national conservation and agricultural production goals.

► The role of nonmarket benefits and costs should be given more emphasis in the development and implementation of soil and water conservation policies.

► Nonagricultural interests should be afforded a greater role in developing and implementing soil and water conservation policies.

► The legitimacy of coercion as an implementation tool to achieve soil and water conservation objectives should be established by policymakers. Agencies responsible for implementing coercive approaches should be authorized and instructed by policymakers to do so.

► Policies to achieve permanent resolution of soil and water pollution problems are needed.

Future Research Needs. Although several studies completed in recent months have focused on the problems associated with implementing the Conservation Title, the contributors to this book identified a number of additional research topics. Successful completion of the following research agenda would provide valuable information to address many of the policy issues just outlined. Some of the research issues identified are as follows:

► Research should be initiated to determine if a single conservation policy can be expected to achieve multiple objectives simultaneously. If compatible policy objectives can be identified, the social and economic costs of implementing multiple objective policies should be measured. Consistency within and between government programs should be assessed.

► A national survey of the general populace should be conducted to determine the relative priority given to soil and water conservation. Because national conservation policy is formulated in the political arena, the total electorate should be involved in the decision-making process. National issues such as maintaining farm income, improving environmental quality, stabilizing commodity prices, improving wildlife habitat, maintaining low consumer prices, and other national goals should be evaluated and ranked in terms of priority.

► Research is needed to identify mechanisms that will facilitate greater cooperation among natural resources agencies. Consideration should be given to creating a single natural resources development agency at the national level to develop and implement natural resources policies and programs.

▶ The impacts of regulatory and economic incentive programs at the farm level should be examined, with particular emphasis on the assessment of social and economic costs of implementing alternative regulatory and incentive approaches.

▶ Research should be initiated to determine the most appropriate means of making landowners aware of Conservation Title programs and regulations. This will be particularly important as the deadline approaches for implementation of conservation compliance. Mass media mechanisms should be contrasted with personal contact.

▶ The social and economic costs of targeting limited soil and water conservation resources on highly sensitive land areas should be researched. Particular attention should be paid to achieving improved water quality while reducing soil loss.

▶ Research is needed to produce agricultural technologies and techniques that maintain high levels of production while simultaneously reducing environmental degradation.

▶ The feasibility of implementing a program that will permanently retire highly erodible land from crop production should be examined. The socioeconomic costs and benefits of such a program should be evaluated in the context of impacts on local community groups.

▶ The socioeconomic impacts of using set-aside land resources for production of alternative crops should be assessed. Aquaculture, commercial recreation activities, and crops produced by low-input agriculture are examples of the types of options that should be evaluated.

▶ The impacts of Conservation Title programs on environmental quality, wildlife habitat, and aesthetic quality have to be documented. Most likely, some of the greatest benefits of Conservation Title programs will be observed in these areas. Researchers should not be compelled to translate the findings from environmental quality studies into monetary value because the validity and reliability of existing methodologies designed to value non-market goods are not well-established at this time.

▶ Willingness of landowners to comply with Conservation Title programs under different socioeconomic conditions should be assessed. If farm subsidy programs are eliminated, land operators probably will be less willing to comply with Conservation Title set-aside contracts.

▶ The utility of the diffusion model to predict participation in Conservation Title programs should be examined. Possibly, the diffusion model will have utility for understanding participation in Conservation Title set-aside programs because participation in such programs is often highly profitable. If an innovation is to be extensively adopted, profitability is essential.

▶ The impact of Conservation Title programs on fish and wildlife should be documented. Preliminary evidence suggests that the impact has been positive, but long-term monitoring is necessary to identify specific outcomes. The monetary and nonmonetary benefits derived from increased recreation opportunities have to be documented.

▶ The impact of Conservation Title programs on the quality of groundwater should be assessed. Long-term diversion of land from crop production most likely will prevent or reduce groundwater contamination in some areas.

▶ A study of the socioeconomic costs and benefits of a water quality enhancement program should be initiated. A program designed specifically to increase water quality will affect land resources and land operators in a different manner than do existing conservation programs.

Summary

The policy issues and research needs identified here clearly indicate that many opportunities exist for academicians, agency personnel, conservation groups, and policymakers to contribute to future soil and water conservation policies and programs. How effectively natural resources researchers, conservationists, and national policymakers address the research and policy questions outlined in this chapter will significantly influence the success or failure of Conservation Title and future conservation efforts.

Relevant research findings, provided in a timely fashion by academicians and agency research staff, will facilitate decision-making, but the ultimate outcome of the policymaking process will be significantly influenced by the willingness of political leaders to formulate soil and water conservation policies that some of the significant actors in the political arena will perceive negatively. Ultimately, decision-makers will be called on to decide whether economic incentives or regulations will be employed to achieve national environmental and agricultural production objectives.

Index